For Sara
Lloyd and Sara
For The joy of seeing you
in Jerusalem

Moshe and Sara

April - 1993

משה ושרה דיין

WITH EYES TOWARD ZION–III

WITH EYES TOWARD ZION–III

WESTERN SOCIETIES
AND THE HOLY LAND

Edited by Moshe Davis and Yehoshua Ben-Arieh

New York
Westport, Connecticut
London

Library of Congress Cataloging-in-Publication Data

With eyes toward Zion—III : Western societies and the Holy Land /
   edited by Moshe Davis and Yehoshua Ben-Arieh.
       p.   cm.
   Based on papers from the Jul. 1990 Workshop of the International
Center for University Teaching of Jewish Civilization, held in
Jerusalem.
   Includes bibliographical references and index.
   ISBN 0–275–93793–3 (alk. paper)
   1. Palestine—Study and teaching—America—History—19th century
—Congresses. 2. Palestine—Study and teaching—Europe
—History—19th century—Congresses. 3. Palestine—Description and
travel—Congresses. 4. Palestine in Christianity—Congresses.
I. Davis, Moshe. II. Ben-Arieh, Yehoshua. III. International
Center for University Teaching of Jewish Civilization. Workshop
(1990 : Jerusalem)
DS101.5.W58   1991
956.94'007—dc20   90–14310

British Library Cataloguing in Publication Data is available.

Library of Congress Catalog Card Number: 90–14310
ISBN: 0–275–93793–3

First published in 1991

Praeger Publishers, One Madison Avenue, New York, NY 10010
An imprint of Greenwood Publishing Group, Inc.

Printed in the United States of America

The paper used in this book complies with the
Permanent Paper Standard issued by the National
Information Standards Organization (Z39.48–1984).

10 9 8 7 6 5 4 3 2 1

In tribute to
LUCY D. MANOFF
for her talent, perseverance, and devotion
to the Institute of Contemporary Jewry
and its America–Holy Land Project

Contents

PART IV
GREAT BRITAIN

AFTERWORD

Illustrations follow page 114.

Acknowledgments

Our gratitude goes to the Jacob Blaustein Fund for American Studies, whose generous grants make possible ongoing research in America–Holy Land Studies; to Rosemary Krensky and Elsie Sang, whose additional support was forthcoming for publication of this volume; to Yohai Goell, Sharon Jacobs, Freda Leavey, Nancy Perlman, and Ora Zimmer, for their special assistance in preparing this multicultural volume for publication; to Elcya and Avi Weiss of *Laser Pages* in Jerusalem, for their service beyond the line of duty; to the Praeger associates: Ron Chambers, editor-in-chief, *par excellence*, Stephen Hatem, production editor, and Alice Vigliani, copy editor; and to the Advisory Committee of the continuing workshops on Holy Land Studies: Yaakov Ariel, academic coordinator; Ran Aaronsohn, Lottie K. Davis, Jonathan Frankel, Ruth Kark, Menahem Kaufman, Leonardo Senkman, and Thomas Stransky.

Abbreviations

AIU	Alliance Israélite Universelle
ASOR	American Schools of Oriental Research; *ASOR Annual*
Bart.	Baronet
BSAJ	British School of Archaeology in Jerusalem
CCC	Correspondance Consulaire et Commerciale
CCSA	Consejo Central Sionista Agentina
CMA	Church Missionary Society
CMG	Commander of the Order of St. Michael & St. George
CP	Correspondance Politique
CPC	Correspondance Politique et Commerciale
CUEJ	Centre universitaire d'études juives
DDR	Deutsche Demokratische Republik
DUEJ	Diplôme universitaire d'études juives
EPHE	Ecole pratique des hautes études
FIPE	Fonds d'investissement pour l'éducation
FSJU	Fonds social juif unifié
HUC	Hebrew Union College–Jewish Institute of Religion
INALCO	Institut national des langues et civilisations orientales
JCA	Jewish Colonization Association
JHSE	Jewish Historical Society of England

LJS	London Society for Promoting Christianity amongst the Jews; also known as London Jews Society
MAE	Ministère des Affaires Etrangères
PEF	Palestine Exploration Fund
PEQ	*Palestine Exploration Quarterly*
RHICOJ	Association pour la recherche sur l'histoire contemporaine des juifs
SUNY	State University of New York
UFR	Unités de Formation et de Recherche
UN	United Nations
WIZO	Women's International Zionist Organization
YMCA	Young Men's Christian Association

OVERVIEW

Introduction: From America–Holy Land Studies to Western Societies and the Holy Land

Moshe Davis

The thrust of this third volume in our continuing series, *With Eyes Toward Zion*, is to move from the conceptual and methodological approaches of America-Holy Land Studies to a comparative analysis of the Holy Land idea in such Western societies as Canada, Iberoamerica, Great Britain, France, and Germany.

The early stages of the America–Holy Land Project are traced in Chapter 2 by Robert T. Handy, the co-director. Beginning with its inception in 1970, he reviews its conceptual design, colloquia, and publications. Deborah Dash Moore's evaluation in Chapter 3 envisages expansion and deepening of the subject from the vantage of contemporary historical and social research.

As the project advanced, the quest for sources spread beyond primary materials in the United States and Israel, into Great Britain and Turkey, resulting in the publication of *With Eyes Toward Zion–II* (1986). An illuminating example of further outgrowth is the recent publication of V.D. Lipman's *Americans and the Holy Land through British Eyes 1820–1917: A Documentary History* (1989).

The present volume introduces a new dimension into Holy Land Studies— namely, international academic participation in the exploration of related data within Western societies, thus illuminating both parallelisms and unique elements. Concrete examples emerging from the respective authors' interpretations are instructive.

THE HOLY LAND IDEA IN COMPARATIVE CONTEXT

The central thesis of Leonardo Senkman's essay, "The Concept of the Holy Land in Iberoamerica," states: "The pervasive influence of the Holy Land idea can be traced *throughout* the cultural history of Iberoamerica'' (Italics added). Does this intrinsic factor apply to all the countries under study?

In the United States, Abraham Karp observes qualifiedly, ''For American Jews and Christians *in the nineteenth century* [Italics added], the Holy Land was both memory and destiny; for Jews, the ancient and future homeland; for Christians, the land of Patriarchs and Prophets, and of the birth, ministry, and passion of the Savior and the site of his Second Advent.'' Yet, in neighboring Canada, the essence of the matter is different. Michael Brown points out that some of the differences between the two North American countries ''are connected to America's role as a new 'promised land' for Jews and other citizens, a role that Canada . . . did not, for the most part, assume.'' Other differences, however, relate to Canada's binational character and quest for distinctiveness.

Continuing with the Anglo-Saxon nexus, Israel Finestein's cogent citation of the early nineteenth-century British travel guide *Palestine or the Holy Land* (1824) underscores the sturdy Biblical–Holy Land–British bond. ''Intellectual curiosity was stimulated by knowledge of the Bible. . . . No reader of the travel guide,'' Judge Finestein concludes, ''could fail to detect the sense of mystery with which the pages endowed the Land of Israel and the People of Israel within the pattern of human history.''

The French liaison has a longer and wider range. On the one hand, as Catherine Nicault notes in her chapter, ''France–Holy Land Studies: Teaching and Research,'' it is rooted in the early Middle Ages, in particular the Crusades; on the other hand, there were ties of a more practical nature, namely, economic and diplomatic. Though relatively modest in scope, the practical connections were more highly developed and more consistent than the spiritual links, although indeed the French authorities provided a great deal of support to the numerous French Catholic institutions in the Holy Land.

Finally, we observe ''The German Protestant Network in the Holy Land.'' Erich Geldbach's twinning formulation of *Heilsgeschichte* and *Heilsgeographie* reveals the basic character of German involvement. Holy history and holy geography are fused. Thus, the Holy Land and the Holy City gained importance in the eyes of ''awakened Christians.'' Nevertheless, while this ideological fusion inspired a movement of German settlement in the Holy Land, it did not reflect mainstream German Protestantism.

Comprehensively, then, our overview of the Holy Land idea in the comparative context of Western societies sustains the generalization of a continuing pervasive Holy Land influence in those countries, notwithstanding significant historical and cultural variations.

COMMON AND DISTINCTIVE COMPONENTS

Parallelisms and unique elements inherent in the represented cultures can be eminently perceived through the four constructs that served as a basis for the overarching America–Holy Land Studies design: diplomatic policy, Christian devotion, Jewish attachment, and cultural aspects. Following that sequence, a select series of concepts are highlighted from the studies in this volume.

Diplomatic Policy: Political Interest, Consular Protection, Economic Missions

Archival resources on these subjects, generally speaking, are vast and virtually untapped. France is an excellent test case. In his bibliographical overview on "French Archives as a Source for the Study of France–Holy Land Relations" (public, Jewish, Christian, and private collections), Ran Aaronsohn cites among other resources the archives of the *Ministère des Affaires Etrangères* (MAE). He emphasizes that the documents of the Foreign Ministry are not limited to political issues; they deal as well with international commerce, domestic trade, and the economic conditions of the local population. In this sense, Aaronsohn provides support for the argument of the other essays in the French section.

Haim Goren's chapter on German libraries and archives is a counterpart to Aaronsohn's, *mutatis mutandis*. Goren informs us that the archives of the German Ministry are described in *A Catalogue of Files and Microfilms of the German Foreign Ministry Archives 1867–1920* (1959). This collection, according to Alex Carmel, surpasses any other archive in the Federal Republic of Germany with respect to holdings on Eretz Israel. An important contribution in Goren's detailed archival report is the fact that the Foreign Ministry archives prior to 1867, housed in East Germany at the *Zentrales Staatsarchiv des Deutsche Demokratische Republik*, Dienststelle Merseburg, contains rich source material on Prussia–Holy Land relations.

The documentation exhibited in the previously mentioned articles, as indeed in the comprehensive archival references throughout this volume, creates unanticipated avenues for historical clarification: for example, what we may term "double illumination" or "correlative documentation"—wherein unpublished sources simultaneously reveal neglected aspects of the historical endeavor, casting new light on the role of individuals and institutions.[1]

To elucidate: In vol. 4 of the *Guide to America–Holy Land Studies*, V. D. Lipman refers to the private papers of Sir John Robert Chancellor (High Commissioner of Palestine, 1928–1931) housed in Rhodes House Library, Oxford.[2] The specific reference is to proposals for a solution to Arab-Jewish friction acceptable to both sides, in correspondence among Chancellor, Judah L. Magnes, and Anglican Bishop George F. Graham-Brown, 1929–1932. Naomi W. Cohen, basing her research primarily on American archival and published material, in her volume *The Year after the Riots: American Responses to the Palestine Crisis of 1929–1930*, utilizes this source for her investigation.[3] This is an example of how parallelism and uniqueness unfold on the intercontinental research trail.

Christian Devotion: The Holy Land in the Historic Christian Tradition; Zion in Christian Denominations

In the thread of Christian historiography, the Holy Land concept does not have one single meaning. André Kaspi, in his summary statement of the French section, puts his finger on the underlying reason: "constraints of vocabulary." Interspersed in this volume—in the articles by Kaspi, Sophie Kessler-Mesguich, Gershon Greenberg, and Rupert Chapman—are several disparate conceptual connotations that emerge from the use of language reflecting, respectively, Christian settings in France, the United States, and England.

Kaspi stresses the fundamental question whether the term "Holy Land" should be employed. Kessler-Mesguich emphasizes that "in England one may use *Holy Land*, but in French *Terre Sainte* has a specifically Christian connotation." Shall it then better be expressed as "Holy Place?"

Gershon Greenberg infers that "Holy Land" is congruous to a "sacred reality." Thus, he explains why some nineteenth-century American missionaries felt obliged to choose the Holy Land as the arena of their vocation. Such individuals as Pliny Fisk and Levi Parsons, Clorinda Minor, and James T. Barclay saw their mission to work for the salvation of the world in the Holy Land as a forerunner to the Second Advent.

In British Protestant Christianity, as exemplified by nineteenth-century archaeologists, a basic perception of *Holy* Land was *Bible* Land. There was, as Chapman emphasizes, "an unprecedented need to establish the historical accuracy of the Bible, as a means of defending its theological accuracy."

These chapters and others in the volume underscore the need for a composite research design in this basic and vital area.

Jewish Attachment: The Holy Land in Jewish Tradition; Eretz Israel in Jewish Communal Life

In his "Comment" on the British section of this volume, Aubrey Newman poses a fundamental question concerning the specific part played by British Jewry in the Holy Land: What was the overarching approach of the Jewish community toward Eretz Israel? While much of that relationship is closely linked with the history of Zionism in Britain—especially during the Mandate period—there is "sufficient that cannot be so viewed and can only be studied within the general context of Britain–Holy Land studies."

This is an important distinction. The manner in which Zionism impacted upon Jewish life in all diasporic communities is a recurring question in modern Jewish historiography. Vital as was Zionism's role in world Jewish continuity, it cannot be equated with the aggregate of Jewish individual and group involvement in Eretz Israel. This is one of Lloyd Gartner's salient thoughts in "Some Reflections on the Present State of Holy Land Studies." For example, all of Moses Montefiore's contributions to the Yishuv notwithstanding, Gartner states, he "was neither a Zionist nor a proto-Zionist."

The part, as pervasive as it may be, should not be confused for the whole; but neither should its organic influence on the totality be gainsaid. To remain in the focus of Moses Montefiore, his intuition of the place of Eretz Israel in the Jewish future was unequivocal, and his belief in the eternal mission of Zion remained steadfast. Consequently, he became so much more than others, a hero figure of nineteenth-century world Jewry.[4]

On the broader scale of Jewish existence, the dynamic interplay of Holy Land concerns with Jewish communal, religious-cultural, and social imperatives, while considered in portions of the book, requires concentrated analysis and definition.

Cultural Aspects: The Holy Land in Thought, Language, Literature and Art, Pilgrimage and Travel

As the contemporary scholar probes the wonder of the *rediscovery* of the Holy Land by the Western world in the nineteenth century, cultural manifestations come to the fore in bold relief. The chapters in this volume are replete with references to the writings of archaeologists, historians, scientists, biblical scholars, novelists, consuls, missionaries, tourists and, above all, settlers and builders of the Land—all attesting to the intrinsic place of the Holy Land in world imagination.

How is one to explain this phenomenon?

An ancient tradition concerning the origin of the cosmos teaches that the Holy Land was first in creation. For centuries, this belief was visually demonstrated by the mapmakers who placed the Holy Land in the very center of the universe, the navel of the earth. With time, even as the scientific facts were established, the tradition remained deeply ingrained in the consciousness, learning, and creativity of Western civilization.

Again, this marked impress can be better comprehended in comparative context. In the United States, for example, what Robert Handy has called "the transferral of Holy Land imagery with all its richness to the New World" became a basic factor early in America's history. It was strongly expressed in literature, hymns, spirituals, oratory, and common parlance. Such concepts as Zion and Jerusalem became synoptic metaphors for the New World. At least fifteen places in the United States are called Zion in almost as many states. Uniquely, Zion City in Illinois was laid out with all its streets bearing biblical names.

To a great extent, the focus of such "transferral" was found in the family circle, as its members drew together to study the "beginnings of mankind" in the pages of the Bible, with Holy Land name places marking the passage of early human events. Remarkable cultural treasures are to be found in the large family Bibles handed down from parent to child with notations added as current commentary. In the family Bibles we find the spiritual-cultural-historical folklore of Western civilization.

Another hue in the cultural spectrum is the place of the study of Hebrew, classical and modern. As Catherine Nicault aptly observes, "If the interest shown in such study is primarily of a biblical nature, then the attraction of the Holy Land is not alien to it." Generally speaking, Hebrew was studied in the Middle Ages in a theological perspective. "Pierre Dubois," Nicault continues, "a thirteenth-century cleric, also considered it a means by which Christendom could take possession of the Holy Land." Even beyond this intense view, some considered Hebrew to be the first human language, and therefore the perfect tongue.

In the French cultural ambience, it is widely accepted that the first Chair of Hebrew was established at the Sorbonne in Paris in 1313. By the mid-sixteenth century, Hebrew was incorporated into the curricula of such Western European universities as Padua and Heidelburg, not to speak of highly developed individual and group studies at the major seats of Christian religious learning. The surge of Hebrew studies in the late nineteenth and twentieth centuries is nothing less' than remarkable, if one is to judge only by the fact that Hebrew is taught today in more than seven hundred institutions of higher learning on all continents of the globe—in colleges, universities, Jewish and Christian institutions, and seminaries.

What has given rise to the interest in Hebrew as language and culture in our times? Certainly, the theological and humanistic source of the Hebraic spirit in Western civilization is a pervasive factor. The most salient force, however, is the emergence of Eretz Israel as the contemporary embodiment of ancient Hebrew civilization—a phenomenon that has fired the imagination of the cultural and intellectual world. The fact that Hebrew is spoken again as a living tongue, and that out of Zion have come forth literary figures, scholars, scientists, and artists, has impelled respect for the language and culture.

A third facet in the Holy Land cultural sphere—the personal dimension—is embossed in creative expression. In the mid-nineteenth century, as scientific study, travel, and settlement developed rapidly, the encounters between Orient and Occident, antiquity and modernity, traditional faith and scientific achievement, produced a large body of literature, art, and music reflecting the individual appreciation of these encounters. Much of this genre is to be found in the sources of travel and pilgrimage. As David Klatzker claims in his essay: "Among all the historical records . . . there are none so vivid and personal as travel accounts." A century and more earlier, Steven Olin, President of Wesleyan University, wrote (in 1844) that "pilgrimage is little less than to be naturalised in the Holy Land."

In the realm of cultural expression particularly, perhaps even more than in the areas of diplomatic policy, Christian devotion, and Jewish attachment to the Holy Land, history and geography met again. In Yehoshua Ben-Arieh's overview of nineteenth-century Western travel literature, he clarifies that the uniqueness of Eretz Israel was felt by most writers of the period. For them, geography and history were mutually illuminating. The Holy Land was "the land of the Old and New Testament. Its destruction and state of desolation had been brought on by divine decree. But it was widely believed and fervently hoped that there would be a new beginning for this Land.''

We present *Eyes–III* looking forward to *Eyes–IV*, based on the papers prepared for the July 1990 Workshop of the International Center for University Teaching of Jewish Civilization. The central theme of this colloquium was "Jerusalem in the Mind of the Western World (1800–1948)," dealing with such categories as diplomacy and presence, religious groups and missions, travelers and explorers, painting and photography. Offering further testimony to Franklin Littell's call for "cooperative international scholarship, which has become the order of the day," the participants presented papers from a variety of historical cultures including Great Britain, Germany, Italy, Poland, the United States, Iberoamerica, and Israel.

This scholarly enterprise was but the first of a contemplated series of colloquia on Jerusalem in anticipation of the celebration in 1996 of the three-thousandth anniversary of its founding by King David—colloquia and publications that, it is expected, will both expand and deepen the realm of Holy Land Studies.

NOTES

1. See my Introduction to *Guide to America–Holy Land Studies 1620–1948, vol. 2: Political Relations and American Zionism*, ed. Nathan M. Kaganoff (New York: Praeger, 1982), xv-xviii.

2. Menahem Kaufman and Mira Levine, eds., *Resource Material in British, Israeli and Turkish Repositories* (New York: Praeger, 1984), 32-33.

3. Detroit: Wayne State University Press, 1988, 182, n.26.

4. See my essay *Sir Moses Montefiore: American Jewry's Ideal*, Pamphlet Series (Cincinnati: American Jewish Archives, 1985).

Chapter 1

Holy Land Views in Nineteenth-Century Western Travel Literature

Yehoshua Ben-Arieh

This chapter examines six different views of the Holy Land in Western nineteenth-century travel literature.[1] Such perceptions lend themselves to comparison and contrast; in some cases they are complementary, in other cases mutually exclusive.

A DIVINE HOLY LAND

For hundreds of years Palestine has been seen by the Western world—both geographically and cartographically—as a holy, ethereal, timeless land. The Divine Presence is thought to dwell in this Land, and the periods when the Jewish and Christian faiths came into being and crystallized are considered to be the most decisive eras in its history.[2]

A religious-mystical perception of the Land and its holy sites—especially Jerusalem—was entertained by the great majority of nineteenth-century authors of travel literature. These roving writers had absorbed a Western Christian culture replete with a wide variety of emotional beliefs and sentimental views about the "Holy Land." In that Land, God Himself ordained laws and commandments, dispatched angels as emissaries, and conducted conversations with human beings; there God was revealed to man. It was in that Land that Jesus descended in the form of man and from that Land returned to the heavens. In Christianity, the holiness of the region derives first and foremost from Jesus' central role in that

This chapter is adapted from the author's Hebrew article by permission of Zalman Shazar Center, publisher of *Transition and Change in Modern Jewish History: A Collection of Articles in Honor of Shmuel Ettinger*.

faith. The New Testament calls for worship of the divine spirit and sanctification of the Land where the divine revelation transpired. The Land is elevated to a metaphysical position, and its material existence is transformed into an abstract concept.[3]

Over the years the view that Jesus' presence sanctified the physical environment, and that one could draw near to God by coming to know and experience that environment, gained currency in Christianity. This idea constituted one of the motivations behind the Crusades and led the Church to regard that undertaking as an integral part of its creed. For Christianity, the sites related to the life of Jesus—travels, associates, and tribulations—are of far greater importance than the earlier holy sites that were already regarded as sacred in Jesus' own lifetime. Christian dogma stressed the role of the holy places in attesting to the experiences of the Christian Messiah.[4]

Many nineteenth-century Europeans found it difficult to make the transition from a transcendental, incorporeal view of the Holy Land to the physical reality of Palestine. This was true not only for those who had merely heard or read about the Land, but also for the many people who had visited it and had come to know it at first hand. Thus, images and perceptions of Palestine as a divine, sanctified Land can be found in the most modern European literature of the nineteenth century.

The very use of the term "Holy Land," which spread steadily in the nineteenth century, is an indication of how deeply the transcendental perception had taken root. This term served to demarcate a particular geographical entity, despite the fact that in many periods of history the Land had no distinctive political status. In the nineteenth century, Palestine was one of several administrative units within the Ottoman Empire. Indeed, only with the inception of the British Mandate period was modern Palestine given concrete borders—and it appears that this development would not have transpired were it not for the existing perception of the Land as a distinct and unique entity, the Holy Land.

One of the Christian theological encyclopedias offered the following explanation for the term "Holy Land": "Name commonly given to Palestine on account of the many places sanctified by the presence of Jesus and identified on the grounds of scriptural documents, history, or legend."[5] However, this Land was holy to three faiths. It was here that both the First and the Second Temples were located (Judaism), the human divinity was born (Christianity), and the Prophet ascended heavenward (Islam). The singularity of the Land bestowed upon it a unique geographical status as the center of the world, a position derived from the fact that it was perceived as having witnessed the revelation of the Divine Presence and having become a focal point for various faiths. In fact, the notation of the Holy Land's centrality originated in Jewish biblical and rabbinical literature, whence it found its way into Christian writings.[6]

The distinction of the Holy Land from other lands, including its important neighbors Egypt and Mesopotamia, inspired numerous attempts in the nineteenth century to discover Palestine's unique geographical features. Many writers stressed the fact that the Land's nourishment depended upon "heavenly rainfall," unlike Mesopotamia and Egypt where agriculture based on river irrigation was practiced. Other writers stressed the significance of its geographic location; that is, the fact that it formed a bridge between two continents and a corridor between Egypt and the Fertile Crescent. Still others noted the extraordinary topographic diversity: high mountains in the north in sharp contrast to deep valleys elsewhere; the lowest spot on earth, the desolate Dead Sea area, as opposed to the green and fertile hills of Hebron, Jerusalem, and Samaria. Finally, there were those who called attention to the desert-like quality of much of the area—the desolation and secretiveness of the Judean desert, and Sinai, the scene of the unique revelation of the Divine Presence.

As a result of the Land's many singular qualities, Western literature on Palestine generally assumed that the geography of the region played an important role in the Land's holiness. Its physical features were held to be conducive to spiritual ideas and explained why it became the cradle of abstract monotheistic thought. In turn, the religions that emerged there bestowed upon the Land a qualitative and eternal holiness.[7]

LAND OF THE BIBLE AND THE HOLY PLACES

A second perception of Palestine was as Land of the Bible and holy places. The area was regarded as a land of divine holiness, but the basis of the perception was historical—namely, that Palestine was *the* land of the Bible.

It was through the Bible that nineteenth-century European thinkers were introduced to the concept of Palestine as a physical entity. The invention of printing, and the translations of the Bible into various European languages during the previous centuries, made possible its widespread distribution, turning it into a central component of Western Christian culture in the early modern period. Christian children were taught from their early years to read the Bible, as well as to hear it being recited in the family, in Sunday school, as part of holiday texts, and during prayers both in churches and in private homes. The Holy Land was the Land that had become familiar through the old Bible tales, whether part of faith or merely of cultural heritage.[8]

As the number of visitors to the Holy Land increased, these people began to search for the sites and scenes with which they were vicariously familiar since childhood. Whether these nineteenth-century travelers were scholars, writers, artists, or simply tourists, the vast majority of them had studied the Bible. They sought not only the spiritual ambience of the Holy Land, but also the locations about which they had heard and read at great length. Their visits served to reinforce their attachment to the Bible, and upon returning home they tended to re-read the portions of the Scriptures dealing with the places they had visited.

Among the travelers to the Holy Land were scholars who attempted to identify biblical sites and locate them on maps that they published. Biblical dictionaries, atlases, maps, books, and articles—both popular and scientific—were printed with great frequency and distributed throughout Europe and the entire Western world.

The scientific spirit led to the development of an empirical approach to the study of the Holy Land, and an attempt to understand biblical events in a tangible manner. The majority of writers were Christians who regarded their scholarly endeavors and the works they produced as part of a search for the roots and early years of the Christian religion.[9]

Well-known Western artists also began visiting the area, with the goal of sketching the holy places and biblical landscapes and making them available to Europeans. The extent to which these drawings became fashionable is demonstrated by the popular practice among nineteenth-century travelers to supplement the written impressions of their trips to the Holy Land with sketches of landscapes; upon the travelers' return, these were submitted to artists for professional renderings. Among the travel books of the period are works in which the drawings of Holy Land landscapes were primary, with the written text merely providing an accompaniment.

Illustrated editions of the Bible also began to appear, containing drawings not only of biblical events, landmarks, and landscapes, but also maps, ethnic types, and architectural designs.[10] The pre-Raphaelite movement in art, whose foremost representative was William Holman Hunt, maintained that in order to sketch the biblical sites with accuracy and detail, one had to visit the Holy Land and witness at first hand the places and types of people mentioned in the Bible.[11]

It was generally believed at the time that the people, dress, and customs of the Middle East had miraculously remained unchanged over the centuries; thus, for artists, they constituted an important link to the biblical past. The Arab sheikh in picturesque garb resembled, the artists felt, the Jewish patriarchs. The Bedouin caravans crossing the desert reminded them of the Israelites carrying the Holy Ark over the same desert. Arab women drawing water from a well recalled the image of Rebecca serving water to Abraham's servant Eliezer.[12] The attempt to identify places bearing Arab names with biblical sites—a popular endeavor at the time—further instilled in the Western world the notion that the Arab society and lifestyle reflected those of the biblical period.[13] Consequently, Palestine turned into a favorite venue for nineteenth-century artists, who diligently searched for traces of biblical life and times.[14]

Another factor that lead people to think of the Land in biblical terms was the rapidly spreading influence of Bible criticism, which reached a peak in the nineteenth century. During the Middle Ages, biblical exegesis had limited itself to literal, moral, and allegoric interpretation. As a result of the Reformation, this type of exegesis gained nearly universal and unchallenged acceptance. However, the scientific materialism that characterized the century, as expressed in Charles Lyell's *Principles of Geology* (1830), and the anti-creation theories advanced by Charles Darwin in his *On the Origin of Species* (1859), encouraged skepticism regarding the unassailable accuracy and credibility of the Bible. Analytical and textual criticism of the Bible became a major challenge as thoughtful believers began to seek a new approach to faith.[15]

The field of biblical criticism continued to expand. Scholars from different schools of thought, particularly Germans, began to publish criticism of the biblical text itself, its composition, and the figures it portrayed. It was suggested that the first biblical personage depicted with historical accuracy was Moses, while the stories of the patriarchs had their origin in various traditions. The New Testament and the figure of Jesus were also subjected to criticism.

These controversies and doubts led, on the one hand, to a diminution of popular faith in the Bible, and even to the complete abandonment of biblical studies by erstwhile believers. On the other hand, they stimulated scientific interest in the Land of the Bible. Devout biblical scholars sought to visit the sites and landscapes of that area, hoping to be convinced about the reality of the biblical stories by familiarizing themselves with the actual environment of those events.[16]

The biblical concept of the Holy Land presented travelers with certain difficulties. For instance, they grappled with the question of how the region depicted in the Bible as "a land of milk and honey" could have degenerated to such a desolate condition. Earlier believers had responded that this development was an incontestable divine curse; but the scientifically minded biblical critics of the nineteenth century attributed the gap between scriptural description and reality to inaccuracy on the part of the Bible. The Scriptures, they claimed, had simply exaggerated the fertility of the Land.

In seeking a scientific explanation, some of the nineteenth-century believers ascribed the woeful transformation of the Land to climatic change. Others claimed that drastically changed social conditions and agricultural methods provided sufficient explanation for the Land's decline. The forests that had once covered the hillsides had been destroyed, as had the terraces that formerly preserved the soil and allowed for its cultivation. This neglect was compounded by fundamental changes in the population and culture. Advocates of this latter theory (which has been accepted up to the present) concluded that there was no contradiction between the biblical description of the Land's natural geographical conditions and the reality that was disclosed in the nineteenth century. Furthermore, they believed that the appearance and the landscapes of the Holy Land in their lifetime served to verify the contents of the Holy Scriptures.[17]

LAND OF ANCIENT HISTORY

Palestine was viewed by Western civilization not only as the Holy Land and the Land of the Bible, but also as part of the ancient world, whether classical Mediterranean (Hellenistic-Roman) or ancient Middle Eastern. Europeans had long evinced respect and esteem for the ancient lands of their history, although they were distant and, in fact, generally unknown. In addition to the Bible, the Europeans were familiar, from the eleventh century on, with the sagas of

Alexander the Great and of other prominent Hellenic figures. In the late Middle Ages interest in these areas increased, and the number of Western visitors to the Mediterranean region and to the Orient rose accordingly—at first to the classical, Hellenistic-Roman world, and afterward to the centers of even earlier civilizations.[18]

In the seventeenth and eighteenth centuries it became fashionable in Europe—especially in England—for young members of the wealthy class to participate in what was known as a "Grand Tour," designed to impart knowledge of neighboring countries, refinement, and prestige. As the Napoleonic wars wreaked havoc in Europe, these tours began to focus on more distant lands; consequently, the number of Europeans visiting the classical world and the ancient Middle East grew. Scholarly societies, archaeological expeditions, philologists, antiquaries, adventurers, the infirm seeking the sun, voyagers wishing to expand their horizons—all set out on journeys to Italy, Greece, Spain, North Africa and Egypt, Turkey, and the Levant. For the most part these trips were made in comfort, with ample—even unnecessary—supplies. A few travelers donned Eastern attire, carried minimal supplies, and penetrated into remote and uncharted areas, encountering numerous difficulties and grave dangers along the way.[19]

A by-product of these journeys was the practice of amassing antiquities and transferring them to the travelers' country of origin. Often these items were placed in prominent museums—for example, the British Museum in London, the Louvre in Paris, museums in Berlin—but they also found their way to private houses and gardens. In England, for example, the practice was to decorate nearly all parks and gardens with ancient statues, capitals, and pottery from Mediterranean and Near Eastern countries.

No feelings of guilt accompanied the act of uprooting these antiquities from their natural milieu. Lord Elgin's marble collection, which included statues taken from the Parthenon in Athens, is but one example of the plunder perpetrated in the belief that the local populace had no interest in preserving their antiquities. One Frenchman likened antiquities to an orchard that by natural right should be in the possession of those who would tend it and reap its benefits. This outlook was shared by wealthy patrons of the arts and by the zealous national administrations of the outstanding European museums. Good relations with the "Sublime Porte"—the Turkish authorities—facilitated this pillage, and precious artifacts were spirited away to safe quarters in Europe. A well-known obelisk from Luxor found its way to the Place de la Concorde in Paris; another obelisk, "Cleopatra's Needle," was moved to the banks of the Thames in London; a third was transferred to New York's Central Park. Private individuals also helped themselves to a share of the spoils. For example, in 1815, William Banks, a British member of Parliament, transferred an Egyptian obelisk to his garden in Dorset.[20]

The antiquities of the Holy Land were also pillaged, as the following examples illustrate. Lucièn Félicièn De-Saulcy, who conducted the first so-called archaeological excavation in the Tomb of the Kings in Jerusalem, moved sarcophagi he had found there to the Louvre; the famous Mesha stone, discovered in Moab, was also housed in the French museum; the Siloam inscription was shipped to a museum in Istanbul. The situation in Iraq-Mesopotamia (Assyria-Babylonia) was no better. Antiquities displayed in the British Museum, the Louvre, the museums in Berlin, and elsewhere attest to the dimensions of the plunder.

On the positive side, the lively interest of the nineteenth century in these lands led to the scientific study of the ancient world, including intensive study of the languages and cultures of the ancient Near East. Exploration of the Egyptian pyramids, the deciphering of the Rosetta stone hieroglyphics (in 1822) by Jean François Champollion, the Layard excavations in Nineveh (during the 1840s), and other developments transformed archaeology from a hunt for antiquities into a basic science for the study of many and varied languages and cultures. Egypt and Mesopotamia, which until the Napoleonic era had been nearly unknown lands from a scientific standpoint, became central subjects of investigation for scholars and other interested parties throughout the world. Similarly, the ancient history of the classical civilizations and of the Near East became a subject of study in the West.[21]

Discoveries in Egypt, Mesopotamia, Asia Minor, and Syria had great emotional appeal for Europeans, primarily because of the affinity of these finds to the Bible and the light they shed on it. Many Europeans still regarded the entire Middle East as the Land of the Bible, and the core of archaeological study in the first half of the nineteenth century was Bible research, with archaeologists stressing this field—partially from motivations of fund raising. In the course of time, however, the study of the great civilizations of antiquity developed into an independent field, eclipsing Bible study. It soon became apparent from the meticulous reconstruction of the history of the ancient empires that Palestine and the Bible played only a minor role in the development of these civilizations. Rarely were places and concepts related to the Holy Land and the Bible mentioned in the Assyrian, Babylonian, and Egyptian documents that were discovered.

Various societies were founded to explore the ancient civilizations as a separate field.[22] In Palestine, archaeological research lagged behind that of the neighboring lands, possibly because of harsher conditions and lack of world-famous sites and monuments. Whatever research was carried out in the Holy Land during the nineteenth century was essentially topographical-historical in nature.[23] European travelers on the Grand Tour, antiquities hunters, and students of ancient civilizations were often accompanied on their trips by artists who strove to provide topographic and ethnographic data on the places and people unfamiliar to the West. Although these artists were in many respects similar to the previously mentioned painters of biblical scenes, their interests were much broader. They began to develop a distinctive style for the portrayal of historic sites and buildings and, faced with a wide variety of foreign landscapes, they adopted new approaches, such as a perspective from above the scene. One can, however, discern an idealized landscape in most nineteenth-century paintings—a style that was established previously by European artists who drew the landscapes of Italy,

Spain, and North Africa. In the nineteenth-century Middle Eastern adaptation of this style, the foreground consisted of local residents or fragments of ruined monuments, usually surrounded by trees or other objects. In the center stood the central subject of the painting—a monastery, mosque, fortress, or the city of Jerusalem—and in the background, at the line where the earth and sky meet, a foggy horizon, clouds, or the sun.[24]

At the same time, the scientific approach that characterized the nineteenth century led to the emergence of a school of realism in which artists sought to record details in an objective manner, while applying esthetic standards. Historical scenes were eternalized on canvas, and the emphasis on detail led the viewer to regard them as truthful representations. However, close inspection reveals numerous inaccuracies.

At times, artists joined the scholars involved in scientific investigation, and they often accompanied archaeologists, documenting the excavation process and drawing the objects that were unearthed. For example, British artist William Simpson, who had formerly been commissioned to portray scenes of the Crimean War, was sent by the British Palestine Exploration Fund to cover the digs carried out in Jerusalem by the renowned British explorer Charles Warren.[25] Palestine was viewed by Western travelers not only as a divine, ethereal, Holy Land, and the Land of the Bible, but also as a historical land, a part of the ancient Middle East.

AN UNKNOWN, DESOLATE, AND DEVASTATED LAND

In addition to the perceptions based on the importance of the area's unique historical past, Western literature, especially in the nineteenth century, also focused on the contemporary condition of Palestine: backward, undeveloped, devastated, desolate, and sparsely populated—all this in contrast to its glorious past and to the West European countries whence came most of those who visited and wrote about that Land.

Following a trip to the region in mid-century, Henry Baker Tristram, among the foremost nineteenth-century researchers of the area, noted his shock upon seeing the extent to which the Holy Land—the land of the Bible with such singular historical significance—had become devastated, desolate, and unknown, and he determined to dedicate himself to the scientific study of Palestine.[26] For example, until the beginning of the nineteenth century there were no maps with accurate measurements of the area as a whole or of its important cities; the location and altitude of the sites and settlements were completely unknown. Many historical sites could not be identified, and the flora and fauna of the land were *terra incognita*, an untouched field. Many areas of the Holy Land had not been visited by West Europeans for hundreds of years.[27]

Scientific study of the Holy Land got under way in the early part of the nineteenth century. Ulrich Jasper Seetzen and Johann Ludwig Burckhardt, pioneers in the exploration of the region, originally traveled to the East with the goal of reaching central Africa and discovering the sources of the Nile. Their expeditions and study in Palestine constituted, at the outset, merely a preparatory stage in this master plan. Burckhardt, in fact, was sent on his mission by the British Association for Promoting the Discovery of Interior Africa. He reached the Levant in the footsteps of his predecessor, Seetzen. Aleppo was his first stop, and from there he proceeded to Palestine.

It was Burckhardt who revealed to Western Europe the exact location of Petra—a disclosure that attracted large numbers of additional scholars and other notable figures from the West. In the course of their explorations, Seetzen and Burckhardt were forced to disguise themselves as Muslims, and they even went so far as to adopt the Islamic faith. Seetzen became known as Sheikh Musa, and Burckhardt as Sheikh Ibrahim. Although they were not acquainted with each other, their *modus operandi* was quite similar. Both were students of the renowned scholar from Göttingen, Professor Johann Friedrich Blumenbach, who had inspired and trained them in the same scientific approach. The two men also met an identical end, each dying in the midst of their travels while preparing for the implementation of their master plan, which was never realized—penetration into the interior of Africa.[28]

Other examples of pioneering studies of the Holy Land were the attempts to explore the Sea of Galilee, the Jordan River, and the Dead Sea. One such project was carried out by a group of Americans headed by Lieutenant William Francis Lynch. In the national atlas of the United States, Lynch's contingent has been designated as the second U.S. scientific expedition to undertake a mission anywhere in the world. This group's work had been preceded by that of individuals who sought to explore the depth and nature of the Sea of Galilee, the course of the Jordan River, and the depth and features of the unique Dead Sea, into which the river flowed. Lynch's expedition, conducted in 1847–1848, was beset with countless dangers, including disease and attacks by Bedouin tribesmen. The group's artist, Lieutenant Dale, was stricken by a fatal ailment, and others also fell seriously ill.[29]

Edward Robinson, one of the most important students of the region in the nineteenth century, laid the foundations for the biblical, historical-geographical, and archaeological investigation of Palestine. He was the first to discover the location of Masada, a quest that numerous earlier scholars had attempted in vain. In Jerusalem he discerned the remains of the well-known arch on the Western Wall, which ever since has been referred to as "Robinson's Arch." He explored the Siloam tunnel and uncovered remnants of the City's third wall, dating from the Second Temple period. Robinson also correctly pinpointed the location of Beersheba (currently Israel's fourth largest city) which, since the period of the Crusades, had been incorrectly identified with the location of Bet-Guvrin.[30]

Additional scores of scholars went to Palestine and contributed to the scientific study of the Land. Their comprehensive research extended the biblical period and was not merely historical-archaeological, but spanned diverse subjects and fields as well. It soon became apparent that significant exploration of the area required the work of teams rather than individuals, however prestigious they might be. Thus, the Palestine Exploration Fund (PEF) was established in London; and similar societies were founded in the United States, Germany, and Russia. French scholars, such as Clermont-Ganneau, also played an important role in the activity of these societies.[31]

During the nineteenth century the European powers intensified their involvement in the political aspects of the region. Geographical details about Palestine and the neighboring lands became important for a variety of reasons, including military motives. Precise data and accurate descriptions, instead of romantic-imaginative versions of the Orient, became increasingly significant. The PEF provided much of the necessary information. After two of its explorers, Charles Wilson and Charles Warren, produced the first precise map of Jerusalem and laid the foundations for archaeological research in the city, especially in the area of the Temple Mount, other members of the PEF drew the first accurate maps of the entire western part of the region, spanning the area from Dan to Beersheba on twenty-six sheets accompanied by three volumes of notes. Afterward, the Arava, Sinai, and parts of Transjordan and the Negev were charted.[32]

The desire to provide an accurate picture of the Land also found expression in nineteenth-century paintings and photographs. Many of the artists specialized in topographic portrayals; others were architects who tended to sketch maps, panoramas, and models of sites, cities, and landscapes in the area. A detailed and accurate model of Jerusalem from the early 1870s was discovered recently. Created by a Hungarian Catholic priest, Stephan Illes, the model is displayed in the Citadel in Jerusalem.[33] This model, and the entire phenomenon of sketching "cosmorama" scenes and creating models of Jerusalem and the sites within it (e.g., the Temple Mount, the Church of the Holy Sepulcher), should be seen as part of a general nineteenth-century trend. Such paintings and models of cities and landscapes, with explanatory texts, were part of exhibits that traveled from town to town and were often displayed in tents set up for this purpose.

In 1796, an Italian naval cadet named Manzoni painted a panorama of Constantinople, depicting with careful detail every major mosque and monument in the city. In 1844, the Austrian artist Hubert Staller painted a breathtaking picture of Constantinople in microscopic detail that would be the envy of a modern tourist equipped with a camera. Staller had been taught by his father, Johann Michael, who in 1829 had painted a stunning panorama of Salzburg, which was taken from city to city by father and son.[34] A detailed panorama of Rome on display at the Victoria and Albert Museum in London provides an example of this art form. With the invention of the camera, new photographic techniques were employed to present Oriental images to the West. Photography took over the role of the artist. The basic approach to the East, however, remained the same.[35]

Scientific discoveries in the Holy Land, the detailed study of its cities and sites, and the spread of this knowledge throughout Western Europe were similar to investigations being undertaken in other remote and unexplored parts of the world. However, the lack of information about contemporary Palestine was particularly striking in light of the West's familiarity with its past.[36]

Some Western researchers, struck by the sheer lack of empirical facts about the Holy Land, went so far as to compare the local Arab populace to the native inhabitants of other lands that had recently been discovered by Europeans. John MacGregor, who had been captured by Bedouin tribesmen in the Hula region while rowing down the Jordan River, painted his captors as American Indians. Claude Renier Conder noted that the Muslims who were natives of the area were generally considered to be on a parallel level with the American Indians and the Australian Aborigines, and he added that, like those two savage groups, the natives in Palestine should also be wiped out to make room for a more progressive and superior race.[37]

AN EXOTIC, ORIENTAL LAND

Still another perception of Palestine was that of an Oriental land, a part of the surrounding Muslim-Arab world. Orientalism had begun to occupy a central niche in European thought and culture in the eighteenth century.[38] In the following century, the romantic perception of the East became more realistic, as a result of (1) historical events that led to the Western countries' growing involvement in the Orient, and (2) the appearance of several key literary works at the beginning of the century, which steered the following generations toward a more scientific approach to the East.[39]

The most significant of these historical events were Napoleon's invasion of the East (1798–1799), the Greek wars (1808–1814; 1821–1828), the construction of the Suez Canal (1859–1869), the Berlin Treaty (1870), acquisition of shares in the Suez Canal by Great Britain (1875), the Turkish-Russian War (1877–1878), and the Sudan War (1882–1885). Foremost among the literary works was *A Thousand and One Arabian Nights*, which by the eighteenth century had already been translated into French and English. These early translations were inaccurate adaptations that attempted to explain and improve upon the stories; three new translations more faithful to the original appeared during the nineteenth century. These tales had a profound influence on the Western cultural world. The anthology won unprecedented popularity; almost all educated Europeans read the tales in their youth and remembered them vividly. Hence, travelers in the area felt as if they were visiting familiar places.

The stories enriched the Western languages with Eastern idioms and imprinted many images of the Oriental lifestyle and customs on Western minds. They also portrayed an accurate picture of Eastern sites: the streets of Baghdad; the gardens and beaches along the Euphrates; Basra, Cairo, and Damascus; the cities with their effervescent bazaars; the mosques. The people—merchants, dervishes, water carriers, letter writers, and fishermen—were described as simple, childlike, and devout.

The stories also contained an imaginary dimension, with magnificent palaces built overnight and moved at will from place to place, cities of copper and black marble, flying steeds, magic carpets, miraculous bottles, young ladies with beautiful eyes, and other wonders. In short, the stories served as a marvelous introduction to the lands of the East and developed a thoroughly Oriental and exotic perception of the region.[40]

In addition to the *Arabian Nights*, many other Arabic stories were translated into European languages, thereby strengthening Eastern influence within Western culture. Lord Byron's poetry was influenced by literature about the East. Disraeli's partly political, partly imaginary novel *Tancred* vividly portrays the landscape of the Orient and depicts the life, customs, and personal traits of Arabs and Jews, of inhabitants of the desert, and of city-dwellers. The writings of Richard Burton created the myth of the exotic and mysterious East. William Makepeace Thackeray and Mark Twain wrote humorous satires on the Oriental population and lifestyle.

Indeed, it seems as if not a single Western writer of the nineteenth century failed to demonstrate, in one fashion or another, that he was well versed in Arabic literature in translation. It also appears that hardly a Western traveler to the East failed to relate or record in some form his impressions of the people, culture, and environment he encountered. Still, each of these travelers viewed the Orient differently. In fact, some of these perceptions were diametrically opposed; some brimmed with acclaim while others expressed complete rejection. These perceptions were also applied to the Muslim scene in Palestine.

Western perceptions of the East were deeply influenced by the belief that the area answered the Europeans' need for an ''exotic'' experience, that is, allowing one's imagination a free rein, unconstrained by fixed conventions. One European artist who often painted Oriental scenes said that visiting the ''exotic East'' was like an excursion into a theatrical world where illusion superseded reality.[41]

The perception of the Orient as emotional and intoxicating attracted tourists to the Middle East. For many, the main attraction of the Muslim world was its image as distant, strange, and entertaining. Western visitors were especially captivated by the Oriental women who seemed unattainable and shrouded in mystery behind their veils. Travelers were fascinated by them, and they often rendered accounts of meetings that were not necessarily based on reality. Harems and places frequented by women, such as bathhouses and Bedouin tents, were often the subjects of stories told back home.

Other items of special interest to Western visitors included both the castles and fortresses of governors, along with the garb worn and customs practiced in these places, and the simple pastoral atmosphere of the Bedouin tribes. Enthusiasm for the East was so great that some of the travelers viewed it as a place of refuge from European civilization. The penetration of the West, and the enormous influence it exerted on the East, were regarded by these people as a potential disaster and a blemish on the pristine and noble beauty of the Orient.[42]

In addition to this romantic approach, political and scholarly interests sought to impart respectability to the study of the Muslim lands within the framework of the West's aspirations to investigate and penetrate the area.

Alongside these positive views, a wide range of critical and hostile opinions of Muslim society were expressed. Many Westerners found fault with the laziness of the local populace. Various nineteenth-century works depict the Arabs as indolent people wasting all their time in idle gossip and smoking narghilas, while about them the splendid monuments of the past fell into ruin. Many saw the Arabs' lack of industriousness as the main reason behind the decline of the Ottoman Empire and the Middle East. Other Arab traits that came under criticism in Western literature were "innate fatalism," "passive submissiveness," and "extreme cruelty." The phrase "barbarism of the Muslim people" appears frequently. Europeans considered Muslims to be ignorant, blindly fanatic, inferior, corrupt (baksheesh was common), dishonest, and capable of extreme cruelty toward non-Muslims. These views found reinforcement in the Turkish-Greek wars and in the slaughter of Christians by the Druze in 1860.[43]

Some Western travelers, although critical of the local inhabitants, also sought positive aspects of the Muslim personality. Alphonse de Lamartine, for example, inveighed against the fatalism of the Muslims but also lauded the depth of their belief, their charitableness, hospitality, patience, and system of justice. He argued at great length that studying the Koran was no less important than studying the New Testament. Many Western visitors noted Muslim devoutness and the unparalleled religious atmosphere prevailing in mosques. This phenomenon could be interpreted either as devotion to the faith or as fanaticism. The Arabs of the desert were viewed as even more religious than their counterparts in the city, and the theme of the Bedouin at prayer in the desert was popular among Western artists. Islamic prayer served to equalize the half-naked fellah and the wealthy effendi with his silk caftan and golden jewelry.[44]

The devoutness of the Muslims, as well as their garb, were regarded as relics of an earlier period. At times they were compared to European practices during the Middle Ages, when a movement within the Roman Catholic Church in France opposed those who sought to compromise between religion and modern science, advocating a return to the complete, natural faith of olden days. In 1870, a "Catholic revival" placed great emphasis on pilgrimages, particularly to the new center in Lourdes, but also to Jerusalem. These Catholic revivalists saw in the Muslim pilgrimage to Mecca a parallel that provided support for their own activities, and they looked approvingly upon Islam, just as they looked wistfully back to the Middle Ages, an era before science challenged religion's supremacy.[45]

The Orient also fascinated Western painters, for reasons beyond the landscapes and the sites of biblical or historical relevance; they found a veritable gold mine in the Oriental ambience. In the eighteenth century, Constantinople and the splendor of the Ottoman sultans had captured the interest of French, Italian, Flemish, and German artists. France was largely responsible for the "turqueries" fashion of this century, and French artists in particular painted the dress, ceremonies, and grandeur of the Ottoman court. At the end of the eighteenth century, English artists also visited Constantinople. Paintings of scenes from Turkey, Egypt, Syria, Palestine, and other parts of the Ottoman Empire were fashionable.[46]

During the nineteenth century the element of realism that was incorporated into paintings of the Orient led to greater exactness, details, and objectivity in the portrayals of Eastern figures and landscapes. An ethnographic approach to painting became apparent in the meticulous depiction of individuals reflecting a variety of types and social groupings, and the precise, minute differences between them. These realist painters went so far as to distinguish between the physiognomies of the different Eastern types: Turks and Egyptians among others. They also noted the differences in architecture and decorative features of Moorish, Mameluk, and Ottoman buildings.

Paintings of the Orient were widely displayed to enthusiastic viewers at international and ethnic exhibitions, the London Royal Academy of Art, and Parisian salons. Collections were also amassed by the nobility and wealthy families. At times, the artists demanded exorbitant prices for their paintings, for they often worked under difficult conditions—due, in part, to the religious opposition of Islam to paintings and sculptures. For example, William Holman Hunt was accused by the local population of selling the portraits he painted to Satan, and in Albania Edward Lear was pronounced to be Satan in person. Painters found it difficult to enter religious edifices and to obtain models, particularly Muslim women.[47] Nonetheless, it seems that the opposition encountered by European artists only served to whet their appetite to capture the Orient on canvas. However, they maintained a dualistic attitude toward their subjects: enthusiastic, but at the same time distant. Muslims at prayer were portrayed as fervent but primitive.

Nineteenth-century Western scholars began to study the fellahin and Bedouin, and to develop other views concerning the origins and religious beliefs of these peoples. Some of them identified in contemporary Arab customs, lifestyle, and folklore influences of the ancient Near East dating back to the pre-Hellenistic period, and even to biblical times.[48] They argued that the population of Syria and, in particular, Palestine had remained essentially Semitic in race and culture for over a thousand years, and that it had withstood the cultural encroachments of all conquerors. The "Unchanging East" was seen to represent the people and culture of the Bible.[49]

This theory had numerous opponents, including the renowned archaeologist William F. Albright, who maintained that Islamic civilization could be traced no farther back than the Hellenistic period, and that Islam itself stemmed from the Judeo-Christian tradition and had little in common with the faiths of the ancient Near East. Albright felt that the gap between Hellenistic-Roman civilization and that of the ancient Orient was far greater than the one separating Islam from Hellenism. Any attempt to ignore this reality, Albright said, was an outright distortion of history.[50] Nevertheless, the school linking the Arab world with the biblical period persisted. Its proponents regarded the local population of Palestine as direct descendants of the Canaanites, Amorites, and other indigenous peoples.[51]

There were also Jewish scholars who searched for a connection between the Arab residents of nineteenth-century Eretz Israel and the Jewish inhabitants of the Land in earlier periods—but their objective was different. They hoped to find an affinity between the two peoples, Arab and Jewish, and they viewed the Arabs as the cultural successors of the Jews rather than of the Canaanites.[52] By contrast, most of the non-Jewish scholars had a political objective—one that exists to this day—namely, to bolster the Arab claim to ownership and primacy in the Middle East, including Palestine. The Arabs were said to succeed the Canaanites, the earliest inhabitants. The Israelites came later, while the modern Jewish population was deemed a foreign implant in the region.[53]

Other than those individuals or groups mentioned above, who focused particularly on Palestine, most scholars viewed that country only as a small and marginal part of the vast expanse of the exotic, Oriental, Middle East. Some of the travelers, scholars, and painters interested in the East failed to write much, or anything, about Palestine. Their major focus lay elsewhere: in Turkey, Egypt, Mesopotamia, Syria, North Africa, and Arabia.[54]

A LAND OF NEW BEGINNINGS

The final perception of Palestine found in nineteenth-century travel literature is that of a land of new beginnings. Three main factors contributed to this view.

The first factor was the group of developments and changes that occurred within the Ottoman Empire as a whole in the nineteenth century, and whose effect upon Palestine was particularly great. These included (1) constitutional reforms that reinstituted the Capitulations laws and led to the establishment of many consulates in Palestine, particularly in Jerusalem, making it possible for foreign citizens residing in Palestine to maintain their original citizenship and to acquire property; (2) increasing involvement in Palestine on the part of European powers and Christian churches; (3) the penetration of modernization and technology into the undeveloped East; (4) changes in the population of Palestine, with an increase in the number of Western pilgrims and other visitors; and (5) the beginnings of a new, Zionist, Jewish immigration (the "New Yishuv"). At times, these developments were not in fact as far-reaching as they appeared to observers, but they generated a sense of new beginnings in the ancient, historic Holy Land, the Land of the Bible.

The second factor was the religious revival within nineteenth-century Christianity. Palestine came to be regarded not only as a land of the past, but also as a land of the future, the "Promised Land." Greater involvement by the Christian Church in the region generated a longing for the Holy Land. This precipitated an increase in the number of pilgrims and accelerated church activity in the area. This awakening was most pronounced among Protestants. The evangelical revival that characterized the first half of the nineteenth century also ushered in various forms of millenarianism and induced diverse groups of Americans, Germans, and Swedes to settle in Palestine in hopes of witnessing the Second Coming.[55] Millenarians also encouraged the return of the Jewish nation to its Land, for they regarded the ingathering of the exiles as the first stage in the process, to be followed by the Jews' acceptance of Jesus, and Jesus' second revelation in the Holy Land. People like Lord Shaftsbury, Colonel Charles Henry Churchill, George Gawler and his son John, Lawrence Oliphant, and many others lent their enthusiastic support to the new beginnings in the Holy Land. These beginnings would introduce changes in the depressing and humiliating situation of the Land under Ottoman rule and would restore it and the ancient nation residing in it to their former glory.[56]

The third factor heralding momentous change was the enormous growth during the nineteenth century of what had been for hundreds of years a very small Jewish community in Palestine. This development was accompanied by ferment in the Jewish world as a whole, a portent of Zionist ideology. Jewish neighborhoods in Jerusalem were built outside the walls of the Old City of Jerusalem; efforts were made to acquire land in Palestine and to establish productive urban and agricultural enterprises; the Jewish community received support from philanthropists such as Moses Montefiore, the Rothschild family, and others; aid was tendered to the settlement of Eretz Israel by Jewish communities and organizations throughout the world; there was a growing new Jewish intelligentsia in Central and Eastern Europe; practical undertakings reflected the messianic hopes of the precursors and followers of Zionism—all these developments reinforced and justified the sense of a new beginning in the Holy Land.

CONCLUSION

These six perceptions of Palestine are to be found in nineteenth-century Western travel literature. Two of them pertained exclusively to Palestine, viewing it *a priori* as a divine Holy Land and as the Land of the Bible and of biblical sites. Two others regarded the Land as an integral part of the broader region in which it was located, whether the ancient Middle East or the Middle East of the nineteenth century. Palestine did not figure prominently in either of the latter two outlooks; it occupied only a small and unimportant corner of the ancient Middle East relative to Egypt, Mesopotamia, and other civilizations in the region. Similarly, within the Middle East of the nineteenth century, Palestine played a minor role vis-à-vis Constantinople, Cairo, Baghdad, Damascus, and other centers of the East.

The two remaining perceptions—like the first and second—focused on the distinctiveness and uniqueness of Palestine. True, other Middle East lands were also utterly desolate and new developments could be discerned there, but the perception of Palestine as a land of new beginnings stemmed from the Land's unique background and ancient history; the depressing condition of the Holy

Land was juxtaposed with its former grandeur. Moreover, the new beginnings bore special significance because they sprang directly from the Land's singular history.

The uniqueness of Palestine was recognized by most nineteenth-century writers; they had no desire to detach themselves from the ancient history of the Land, and they viewed the fact that Palestine was organically part of a much larger region as a temporary phenomenon. Palestine was different from the rest of the Ottoman Empire. It was the Holy Land, the Land of the Old and New Testament. Its destruction and state of desolation had been brought on by divine decree. But it was widely believed and fervently hoped that there would be a new beginning for this Land.

NOTES

1. For a review of the scope and character of nineteenth-century literature on Western travel to Palestine, see Yehoshua Ben-Arieh, *The Rediscovery of the Land in the Nineteenth Century* (Jerusalem and Detroit: Magnes Press and Wayne State University Press, 1979).

2. Izak Schattner, *The Map of Palestine and Its History* (Jerusalem: Bialik Institute, 1951, Hebrew), 159.

3. George L. Robinson, *The Biblical Doctrine of Holiness* (Winona Lake, Ind.: Winona Publishing, 1903), 34.

4. William D. Davies, *The Gospel and the Land* (Berkeley: University of California Press, 1974); Frank W. Epp, *Whose Land Is Palestine: The Middle East Problem in Historical Perspective* (Grand Rapids, Mich.: W. B. Eerdmans, 1974), 87; Lester I. Vogel, "Zion as Place and Past—An American Myth: Ottoman Palestine in the American Mind Perceived through Protestant Consciousness and Experience" (Ph.D. diss., George Washington University, 1984), 24-26.

5. G. A. Barrois, *Twentieth Century Encyclopedia of Religious Knowledge* (Grand Rapids, Mich., 1955), 523.

6. Mercea Eliade, *The Sacred and the Profane* (New York: Harcourt Brace, 1959), p. 199; L. I. Vogel (above, n.4), pp. 21, 23.

7. See, for example, George A. Barton, *Archaeology and the Bible* (Philadelphia: American Sunday School Union, 1927), 94; Arthur P. Stanley, *Sinai and Palestine in Connection with Their History* (London: J. Murray, 1856), Preface; George A. Smith, *Historical Geography of the Holy Land*, 26th ed. (London: Hodder and Stoughton, 1935), Preface.

8. See, for example, Edward Robinson and E. Smith, *Biblical Researches in Palestine and in the Adjacent Regions* (London: J. Murray, 1841), 46.

9. L. I. Vogel (above, n.4), pp. 40-45.

10. James W. Parkes, *A History of Palestine from 135 A.D. to Modern Times* (London: Gollancz, 1949), 215-16; Thomas H. Horne, *The Biblical Keepsake: Or Landscape Illustrations of the Holy Scriptures* (London: J. Murray, 1836); Y. Ben-Arieh (above, n.1), pp. 15-16.

11. W. Holman Hunt, *Pre-Raphaelitism and the Pre-Raphaelite Brotherhood* (London: MacMillan, 1905); Andrea Rose, *The Pre-Raphaelites* (Oxford: Phaidon, 1981); M.

Bennet, *Catalogue of Exhibition, William Holman Hunt* (Liverpool/London: Walker Art Gallery & Victoria and Albert Museum, 1969).

12. Malcolm Warner, "The Question of Faith: Orientalism, Christianity and Islam," in *The Orientalists: Delacroix to Matisse, European Painters in North-Africa and the Near-East*, ed. Mary-Anne Stevens (London: Royal Academy of Arts, 1984), 32-39 (hereafter: *Orientalists*).

13. J. W. Parkes (above, n.10), pp. 232-33.

14. Sarah Searight, *The British in the Middle East*, 2d ed. (London: Weidenfeld & Nicolson, 1979), 231-51.

15. M. Warner (above, n.12), pp. 32-39.

16. L. I. Vogel (above, n.4), pp. 40-46, and sources referred to in the text.

17. Izak Schattner, "Ideas on the Physical Geography of Palestine in the Early 19th Century," *Eretz-Israel* 2 (1953, Hebrew): 41-49; Y. Ben-Arieh (above, n.1), pp. 100-105, 137-40.

18. Marie E. de Meester, *Oriental Influences in English Literature of the Nineteenth Century* (Heidelberg: C. Winter, 1915), Preface.

19. *Travellers beyond the Grand Tour: Catalogue* (London: Fine Art Society, 1980) (hereafter: *Grand Tour Catalogue*).

20. S. Searight (above, n.14), pp. 231-51.

21. Robert Irwin, "The Orient and the West from Bonaparte to T. E. Lawrence," in *Orientalists* (above, n.12), pp. 24-26.

22. For details on the founding of the Egyptological Society of London and the first stages of Egyptology, see, for example, Peter A. Clayton, *The Rediscovery of Ancient Egypt: Artists and Travellers in the 19th Century* (London: Thames & Hudson, 1982).

23. S. Searight (above, n.14), pp. 213-14.

24. Mary-Anne Stevens, "Western Art and Its Encounter with the Islamic World," in *Orientalists* (above, n.12) pp. 15-23.

25. Several of Simpson's original paintings are in the Palestine Exploration Fund Archives in London. Also see the Fund's internal publication, *Catalogue of Palestine in Pictures*, which contains a brief report on Simpson.

26. Y. Ben-Arieh (above, n.1), pp. 161–63; Henry B. Tristram, *The Land of Israel: A Journal of Travels in Palestine* (London: Society for Promoting Christain Knowledge, 1865).

27. Y. Ben-Arieh (above, n.1), pp. 14-16 and passim.

28. Yehoshua Ben-Arieh, "Pioneering Scientific Exploration in the Holy Land at the Beginning of the Nineteenth Century," *Terrae Incognitae: The Annals of the Society for History of Discoveries* 4 (1972): 95-100.

29. Yehoshua Ben-Arieh, "Lynch's Expedition to the Dead Sea (1847–48)," *Prologue: The Journal of the National Archives* 5 (1973): 14-21.

30. Y. Ben-Arieh (above, n.1), pp. 68-77.

31. Ibid., pp. 177-215; V. D. Lipman, "The Origins of the Palestine Exploration Fund," *Palestine Exploration Quarterly* 120 (1988): 45-54.

32. Y. Ben-Arieh (above, n.1), pp. 177-215.

33. Rehav Rubin, "The Search for Stephan Illes," *Eretz Magazine* (Autumn 1985): 44-48; Rehav Rubin and Moti Yair, "The Maps of Stephan Illes: A Cartographer of Jerusalem in the Nineteenth Century," *Cathedra* 36 (1985, Hebrew): 63-72.

34. *Grand Tour Catalogue* (above, n.19), p. 31.

35. Yehoshua Ben-Arieh, "Nineteenth Century Western Travel Literature on Eretz-

Israel: A Historical Source and a Cultural Phenomenon," *Cathedra* 40 (1986, Hebrew): 159-88. For details on the introduction of photography in Palestine, see Yeshayahu Nir, *The Bible and the Image: The History of Photography in the Holy Land 1839-1899* (Philadelphia: University of Pennsylvania Press, 1985).

36. Jacob de Haas, *History of Palestine: The Last Two Thousand Years* (New York: Macmillian, 1934). For a work that emphasized Palestine's destruction and desolation, citing numerous quotations from ninteenth-century travel literature, see Saul S. Friedman, *Land of Dust: Palestine at the Turn of the Century* (Washington, D.C.: University Press of America, 1982); also see David S. Landes, "Palestine before the Zionists," *Commentary* 61 (February 1976): 47-56; (May 1976): 22.

37. J. de Haas (above, n.36), p. 386, quotes Conder; John MacGregor, *The Rob Roy on the Jordan* (London: J. Murray, 1870), Frontispiece.

38. The term "Orientalism" has had different usages: Arberry applied it to students of the languages and literature of the Eastern lands; Said adopted it to attack Westerners who, he felt, offered incorrect explanations of the East. See A. J. Arberry, *British Orientalists* (London: William Collins, 1943); Edward W. Said, *Orientalism* (New York: Pantheon, 1978). In this chapter, the term "Orientalism" is used to denote interest in, and study of, the Islamic lands of the Middle East in the nineteenth century.

39. M. E. de Meester (above, n.18).

40. M. A. Stevens (above, n.24).

41. Ibid.

42. The best-known example is that of Lady Hester Stanhope, who built her home on Mount Lebanon.

43. M. Warner (above, n.12); see also, for example, the opinions of the well-known artist David Roberts as expressed in his work, *The Holy Land, Syria, Idumea, Arabia, Egypt & Nubia* (London: F. G. Moon, 1842-1849).

44. M. Warner (above, n.12); M. A. Stevens (above, n.24).

45. M. Warner (above, n.12).

46. *Grand Tour Catalogue* (above, n.19), p. 27.

47. Caroline Bugler, "Innocents Abroad: Nineteenth Century Artists and Travellers in North-Africa and the Near-East," in *Orientalists* (above, n.12), pp. 27-31.

48. J. W. Parkes (above, n.10), pp. 232-33.

49. L. I. Vogel (above, n.4), pp. 398-404, and sources cited there, especially Samuel I. Curtiss, *Primitive Semitic Religion Today* (Chicago: F. H Revell, 1902).

50. William F. Albright, *History, Archaeology and Christian Humanism* (New York: McGraw Hill, 1964), 157-77.

51. L. I. Vogel (above, n.4); Elihu Grant, *The People of Palestine* (Philadelphia: J. B. Lippincott, c. 1921); idem, *Palestine, Our Holy Land* (Baltimore: typ., J H. Furst, 1940); Elizabeth A. Finn, *Palestine Peasantry: Notes on their Clans, Warfare, Religion and Law* (London: Marshall, 1923).

52. See, for example: David Ben-Gurion and Izhak Ben-Zvi, *Eretz Israel* (New York: Poalei Zion, 1918, Yiddish). I am grateful to Dr. Ran Aaronsohn, who called my attention to the writings of Yisrael Belkind on this subject, in which he advocated the assimilation of the Arab population into the Jewish community. See Ran Aaronsohn, ed., *In the Path of the Biluim: Memoirs of Yisrael Belkind* (Tel Aviv: Ministry of Defense, 1983, Hebrew); a listing of Belkind's writings appears at the end of the volume.

53. M. A. Aamiry, *Jerusalem: Arab Origin and Heritage* (London: Longman, 1978);

Frances E. Newton, *Fifty Years in Palestine* (Wrotham, England: Coldharbour Press, 1948), 174-75.

54. Three well-known Orientalists who did not write about Palestine are the subject of Thomas J. Assad, *Three Victorian Travellers: Burton, Blunt, Doughty* (London: Routledge & K. Paul, 1964).

55. Ruth Kark, "Millenarism and Agricultural Settlement in the Holy Land in the Nineteenth Century," *Journal of Historical Geography* 9 (1983): 47-62.

56. Barbara Tuchman, *Bible and Sword: England and Palestine from the Bronze Age to Balfour* (London: A. Redman, 1957), chaps, 10-12; Albert M. Hyamson, *British Projects for the Restoration of the Jews* (London: British Palestine Committee, 1917).

PART I

NORTH AMERICA

Chapter 2

The America–Holy Land Studies Project: A Personal Statement

Robert T. Handy

When I take down any of the many volumes produced under the auspices of the America–Holy Land Studies project, I use it as I would any other scholarly work, normally without reflecting on how the book came to be. That we need a set of source books, bibliographical guides, and collections of stimulating essays on the historical relationship between the United States and the Holy Land seems obvious enough, and so we accept and use the materials that have been prepared as given. However, as I look over the long row of books on America–Holy Land Studies published since 1977, I am reminded of words Herbert Butterfield once wrote:

> When we look back upon the past we see things fixed and frozen as they happened, and they become rigid in our minds, so that we think they must always have been inevitable—we can hardly imagine how anything else could have happened. But when we look to the future, while it is still fluid, we can hardly fail to realize its unspeakable liquidity.[1]

More than two decades of planning, thinking, consulting, testing, organizing, and fund raising lie behind the impressive set of unpublished materials that have appeared over the last ten years. Only slowly in that earlier period of "liquidity" did the conceptualization of the project emerge, finally to bear rich fruit.

Professor Moshe Davis has been the instrumental force for the publication of these scholarly materials, that have opened up a fascinating field of study and have gathered a widening circle of interested scholars. In 1956, while he was teaching at the Jewish Theological Seminary of America, he edited a book entitled

Israel: Its Role in Civilization, of which the fourth part was "America and Israel." In the five essays gathered under that title one can already discern some of the foundation stones on which the project was to be built. Two of those presentations were by persons who were to become closely associated with Davis as co-directors as the project unfolded. The late Selig Adler, professor of history at the State University of New York at Buffalo, wrote on "Backgrounds of American Policy toward Zion," utilizing his vast knowledge of American dip- lomatic history as he traced in detail the steps that led up to Truman's speedy recognition of Israel in 1948. I contributed an article on "Zion in American Christian Movements," pointing to various, often changing uses of the concept of Zion in the history of Christian thought and life in the United States.[2] In this way a partnership was begun that guided the America–Holy Land Studies project to maturity.

Three years after the publication of that book, Davis moved to Israel to teach American Jewish history and to establish the Institute of Contemporary Jewry at the Hebrew University of Jerusalem. Along with various other projects, Davis pursued his interest in America–Holy Land Studies, conducting a variety of conferences in Israel and the United States on this theme, referring to it in addresses and meetings, and whenever possible involving his partners and others who shared interest in and knowledge of the field. A fruitful example is the joint seminar we taught under the sponsorship of the Jewish Theological Seminary and the Union Theological Seminary.

Gradually, the outlines of the project took shape. It was decided to approach the field in a thoroughly scholarly and primarily historical way, to make 1948 the terminal date of study, to use the term "Holy Land" for the region that has long had an aura of holiness in varying degrees for three major faiths, and to open the project to interested scholars of all traditions. A working hypothesis was that the theme of Holy Land, or Zion, has long been used with somewhat differing but overlapping meanings in both Jewish and Christian history, that it is part of the continuing spiritual history of America, and that it illuminates the interplay of ideas among diverse religious and cultural elements in the United States. Administratively, America–Holy Land Studies became a joint project of the American Jewish Historical Society and the Institute of Contemporary Jewry. The labors of the society's director, Bernard Wax, of editorial coordinators Nathan Kaganoff (U.S.) and Menahem Kaufman (Israel), and of coordinator Lucy D. Manoff (U.S.) have been very important in guiding the events and producing the publications of the project.

A major step in the process of defining an undeveloped and neglected field of historical study was an informal colloquium of some thirty-five scholars held in 1970 at Union Theological Seminary.[3] As the project matured, it was found that an important task was the identification of bibliographical materials. Two teams of researchers were formed to gather and annotate the needed references, one in Israel led by Yohai Goell of the Institute of Contemporary Jewry of the Hebrew University, and the other in the United States directed by Nathan M.

Kaganoff, librarian of the American Jewish Historical Society. Once again, the results of the preliminary work were put into pamphlet form as specimen pages of a projected multivolume bibliographical guide; the section chosen was on the individual and institutional presence of America in the Holy Land from 1620 to 1948.[4] These early pamphlets proved to be useful in calling attention to the project as it was being defined, and in enlisting older and younger scholars to participate in it. In preparation for a major colloquium, a representative consultative committee met in 1974 in New York to test the methodology that was being developed.

Finally, twenty years after the work of defining and shaping a relatively new field for scholarly research and interpretation began, the first Scholars Colloquium on America–Holy Land Studies met on September 8–9, 1975 at (and with the co-sponsorship of) the National Archives and Records Service in Washington, D.C. The carefully edited papers of the colloquium, a list of participants, a bibliography on Americans in the Holy Land for the years 1850–1900 (compiled by Yohai Goell and Martha B. Katz-Hyman), along with some illustrative texts, were published in book form, *With Eyes Toward Zion*. In the introduction and in the opening paper, "The Holy Land in American Spiritual History," Davis presented the results of the long process of the project's definition and outlined its four major categories and subthemes as diplomatic policy, Christian devotion, Jewish attachment, and cultural aspects. Among other matters, he stated:

> The concept *spiritual*, as I understand it, is not a synonym for *religious*, but encompasses the spectrum of religious, cultural, and ethnic history—the accumulated moral, ethical, and creative decisions made by individuals and groups. In this sense, the America–Holy Land theme is integral to America's spiritual history. . . . Devotion to Zion has been shared by Americans of diverse backgrounds and cultural orientations. Attachment to the Holy Land extends into American homes, patterns of faith, and education, illuminating the interplay of ideas among different religions and cultures. Here many varied elements meet, sometimes antithetically, but most often cooperatively.[5]

In view of the venue of the colloquium, a paper identifying resources for further research and interpretation was prepared by Milton O. Gustafson, then chief of the diplomatic branch of the National Archives.[6] In an article in the *Washington Star*, a staff writer summarized several of the papers, observing that if the most careful academic ethic were not followed, the project could be used as a political platform, but he concluded: "Notwithstanding some inherent dangers—and there always will be political dangers no matter what phase of studies one takes regarding the Holy Land—this field of study of the relationship of Americans to the Holy Land should be encouraged."[7] The warning about a strict academic ethic was and has continued to be heeded, but one reviewer very prominent in politics at the time, Robert F. Drinan, observed in his review of the book, after noting the 1948 terminal date: "Those who absorb the rich new material in this book will be well equipped to explain more persuasively America's relationship to the Holy Land since 1948.''[8] Most reviews included some comment similar to the one with which Franklin H. Littell concluded his remarks in the journal of the American Society of Church History: "This book is a valuable introduction to one of the most important recurring themes in America's spiritual history.''[9]

The report of the 1975 colloquium was the only "original" volume in what was otherwise a reprint series of 72 books on America and the Holy Land, which appeared in 1977. Five of the reprints were original anthologies made up of some important pieces of less than book length; the rest were reproduced from works published between 1828 and 1950. Selected from a list of some 300 possibilities, the books contained studies and travel accounts by noted Christian and Jewish authors, including archaeologists, historians, scientists, biblical scholars, novelists, consuls, missionaries, settlers, and builders of the Land; some were works famous in their time but long out of print. A few scholarly tomes mingle with popular writings—as, for example, Edward Robinson's remarkable contribution to the geography of the Holy Land, *Biblical Researches in Palestine, Mount Sinai and Arabia Petraea*, originally published in 1841.[10]

In an interview, Davis observed that among the criteria for the reprint series were readability and significance for understanding the transmission of culture. He stressed that the series was not designed to promote the Zionist point of view: "We tried to play fair. . . . Someone like Harry Emerson Fosdick [*A Pilgrimage to Palestine*] was far from favoring the idea of a Jewish state. But his work is of high literary, historical, and philosophical value—and of course it was included.''[11] The new availability of important works from the past was a boon to researchers in this expanding field, and to professors of religion and history who have developed courses directly or indirectly related to the theme of America–Holy Land studies.

Early in the history of the project it was recognized that many other relevant books, periodicals, reports, and documents were located in specialized archives that were not readily available. The bibliographical researchers on the two teams previously mentioned undertook precise and demanding spadework in many libraries, archives, and institutions, and in the early 1980s the rich crop was harvested as the first of four volumes under the title *Guide to America–Holy Land Studies* (after the first volume, the dates 1620–1948 were added to the series title). Each volume had a distinctive theme, and each was introduced by Moshe Davis as the project director. The first three were meticulously edited by Nathan M. Kaganoff, and they were focused respectively on American presence (1980), political relations and American Zionism (1982), and economic relations and philanthropy (1983). The fourth volume of the *Guide* was edited by Mehahem Kaufman and Mira Levine (1984); it bore the subtitle *Resource Material in British, Israeli and Turkish Repositories*, and it represented a significant widening of the bibliographical base of the project. Each book includes a list of the researchers and of the repositories explored. The first volume was published by

Arno Press; the following three by New York's Praeger Publishers, which has since become the project's publishing channel.

At least two review articles considered all four volumes. Ava F. Kahn had "field-tested" the *Guides* with good results, finding them "an amazing new tool for historians working in the fields of American and Israeli history, or in the newly defined field of America–Holy Land studies." The reviewer regretted only that the coverage did not extend through the 1970s, but it seems fair to add that as the *Guide* is called "an excellent model for anyone planning such an archival tool," it is usable for anyone who might like to take on that added task.[12] Michael Brown's review in *Jewish Social Studies* pointed to a few problems and omissions, but he found that the *Guide* is a seminal work, "sowing the seeds of future scholarship relating to the America–Holy Land connection for generations to come." He anticipated that "now standard views will alter, when all of these documents are digested."[13]

In my role as a co-director of the project, I have served as a resource person for the Christian aspects of the studies and have undertaken some research and writing appropriate to that end. An unexpected benefit for my teaching and writing in the field of American religious history was the deeper knowledge of and feeling for Judaism and the Jewish people gained as I worked alongside Jewish scholars on historical materials of mutual interest.[14] A chapter on "Sources for Understanding American Christian Attitudes toward the Holy Land, 1800–1950" in *With Eyes Toward Zion* was followed by the editing and introducing of a volume of sources on *The Holy Land in American Protestant Life, 1800–1948*. A reviewer indicated that from the book, one gains

> a better understanding of the complex nature of American Protestant attitudes, from biblically based pro-Zionist positions to the pro-Arab sympathies of a number of nineteenth-century biblical archaeologists whose earliest contacts within Palestine were with Arabs. One also gains insight into the reasons why so many American Protestants felt an attachment to the Holy Land and what those who traveled or lived there hoped to accomplish. Finally, one is offered a rare glimpse of Arab-Jewish relations within Palestine prior to the founding of the State of Israel and or black attitudes toward Zionism and toward the sufferings of the Jewish people.[15]

Reviews pointed out limitations as well as values in the book; for example, John M. Mulder wrote, "One might have expected Handy to begin with the colonial mythologies of Israel, but there is ample material on this issue; one also might regret that he cut off his selections with the creation of the state of Israel in 1948, but the richness of the collection indicates that the present configuration of attitudes has a lineage."[16] William R. Hutchinson observed that "Judging from these selections, the exciting and portentous American experience of the Holy Land produced, in almost every genre, a curiously tedious literature," but in conclusion he noted that the work "is nonetheless a pioneering venture for which teachers in a number of fields will be grateful.''[17] Indeed, making primary materials related to America and the Holy Land available to serious students and scholars has been a major aim of all the publications of the project from its inception.

The Second International Scholars Colloquium on America–Holy Land Studies was again held at the National Archives in Washington, D.C. from August 30 to September 1, 1983. Nearly twice as many contributors and participants were involved than had been at the first. Topics that had been part of the first colloquium were given further consideration in the light of continuing work and of the research into materials in British, Turkish, and Israeli repositories. Davis' opening statement emphasized that the basic research was contributing to the expansion of teaching and study about America and the Holy Land in universities; papers reported on educational experiences in the growing field. Presentations on the meaning of the Holy Land for various American groups such as blacks, evangelical Protestants, Catholics, and Mormons elaborated on matters briefly covered eight years before.

A remarkable widening of the horizons was apparent as materials from British and Turkish sources were richly cited in papers that illuminated the America–Holy Land relationship through outside observations. At the same time, the deepening research into archives in Israel broadened the scope of the studies so that it became more fully a two-way street—not primarily a view of the Holy Land from the American perspective, but also a consideration of America through the eyes of those who lived and worked in the Palestine of the Ottoman and Mandate periods: American consuls, writers in Hebrew periodicals, and travelers from the Holy Land to America. Those who study the motivations of persons who went on pilgrimages and travels to the Holy Land—or who lived and worked there for a time as scholars, consuls, and settlers—will be quite surprised to see how these same people were viewed by the resident populations! It is equally as fascinating to look at America through the eyes of visitors *from* the Holy Land.

The volume that emerged from the second colloquium, containing the papers and complete documentation, was nearly twice as long as the first: *With Eyes Toward Zion–II.*[18] It is an impressive progress report, reinforces the *Guides* in pointing to vast new resources that need continuing research and interpretation, and raises many fresh topics for investigation and analysis; it calls attention to the need and value of continued study in a now well-defined field. The entire America–Holy Land Project has highlighted the importance of a somewhat neglected area of scholarly study, raised significant questions, and produced an impressive array of materials that invite younger and older scholars from various backgrounds and points of view to devote part, or in some cases all, of their creative time to America–Holy Land Studies. The growing body of materials and their interpretation demonstrates that a united field in which American history meets the Jewish and Christian traditions has been firmly established.

NOTES

1. Herbert Butterfield, *Christianity and History* (New York: Charles Scribner's Sons, 1950), 110.

2. Moshe Davis, ed., *Israel: Its Role in Civilization* (1956; reprint, New York: Arno Press, 1977), pt. 4, pp. 229-322. The two papers cited are on pp. 251-83 and 284-97.

3. "America and the Holy Land: A Colloquium," *American Jewish Historical Quarterly* 62 (September, 1972); reprinted as a pamphlet by the Institute of Contemporary Jewry, 1972.

4. Moshe Davis, ed., *Guide for America–Holy Land Studies: Section on American Individual and Institutional Presence, 1620–1948—Specimen Pages* (Jerusalem: Institute of Contemporary Jewry, Hebrew University of Jerusalem, 1973).

5. Moshe Davis, ed., *With Eyes Toward Zion: Scholars Colloquium on America–Holy Land Studies* (New York: Arno Press, 1977), xvii-xxii, 3-33, quotations on pp. 3, 4.

6. Milton Gustafson, "Records in the National Archives relating to America and the Holy Land," ibid., 129-52.

7. William F. Willoughby, *Washington Star*, 21 September 1975.

8. *Moment* 3 (October 1978): 40.

9. *Church History* 49 (March 1980): 106.

10. The reprint series was published by Arno Press. Since that firm went out of business, copies of all the works published for the project by Arno through 1981 are available from the Ayer Company, P.O. Box 958, 382 Main St., Salem, NH 03079, phone 603-898-1200, as long as supplies last.

11. Quoted by Matthew Nesvisky, "American Responses to the Land of the Bible," *Jerusalem Post*, 12 September 1977.

12. *Public Historian* 6 (Fall 1984): 110-14.

13. *Jewish Social Studies* 47 (Summer/Fall 1985): 337-39.

14. I sought to spell this out in an article written in the project's formative years: "Studies in the Interrelationships between America and the Holy Land: A Fruitful Field for Interdisciplinary and Interfaith Cooperation," *Journal of Church and State* 13 (Spring 1971): 283–301; reprinted in James E. Wood, Jr., ed., *Jewish-Christian Relations in Today's World* (Waco, Tex.: Markham Press Fund of Baylor University Press, 1971), 105-25.

15. Ellen M. Umaͦᵤ   *American Jewish Archives* 36 (April 1984): 64-65.

16. *Church History* 52 (September 1983): 420.

17. *Catholic Historical Review* 69 (January 1983): 119. David Klatzker, in his study "American Christian Travelers to the Holy Land, 1821–1939" (Ph.D. diss., Temple University, 1987), has suggested that a clue to the repetitiveness of such writings may reflect the fact that the authors tended to see what they sought to see and utilized familiar stereotypes in their accounts. See also Klatzker's chapter in this volume.

18. Moshe Davis, ed., *With Eyes Toward Zion–II: Themes and Sources in the Archives of the United States, Great Britain, Turkey and Israel* (New York: Praeger, 1986.)

Chapter 3

Studying America and the Holy Land: Prospects, Pitfalls, and Perspectives

Deborah Dash Moore

The field of America–Holy Land Studies emerged within the context of the burgeoning of new areas of academic study during the last several decades. In the field of history, the major discipline to which scholars of America and the Holy Land initially had recourse, innovation extended to a range of methodologies applied to increasingly diverse subjects. The "new history," the appellation given fields within social history, reflected an ever-broadening consciousness regarding the dimensions of human activity. No longer content to chronicle political events, the lives of great men, significant intellectual trends, and major economic transformations, historians discovered urban history, immigration and ethnic history, black history, women's history, family history.[1] They also provoked debate over traditional approaches to standard historical topics, such as politics and diplomacy, and challenged the assumptions of such established fields of inquiry as labor history. Historians even made the elusive subject of gender and sexuality an area for research. Many of these fields grew because of their advocates' hidden and not-so-hidden agendas and have come under attack by proponents of the old history.[2] Nonetheless, social history widened the scope of historical research and contributed to our understanding of the past.

America–Holy Land Studies have blended the traditional methods of the old history with the innovative subject matter of the new history. If the focus upon the Land of Israel in the nineteenth and first half of the twentieth centuries reflects the heightened American fascination with the State of Israel in the wake of the Six Day War of 1967, the excavation of archival sources for diplomatic, religious, and cultural history indicates a disavowal of any political agenda. The first published narrative historical accounts of diplomatic and religious interaction enhanced the legitimacy of America–Holy Land Studies through the application of conventional historical methods.[3] The decisions to divide the field into four major categories—diplomatic policy, Christian devotion, Jewish involvement, and cultural attachment—and to reprint a large number of volumes to make a body of material available to students strengthened the commitment to historical analysis. Yet these very efforts to secure the study of America and the Holy Land upon firm ground have contributed to a loosening of the constraints of conventional history in the discussion of specific topics. Scholars writing in *With Eyes Toward Zion–II* characteristically stepped beyond the boundaries of the four categories. In their discussions, for example, of the impact of Christian devotion upon diplomatic policy, or the influence of Jewish involvement on Christian religious thought, they have introduced an interdisciplinary posture.[4] The prospects of interdisciplinary America–Holy Land Studies enlarge the scope of the field and the range of scholars who would find such research attractive. Significantly, the same volume includes the work of historical geographers and recognizes the importance of visual evidence.[5]

In considering the prospects for interdisciplinary research, America–Holy Land Studies need not pioneer completely uncharted methodological territory. Area studies in general, and American studies in particular, offer several useful models of interdisciplinary approaches, both theoretical and substantive. American studies scholars also have acquired a measure of self-consciousness and self-reflectiveness that highlights the pitfalls facing interdisciplinary endeavors.[6] Their continuing calls for comparative and cross-cultural analysis reveal the dangers of American exceptionalism. Given the unique position occupied by the Holy Land in the Western religious imagination, such warnings can similarly remind scholars of America and the Holy Land of the need for caution. The openness of American studies to the new history, its willingness to explore such once marginal topics as sports and popular culture, and its ready embrace of any theoretical approach that promises fresh insight make it a provocative source of themes and methods for the next stage of America–Holy Land Studies. Needless to say, the future always builds upon the past, and that truism is nowhere more relevant than in the realm of scholarship.

Since cultural attachment has received the least attention of the four established categories of America–Holy Land Studies, it offers a most promising area for research. The wealth and diversity of sources available—including travelers' accounts, photographs, *belles lettres*, poetry, paintings, sculpture, architecture, as well as scientific exploration and archaeological discoveries—probably account for the relative lack of scholarship. So many diverse documents—as Yehoshua Ben-Arieh notes, there were at least 5,000 published items on Palestine from 1800 to 1878 alone—challenge the researcher to provide a coherent framework for discussion. Furthermore, the most interesting possibilities lie in examining the interrelationship of several of these cultural sources, in comparative analyses in addition to description. Fortunately, Ben-Arieh's narrative account and categorization of nineteenth-century travelers' accounts provides a solid foundation not only for historical geographers. His periodization, especially his dating of the beginning of modernization in Palestine in 1865, should help scholars who approach the travel literature from an American perspective to juxtapose American with Holy Land political realities.[7]

In contrast to Ben-Arieh's primary interest in Palestine and its history, David Klatzker's dissertation "American Christian Travelers to the Holy Land, 1821–1939" uses the travel literature to focus on the attitudes of American Christians toward Jews and Zionism. Klatzker explores one substantial body of cultural material and integrates the variety of sources through a typology of responses to the Holy Land. He also takes account of the growing interest in the business and culture of travel.[8] The latter topic would be worth exploring in its own right, especially in comparison with other popular places to visit.[9]

The issues of pilgrimage versus travel and of the secularization of pilgrimage in the modern world provide yet another framework for extending the discussion of cultural attachment. The anthropologist Victor Turner suggests the importance of pilgrimage in the salvation religions, arguing that "pilgrimage is to a voluntaristic, what initiation is to an obligatory, system."[10] Pilgrims undergo "a separation from a relatively fixed state of life and social status" and pass into what Turner defines as a "liminal or threshold phase," for which none of the rules "and few of the experiences of their previous existence had prepared them."[11] The application of these anthropological categories to the rich travel accounts would illuminate the nature of American religious attachment to the Holy Land and the impact of secularization upon those sentiments.

While travel literature, photography, and scientific expeditions have received some scholarly attention, architecture appears not yet to have found its historian, one who could examine the mutual influence between America and the Holy Land. Holy Land buildings provided a model of religious architecture for architects of American churches and synagogues, and American style and innovation had an impact upon construction in the Holy Land. The attraction of the "Oriental" as representing an exalted spirituality can be contrasted to the appeal of Greek classicism for both Christians and Jews in the United States. A discussion of what Edward Said calls the "domestications of the exotic" potentially could defuse the polemics surrounding Orientalism by considering concrete examples of cultural exchange.[12] The process of cultural borrowing and reciprocity deserves the attention of scholars of America–Holy Land studies.

One example of the complexities of cultural exchange that illustrates specifically what could be done with comparable sources can be found in the current research of Ilan Troen of Ben Gurion University. In the process of studying the urban history of Palestine during the Mandate period, Troen has uncovered a complex international network of cultural exchange that decisively shaped the structure, situation, and style of most contemporary Israeli cities.[13] He highlights several key elements contributing to urban growth, including the British garden cities ideology that reached Palestine through Mandate administrators, the Bauhaus international style in architecture that arrived in Palestine with German

Jewish refugees from Hitler, and the "new towns" philosophy that was popular throughout Europe in the 1920s. These intersected both with Zionist theory regarding immigration and population growth and with archaeological discoveries proving the existence of sizable cities during biblical times. These varied cultural influences legitimated the rapid urban expansion that occurred during the Mandate period, affected the location of cities as regional centers, influenced the structural pattern of urban growth to reflect garden city theories, and determined the cities' modern architectural style. Tel Aviv, as the "white city," provides the preeminent but not the only example.[14] Although Troen does not explore reciprocal influence, he provides a model of cultural interaction.

Another way to examine cultural evidence is to read the landscape itself. Ben-Arieh argues that the available material makes it "possible for us to reconstruct the physical and social landscape" of nineteenth-century Palestine.[15] The interpretation of cultural landscape serves as a companion to social history because of its focus on the vernacular. Landscapes are codes that require deciphering. But the effort is worthwhile because landscapes also encode the symbolic; they are "expressions of cultural values, social behavior, and individual actions worked upon particular localities over a span of time."[16] The cultural landscape refers to the human landscape and represents an enormous collective investment. Scholars recognize that people will not change their landscape unless under pressure to do so; thus the corollary, that changes in the look of the cultural landscape indicate major cultural upheavals.[17] Given the transformation of the landscape of the Holy Land during the nineteenth and twentieth centuries, efforts to interpret the differences would yield unexpected insights. The uncovering of ancient archaeological remains and the building of new cities, the preservation of areas of natural beauty, and the transformation of desert wilderness into cultivated settlements constitute a biography of the landscape that deserves scholarly attention. Americans contributed to these processes through their words and deeds. They helped to discover the landscape of the Holy Land, to make it accessible, and to exploit it in as yet undocumented ways.

The exploration of the cultural landscape of the Holy Land through the methodology of landscape interpretation does not preclude analysis of the symbolic landscape of the Holy Land. In fact, scholars could compare the reality with the many images of the symbolic landscape. Travel brochures and advertisements often upgrade the image of reality and influence the actual landscape to conform with their prescription. The land itself deserves study as a text. The fascination with deconstruction has opened possibilities to interpret the landscape of the Holy Land and to "read" its sacred text. Of course, more traditional explorations of symbol, image, and myth continue to be important.

Scholars would find it rewarding to uncover the meanings of the frontier in the literature of the Holy Land. The frontier theme, so popular in America, need not be confined to literary materials; it may provide a useful lens for an approach to diplomatic policy.[18] It has already been noted how different groups of Americans share metaphors generated by the Holy Land, and the groundwork has been laid for a comparative analysis of the meanings of these metaphors, their uses by different religious groups, and especially the conflict over their control. The language of culture shapes and is shaped by the political struggles of groups contending for influence. Through an examination of who controls and who contests the metaphors of the Holy Land, we might gain greater insight into the politics of perception.

One model of such a study could draw upon the approach of Howard Mumford Jones and Hugh Honour, using American images of the Holy Land rather than European images of the new "golden land."[19] Both Jones and Honour explore the subject of perceptions and the relationship of myth and image to reality, through artistic and literary sources. Jones juxtaposes the image of the New World with its anti-image, and then he examines the transplantation and modification of the Renaissance culture in America. Honour treats such topics as the land of allegory, the power of first impressions, the exotic land, the savage natives, and the land of the future. He devotes attention to the types of people found in the New World as well as to images of the land itself. He also uses varied visual materials as evidence for his analysis, an approach that could have a counterpart in the study of America and the Holy Land. Such a model of cultural analysis would present the vivid panoply of meanings associated with the Holy Land by Americans and would suggest analytic categories drawn from cultural studies. Since it also calls for the integration of visual and written sources that have largely been studied separately—with the former used to illustrate the latter—the model encourages scholars to examine the cognitive dissonances between image and reality.

Not all studies of cultural attachment need embrace new methodology or even the interdisciplinary ideals of American studies. There is room, and a need, for solid institutional histories of American organizations in the Holy Land. Within the historical framework, the genesis, growth, transplantation, and development of several important American institutions could be discussed. The role of religion and ideology, the significance of individual figures and their impact upon the social contours of the Holy Land could be treated. Among the institutions worthy of a study of their American origins and Holy Land histories are the American School of Oriental Research (now the Albright Institute for Near East Research), the Rockefeller Museum, Hadassah Hospital, the American Colony, the American Zion Commonwealth, and the B'nai B'rith. Each of these requires a historian sensitive to their particularities yet aware of the context of America–Holy Land relations, and able to draw upon the preliminary completed research. The pitfall of narrowness must be avoided, and the theme of cultural exchange must be held in view while the richness of unique detail is elaborated. The challenge is to speak to a variety of audiences despite the specific focus of the historical account.

Unlike the category of cultural attachment, Jewish involvement in the Holy Land has received substantial attention from scholars. A wealth of studies consider American Zionism, Jewish political activity in behalf of Palestine, American Jewish philanthropic support, religious interpretations of the meaning of Zion, and the Jewish return to the Land. Scholars have been more reluctant to examine the reciprocity of influence between American Jews and members of the Yishuv. Because there was movement across the ocean in both directions, studies of Jewish involvement in the Holy Land would benefit from research on a number of Zionist figures who lived in Mandate Palestine and in America. These individuals attempted to transplant American values and to shape the contours of the Yishuv. Michael Brown's essay on the reaction of Zionist leaders who lived in the United States after being exiled from Palestine during World War I indicates the importance of the reciprocal interrelationship.[20] His article points to a dramatic disillusionment with the United States as a result of the experience of living there; a parallel study of *shlihim* (emissaries) to the United States would be fruitful. How did the years spent in America influence these leaders, modifying not only their perceptions of America but their subsequent political behavior? What impact did the *shlihim* have upon American Zionists and, more broadly, upon American Jews?

Although American Zionists, as individuals, had considerably less influence than the European Zionist leaders who settled in Palestine, they deserve more attention than they have yet received. Bernard Rosenblatt, for example, a second-rank leader in the American Zionist movement, an adept in American Tammany Hall politics, a progressive social thinker—also a skilled lawyer, businessman, and entrepreneur—initiated a number of important business enterprises in Palestine through the American Zion Commonwealth, which he founded in 1915.[21] Rosenblatt and his wife, Gertrude Goldstein, a founder of Hadassah, lived in Haifa during the interwar years with their two sons. From his house on Hadar HaCarmel, Rosenblatt participated in international Zionist politics, engaged in several important land purchases (including the land around Haifa Bay), invested in the Tiberias Hot Springs Company, and advocated the importance of having capital as well as settlers directed to the Land of Israel. Rosenblatt's experience in Palestine, coupled with his education and youth in the United States, influenced an important book he wrote in favor of a Jewish commonwealth in a federated Palestine. The book combined the values of his two worlds and helped to popularize the term "commonwealth" among American Zionists.[22] As this brief summary indicates, a dual biography of Rosenblatt and Goldstein has the potential to illuminate the complex interaction of American Jews and the Holy Land.

Most American Jews did not live for an extended period in the Holy Land, but a number came there to study. There is room to expand Robert Handy's thoughtful suggestion that attention be paid to the impact of time spent studying in the Holy Land upon biblical scholarship.[23] Students also came to the Holy Land to study in other areas, especially in scientific and technical research. What effect did their period of study in the Holy Land have upon them and their scholarship?

The educational experience of American Jews constitutes another area of reciprocal influence. American Jews supported educational institutions in the

Holy Land, and they also propagated educational theories that often conflicted with the methods developed by European Jews in their institutions. A number of influential educators traveled in both directions across the seas. A comparative study of Samson Benderly, Alexander Dushkin, and Isaac Berkson would be instructive. It is important to recognize that their interaction and impact upon educational trends in the United States and Mandate Palestine occurred within the context of America–Holy Land relations. Too often, migration marks the end of scholarly interest; scholars need to tell the story of what happened in both America and the Holy Land.[24] Arthur Goren's perceptive biography of Judah Magnes addresses directly the issues of transplantation and cultural migration. He also indicates the scope of Magnes' influence upon the early years of the Hebrew University.[25]

Another excellent suggestion made by Robert Handy deserves to be underlined: Scholars need to devote research to women in America–Holy Land Studies. This concern transcends the four research categories noted earlier, because women have been significant figures in each category of study. Individual women and women's organizations have decisively shaped Holy Land institutions and social patterns. While scholars have studied the activities of a handful of influential American Jewish women—especially Golda Meir and Henrietta Szold—they have paid scant attention to American women's organizations or to the experience of those women who came to the Holy Land to work or settle. We do not know how gender affected their perceptions and encounters with the Holy Land. In this area we tend to assume that what men did or saw or thought comprised the total experience. Yet a path-breaking historical account of the women's farm at Kinneret by the historian Margalit Shilo reveals how different women's experiences were, even when the women were motivated by values they shared with male pioneers.[26]

The sources indicate the prominent participation of women—American Jews, Christian missionaries, religious visionaries, philanthropic activists—in a wide array of Holy Land endeavors, but research has yet to interpret why they came and how they achieved so much. Scholars have not applied their skills to understand how women were transformed by their experience in the Holy Land and how the religious dimensions of their lives were affected by the image and reality of the Holy Land. Here, surely, is a missing chapter waiting to be written.

Initial studies on the subject of Christian devotion have identified the diverse Christian communities and have demonstrated the value of exploring the meaning of the Holy Land for each. Scholars now face the task of delving deeper into the relationships between the religious and secular. For example, in the early twentieth century black nationalists as well as black preachers drew upon the inspiration of the Holy Land. However, the former found a model in Zionism that differed substantially from the latter's religious interpretation. An examination of the internal dialogue between nationalists and religious leaders within the black community suggests one way of focusing upon the conflict over the control of Holy Land metaphors mentioned earlier.

Another topic that would encourage deeper analysis of Christian religious thought is the subject of Land theology. Scholars of Judaism have recently directed more attention to this dimension of Jewish theology, probably in response to its increasing prominence in current politics.[27] Political struggles aside, Christian theologies of the Holy Land warrant serious analysis and interpretation. As in the cultural realm, comparative work would be most valuable since the European churches often differed from their American counterparts.

Research in the last category of America–Holy Land Studies, diplomatic policy, follows traditional lines. Nonetheless, opportunities exist for more extensive research, especially if a scholar is willing to examine the political and economic fringes of diplomacy. The recent study by Naomi W. Cohen of the Arab riots in Palestine in 1929 and the American response to them is a good example of such expanded research.[28] Other related topics include financial investment, policy planning, and trade relations between America and the Holy Land. Diplomacy regulated these activities, and individuals who had an economic stake in trade undoubtedly tried to insure favorable diplomatic conditions. Although the scope of American investment and trade with the Holy Land was not large in the nineteenth century, contacts and commitments grew in the twentieth century. The role of American Jews in promoting such economic ties cannot be overlooked. The subject of economic relations with the Holy Land involves a complex mix of colonialism, capitalism, philanthropy, and politics in constantly shifting proportions.

The problems faced by scholars conducting research in America–Holy Land Studies stem not only from the newness of the field but from the diversity of sources and the need to speak to often disparate audiences. Although history offers a connective framework, the recent upheavals within that discipline contribute to the frustration of fragmentation. Had each of the sixteen authors of chapters in the volume *With Eyes Toward Zion–II* sought a journal in which to publish his or her essay, there would have been probably over half a dozen journals represented. If scholars of America and the Holy Land want to reach a larger audience, they must seek out peers in an array of forums. These difficulties might well be overcome through collaborative research. The concept of co-authorship is established in the social sciences, but it has not met with a warm reception among historians and scholars of cultural change. America–Holy Land Studies offers an arena for such cooperation. It would produce genuine dialogue regarding the topic investigated and enhance the attractiveness of the field, since each scholar would be encouraged to bring his or her own resources to the investigation. Thus, the long process of mastering a new field would be accelerated and the problem of speaking to several audiences at least partially overcome.

Despite the problems, the prospects remain good for enlarging the field of America–Holy Land Studies. The cross-cultural and interdisciplinary perspectives generated by the concept of area studies do not preclude alternative approaches influenced by other fields. Ultimately, it will be the variety of scholars, students, and researchers attracted to the study of America and the Holy Land that will determine its future course.

NOTES

1. The best summary discussion of the theory, method, and substance of the new social history appears in the tenth anniversary issue of the *Journal of Social History* 4 (Winter 1976). See also Theodore K. Rabb and Robert I. Rotberg, eds., *The New History: The 1980's and Beyond: Studies in Interdisciplinary History* (Princeton: Princeton University Press, 1982).

2. Gertrude Himmelfarb, *The New History and the Old* (Cambridge, Mass.: Belknap Press of Harvard University Press, 1987).

3. See Moshe Davis, ed., *With Eyes Toward Zion* (New York: Arno Press, 1977).

4. Israel Finestein, "Early and Middle 19th Century British Opinion on the Restoration of the Jews: Contrast with America," and David A. Rausch, "Evangelical Protestant Americans," in *With Eyes Toward Zion-II*, ed. Moshe Davis (New York: Praeger, 1983).

5. See Ruth Kark, "Annual Reports of United States Consuls in the Holy Land as a Source for the Study of 19th-Century Eretz Israel" and Yehoshua Ben-Arieh, "Nineteenth-Century Hebrew Periodicals as a Source for America-Holy Land Studies" in M. Davis (above, n.4).

6. For a discussion of trends, see the annual bibliography issue of *American Quarterly* 35, no. 3 (1983).

7. Yehoshua Ben-Arieh, *The Rediscovery of the Holy Land in the Nineteenth Century* (Jerusalem and Detroit: Magnes Press and Wayne State University Press, 1979), 9-10, 15.

8. David Klatzker, "American Christian Travelers to the Holy Land, 1821–1939" (Ph.D. diss., Temple University, 1987).

9. Italy, for example. Paul R. Baker, *The Fortunate Pilgrims: Americans in Italy 1800–1860* (Cambridge, Mass.: Harvard University Press, 1964).

10. Victor Turner, *Process, Performance and Pilgrimage* (New Delhi: Concept Publishing, 1979), 131.

11. Ibid., 122.

12. Edward W. Said, *Orientalism* (New York: Pantheon Books, 1978), 60. For a discussion of Said's arguments, see David S. Landes, "Passionate Pilgrims and Others: Visitors to the Holy Land in the 19th Century," in M. Davis (above, n.4), pp. 15-18.

13. The following discussion draws upon a presentation at the Columbia Urban History Seminar, April 1987.

14. Mikhael Levine, *White City: Gems of the International Style in Israel* (Tel Aviv: Tel Aviv Museum, 1984, Hebrew).

15. Y. Ben-Arieh (above, n.7), p. 5.

16. P. J. Hugill in the editor's introduction to *The Interpretation of Ordinary Landscapes*, ed. E. W. Meinig (New York: Oxford University Press, 1979), 4.

17. Pierce F. Lewis, "Axioms for Reading the Landscape," ibid., 11-15.

18. The classic study of the American frontier is Henry Nash Smith, *Virgin Land: The American West as Symbol and Myth* (New York: Vintage, 1950). See also Arthur

K. Moore, *The Frontier Mind: A Cultural Analysis of the Kentucky Frontiersman* (Lexington: University of Kentucky Press, 1957).

19. Howard Mumford Jones, *O Strange New World* (New York: Viking, 1952); Hugh Honour, *The New Golden Land: European Images of America from the Discoveries to the Present Time* (New York: Pantheon, 1975).

20. Michael Brown, "Some Early 19th-Century Holy Land 'Travelers' to America: Sources and Contexts," in M. Davis (above, n.4), pp. 230-50. Many of the better-known "travelers" to America were there during the first two decades of the 20th century.

21. See his fascinating autobiography, *Two Generations of Zionism* (New York: Shengold, 1967).

22. Bernard Rosenblatt, *Federated Palestine and the Jewish Commonwealth* (New York: Scopus Publishing, 1941).

23. Robert T. Handy, "America and the Holy Land: Perspectives and Prospectives," in M. Davis (above, n.4), p. 393.

24. In my own book on B'nai B'rith I gave short shrift to its transplantation to the Holy Land, a serious shortcoming. But the establishment of this American Jewish fraternal organization, albeit through the migration of European Jewish members rather than Americans, sparked such significant American innovations as the introduction of public libraries. See *B'nai B'rith and the Challenge of Ethnic Leadership* (Albany: SUNY Press, 1981).

25. Arthur A. Goren, *Dissenter in Zion* (Cambridge, Mass.: Harvard University Press, 1982).

26. Margalit Shilo, "The Women's Farm at Kinneret, 1911–1917: A Solution to the Problem of the Working Woman in the Second Aliya," *Jerusalem Cathedra* (1981): 246-83.

27. Lawrence Hoffman, ed., *The Land of Israel, Jewish Perspectives* (Notre Dame, Ind.: University of Notre Dame Press, 1986).

28. Naomi W. Cohen, *The Year after the Riots: American Responses to the Palestine Crisis of 1929–1930* (Detroit: Wayne State University Press, 1988).

Chapter 4

America–Holy Land and Religious Studies: On Expressing a Sacred Reality

Gershon Greenberg

America–Holy Land Studies has been described as a corridor field or subdiscipline; that is, a composite of two or more standard disciplines.[1] In the university, however, the subject is located administratively within a single discipline. For pragmatic reasons the data need to relate closely to a standard discipline. My own text, *Holy Land and Religious America*, attempts to present America–Holy Land relations in the language of Religious Studies.[2]

The structure in which the material is presented reflects the conviction that the history of religious consciousness is inherently dialectical. The period of the seventeenth through early nineteenth century is presented as the thesis, the nineteenth century as the antithesis, and the twentieth century through 1948—which is as far as the field of America–Holy Land Studies goes—as the synthesis.

A CHRONOLOGICAL DIALECTIC

Seventeenth through Early Nineteenth Century

The history of the America–Holy Land relationship begins with the thesis of America as Holy Land (Zion). The Puritans transfer the Holy Land reality to America, as if it were a sacred territory that could be disconnected from its geographical ties. The Sephardic Jews take the transfer farther. They find scriptural (i.e., Holy Land) ramifications in the American Revolution and regard the victory as precipitating the messianic coming in Holy Land/Eretz Israel. Meanwhile, early settlers project the Holy Land onto the geography of America; eventually, there are over one thousand places with biblical and Holy Land names. The Land is also projected onto native Americans;[3] from missionary John Eliot (1609–1690) to present-day Mormons, American Indians have been identified continually as descendants of the Ten Lost Tribes.

Nineteenth Century

In the nineteenth century, the thesis gradually gives way to its antithesis, the Holy Land (Zion)/Eretz Israel. The first "consul" to Jerusalem, Warder Cresson, goes there in 1844 to help precipitate the millennium. Presbyterian journalist William Cowper Prime in 1855–1856, author Herman Melville (whose family belongs to the Dutch Reformed Church) in 1857, Episcopalian priest John Fulton in the 1880s, and Presbyterian minister Thomas de Witt Talmage in 1880—are all pilgrims to Eretz Israel for whom historical experience blends with scriptural timelessness, confirming Zion's reality in Eretz Israel. In the early 1820s, Congregational Church missionaries Pliny Fisk, Levi Parsons, and Jonas King seek to convert Jews living in Eretz Israel and thereby enable the advent of the Christian millennium there. American consuls Victor Beauboucher (1865–1869), Frank De Hass (1874–1877), Selah Merrill (1886–1891), and Edwin Sherman Wallace (1891–1893) all explore the history of the Land and its peoples as they identify with the Land of Scripture.

Among the nineteenth-century travelers, black American Christians are represented by David Dorr in 1853, Charles T. Walker in 1891, and Daniel P. Seaton in 1893(?), who travel to Eretz Israel as pilgrims to the Holy Sepulcher and Calvary. They also search for testimony to the biblical myth of exile, enslavement, and redemption, with which blacks identify.

Christian Fundamentalists are committed to restoring the Land of Scripture to the Jews, to enable Christ's Second Coming to the Land. In 1834, once Mormon Zion begins to take hold in America, Joseph Smith announces that Orson Hyde will go to Jerusalem to prepare for the ingathering of the Jews.

In nineteenth-century American Judaism, Bernhard Felsenthal, Caspar Levias, and William Fineschreiber begin to alter Reform's monolithic non-Zionist stance. Historical/Conservative Judaism interprets America as a supporting factor for Holy Land (Zion)/Eretz Israel. In Orthodox Judaism, the traditional position of a miraculous return to Zion changes to the Zionist positions of Ralph B. Raphael (1893) and Shimon Yitzchak Finkelstein (1899), both of whom wrote in Hebrew.

Twentieth Century

In the twentieth century the thesis of Holy Land (Zion)/America and antithesis of Holy Land (Zion)/Eretz Israel become synthesized, to the extent that both positions prevail simultaneously. Protestant Liberals vary in their support of a Jewish state depending upon how Jews and Arabs appear to relate to the universal (i.e., American) principles of freedom, democracy, and morality. Catholics are generally anti-Zionist; a Jewish state threatens their holy places and the experience of Christ's life, death, and resurrection that they provide. A state would lend credibility to those allegedly responsible for the death of Christ and would foster modernization, which upsets the idyllic image of the scriptural Holy Land. With the exception of small elements in Reform and ultra-Orthodoxy, twentieth-century Judaism becomes Zionist. The Mormons crystallize the synthesis by speaking of Zion in America as well as in Eretz Israel.

COMMON RELIGIOUS POSITIONS AND THEIR JEWISH AND CHRISTIAN FORMS

Our assumption is that Zion is a sacred, spiritual territory. The territory lends itself to two overarching inquiries, in the context of which the various positions may be classified. Each position yields a variety of Jewish and Christian forms. The fact that, with very few exceptions, the forms are common to both Judaism and Christianity reinforces in turn the assumption of the one sacred territory.

The first inquiry: *What is the role of human or divine initiative in the onset of Zion?* Altogether, five positions may be discerned. Namely, "Zion" is either America, Eretz Israel, or both; and "Jerusalem" is either "above" (celestial) or "below" (terrestrial).

Holy Land (Zion) Is America

In the Puritan form of America-as-Zion, the Pilgrims' entry into America is a divine action. Governor William Bradford declares on Cape Cod in 1646:

> May not the people of God now say (and these poor people among the rest), the Lord hath brought forth our righteousness. Come let us declare in Zion the word of the Lord our God (*Jeremiah* 51:10). . . . Are not these Jebusites overcome that have vexed the people Israel so long, even holding Jerusalem till David's days? . . . The tyrannous bishops are ejected, their courts dissolved, their canons forceless, and all their superstitions discarded, their service cashiered, their ceremonies useless and despised, their plots for popery prevented, and returned to Rome from whence they came. . . . But who hath done it? Who, even he that sitteth on the white horse who is called faithful and true and judgeth and fighteth righteously (*Revelations* 19:11).[4]

A Jewish form of America-as-Zion is found among Reform Jews such as Gustavus Poznanski in 1841, Isaac Mayer Wise in 1852, David Einhorn in 1855, and Isaac W. Bernheim in 1921. For example, David Einhorn arrives in America and expresses gratitude to God for having brought him to the promised land of Canaan, where Torah principles are fulfilled, where Washington, D.C. is the new Jerusalem, and the capitol building the new temple sanctuary.[5]

Holy Land (Zion) Is Eretz Israel

In a first form, Orthodox Jews Abraham J. G. Lesser (1834–1925) and Baruch Meir Klein (1873–1932), with their pre-Emancipation concept of redemption, view the homeland as realized through divine initiative, with man as God's instrument. The Catholics, in turn, think in terms of divine history; they reject the historical development of Eretz Israel and consider it as a place for pilgrimage and reenactment of the life and crucifixion of Jesus.

A second form acknowledges human participation in Zion, in a passive way. Christian missionary Levi Parsons is called upon to become part of the forward surge of Christian history toward the Second Coming by converting Jews. He goes to Eretz Israel to "besiege a great empire of sin, where satan from ancient times has held undisputed possession of his strongholds."[6] Similarly, Fundamentalist colonist Clorinda Minor of Philadelphia relates in 1851:

> I was directed towards Jerusalem, though I had no outward reason for expectation, or spiritual profit for myself or others *there*. Long and agonizing was my inward struggle against the thought of going. Outwardly, I had *everything to lose*, and suffer; and inwardly, nothing apparently to gain; but the conviction of my soul increased every hour that God was calling me to go![7]

In this second form we have been unable to find a Jewish counterpart.

In a third form, there is active human participation in Zion, within a divine context. Warder Cresson detects signs of the restoration and declares:

> Let us enter into the plans of Divine Providence; let us cooperate in accomplishing the prophecies, which announce so clearly the restoration of the Jews, and *let us remember there are special blessings attached to this work*.
> ... When this time [to favor Zion] has fully come, woe, woe to that man that is found fighting against God, by supporting their different Zions [the Catholic] one at Rome, another [that of the Mormons] at Nauvoo.[8]

Cresson has himself appointed consul to Jerusalem and subsequently tries to restore the Land through agricultural development.

Orthodox Rabbi Joseph Levin (1870–1936) also reflects this third form:

> The truth is that authentic redemption will come only from God. For only He is the Redeemer. But we are not to rely on miracles when we can save ourselves in a natural way. If we consolidate ourselves into one body and one soul with one longing, if our views are harmonized without exception, we can [have reason to] hope that the authentic Saviour will come and bring authentic redemption upon his wings.[9]

Synthesis of Eretz Israel and America

On the Jewish side, secular Zionism provides a this-worldly form of synthesis. Louis D. Brandeis offers this pragmatic expression in 1941:

There is no inconsistency between loyalty to America and loyalty to Jewry. The Jewish spirit, the product of our religion and experiences, is essentially modern and essentially American. Not since the destruction of the Temple, have the Jews in spirit and in ideals been so fully in harmony with the noblest aspirations of the country in which they lived. . . . Indeed, loyalty to America demands rather that each American Jew become a Zionist.[10]

Similarly, Horace Kallen wants a "Hebraic" state. Hebraism is a comprehensive concept that includes Jewish history, ethnic solidarity, and language. Religion is one component, and it refers basically to the American principle that all men are created equal and have inalienable rights. Horace Kallen's "Pittsburgh Program" (1918) describes a state based upon social justice, where individual life, liberty, and happiness are secure; natural resources are controlled; and there is free public education in the name of economic and social democracy. There will be free expression, political and civil equality, and equality of opportunity.[11]

In contrast, the black American Christian form of synthesized Zion transcends those of America and Eretz Israel. Zion begins beyond the limits of both geographical entities; there is little hope that either or both can contain the Holy Land. The *AME Church Review* of 1918 states:

It would seem that, at last, after the lapse of centuries, we are arriving at the Golden Age of the fulfillment of prophecies, of visions and of dreams. May the Jews find their chief joy not in returning to Jerusalem to build the foundations of a Jewish state where once the throne of David was, but rather in the homecoming of all their exiles to Him who opened in the house of King David a fountain for sin and all uncleanness. May the Christians not return to Jerusalem simply to cherish the sacred places, hallowed by the footprints of Jesus, but in neighborliness, in brotherhood, in justice, righteousness and peace, may they truly honor Him by walking according to His commandment and His will.[12]

The Mormons share the perception of an ultimate, transcendental, synthesized Zion. Zion in America and Zion in Eretz Israel are dual pillars from which transcendental Zion may be reached. Mormons believe that in the future there will be two "space-time capitals" of God's kingdom on earth—Jerusalem in Eretz Israel, and a New Jerusalem in America. Together, they produce a "universalized covenant community."[13]

"Jerusalem above" (Celestial Jerusalem)[14]

Christian missionary Pliny Fisk describes the ahistorical kingdom as follows:

I look at the dome which covers the tomb, and thought of the death and resurrection of my Lord and burst into tears. . . . It seemed then as if Jesus Christ the Son of God had really suffered, died and risen from the dead [and this] dwindled as it were to a moment [with me].[15]

Reform Zionist Abba Hillel Silver (1893–1963) speaks of the establishment of the Jewish state in these mythic terms:

> The inescapable logic of events! When all the doors of the world will be closed to our people, then the hand of destiny will force open the door of Palestine. And that hour is rapidly approaching. . . . What is really moving us toward Palestine, and why is our movement irresistible? Our Sages say [in *Mekhilta Beshallach Pesikta* 24b] that two Arks led the Children of Israel through the wilderness on to the Promised Land: The Ark wherein lay the dead body of Joseph, and the Ark of the Covenant. Two Arks! The Ark of death and the Ark of faith![16]

The celestial Jerusalem mindset is applied to anti-Zionism in 1948 by ultra-Orthodox Rabbi Joel Teitelbaum:

> *Sanhedrin* 98a states explicitly that the son of David will not come until even the slightest traces of sovereignty are removed. Anyone who participates in promoting sovereignty contributes to hindering the coming of the Messiah. There is nothing worse. Stupid people call sovereignty redemption. No! It hinders redemption. . . . Let us wait [passively] each day for the complete redemption. [Redemption takes place] through the coming of the son of David, as a manifestation of the Creator's will. He is omnipotent. He can do everything in a single moment [i.e., outside human time].[17]

"Jerusalem below" (Terrestrial Jerusalem)

This position is represented in Judaism by Ralph B. Raphael. He plans for a vanguard of pioneers to Eretz Israel and a government with Turkish control over external affairs and Jewish control over internal activities. He urges mass immigration with a goal of two million by the early 1940s. Together with agricultural development, this will assure *de facto* justification of a sovereign state. Once all this is under way, *teshuvah* (repentant return to God) and redemption will take place.[18] Liberal Christian Reinhold Niebuhr (1892–1972) calls to establish a Jewish state immediately and unconditionally, in the name of the ideals of freedom, social justice, and the right to a particular national identity.[19]

The second inquiry: *What is the sequence of the redemptive process?* The common Holy Land (Zion) urge within American Judaism and Christianity lends itself to eight positions regarding the sequence of the redemptive process, secular and religious.

America as a Negative Factor for Zion/Eretz Israel

Here the hope that America will become Zion is dashed. Return to the Land of Israel is sought, for it is here that Zion's source and the original enunciation of its ideals are located. Clorinda Minor, of Puritan ancestry, expects the millennium to be realized in America in 1843:

> I had entire confidence in the Scriptures and received their most literal and definite sense, in regard to present practical duty and future promise. In the latter part of these [twenty-four years in the Congregational Church], I began to realize a great discrepancy, between the religion, and form of godliness in this age.[20]

Minor concludes that the "day of preparation" must precede Christ's coming. This means going to the Land of Israel. She travels there and establishes Mt. Hope Colony in 1851.

Warder Cresson, during his Mormon period, presumably had hopes for Zion in America. But he also feels called upon by God to separate legalistic externals from the gospel of the soul; he attacks American materialism, self indulgence, and slavery.[21]

Herman Melville visits Palestine in 1857 "in an effort to recapture the true spirit of Christianity," which had disappeared from America.[22] Among the Jews, Horace Kallen looks to the Hebraic homeland to realize the ideals of the Jeffersonian liberal, just, socialist, democracy that remained unrealized in America.

America as a Positive Factor for Zion/Eretz Israel

America is also a positive force for establishing a Jewish homeland. For the eighteenth century Sephardic Jewish congregants of Shearith Israel, the victory of American revolutionaries implies the onset of redemption centered in Eretz Israel.[23] After the Balfour Declaration in 1917, Orthodox Rabbi Chaim Hirschensohn writes that democratic American institutions are indispensable models for developing covenant-centered *halakhah* in the Holy Land.[24]

No Christian counterpart appears to exist for this attitudinal form.

The Universal Positive Impact of Restoring Eretz Israel

Some see the restoration as having positive ramifications for all humanity. For example, H. Pereira Mendes of the Historical School of Judaism writes in 1899:

> To establish a Jewish state for spiritual purposes is more than necessary. It is essential for the existence of society, for human liberty, and for humanity's progress. . . . [A] Jewish state is a spiritual centre, whence spirituality shall radiate to the end of the world.[25]

Similarly, A. A. Berle, a liberal Protestant, asserts in 1918 that by establishing a Jewish "social commonwealth,"

Israel will find itself and that portion of it which has lost the way. [It] will hear again the fresh utterance of the ancient law, "Hear, O Israel" [and] will see before its eyes the blazing beacons that point toward the solidarity and unity of the ancient kindred. This will be a wonderful thing for Israel, but it will be not less wonderful for the rest of the world. Under the influence of the religionizing of the Jew himself there will also come an idealizing of his purposes, which will be one of the most serviceable agencies for world happiness and culture imaginable.[26]

The Universal Negative Impact of Restoring Eretz Israel

Others regard the restoration as a negative act, with implications beyond the boundaries of Eretz Israel. In 1892, Leo Franklin, a Reform Jew, speaks of a "national hermitage" and historical regression:

Seclusion may be fit environment for the savage beast, to whose existence there is no spiritual or intellectual side. . . . Only savages can boast of pure unmixed race, but in the veins of civilized man there runs mingled the blood of such a multitude of races that purity is a reproach rather than a cause of self laudation.[27]

Another Reform Jew, Hyman G. Enelow, in 1900 speaks of theological regression:

Zionism, apart from its secular connotation, should be considered as a dogma of an effete Jewish theology. It was rooted in an ancient conception relating to the power and limitations of the gods. "In antique religion," says [William] Robertson Smith [*Religion of the Semites* (London, 1894), pp. 91 ff.], "gods as well as men have a physical environment on and through which their activity is conditioned." They are thus conceived not only as limited in sphere and sway by the bounds of their particular countries, but also as having fixed residences, homes—executive mansions, as it were.[28]

Among the Christians, the negative form is expressed in 1927 by a Liberal Protestant, Harry Emerson Fosdick, in his criticism of Zionist nationalism:

We Americans, Jewish Americans as well as Christian Americans, do not always realize that the central passion of the Zionists is not religious. Nationalism, not religion, is the dominant factor. And it is rather discouraging that today, when nationalism has been shown to be a Caesar, a false God which we have been worshipping and magnifying past all reason, that this Jewish experiment should be started with nationalism as its fundamental basis.[29]

The Particular Positive Impact of Restoring Eretz Israel

In terms of Zion's ideals, some believe the establishment of a Jewish homeland to have beneficial effects on the indigenous population. Orthodox Rabbi Shimon Yitzchak Finkelstein states:

Each land differs from the next. One land produces merchants and trades in the land. Another produces those who do actual labor. Another produces scholars and authors. . . . Some places promote involvement with Torah and walking in God's ways. Therefore it is said, "Whoever lives in the Land of Israel may be considered to have a God, but whoever lives outside the Land may be regarded as one who has no God" [Talmud Bavli, *Ketubbot* 110b]. . . . In every place where Rabbi Yohanan dwells in the Land he feels in his soul that God is present [*Rosh Hashanah* 31a]. . . . Rab Hiyya Bar Gamada kisses the sand of our Land [*Ketubbot* 112b]. Only in the Land is there the source of Torah, and an atmosphere of anticipating [its realization].[30]

Presbyterian Consul Edwin Sherman Wallace speaks of the Land and the Jewish people waiting for each other. The restored land will hopefully produce a restored Judaism, one spiritualized by Christianity:

Christianity and Judaism are radically the same religion. We believe that Christianity has the real life—the life of the spirit—a stage of development to which Judaism has not attained but [to which] Judaism will advance; that when it has reached the spiritual stage the "wall of partition" will be broken down and a union will be effected in religion nearer the divine ideal than this world has yet witnessed, whose adherents shall be "Israelites indeed."[31]

The Particular Negative Impact of Restoring Eretz Israel

Others believe that contemporary Jewish reality in the Land of Israel compromises the ideals of Zion. Christian Consul Albert Rhodes considers Jews in Palestine to be lacking in manhood:

[W]hen a Jew is converted, a transformation takes place in his appearance. The filthy gown, slatternly shoes, and furred caps are thrown aside, and the dangling frontlocks are shorn. From a thorough scouring, his complexion assumes a different hue. He is seen in clean linen and a good plain suit of European clothes. He has a more civilized air, and partly loses his excessive Jewish humility, which made him cringe and bow before every passer-by. He walks erect. In short, [he again] receives his lost manhood.[32]

Baruch Meir Klein, an Orthodox Jew originally from Munkacz, Hungary, attacks secular Jews in Eretz Israel for separating Jewish nationality from Torah. They defy *mitzvot*, eating *trayfah* (prohibited foods) in Jerusalem itself. Klein asserts: "I am content, for my part, living in exile among the *Goyyim*. I have no need to be in exile [in Eretz Israel] with Jews who are anti-semitic Zionists."[33]

Apocalyptic Eretz Israel

Among the Christians, James T. Barclay of the American Christian Missionary Society claims in 1858 that the destruction of the antichrist and the salvation of the world require the conversion of the Jew in the Land of Israel.[34] In 1888, Ellen G. White of the Seventh Day Adventists describes how Jesus will return to earth at the millennium to battle satan's forces:

In the fate of the chosen city we may behold the doom of a world that has rejected God's mercy and trampled upon His law. Dark are the records of human misery that earth has witnessed during its long centuries of crime. But a scene yet darker is presented in the revelation of the future . . . when the restraining Spirit of God shall be wholly withdrawn from the wicked, no longer to hold in check the outburst of human passion and satanic wrath! But in that day, as in the time of Jerusalem's destruction, God's people will be delivered. . . . Then shall they that obey not the Gospel be consumed with the spirit of His mouth, and be destroyed with the brightness of His coming.[35]

The Lubavitcher Hasidim speak in 1945 of a redemption era "nightmare" centered around Eretz Israel:

All the filth and its producers on earth are now about to be purified. A great divine "mop", drenched in blood and tears will wash away [all the] human filth from the earth. No one is exempt—no particular class, race, land, or leader. Big and small will be washed away. Great empires are in as much danger as the smallest country. Entire races have no greater standing, when it comes to the mop, than do killer groups. The only passports recognized by the great "cleaner" of the world are those which are stamped. The only survivors will be those who neither dirtied the world nor even considered dirtying it.[36]

Disjunction between the Zion Ideal and Eretz Israel Reality

Herman Melville describes the Holy Sepulcher as a sickening cheat, surrounded by the "least nameable filth of a barbarous city." The whole city "looks at you like a cold grey eye in a cold grey man."[37] Presbyterian pilgrim Thomas de Witt Talmage is distressed by the reality of "Christland." It withers under the accursed nation of Turkey. The darkness of Islam precludes modern civilization and free thought:

If the Sultan of Turkey attempted to visit Jerusalem, he would never get back again [to Turkey]. All Palestine hates him. I saw him go to the mosque for prayers in his own city of Constantinople, and saw seven thousand armed men riding out to protect him. Expensive prayers! Of course that government wants no better harbor at Joppa. May God remove that curse of nations, that old hag of the centuries, the Turkish Government! For its everlasting insult to God and woman, let it perish![38]

A Jewish example of this view is the 1933 statement of Orthodox Rabbi Chaim Hirschensohn:

It is not the land, God forbid, that has lost its holiness. That lasts forever. There is another danger. Zionism attracts many materialists. If the sickness [of careerism] spreads to the land of Israel, we are all lost. We will be, God forbid, like all the nations. . . . It is our land, the inheritance of our fathers. We must not end up murmuring in [Eretz] Israel itself, "Where, o where is the Holy Land? My spirit longs for it."[39]

OBSERVATION

We believe that America–Holy Land Studies can be located academically within Religious Studies if it shares the language of that discipline. We begin with the concept of sacred territory and trace its dialectical journey through American religious history. We attempt to show, first, the positions in this territory, and then the specific formations manifested by Judaism and by Christianity. The sacred territory concept lends itself to two overarching questions, (1) about human or divine initiative in the return to Zion, and (2) about the sequence of the redemptive process. The first question is answered in terms of positions identifying Zion in America, and in Eretz Israel, both "above" or "below." The second is answered in terms of America's role in the vision of the Land of Israel as Zion, and in terms of the positive or negative, universal or particular, impact of restoring the Land of Israel. With few exceptions, these positions have Judaic and Christian forms.

In Religious Studies, the reality of the religious quest is assumed. The various religions are regarded as particular manifestations of the universal reality. In this respect, we have found the topic of America–Holy Land relations to be at home in the academic discipline.

NOTES

1. The terms "Holy Land" and "Zion" will be used interchangeably. They do not necessarily mean the geographic area of the Land of Israel (Eretz Israel). For purposes of clarity, I employ the formulas Holy Land (Zion)/Eretz Israel and Holy Land (Zion)/ America.

2. Experimental edition, June 1988.

3. When referring to Eretz Israel, the term "Land" used by itself is capitalized.

4. William Bradford, *History of Plymouth Plantation 1620–1647* (Boston: Houghton Mifflin, 1912), 15–16.

5. Gustavus Poznanski, cited in *Charleston Courier*, 20 March 1841; Isaac Mayer Wise, *The End of Popes, Nobles and Kings—Or, The Progress of Civilization* (New York: J. Muhlhaeuser, 1852), 20; Max Lilienthal, "The Platform of Judaism," in *Max Lilienthal, American Rabbi*, ed. David Philipson (New York: Bloch Publishing, 1915), 457; Isaac W. Bernheim, *The Reform Church of American Israelites* (Buffalo, N.Y., 1921), 6; Gershon Greenberg, "David Einhorn's Conception of History," *American Jewish Historical Quarterly* 63, no. 2 (December 1973): 160-84.

6. Alvin Bond, *Memoir of the Rev. Pliny Fisk, A.M., Late Missionary to Palestine* (1828; reprint, New York: Arno Press, 1977), iii-v.

7. Clorinda S. Minor and Charles Minor, *Meshullam! Or, Tidings from Jerusalem from the Journal of A Believer Recently Returned from the Holy Land* (1851; reprint, New York: Arno Press, 1977), vi-xi.

8. Warder Cresson, *Jerusalem the Centre and Joy of the Whole Earth* (Philadelphia: J. Harding, 1844), 7-8.

9. Joseph Levin, "Sermon on Zion," in *The Lessons of Joseph* (New York: A. Ch. Rosenberg, 1906, Hebrew), 76.

10. Louis Brandeis, "The Jewish Problem—How to Solve it," *Maccabaean* (June 1915): 105-10.

11. Horace M. Kallen, "Zionism and the Struggle for Democracy," *Nation*, 23 September 1915; idem, "Constitutional Foundations of the New Zion." *Maccabaean* (April, May 1918), as cited in Sarah Schmidt, "Messianic Pragmatism: The Zionism of Horace M. Kallen," *Judaism* 25, no. 2 (April 1976): 217-29. See also Sarah Schmidt, "Toward the Pittsburgh Program: Horace M. Kallen, Philosopher of an American Zionism," *Herzl Year Book* 8 (1978): 18-36.

12. *AME Church Review* 34, no. 3 (January 1918): 179-80, cited in Albert Raboteau, "Black Americans," in *With Eyes Toward Zion–II*, ed. Moshe Davis (New York: Praeger, 1986), 319. See also Timothy I. Smith, "Slavery and Theology, the Emergence of Black Christian Consciousness in Nineteenth-Century America," *Church History* 41, no. 4 (December 1972): 497-514.

13. Truman G. Madsen, *The Mormon Attitude toward Zionism*, Series of Lectures on Zionism, no. 5 (Haifa: University of Haifa, 1981), 2-3.

14. See Yehoshua Prawer, "Jerusalem, Capital of the Crusader Kingdom," in *Judah and Jerusalem: The Twelfth Archaeological Convention* (Jerusalem: Jewish Palestine Exploration Society, 1957, Hebrew), 92-93.

15. A. Bond (above, n. 6), p. 286.

16. Abba Hillel Silver, "The Conspiracy of Silence," in *Vision and Victory* (New York: Zionist Organization of America, 1949), 7.

17. Joel Teitelbaum, "Concerning a Government for Israel—Before the Coming of the Messiah," in *The Words of Joel, Letters I* (Brooklyn, N.Y.: Yerushalayim, 1980–81, Hebrew), 89.

18. Ralph B. Raphael, *The Question of the Jews* (New York: Ephraim Deinard, 1893).

19. Reinhold Niebuhr, "Jews after the War," *Nation*, 21 February 1942: 214-16; 28 February 1942: 253-55; Franklin H. Littell, "Reinhold Niebuhr and the Jewish People," International Niebuhr Symposium, Kings College, London, 20 September 1984.

20. C. S. Minor (above, n.7), p. 3.

21. See Frank Fox, "Quaker, Shaker, Rabbi—Warder Cresson, The Story of a Philadelphia Mystic," *Pennsylvania Magazine of History and Biography* 95 (April 1971): 147–94. Fox cites Warder Cresson, *A Humble and Affectionate Address to the Select Members of the Abington Quarterly Meeting* (Philadelphia, 1827); idem, *Babylon the Great Is Falling! The Morning Star or Light from on High, Written in Defense of the Rights of the Poor and Oppressed* (Philadelphia, 1830).

22. William Braswell, *Melville's Religious Thought* (Durham, N.C.: Duke University, 1943), 108-9.

23. Prayer in Hebrew, composed by Rabbi Hendla-Iehochanan Van Oettingen-Jacob Cohen, *Publications of the American Jewish Historical Society (PAJHS)* 27 (1920): 34-37.

24. Chaim Hirschensohn, [*The Procession of My God*] *My King Into The Sanctuary* [Psalms 64:25], 6 vols. (St. Louis: Moinester, 1919, 1921, 1923, Hebrew). See Eliezer Schweid, "Democratic State Based on Halakhah," in *Democracy and Halakhah* (Jerusalem: Magnes Press, 1978, Hebrew), 59-89.

25. "Should a Jewish state be established?" Quotation from H. Pereira Mendes, "As to a Jewish State," *American Hebrew* 64 (January 13, 1899): 392.

26. Adolph Augustus Berle, *The World Significance of a Jewish State* (New York: M. Kennerley, 1918), 45-46.

27. Leo Franklin, "A Danger and a Duty Suggested by the Zionist Agitation," *Hebrew Union College Journal (HUC Journal)* 2 (1897-1898): 142-47.

28. Hyman Enelow, "Zionism as a Theologic Dogma," *HUC Journal* 5, no. 5/6 (1900): 111.

29. "Fosdick Sees Ruin Ahead for Zionism," *New York Times*, 25 May 1927, p. 8.

30. Shimon Yitzchak Finkelstein, *Harvest of Grapes* (Chicago: Eliezar Maites, 1899, Hebrew), 24.

31. Robert T. Handy, ed., *The Holy Land in American Protestant Life* (New York: Arno Press, 1981), 163, cited from Edwin Sherman Wallace, *Jerusalem the Holy: A Brief History of Ancient Jerusalem, with an Account of the Modern City and Its Condition, Political, Religious and Social* (1898; reprint, New York: Arno Press, 1977).

32. Albert Rhodes, *Jerusalem As It Is* (London: J. Maxwell, 1865), 458.

33. Baruch Meir Klein, *Pray for the Peace of Jerusalem* (New York: Philip Publishing, 1918, Yiddish), 28.

34. James T. Barclay, *The City of the Great King* (1858; reprint, New York: Arno Press, 1977), 581.

35. Ellen G. White, "Destruction of Jerusalem," in *The Great Controversy between Christ and Satan* (Oakland, Calif.: Pacific Press, 1888), 36-37. See also idem, "Salvation of the Jews," in *The Acts of the Apostles* (Mountain View, Calif.: Pacific Press, 1911), 372-82.

36. "From the Editor: A Thousand Nightmares—One Explanation," *Hakriyyah Vehakedushah* 5, no. 54 (March 1945, Yiddish): 4.

37. Herman Melville, *Journal of a Visit to Europe and the Levant, October 11, 1856—May 6, 1857*, ed. Howard C. Horsford (Princeton, N.J.: Princeton University Press, 1955), 155-60.

38. R. T. Handy (above, n.31), pp. 124-25, cited from Thomas De Witt Talmage, *Talmage on Palestine* (1890; reprint, New York: Arno Press, 1977).

39. Chaim Hirschensohn, "Where O Where Is the Holy Land? My Spirit Longs For It," *Year Book of the Federation of Palestine Jews of America* (1933, Hebrew): 20-21.

Chapter 5

American Christian Travelers to the Holy Land, 1821–1939

David Klatzker

In the early 1970s, when "America and the Holy Land" was first articulated as a field of research and teaching, American travel to the Land was identified as a discipline deserving of study.[1]

Among all the historical records that one could use to examine Christian attitudes, there are none so vivid and personal as travel accounts. Narratives written by Americans who visited the Holy Land shed light on many aspects of American religion and popular culture, and on American Christian attitudes toward the Jews. Although most travelers were primarily interested in the factual description of the Land, they also sought to explain its spiritual significance. For them, the Holy Land was a kind of touchstone, a means of defining what it meant to be an American and a Christian.

Although estimates of book sales in the nineteenth century are for the most part mere guesses (few records are available), it is clear that travel literature enjoyed wide popularity, coming in close second only to that enjoyed by novels. (It might be asserted that travel narratives are a characteristically middle-class form of writing; the American middle class was concerned with integrating other peoples and places into its worldview.) Holy Land travels comprised a significant portion of this literature. Between the 1820s and the 1930s, American travelers to the Holy Land published hundreds of travel books and articles in journals and newspapers.[2]

Before the 1860s, when travel was more of an adventure, most Holy Land travelers were young men. In the latter half of the nineteenth century, there were more middle-aged travelers, and more women. Above-average affluence was required to travel to the Holy Land, and a sizeable number of Americans enjoyed the means to go abroad in the post–Civil War period.[3] Many clergymen flocked to the Holy Land, not only because of its holiness, but also due to their "sore throats and liberal congregations"[4]—in other words, they sought to improve their health and add to the prestige of their churches.

During the nineteenth century, a tourist infrastructure evolved to meet the needs of Western visitors. Not surprisingly, Americans developed their own support system in the Holy Land. Rolla Floyd, a member of the short-lived Adams Colony in Jaffa (1866–1868), remained in Palestine and became one of the best-known dragomans (translator-guides) and tour operators. Other Americans were also active in the fledgling Holy Land tourist industry, notably cruise operators Frank and Herbert Clark, who grew up in the Adams Colony. The adventist-communitarian American Colony in Jerusalem (which functioned as a commune from 1881 until the 1930s, when it was incorporated into an independent association) operated a hotel, sold souvenirs, and published photographs as well as tour books. The Colony served as a strong attraction for visitors by virtue of its familiar American hospitality; it was "a little America in a Moslem world."[5]

Contrary to the popular notion that travel changes the traveler, the overwhelming evidence is that few travelers were transformed by their visits. Only a small number managed to transcend their religious and cultural biases. Holy Land travel literature is monumentally repetitive. Travel writing was so much a matter of convention that it is sometimes difficult to prove that a given writer actually visited the Holy Land. Travelers shaped and selected their impressions of the Land to fit preconceived patterns in the hope of finding a receptive audience for their travel reports.[6]

However, the fact that most Americans shared certain stereotypes of the Holy Land does not mean that all travelers resolved the distinctiveness and significance of the Land in the same way. A synoptic comparison of travel accounts often discloses differences in focus between one account and another. These differences reflect the great diversity of American Christian subcultures. The implicit and explicit "conversations" between travel accounts—the fact that different sorts of travelers emphasized diverse aspects of their Holy Land experience, and in their memoirs frequently argued with each other about the meaning of the Land— helps to sort the authors into distinct groups. My research has focused on five of these groups: "genteel" travelers, "debunkers," millenarians, blacks, and Roman Catholics. The distinctions between them are often blurred; for instance, black and Roman Catholic travel narratives are sometimes indistinguishable from those of white Protestants. Yet there can be no doubt that the various groups existed and that they throw interesting light on travelers and their sense of self.

GENTEEL TRAVELERS

By genteel travelers I refer to bourgeois evangelical Protestants, the standard bearers of Victorian culture. The gentry was an elite group, yet open to anyone with the proper education and self-discipline. Members of this social class typically traveled to the Holy Land to confirm and refresh their values. To be sure, tours of the Mediterranean, Egypt, and the Holy Land might combine "fun in the sun," romantic Orientalism, and religious motives for travel. But absorbing the biblical atmosphere of the Holy Land was usually given as principal justification for such trips.

It is revealing that one genteel preacher recommended a trip to the Holy Land chiefly as a way to renew one's interest in the Bible.[7] The truth is that the Bible could be a difficult and even boring book for clergymen as well as laypeople. Travel writing was typically viewed as a teaching tool; if it did not provide a forum for serious theology, it at least helped to provide religious knowledge and spiritual uplift. Genteel authors created a new genre of travelogues: moralistic travel books for children, with titles such as *A Family Flight over Egypt and Syria* and *Three Vassar Girls in the Holy Land*. These books emphasized Protestant piety and middle-class ideals, while making the necessary allowances for a child's right to read for pleasure.[8]

Whether writing for children or adults, most of the genteel travelers emphasized the "nicer" side of their trips—not Orthodox or Catholic "superstition" in the Holy Land, not flies and filth, but picturesque scenes of Oriental life. The phenomenal popularity of artistic photographs—virtually tens of thousands of negatives survive—attests to the marketability of the sentimental conception of the Holy Land. Photographers, including a number of Americans, offered posed scenes of natives in costumes imagined to be identical with those of Jesus' day, ethereal views of domes and minarets, and landscapes that added a dimension of otherworldliness not present in nature.[9]

There was another kind of stereotyping common to genteel travelers: descriptions directed toward arousing the reader's sympathy for the wretched natives of the Holy Land. In *Home of the Bible*, the "feminist" writer Mary Terhune intended to evoke pity for downtrodden Oriental women.[10] Travelers like Terhune could seldom enjoy the foreignness of the Holy Land, for it crushed their refined sensibilities.

In contrast to the detractors of the Holy Land, who often emphasized its desolation as proof that it had been cursed, many genteel observers emphasized the splendor of the Land. The famous Presbyterian preacher T. De Witt Talmage declared:

> How any man can be disappointed with the Holy Land I cannot understand. Some of the Palestinian tourists have been chiefly impressed by the fleas, the filth, and the beggars. To me, the scenery, if it had no sacred associations, would be appealingly majestic. There is nothing in America or Europe that surpasses it for a mingling of beauty and grandeur.[11]

Another genteel traveler, Robert Hichens, reported that the Holy Land was an "Arcady of the East," offering release from the pressures of modern life. "Cares drop away, are lost among the innocent wild flowers; fears, anxieties disperse on the gentle, caressing breeze,'' he wrote.[12] It is not hard to conceive that underlying this artificial glorification of the rural landscape was a critique of the technology, urbanization, and speed that had invaded American life.

All travelers to the Holy Land were forced to decide how literally they would interpret the scriptural claims of the Land and the Jews. Genteel visitors tended to believe in the prophecies that the People of Israel would eventually return to their homeland, and they often declared their sympathy for the troubles of the Jews. Despite this proto-Zionist inclination, however, they sometimes expressed sharp skepticism as to the practicality of a Jewish restoration in their own day. It must be admitted that their doubts were realistic. But at times their hesitancy about the fledgling Zionist movement may have been a way of expressing their displeasure that the Oriental Jews had failed to assimilate into Western culture; it was probably also a means of voicing their apprehension that ''progress'' would ruin the romantic land of Jesus. A genteel traveler of the 1920s, Carlyle Channing Davis, feared that ''the history of Southern California will be repeated in Palestine''; he declared that ''the world can well afford to preserve Palestine as it was in the days of Jesus.''[13]

It seems reasonable to suggest that the missionary rhetoric characteristic of the genteel travelers—their zeal to spread the ideals of Protestantism, democracy, rural stability, and simple living—was connected with their efforts to persuade themselves and other Americans that they were still the ''American Israel,'' a chosen people with a special code of behavior and a land of promise of their own. To the extent that these travelers kept alive a sense of the original Puritan idea—that is, to the degree that they sacralized America and the American way of life—they could reverence the Holy Land, but could not declare it central to their lives. The implied focus of the genteel travelers was not the Holy Land, but rather their audience of ''civilized'' Americans.

THE DEBUNKERS

Those travelers whom I have labeled the ''debunkers'' found the moralism and sentimentalism of the genteel travelers an easy target for satire. A key concern of the debunkers was the so-called feminization of American culture, the alleged domination of letters and spirituality by ladies, preachers, and missionaries. Whether this critique was in fact justified is hotly debated among scholars in American studies today.[14] In any case, for these fault-finding travelers, a visit to the Holy Land afforded a golden opportunity to attack what they perceived as self-indulgent emotionalism and ''tendermindedness'' in religion and culture.

Perceptive readers saw the theme quite clearly. In a review of John Franklin Swift's debunking *Going to Jericho* (1868), Bret Harte bravely declared that the era of ''feeble moralizing'' and ''romance'' in travel writing was drawing to a close: ''Sentimental musings on foreign scenes are just now restricted to the private diaries of young and impressionable ladies, and clergymen with affections of the bronchial tubes, whose hearts and mucous membranes are equally susceptible."[15]

The massive success of Mark Twain's burlesque travelogue of 1869, *The Innocents Abroad* (despite Twain's own misgivings over the book's irreverence),[16] and the relative celebrity of later debunkers indicate that many Americans were prepared to mock the images of the Holy Land that they had learned in Sunday school, or at least had fantasies of escape from the hold of traditional religion. The impiety serves as a reminder that the nineteenth century was not only a great period for missionizing at home and abroad, but was also a time of substantial secularization. For example, the freethinker DeRobigne Mortimer Bennett mocked the tiny, unsightly "Land of Yaweh" in order to diminish the scriptural God. "Can it be," he asked, "that this is all there is of the land which such a noise and a fuss have been made about? Can it be that this little seven-by-five country was all that the deity who had created the whole earth and all the suns and stars cared for or selected?"[17] Alongside their aggressive secularism, debunking travelers like Bennett were usually firm believers in the American "civil religion"; they maintained that the resplendent expanses of America provided the ideal against which all other countries should be judged.

An interesting pattern seems to emerge regarding the debunkers' approach to the Jews and Zionism. The Jews of the Old Yishuv, the pietists who lived mainly on charity, were marked for ridicule because they appeared puny in comparison to their heroic biblical ancestors. Yet the self-confident pioneers of the New Yishuv were regarded as an entirely different breed of Jew. H. L. Mencken described the *halutzim* as "realistic and enterprising fellows who look like Americans even when they are Palestinians or Roumanians."[18]

MILLENARIAN TRAVELERS

Millenarianism—in broad terms, the belief that space and time are bursting with significance—was rife in nineteenth-century America. It might be said that many Protestant millenarians were more attracted to space than to time, for many assumed that the return of Jesus to earth would transpire only after his followers had prepared this-worldly kingdoms in the places of God's choosing. Thus, although a belief in the national restoration of the Jews was shared by many Americans, both millenarians and non-millenarians, only the latter saw no contradiction at all in actively supporting Jewish efforts to settle in the Holy Land while constructing their own Zions in America.[19]

The remarkable 1841 journey of Mormon disciple Orson Hyde, from Nauvoo, Illinois, to Jerusalem to dedicate the Holy Land for the return of the Jews, has often been recounted as proof of the importance to the early Mormons of the concept of the restoration of the Jews. Yet the story of early Mormon Zionism is not entirely simple and straightforward.[20] Moreover, it appears that once the gathering of the "saints" to "Zion" in the American West was nearly complete, and Mormon-Gentile relations had been normalized, there was a shift in Mormon interest in the return of the Jews to Jerusalem. Many Mormon travelers seem to have regarded the development of the Zionist movement less as an indication that the millennium was near than as an opportunity to affirm the prophetic truth of their own modern Mormon scriptures, and the validity of the claims to divine inspiration made by the church leadership at a time of transition between generations.[21]

Before World War I, when there were few signs to indicate that the backward Holy Land was about to return to the supposed peace and plenitude of biblical days, millenarian travelers, especially the "dispensationalists," sometimes exaggerated the extent of Western influence and the success of the Jewish colonists.[22] Although millenarians typically focused on the Holy Land itself rather than on America and its culture (in sharp contrast to the general focus on genteel and debunking travelers), there can be no doubt that their interpretation of current events in British Palestine played an important role in the polemic struggle of "Liberals" and "Fundamentalists" in America in the 1920s and 1930s. Millenarian travelers were able to take comfort from the literal fulfillment of prophecy by the Zionist movement, although some still felt it necessary to stretch the truth about the Jews and the Land.[23] Yet most millenarians expected a violent future for the Holy Land and insisted that the ultimate success of the Jews would depend on their acceptance of Jesus as the Messiah. Moreover, in contrast to more recent visionaries, nineteenth- and early twentieth-century millenarians appear to have had relatively little interest in influencing American political opinion regarding Zionism; in their scenario of the future, God alone would direct the course of events.

BLACK TRAVELERS

The travel accounts of black Americans provide a somewhat surprising picture of black religion and culture. For the most part, their travel writings are indistinguishable from those of white Protestants; it might even be argued that blacks should not be classified as a separate group of travelers. There are surprisingly few signs of identification with the suffering and striving of the biblical Hebrews or with their modern descendants, and even the anticipated comparisons of racist America to Egypt seems absent. This unexpected divergence from the typical qualities of black Christianity probably stems from the fact that black travelers were in no way typical—they came from the economic and political elite of their people. Most likely they hoped that whites would read their travel accounts, and therefore they adopted many of the conventions and limitations of white travel literature. Black travelers could stress the hedonistic joys of travel or could use their travel impressions to enliven sermons on typical evangelical themes.[24] Yet it appears that they seldom felt free enough to give a meaningful expression of their feelings as black people.

Adam Clayton Powell, Sr.'s account of his 1939 pilgrimage to the Holy Land, *Palestine and Saints in Caesar's Household*, is the exception to the rule. Perhaps because he explicitly addressed his book to blacks rather than to a mixed readership, Powell was able to mine the rich black Christian heritage to articulate his love of the Holy Land and his empathic approach to the Jewish problem. For example, the trip from Cairo to Jaffa reminded Powell of the account of how the Hebrews borrowed gold and silver from the Egyptians (Exodus 11:2). That led him to a story told by Booker T. Washington about a black slave who ate his master's animals: "You owns the chicken and you owns me," said the slave; "You has a little less chicken and a little more Negro." By way of extension, Powell then explained that Jewish salesmen are unable to get fair prices from Gentiles and are sometimes forced to ask for higher prices knowing that the Gentiles expect them to begin the so-called "jewing process."[25] In this clever way, Powell tried to deconstruct the prejudices of his readers.

CATHOLIC TRAVELERS

In accordance with the traditional religious focus of Catholic journeys to sacred places, American Catholic travelers to the Holy Land emphasized the difference between superficial tourism and intensely conscious pilgrimage. The multitude of challenges faced by the Catholic Church in voluntaristic America necessitated a concentration on organization and piety. While Protestant critics might assign pilgrimages to the peripheral zone of spirituality, Catholics (especially the Franciscan order) tried to take advantage of the opportunities such trips afforded to strengthen faith and a sense of community.[26]

An American Catholic traveler made a revealing comment a few years after the period of this study:

> Whatever it was—I felt incapable of pinning it down—the Catholic seemed not fully at home in Palestine, like someone returning to a long neglected family and not knowing how to act. . . . In Catholic life as it is actually lived in the United States, there is little realization of the deep connection between Catholicism and Palestine; between Catholicism and Rome, yes. But somewhere along the line, a once firm grip on that ancient land at the eastern Mediterranean has been lost.[27]

Travel narratives provide evidence that Catholics viewed Rome and Jerusalem from different perspectives. For example, John W. Brennan, a Catholic pilgrim to both cities sometime in the late 1920s, wrote that Rome's special appeal was its "conservatism." Encountering a flock of children in the street, he was happily reminded that "progressive" ideas like birth control had no place in the Eternal City. Brennan was also attracted to Rome because of its "catholicity"; he remarked that many different languages spoken at the Vatican remind the pilgrim that he has arrived at the very "heart" of the world-church. Brennan was intrigued by the biblical associations of Jerusalem, "an Open Sesame to a treasure house of vivid memories," but in contrast to Rome, he found relatively little to write about in the Holy Land.[28] In other words, because it was the headquarters of the world-church, Rome was "first among equals" as a pilgrimage center. The popular Catholic notion that the Bible was in some sense a "Protestant book" probably also contributed to the weakening of Jerusalem's appeal. In one respect, however, both Rome and Jerusalem were equally disadvantaged: The need to develop parish churches and other institutions at home meant that pilgrimage abroad could never rise to the top of the list of communal priorities, although it always remained an attractive option for individual Catholics.

Pious Catholic travelers enthusiastically described the spiritual benefits of visiting the holy places and seized every chance to correct Protestant "misrepresentations." They declared the Jews to be materialistic and intolerant, as well as pitiable, thus confirming stereotypes that were shared by many Protestants. But Catholic travelers were occasionally more extreme than Protestants, with some Catholics referring to the Jews' guilt in the crucifixion and expressing dark suspicions that the Zionists aimed to expropriate the native Christians and control the holy places.[29] These negative views corroborate the notion that pilgrimage served an essentially conservative function for Catholics, reinforcing their traditional images of the Holy Land and its inhabitants.[30]

CONCLUSIONS

In contrast to many places around the world in the era of mass tourism, the Holy Land never succumbed to the touristic phenomenon of "placelessness"—in other words, the Land retained its distinctiveness for travelers. Jerusalem might begin to offer Western amenities, but it could never be considered just another place to visit. Although travelers held a variety of views regarding its centrality, Jerusalem was always the "holy" city.

Perhaps scholars need to pay close, more analytic attention to the notion that Jesus is the true central symbol of Christianity. W. D. Davies has suggested (with special reference to the Fourth Gospel) that "the person of Jesus becomes 'the place' which replaces all holy places" or Christians; to be "in Christ" (which has been variously interpreted) is to be in the land of the Christians.[31] It was the holiness of the place that attracted most travelers; the travel memoirs of Americans offer eloquent testimony to the desire of all sorts of Christians to make physical contact with the Land of the Prophets and of Jesus.[32]

To what extent did travel to the Holy Land encourage better interfaith relations? Debunking travelers, as well as many nondenominational Protestants who sought God in a private way, often gleefully demonstrated how unchristian Christianity had become in the land of its origin. Mark Twain described how priests from all of the denominations occupying the Holy Sepulcher are entitled to enter the Chapel of the Finding of the Cross "to weep and pray and worship the gentle Redeemer. Two different congregations are not allowed to enter at the same time, however, because they always fight." Yet Twain, who confessed that he was not always well disposed toward Catholics, also expressed his "honest gratitude" for the unselfish hospitality of the convent fathers toward weary

travelers.[33] Travelers who were ardent supporters of interdenominational cooperation in America had their ecumenical interests "illustrated and confirmed"
by their journeys to the Holy Land; for example, Philip Schaff and Harry Emerson
Fosdick eagerly sought out Protestants of many different churches for fellowship
in Jerusalem—and yet both objected to the "triviality" of the Orthodox ceremonies that they witnessed. "And this is Christianity in the land of Christ!"
exclaimed Fosdick.[34]

It seems reasonable to conclude that tourism/pilgrimage to the Holy Land
emphasized *communitas* and developed an implicit critique of social strife; and
yet it is clear that authentic tolerance toward world religions (Eastern Christianity,
Judaism, Islam) grew very slowly in America, even within the reality of radical
religious pluralism. Until sometime after 1948, most Americans could probably
not view Jerusalem as a center of ecumenism in a positive light; one wonders
how many may still find difficulty doing so.

In short, the huge mass of writings produced by American Christian travelers
to the Holy Land helped their countrymen to articulate the nature of their attachment to the Bible, heightened their awareness of the fact that Americans
belonged to a variety of different social groups and subcultures, and provided
them with a forum for the discussion of the Jews' place in the contemporary
landscape. Travel literature is a prism that reflects many significant American
social and cultural trends; in truth, travel writings often reveal less about the
Land than about the religious and cultural identities of the travelers who authored
them—their motives, justifications, disappointments, and satisfactions. Although
not all travelers to the Holy Land succeeded in developing self-understanding,
their quest was a metaphor of their time.

NOTES

1. See the comments by Moshe Davis and Robert T. Handy, "America and the Holy
Land: A Colloquium," *American Jewish Historical Quarterly* 62 (1972): 5–62. My
interest in the topic was sparked by Professor Davis' graduate seminar on "America–
Holy Land Studies" at the Hebrew University of Jerusalem. It developed into my doctoral
dissertation on "American Christian Travelers to the Holy Land," at Temple University,
under the direction of Professor Franklin H. Littell.

2. See David Klatzker, "American Christian Travelers to the Holy Land, 1821–
1939" (Ph.D. diss., Temple University, 1987), for an extensive bibliography of primary
sources. Many of the seventy-two volumes in the Arno Press reprint series, "America
and the Holy Land," deal with travel to the Holy Land. For some representative selections
from those texts, with historical commentary, see Robert T. Handy, ed., *The Holy Land
in American Protestant Life, 1800–1948: A Documentary History* (New York: Arno Press,
1981).

The time frame of my study covers the first century of American travel to the Holy
Land, from the earliest published travel letters from Jerusalem (the missionary reports of
Pliny Fisk and Levi Parsons in 1821) to the effective closure of tourist traffic at the onset
of World War II.

3. In the postbellum period, larger and faster steamships reduced the cost of travel considerably; at times, fares dropped so low that the shipping firms incurred deficits in order to stay competitive. In the 1880s and 1890s, budget-minded travelers sailing second-class could make a brief trip to Egypt and the Holy Land for as little as $500 round-trip from the United States, expenses included. First-class travel was also relatively inexpensive. Travel-guide writer W. Pembroke Fetridge (1897) estimated the expenses for nearly a full year of first-class wandering:

Passage to London	$100
Passage to Alexandria and Cairo	130
Return	240
Three weeks on the Nile	200
Two months in Palestine at $8 per day	480
Seven months in cheap countries at $4.60 per day	970
	$2120

Fetridge noted that a prepaid Cook's tour (also first-class) would cost about one-third less. See Allison Lockwood, *Passionate Pilgrims: The American Traveler in Great Britain, 1800-1914* (New York: Cornwall Books, 1981), 145-72, 295-313; Warren Tute, *Atlantic Conquest* (Boston: Little, Brown & Co., 1962), 49-50, 52, 111-12; Hezekiah Butterworth, *Zigzag Journeys in the Levant with a Talmudist Story-Teller* (Boston: Estes and Lauriat, 1886), 67-72; W. Pembroke Fetridge, *The American Travellers' Guides: Hand-Books for Travellers to Europe and the East*, vol. 1 (New York: Fetridge & Co., 1897), xxvi-xxvii.

The real incomes of Americans rose over this period: From 1860 to 1880, average wages increased by 43 percent, while prices went up only 10 percent. Between 1890 and 1915, wages went up 50 percent, and prices 35 percent. Many Americans were affluent enough to travel. See Hugh De Santis, "The Democratization of Travel: The Travel Agent in American History," *Journal of American Culture* 1 (Spring 1978): 1-17.

4. O. R. Burchard, *Two Months in Europe: A Record of a Summer Vacation Abroad* (Syracuse, N.Y.: Davis, Bardeen & Co., 1897), 1.

5. On Floyd, see Helen Palmer Parsons, ed., *Letters from Palestine, 1868–1912, Written by Rolla Floyd* (Dexter, Maine: privately printed, 1981). Floyd is mentioned in numerous American travel books. On the Clark brothers, there is an interesting letter from Mrs. Clorinda Clark to Prime Minister David Ben-Gurion (10 May 1950), copy in YMCA Archives, Jerusalem; see also Paul S. Junkin, *A Cruise Around the World* (Creston, Iowa: Advertiser-Gazette, 1910). Regarding the American Colony, see Bertha S. Vester, "Jerusalem, My Home," *National Geographic* 126 (1964): 826-47; idem, *Our Jerusalem: An American Family in the Holy City, 1881-1949* (1950; reprint, New York: Arno Press, 1977); Paul Elmen, "The American Swedish Kibbutz," *Swedish Pioneer Historical Quarterly* 32 (1981): 205-18; Helga Dudman, *Street People* (Jerusalem: Jerusalem Post/Carta, 1982), 83–104; Dov Gavish, "The American Colony and Its Photographers," in *Sefer Zev Vilnay*, ed. Ely Schiller (Jerusalem: Ariel, 1984, Hebrew), 127-44. The quotation is taken from Edward Ruskin Welch, *A Palestine Pilgrimage* (Asheville, N.C.: Asheville Advocate, 1922), 88.

6. Mark Twain pointed out that Presbyterian travelers "found a Presbyterian Pal-

estine, and they had already made up their minds to find no other, though possibly they did not know it, being blinded by their zeal. Others were Baptists, seeking Baptist evidences and a Baptist Palestine. Others were Catholics, Methodists, Episcopalians, seeking evidences endorsing their several creeds and a Catholic, a Methodist, an Episcopalian Palestine. Honest as these men's intentions may have been, they were full of partialities and prejudices, they entered the country with their verdicts already prepared, and they could no more write dispassionately and impartially about it than they could about their own wives and children." *The Innocents Abroad, or The New Pilgrims' Progress* (Hartford: American Publishing Co., 1869), chap. 48.

7. A. A. Murphy, "Homiletic Advantages of a Trip to the Holy Land," *Homiletic Review* 21 (1891): 86-87.

8. On this new genre of children's literature, see Virginia Haviland, "The Travelogue Storybook of the Nineteenth Century," in *The Hewins Lectures*, ed. Siri Andrews (Boston: Horn Book, 1963), 25-63. See also Edward Everett Hale and Susan Hale, *A Family Flight over Egypt and Syria* (Boston: D. Lothrop, 1882); Elizabeth W. Champney, *Three Vassar Girls in the Holy Land* (Boston: Estes and Lauriat, 1892).

9. On nineteenth-century photography, see Eyal Onne, *Photographic Heritage of the Holy Land, 1839–1914* (Manchester: Institute of Advanced Studies, Manchester Polytechnic, 1980); Yeshayahu Nir, *The Bible and the Image: The History of Photography in the Holy Land, 1839–1899* (Philadelphia: University of Pennsylvania Press, 1985).

10. Mary Harland [pseud. for Mary Virginia Terhune], *Home of the Bible: A Womans Vision of the Master's Land* (Philadelphia: Historical Publishing Co., 1895).

11. Thomas De Witt Talmage, *The Oriental World* (Chicago: J. J. Moore, 1897), 72.

12. Robert Hichens, "The Holy Land," *Century* 80 (1910): 4.

13. Carlyle Channing Davis, *The Holy Land: Before and After the World War: Tracings of Its Weirdly Tragic History and Redemption* (Boston: Roxburgh Publishing Co., 1920), 171-72.

14. For scholarly arguments that nineteenth-century American culture had become "feminized," see Ann Douglas, *The Feminization of the American Culture* (New York: Alfred A. Knopf, 1977); Alfred Habegger, *Gender, Fantasy and Realism in American Literature* (New York: Columbia University Press, 1982). For opposing statements, arguing that American literature and religion showed signs of having become both more "feminine" and more "masculine," see Nina Baym, *Woman's Fiction: A Guide to Novels by and About Women: 1820–1870* (Ithaca: Cornell University Press, 1978); David Schuyler, "Inventing a Feminine Past," *New England Quarterly* 5 (September 1978): 291-308; David S. Reynolds, "The Feminization Controversy: Sexual Stereotypes and the Paradoxes of Piety in Nineteenth-Century America," *New England Quarterly* 53 (March 1980): 96-106; Mary G. De Jong, " 'I Want to be Like Jesus': The Self-Defining Power of Evangelical Hymnody," *Journal of the American Academy of Religion* 54 (Fall 1986): 461-93.

15. "Current Literature," *Overland Monthly* 1 (July 1868): 101.

16. Twain apparently sought financial success and genteel respectability, although the latter was not within his grasp. He wrote his publisher that the "irreverence of the volume appears to be a tip-top good feature of it, (financially) diplomatically speaking, though I wish with all my heart there wasn't an irreverent passage in it" (Hamlin Hill, ed., *Mark Twain: Letters to His Publishers* [Berkeley and Los Angeles: University of California Press, 1967], 28). For a valuable study of the reception of *The Innocents Abroad*, see Louis J. Budd, *Our Mark Twain* (Philadelphia: University of Pennsylvania Press, 1983), chap. 30.

chap. 30.

Unlike most other travelogues of the era, reliable records of the book's sales exist. It was the most popular travel book ever written by an American, selling at least half a million copies in Twain's lifetime. See James D. Hart, *The Popular Book: A History of America's Literary Taste* (New York: Oxford University Press, 1950), 147.

17. DeRobigne M. Bennett, *A Truth Seeker around the World*, 4 vols. (New York: D. M. Bennett, 1882), 2: 123.

18. H. L. Mencken, *Erez Israel* (New York: B. F. Safran at the New School, 1935), 10. Mencken made a surprisingly cheerful visit to the Holy Land in 1934, although there was a negative undertone to some of his comments about the future of Zionism; as a result, his travel articles were criticized by the Baltimore Jewish community. On this controversy, see Carl Bode, ed., *The New Mencken Letters* (New York: Dial Press, 1977), 304-10; see also Robert Kanigel, "Did H. L. Mencken Hate the Jews?" *Menckeniana* 73 (Spring 1980): 1–7; Gwinn Owens, "Mencken and the Jews, Revisited," *Menckeniana* 74 (Summer 1980): 6-10.

19. For background, see Robert Kieran Whalen, "Millenarianism and Millennialism in America, 1790-1880" (Ph.D. diss., State University of New York at Stony Brook, 1972), chap. 2.

20. The *Book of Mormon* is undeniably packed with references to the return of the Jews to their land. It is also reported that early Mormon missionaries to England, who might have been expected to focus on the promise of America, spoke mainly about the restoration of the Jews to Jerusalem. See W. H. Oliver, *Prophets and Millennialists: The Uses of Biblical Prophecy in England from the 1790s to the 1840s* (Auckland, New Zealand: Auckland University Press, 1978), 222-25. However, in the collection of direct revelations granted to Joseph Smith and canonized as Mormon scriptures, the *Doctrine and Covenants*—a work probably more important for early Mormon belief than the *Book of Mormon*—the emphasis is plainly on the Mormons' own "gathering" to "Zion" in America. The Mormons, like the ancient Israelites, were promised a land flowing with milk and honey; see *The Doctrine and Covenants of the Church of Jesus Christ of Latter-Day Saints*, rev. ed. (Salt Lake City: Church of Jesus Christ of Latter-Day Saints, 1921), 38: 18-19, 57: 1-4. See also Melodie Moench, "Nineteenth-Century Mormons: The New Israel," *Dialogue* 12 (Spring 1979): 42-56.

21. The Holy Land visit of Mormon official Anton H. Lund (1898) is an example of how later church leaders were eager to make use of Orson Hyde's mission, part of the Mormon collective memory, to back up their claims to prophetic truth, yet were cautious enough not to make Zionism appear as the literal fulfillment of the Mormon millennial hope. Lund reported that "The prophet Joseph was inspired to send Brother Hyde to that land, and look at the change! A spirit has come over the Jews, over the House of Israel, to gather to that land. This was not felt by them before but since that time." However, Lund noted, the Zionists were not "gathering in faith" as required by Mormon doctrine— that is, the Jewish settlers were not attracted to Jesus. See *Annual Conference Report* (Salt Lake City: Deseret News Publishing Co., 1898), 10-13.

22. For example, the famed Baptist pastor and social reformer Russell H. Conwell declared that "Jerusalem has steadily bowed to the teachings of the disciples of Jesus, until it seems almost ready to kneel at his feet." He claimed to find tolerance, love, and social progress everywhere in the Holy Land in 1898. "The New Palestine," *Sunday School Times*, 14 May 1898, p. 315.

23. A typical claim concerned increased rainfall in the Holy Land in recent years;

rainfall figures were frequently fabricated or manipulated by millenarian travel writers. See Dwight Julian Wilson, "Armageddon Now! The Premillenarian Response to Russia and Israel Since 1917" (Ph.D. diss., University of California at Santa Cruz, 1975), p. 45.

24. David F. Dorr was utterly bored by the primitive Holy Land, in contrast to sophisticated Europe; see his *A Colored Man Around the World* (Cleveland, Ohio: privately printed, 1858). Although he identified himself as an escaped slave and frequently worked comments on racial injustice into his chapters, Dorr never mentioned Canaan or Egypt with reference to his Holy Land experiences. Baptist preacher Charles T. Walker emphasized sin and redemption in his travel memoir, *A Colored Man Abroad: What He Was and Heard in the Holy Land and Europe* (Augusta, Ga.: John M. Weigle & Co., 1892).

25. Adam Clayton Powell, Sr., *Palestine and Saints in Caesar's Household* (New York: Richard R. Smith, 1939), 14-15.

26. Father Charles A. Vissani of the Franciscan Commissariat of the Holy Land led the first organized Catholic pilgrimage from the United States to Jerusalem in 1889; see Rev. James Pfeiffer, *First American Catholic Pilgrimage to Palestine 1889* (Cincinnati: Joseph Berning & Co., 1892). The Franciscan Commissariat raised funds to build a 100-room addition to the Casa Nova Hostel in Jerusalem, a new pilgrim house ("Our Lady of America") in Nazareth, and the Basilica of the Transfiguration on Mt. Tabor. Construction was not limited to the Holy Land. The Monastery of Mount St. Sepulchre ("The Holy Land of America") was erected on land near the Catholic University of America in Washington, D.C., in 1899. It contains exact replicas of many of the traditional holy places in Bethlehem and Jerusalem. Large group pilgrimages to this American shrine were organized on a yearly basis, perhaps serving as a vicarious substitute for visits to the original sites; see *Guide to the Franciscan Monastery, Washington, D.C.; A Pilgrimage to the Holy Land of America, Together with Many Interesting Facts about the Order of St. Francis and Its Work in the Holy Land and America* (Washington, D.C.: National Capitol Press, 1934).

27. Thomas F. Troy, "Tourist or Pilgrim?" *Crusader's Almanac* 54, no. 3 (1946): 7.

28. John W. Brennan, C.Ss.R., *The Student Abroad* (Boston: Stratford Co., 1928), 31, 120, 399.

29. Nineteenth-century Catholic travel literature was sometimes grotesque in its portrayal of the Jew. A young Philadelphia Catholic was deeply moved by a visit to "Calvary": "One could almost imagine that he heard the unbelieving Jews breaking the stillness with jibes and sneers, crying out: 'If He be the King of Israel, let Him come down from the cross!'" See William H. Bergan, *Busy Thoughts of a Traveler in the Orient* (n.p., [1874]), 78. Zionism was the special target of the Franciscan journal, *The Crusader's Almanac*, in the twentieth century; for example, it declared that Arab riots against the Jews were justified, since the Jews came "not as settlers, but as out-and-out invaders, whose ultimate purpose [was] to oust the present inhabitants and set up for themselves a kingdom of priests." *Crusader's Almanac* 29, no. 1 (1920): 42.

30. See David Klatzker, "American Catholic Travelers to the Holy Land, 1861–1929," *Catholic Historical Review* 74 (January 1988): 55-74.

31. W. D. Davies, *The Gospel and the Land: Early Christianity and Jewish Territorial Doctrine* (Berkeley and Los Angeles: University of California Press, 1974), 318; see also 217-19, 256, 368.

32. Although I have not attempted to quantify the number of Zion or Hebrew Bible

sites, and Jesus sites related to the Apostolic Writings, described in American Christian travel narratives, it appears that the main concern of most travelers was to visit the locales associated with Jesus in Jerusalem, Bethlehem, and the Galilee. For the most part, Jesus' historical presence in the Holy Land, rather than Jewish *realia*, carried over into Christianity, attracted travelers, and made the land "holy" in their eyes.

33. Mark Twain (above, n.6), chaps. 53, 55.

34. "Illustrated and confirmed," quotation from Robert T. Handy, "Holy Land Experiences of Two Pioneers of Christian Ecumenism: Schaff and Mott," in *Contemporary Jewry: Essays in Honor of Moshe Davis*, ed. Geoffrey Wigoder (Jerusalem: Institute of Contemporary Jewry, Hebrew University of Jerusalem, 1984), 66.

Philip Schaff wrote that he was "pained and shocked by the base superstition and empty formalism" of the Oriental churches. Philip Schaff, *Through Bible Lands: Notes of Travel in Egypt, the Desert, and Palestine* (1878; reprint, New York: Arno Press, 1977), 233.

"And this is Christianity . . . " Quotation from Henry Emerson Fosdick, *A Pilgrimage to Palestine* (1927; reprint, New York: Arno Press, 1977), 264.

Chapter 6

Canada and the Holy Land: Some North American Similarities and Differences

Michael Brown

Common wisdom, among Americans at least, has often been that Canada is an extension of the United States geographically and culturally, and that only accidents of history have kept the two countries distinct politically. That assumption has frequently been made with regard to Canada's Holy Land connections, and with some justice. As the Canadian correspondent of an American Zionist journal put it in 1917: "Whatever happens in the United States [that is in any way related to Jews] eventually makes its way across the border and happens in Canada, too."[1]

Some aspects of the Canada–Holy Land relationship, however, have little to do with the United States and much to do with Canada's binational make-up and ongoing relationship with Great Britain. In fact, three elements, the American connection, British relationship, and binationalism have contributed over the years to shaping the character of Canada's ties to the Holy Land.

AMERICAN CONNECTION

Among the aspects of America–Holy Land relations over the years that have had their Canadian counterpart or involved direct Canadian participation are (1) Biblicism, interest in the Holy Land, and affinity to Judaism, all of which are characteristic of English-speaking Protestants; (2) joint American-Canadian church, Zionist, and secular-scientific undertakings related to the Holy Land; and (3) the emergence of a sympathetic attitude toward Zionism among certain liberal groups. A few examples may be instructive.

In English Canada, as in the United States, localities were given biblical names by early Protestant settlers more at home with the geography of the Holy Land than with that of their own country. In Ontario, for example, there are places called Bethany, Jaffa, and Sharon, two named Salem, and another, Mount Salem. Hebron, Goshen, Jordan Falls, and East Jordan are in Nova Scotia. And there are others elsewhere.[2]

As was the case with American literature, nineteenth-century English Canadian literature provided many examples of authors influenced by Bible stories and geography, which they knew from English and American literature as well as from the Bible itself.[3] The first issue of the *Mercantile Journal of Quebec* (4 September 1816) included an anonymous article entitled "Jerusalem, Sketch of the Most Ancient City in the World." Early Canadian schoolbooks exhorted youngsters to cherish the Holy Land. *The Fourth Book of Lessons for the Use of Schools*, for example, described the Holy Land as a place with

> a record of events such as have not come to pass in any other land, monuments
> of belief denied to all other nations, hopes not elsewhere cherished, but which
> nevertheless are connected with the destiny of the whole human race and stretch
> forward to the consummation of all terrestrial things.[4]

Charles Heavysege wrote ponderous verse dramas on biblical themes, such as the fifteen-act "Saul" (1857–1869) and "Jephthah's Daughter" (1867), as well as shorter poetry, such as his "Sonnets: Jezebel" (1867). Rev. John Douglas Borthwick of Montreal published an anthology of poetry based on the Bible, *The Harp of Canaan*, which had appeared in a second edition by 1871. Thomas Talbot's *The Hebrews at Home* (Montreal, 1874) was a popular work on the customs of the ancient Hebrews. More scholarly were the works of John William Dawson, longtime president of McGill University. Dawson lectured a great deal in the United States and provided a living Holy Land link between that country and its northern neighbor. He delivered the Phi Beta Kappa Oration at the Harvard commencement in 1875 and in the same year published *Nature and the Bible* in New York.

In the years before movies and television, travel literature provided one of the most popular vehicles of escape. Accounts of Holy Land travels offered inspiration as well as adventure and were as widely read in Canada as in the United States. Over the years Canadians read the descriptions of journeys written by Mark Twain, Herman Melville, and other lesser American writers, such as Henry Van Dyke, the maverick Presbyterian minister and Princeton literature professor, whose *Out-of-Doors in the Holy Land* was published simultaneously in Toronto and New York in 1908.

Of no less significance than literature as a medium for American-Canadian interchange on Holy Land affairs have been the joint activities of Canadians and Americans in both the evangelical movement and the Zionist movement. Evangelical Christians have worked in unison throughout North America. Beginning in 1878, American fundamentalists held a series of International Prophetic Conferences; a major issue on their agenda was the restoration of the Jews to the Holy Land. Canadians were present at these gatherings and presumably brought back to Canada a considerable measure of the Americans' enthusiasm.[5] Prominent American evangelists, such as Dwight L. Moody, preached regularly in Canada, often touching on the subjects of the Holy Land and Jewish restoration—as well as the conversion of the Jews.[6] A Canadian, Rev. A. E. Thompson, served as pastor of the American Church in Jerusalem until he was expelled by the Turks during World War I. After the capture of the Holy City by the British, Thompson appeared frequently in the United States to tell fellow Christians about "the Jewish colonies" in the Holy Land, which were "turning the wilderness into a very garden of the Lord," and thus were preparing the way for restoration and the Second Coming.[7]

The extensive contacts and interchanges of Americans and Canadians involved in Zionism have been catalogued elsewhere.[8] Although some Canadian Zionist organizations have been heavily dependent on their American counterparts, Zionism in Canada, since its earliest days, has generally maintained its independence from the American movement while cooperating with it. Something of an exception to the rule is Canadian Hadassah–WIZO, the women's Zionist organization. Hadassah was founded in the United Sates in 1912, and soon afterward Canadian women made contact with the Americans regarding the establishment of a chapter in Canada. Canadians attended the American Hadassah convention in 1914; in 1917 and again in 1919 Henrietta Szold, the founder of the group, visited Canada to assist the Canadians. In the end, however, the Canadians affiliated with the Women's International Zionist Organization (WIZO) founded in London in 1920, partly because of the intervention of Vera (Mrs. Chaim) Weizmann and partly out of a desire to remain independent of the Americans.[9] Szold was not sensitive to the issue of Canadian nationalism and could not understand how she might be viewed as an American imperialist. She never forgave the Canadians, especially Lillian (Mrs. Archibald) Freiman, the president of Canadian Hadassah–WIZO, for what she regarded as their treachery. Szold felt that she and "Hadassah in America" had given their "effective and wholly unselfish aid" to the Canadians. She broke off relations with them in the early 1920s in the belief that "forebearance further [for their ingratitude] would hardly be a virtue."[10] Relations between the two groups remained cool for many years.

One other aspect of North American relationships with the Holy Land deserves mention here—namely, the strain of idealistic and pluralistic liberalism often found in both Canada and the United States. Over the years, the atmosphere with regard to Jews in both countries has varied. Until the 1960s, at least, the United States tended to be rather more open to ethnic minorities and to religious differences. In both countries at all times, however, there have been outspoken champions of Jewish rights and especially of Zionism—more, perhaps, than anywhere else with the possible exception of Britain. Frequently, Canadian and American idealists influenced each other.

In the United States in the 1930s and 1940s, this tradition was best exemplified by liberal Protestant clergymen such as John Haynes Holmes and Reinhold Niebuhr, who were both well known in Canada.[11] North of the border its outstanding exponent was Arthur Wentworth Roebuck (1878–1971). Roebuck, who could trace his impeccably WASP (White Anglo-Saxon Protestant) family roots back some four centuries, worked his way up from rather humble beginnings to positions as Liberal member of the Ontario and then federal Parliament from 1934 to 1945, minister of labor and attorney general in Ontario in the mid-1930s, and was appointed to the Senate in 1945. A liberal in every sense of the word—too much so for the leaders of his own Liberal Party, who kept him at arm's length—Roebuck fought the monopolies and the union busters, and he sympathized with the lot of blacks, Chinese, and other disadvantaged groups.[12] He was particularly outspoken in his support for Jews, many of whom lived in the ridings he represented. In his usual forthright way, Roebuck described his relationship with the Jewish community. Although the Jews "were not sufficiently numerous to assure my election," he explained retrospectively in 1963, they

> were the most numerous and powerful of the groups other than my own, British, and their friendship and generosity knew no bounds. In addition to their election drive, they contributed handsomely to my campaign fund. I feel that I have justified their confidence. Like Churchill, I am a Christian Zionist.[13]

Roebuck's Zionist activities were wide-ranging. As attorney general of Ontario, he extended greetings to the twenty-fourth Canadian Zionist convention in 1935. In 1947 he spoke in New York at the opening of a Palestine exhibit. He advocated Canadian support for the Jewish National Home in Parliament, and he arranged an interview in 1944 for Nahum Goldmann, head of the World Jewish Congress, with Prime Minister Mackenzie King in a futile attempt to bring King over to the Zionist cause.[14]

Notwithstanding their extensive contacts with regard to Holy Land matters, and parallel developments in the two countries, there have been differences in the relations of Canada and the United States with the Holy Land. Some of these differences are connected to America's role as a new "promised land" for Jews and for other citizens, a role that Canada, like most countries of immigration, did not for the most part assume. Other differences stemmed from Canada's ties to Great Britain; still others are related to the binational character of Canada. Although full analysis of the issues is impossible here, an indication of their nature, pointing the way to future study, is in order.

From Puritan times, Americans have thought of their country as a new promised land. Immigrants came to America believing that it was the divinely appointed new Zion supplanting the old Zion, now little more than an antique memory. Many in Europe and elsewhere who did not emigrate also considered America to be the new hope of the world, replacing Jerusalem as the "city on the hill'' and the "light unto the nations." America was also a new and better "land of milk and honey," potentially far more bountiful than the barren Holy Land of contemporary reality could ever hope to be. To Jews, the notion of America as a new land of promise was especially congenial. The United States offered them a degree of spiritual freedom, social equality, and material opportunity unattainable in other places.[15] To Zionists and to Christian restorationists, however, America offered a competing and often more attractive vision to replace that of a restored Jewry in its ancient land. For many, the Holy Land became over the years a mere symbol and the stuff of history, displaced from its role in contemporary affairs by the New World colossus.

Some Canadians, such as Adolphus Mordecai Hart, a historian-politician and grandson of the country's pioneer Jewish settler Aaron Hart, have shared the view of America as the "triumph of human right."[16] On the whole, however, Canadians' sense of their own distinctness has precluded wholehearted endorsement of America as the new Zion. From time to time Canadians have articulated a mission for their own country. Seldom, however, were such notions invested with the universal, religious implications ascribed to America's role as the new promised land, nor did they resonate with biblical tones.[17] To be sure, many Canadians, especially English Canadian Protestants—like American and other Protestants—have tended to view their personal experiences, and even those of their own communities, as replays of biblical events. In their view, the Bible speaks intimately of contemporary issues. Few, if any, however, projected that vision onto a national screen in Canada. Canada could be, as the London *Jewish Chronicle* remarked in 1907, "a minor land of promise,"[18] but it could never be the promised land. Thus, there is less Holy Land imagery in Canada than in the United States, and less competition for the attachment to the Holy Land in its present-day reality. An exception to this rule was Henry Wentworth Monk (1827–1896), the foremost leader of the British-Israel movement, which promoted the notion that the Anglo-Saxon peoples were the descendants of the Ten Lost Tribes of Israel, destined to lead a restoration of themselves and of the other two tribes (i.e., the Jews or "visible Israelites") to the Holy Land as preparation for the Second Coming of Jesus. Monk believed that with its confederation in 1867, Canada had become a possible symbol of a new, harmonious world order; and for a time he envisioned Ottawa as the new Jerusalem. Corruption and violence in the post–Civil War United States strengthened Monk in these convictions.[19]

If Americans have tended to see their own history as a new version of biblical experience, increasing involvement in the Middle East has led them to view events in that part of the world as a revised version of American history. The pioneering values of the Zionist settlers and their attachment to the Bible were admired nostalgically by Americans who yearned for their lost national youth. The Jews' experience with "savages" in an untamed land also seemed familiar. Molly Lyons Bar-David, a Canadian from the prairies who settled in the Holy Land in the mid-1930s, articulated this peculiarly American vision clearly. She noted that in the American West "the women were familiar with weapons . . . [and] would not have been prevented at a stockade from mowing down scalping Iroquois." She believed the situation in the Holy Land to be analogous.[20] Most Canadians, however, perceived no correspondence between Canadian and Holy Land historical experiences.

There is yet one more way in which Americans have become involved in Holy Land affairs that has no parallel in Canada. This connection stems less from history and theology than from geopolitics. Early in its history the United States began to acquire a sense of being a great power. Although it was often reluctant to become entangled in world affairs as great powers must, such involvement proved inevitable. In the Middle East in general, and in the Holy Land in particular, American entanglement grew steadily, if erratically, from the mid-nineteenth century on. By the end of World War II, the United States had become the chief player in the game of Holy Land politics.

Canada, on the other hand, has never had a sense of itself as a great power, and until well after World War II, her interest in affairs outside Europe and the United States was quite limited. Illustrative was the complete ignorance of the Balfour Declaration on the part of Sir Joseph Pope, undersecretary of state for external affairs and Canada's senior civil servant in the area of foreign relations, days after the issuance of the Declaration and months after the visit to Ottawa of Arthur Balfour to discuss it.[21] During the struggle for Israel's statehood and thereafter, Canada did become involved in Holy Land affairs, and over time it came to support Israel only somewhat less enthusiastically than the United States, chiefly in the diplomatic arena and in facilitating the transfer of funds raised by Canadian Jews for the state. Some see this development as evidence of the Americanization of Canadian foreign policy.

BRITISH RELATIONSHIP

Perhaps the main reason for Canada's differences from the United States is her loyalist tradition. Here, too, place names are instructive. More striking in Canada than the incidence of biblical place names, and more telling with regard to the self-image of the country's founders, is the much higher incidence of names with British associations. From Halifax in Nova Scotia to Victoria in British Columbia, from Hull and Victoriaville in Quebec to Kingston, Windsor, Hamilton, and London in Ontario, Regina and Prince Albert in Saskatchewan, British place names abound. The names of four of the ten provinces and of thousands of institutions are testimony to continuing ties to the British crown. The British heritage and connection are parts of Canada's identity; these have had much to do with shaping her involvement with the Holy Land.

Many of the people who sparked interest in the Holy Land and in Canada over the years had acquired their enthusiasm in Britain. Charles Alexander Brodie Brockwell, who was a professor of Hebrew and Semitic languages at McGill University in Montreal from 1906 to 1937, served as a catalyst for interest in the Holy Land on campus and sometimes spoke at off-campus Zionist events. Brockwell was an Anglican clergyman, born and educated in Britain, who returned there when he retired from McGill.[22] Arthur Roebuck, although Canadian born, maintained close ties with his family in Britain and considered himself to be of British stock.[23] And there was, of course, novelist John Buchan, who, as Lord Tweedsmuir, served as governor-general of Canada from 1936 until his death in 1940. Buchan's interest in Zionism had been "aroused" by Arthur Balfour.[24] While a member of the British Parliament, Buchan had served a term as chairman of the House of Commons Pro-Palestine Committee. In Canada both he and his wife spoke publicly in favor of Zionism, lending the cause the cachet of the crown. Occasionally Buchan intervened politically on behalf of the Zionists.[25] Except for his stay in Canada, his experiences during World War I, and his foreign travels, Buchan lived all his life in Britain.

Of greater importance than the presence in Canada of Britishers promoting interest in the Holy Land has been the influence of British culture and institutions. The British-Israel movement is an outstanding example. The founding father of the movement, Richard Brothers (1757–1824), as well as his successor, Henry Wentworth Monk, were both natives of British North America; they devoted much of their political and proselytizing efforts to the British Isles, creating an important Holy Land link between Canada and Great Britain. Monk believed that peace would come to the world only when justice was done to Jews; to him such justice meant, primarily, restoring them to their ancient homeland under the tutelage of Great Britain. At a utopian colony on the shores of Lake Erie, Monk met Laurence Oliphant, a staunch British advocate of Jewish restoration, who was later active in helping to resettle Jews fleeing the Russian pogroms of the 1880s. Thus British Israelites in Canada became associated with practical efforts to settle Jews in the Holy Land. Brothers promoted the notion of the Davidic lineage of certain prominent Britons. Among these was Sir Gilbert Elliot, first earl of Monto and the great-grandfather of the fourth earl, who served as a governor-general of Canada from 1898 to 1904.

By the turn of the century, the British-Israel movement had some two million adherents in Britain, Canada, and the United States, and it was contributing considerably to heightening consciousness of the Holy Land in all three countries. Evidence of its continued presence in Canada is the experience of Yitzhak Eleazari-Volcani, who arrived in 1920 as an emissary of the Jewish labor movement in the Holy Land. "At the border," Eleazari-Volcani reported,

> an old official checked our papers. . . . "Oh!" [he exclaimed.] "This is the first time a Jerusalemite has ever crossed the border here, a real Jerusalemite!" The official explained that he was himself of Israelite stock and belonged to the lost ten tribes. He wanted to take me to his house and give me some literature about his sect.[26]

More mainstream cultural currents related to the Holy Land also made their way across the water from the mother country during the nineteenth century.

The best-selling novels of Disraeli were widely read in Canada; and many Canadians, like people elsewhere, came to believe that he would be the instrument of a Jewish restoration to the Holy Land. One such was the Reverend J. W. Beaumont of the Anglican Diocese of Huron, Ontario, whose 1876 pamphlet, *Judaea for the Jews*, proposed a "joint protectorate [over the Holy Land] of the great Christian powers" of Europe under the leadership of Britain.[27]

Accounts of the Holy Land travels of Britons, like those of Americans, were read avidly in Canada. At least one, *Eöthen, or Traces of Travel*, by Alexander William Kinglake, was printed in a separate Canadian edition in 1871. The most influential work of English literature to deal with the restoration of the Jews was George Eliot's *Daniel Deronda* (1876). The novel was published throughout the English-speaking world and appeared in separate editions in Toronto and Montreal in 1876. The *New Dominion Monthly* printed long extracts from the book, calling it "the great novel of the year."[28] Eliot quickly found a Canadian imitator—Montreal novelist Mary Ellen Ross. Ross's novel, *The Legend of the Holy Stone*, praises Jews in general as "by far the most remarkable of all the earth's tribes," and the inhabitants of Jerusalem in particular as people who readily extend "brotherly welcome" and support to fellow Jews, despite their straitened circumstances.[29] Even scholars, such as Professor John Clark Murray of the University of Toronto, translator of the *Autobiography of Solomon Maimon*, claimed to have been influenced by Eliot's book.

Canadians' scientific interest in the Holy Land was often connected to the activities of individuals and societies in the mother country. J. William Dawson published his *Modern Science in Bible Lands* (Montreal, 1888) in Canada, and other works, as noted earlier, in the United States. *Egypt and Syria* (London, 1885), however, was published in England. The Palestine Exploration Fund (PEF), founded in 1865 with the scientific validation of the Bible as one of its original goals, attracted prominent scholars, churchmen, and even the Queen herself to its ranks. Within a few years of its establishment, the PEF was regularly receiving donations from subscribers in Toronto and Woodstock, Ontario, and from others in Nova Scotia, New Brunswick, and Prince Edward Island. In 1873 its book-length report of accomplishments to date, *Our Work in Palestine*, was published in a Canadian edition by Adam, Stevenson & Co. of Toronto.

What is particularly striking about the PEF activities in Canada is the caliber of the people involved. Subscribers included Hon. William Henry Draper and Hon. John Hawkins Hagarty, both of whom served as chief justice of Ontario. (Draper was born in England and Hagarty in Dublin, two more instances of Canadians of British origin active in Holy Land affairs.) Another subscriber was Rev. Egerton Ryerson, a Methodist clergyman, the first president of the University of Victoria College (now part of the University of Toronto), and longtime chief superintendent of education for the province of Ontario. The PEF Canadian bursar in the 1870s was Hon. G. W. Allan, who served as mayor of Toronto for a short term, as chancellor of the University of Trinity College (now also a part of the University of Toronto), as a member of the Senate of Canada, and as founding member and sometime president of the Royal Canadian Institute. Allan had celebrated his admission to the bar in 1846 by embarking on a Grand Tour of Europe and the Middle East. Sightseeing led to scientific investigation and a fellowship in the Royal Geographical Society of England. In the PEF he was able to combine his religious concerns and scientific interests. Allan was president of the Upper Canada Bible Society for over twenty years.[30]

For Canadian Jews, no less than for Christians, the British connection was of considerable importance in their Holy Land affairs. Canadian Zionists "always felt a special kinship for the British Zionist Federation."[31] Especially in the early days of the movement they worked closely with the British Federation, as the previously described incident with American Hadassah illustrates. The closeness to Britain stemmed partly from the natural imperial connection, partly from appreciation for the widespread support for Jewish restoration expressed in Britain throughout the nineteenth and early twentieth centuries.

After the British conquest of Palestine, Canada–Holy Land relations assumed a somewhat different aspect. A number of Canadians participated in the British military campaign in Palestine. William Sebag-Montefiore was a British Jew who had resigned his army commission in 1912 and emigrated to Canada. At the outbreak of the war he rejoined his regiment and later fought in Europe and in Palestine; after the war he returned to Montreal. Several hundred Canadians fought in the British units known as the Jewish Legion, among them Bernard Joseph of Montreal. As Dov Yosef he went on to a distinguished career in the Jewish civil service during the Mandate period and subsequently in the Israeli government.[32] Over the years other Canadians settled in the Holy Land, creating a small but noticeable Canadian presence. (Since 1948, a considerable number of Israelis have settled in Canada, creating a Holy Land presence there!)

By the inclusion of the Balfour Declaration, the League of Nations Mandate made Zionism British policy and, to some degree, the policy of the various constituents of the British Empire, including Canada. Before World War I, Canadian government officials had endorsed Zionism on a number of occasions; Sir Robert Borden's wartime government was regarded as firm in support of the movement.[33] Ironically, during the Mandate period, the Canadian government backed away from the increasingly thorny Zionist issue even more rapidly than the British government. In 1934, Prime Minister R. B. Bennett lent some support by opening the United Palestine Appeal with a nationwide radio address. However, his successor, William Lyon Mackenzie King, said and did little to give comfort to the Zionists, despite his association with Ottawa department store magnate Archibald Freiman, who headed the Canadian Zionist movement from 1921 to his death in 1944. One way in which King's government avoided support for the Zionists, without openly declaring its opposition to their aims, was to assert the then still plausible claim that it was properly leaving Holy Land affairs to the British.[34]

If the Balfour Declaration and the British Mandate did little to awaken sympathy for Zionism in Canadian government circles, they were of major significance in enabling Canadian Zionists to present their movement to the public as a patriotic enterprise in harmony with national (or imperial) interests. Unlike American Zionists, Canadians had no need to wrestle with the question of dual loyalty.[35] In his presidential message to the Federation of Zionist Societies in Canada in 1917, Clarence De Sola—the son of a British-born father and himself an ardent, lifelong Anglophile—gloried in "the fact of the entry of the British into the precincts of the Holy Land." He expressed confidence that "Britain would uphold the Jewish right to Palestine."[36] Throughout the interwar period, perhaps as an antidote to government apathy, Canadian Zionists emphasized Britain's ties to Zionism. In 1935 Canadian Zionists planted a forest in the Holy Land in honor of the twenty-fifth anniversary of the accession of King George V to the throne. On that occasion the *Canadian Zionist*, the official publication of the movement, reminded readers that "Canadian Jewry has always been distinguished for its loyalty to the throne and the constitution, and in paying tribute to His Majesty they will take special pleasure in linking perpetually the name of their beloved sovereign with the land of Palestine."[37]

The British/Canadian/Jewish connection to the Holy Land was recognized by Gentiles no less than by Jews. In 1917 both the Toronto *Globe* and the *World* rejoiced in the British capture of Jerusalem, an event that the papers took to be "favorable to Zionism."[38] In the 1934 radio address mentioned earlier, Prime Minister Bennett asserted that with the Balfour Declaration and the conquest of Palestine by Britain, "Scriptural prophecy was being fulfilled." Moreover, he said, "recent political and social upheavals in Europe [made] . . . Palestine . . . the only haven of refuge" for Jews.[39] A special twist to the three-way link was the notion that Canada—both as a binational country and as a British dominion— might serve as a model for a future independent state in Palestine. Henry Wentworth Monk and Senator Arthur Roebuck both advocated Palestine becoming a British dominion like Canada;[40] and many Jews found the idea attractive as well. During a speaking tour of Canada in 1935, maximalist Zionist Vladimir Jabotinsky claimed that "dominion status similar to that enjoyed by Canada would eventually be very satisfactory in Palestine." At that date he still expected England to take a "leading role in giving the Jewish people a homeland." *The Canadian Zionist* also endorsed the domination notion. Even after Israel had become independent in a struggle against both the British and the Arabs, Molly Lyons Bar-David felt "sorry that Israel had not emerged as a seventh dominion."[41]

BINATIONALISM

An additional aspect of the Canadian historical experience bears mention here; that is, the binational character of the country. Since the British conquest of Canada in 1759, considerable tension has existed between French Canadians and English Canadians; it is manifested in culture, politics, religion, language, and most other areas of national life. Often in Canada, as Lewis Carroll put it, "The farther off from England, the nearer is to France." The rule obtains with regard to Holy Land affairs no less than with other issues. For the most part, enthusiasm regarding the Holy Land, and especially regarding the Jewish connection with it, has been mainly a feature of English Canadian society. Some French Canadians have written about the Holy Land, made pilgrimages there, and even established a Canadian commissariat for the Holy Land. Most, however, have been apathetic about Holy Land happenings and antagonistic toward Jewish restoration and Zionism. A comparison of French and English Canadian pilgrim literature is instructive.

Beginning with G. L. Abbé's *La Terre Sainte ou Lieux Celébrès dans l'Histoire Sainte* (Montreal, 1841), French Canadian pilgrim books have appeared with regularity over the years. These include Abbé Léon Gingras' *L'Orient, ou Voyage en Egypte, en Arabie, en Terre Sainte, en Turkie, et Grèce* (Quebec, 1847); Abbé Léon Provancher's *De Québec à Jérusalem* (Quebec, 1884); Abbé J. F. C. De la Planche's *Le Pèlerin de Terre Sainte* (Quebec, 1887); Abbé Jean François Dupuis' *Rome et Jérusalem* (Quebec, 1895); Abbé Henri Cimon's *Aux Vieux Pays* (Montreal, 1895, 1917); Abbé Frédéric de Ghyvelde's *Album de Terre Sainte* (Quebec, 1905); Frère Joseph A. l'Archévêque's *Vers la Terre Sainte* (Montreal, 1911), as well as *Premier Pèlerinage Officiel des Canadiens en Terre Sainte sous la Direction Spirituelle du Très Révérend Père Mathieu-Marie de l'Ordre des Frères Mineurs* (Montreal, 1922). In its approach to Jews and the Holy Land, l'Archévêque's writing is representative. He describes Holy Land Jews as having "crooked noses . . . stooped backs . . . ghastly faces." They were, he asserted, "people of appalling debilitation" exhibiting "degeneracy peculiar to their race." According to l'Archévêque, "any true Jew" has but one "life" and "happiness," that is, "to dominate."[42]

The works of English Canadian pilgrims almost invariably strike a different note. These include J. Bell Forsyth's *A Few Months in the East; or, A Glimpse of the Red, the Dead, and the Black Seas* (Quebec, 1861); Thomas Stirson Jarvis' *Letters from East Longitudes* (Toronto, 1875); Marian Keith's[43] *Under the Grey Olives* (Toronto, 1927), which grew out of a trip to the Holy Land with a group of American tourists; and *The Bethlehem Road* (Toronto, 1933) by Rev. Herbert Henry Bingham, minister of Toronto's fashionable Walmer Road Baptist Church. Forsyth's early work set the tone for his successors. He admired the Jews of the Holy Land, who "continue . . . to live in hope," and found the synagogue services he attended "very interesting." He described the Jewish Quarter of Jerusalem as "the most filthy and uninteresting part of the city," but even that perception is stated in a matter-of-fact tone without animus.[44]

Antonio Hout and Mary Esther MacGregor visited the Holy Land at almost the same time, the former in 1928 and the latter a year earlier. Hout was a French Canadian and a Roman Catholic priest. MacGregor, an English Canadian, was the daughter of a Protestant minister and the wife of another. Their contrasting reactions to what they saw, and especially to Jews, are characteristic of the two peoples they represented. MacGregor commented on "the passionate love the Jew has for his country," on the town of Jaffa "where Solomon's myriad workmen floated the mighty timbers for the temple on Mount Moriah," on the "beginnings of the great Jewish university," and, noting the connection with Britain, "the prosperous new Jewish colony of Balfouria, named after Lord Balfour."[45] Hout, who had some years earlier tried to substantiate the charge that Jews practiced ritual murder, claimed that the Zionist settlers in the Holy Land were all communists, a "fact" for which he adduced clear evidence—the red tile roofs of the Jewish houses of Jerusalem.[46] In more recent times, too, sympathy for Zionism and for Israel has been much greater in English Canada than in Quebec.[47]

Partly, then, as a result of the tensions between French Canadians and English Canadians, the two groups have had very different attitudes toward the Holy Land, especially with regard to its Jewish component. But it must be said that English Canada, too, has often exhibited hostility toward Jews and apathy toward the Holy Land. Such attitudes, in turn, have affected the relationship of Canadian Jews to the Holy Land. In general, the Jews' relationship to Zionism and to the Holy Land is a function of the degree to which they feel at home in the countries where they live.[48] Until 1948, Zionism was relatively weak and anti-Zionism was strong in the United States. In Canada anti-Zionism has been virtually unknown and Zionism more successful than in most other countries. Notwithstanding the present very firm attachment of American Jews to Israel, they still seem to consider their own country to be the promised land. In contrast, Canadian Jews, historically scattered over a vast land and relatively few in number, rejected by French Canadians and not altogether accepted by English Canadians, have not—until very recently—felt correspondingly at home in their country. In fact, Zionism more than anything else made them into a community and represented them to the outside world. Although this has changed somewhat in the last few decades, the Holy Land has remained the promised land of Canadian Jews.

It can be seen, then, that with regard to the Holy Land, North America has not been all of a piece. There are many similarities between Canada and the United States, institutional and individual interconnections, and corresponding developments in the two countries. Perhaps more significant, however, are the ways in which Canadians' relations with the Holy Land over the years have differed from those of Americans, reflecting different social and historical developments in the two countries.

NOTES

1. David Rubin, "Letters from Canada," *Halbri*, 23 March 1917, pp. 9-10; 30 March 1917, p. 10 (Hebrew).

2. Cf. Moshe Davis, "The Holy Land in American Spiritual History," in *With Eyes Toward Zion*, ed. Moshe Davis (New York: Arno Press, 1977), 3-33; also "Biblical Place-Names," 246-52.

3. See Robert T. Handy, "Sources for Understanding American Christian Attitudes

toward the Holy Land, 1800-1950,'' in M. Davis (above, n.2), pp. 34-56.

4. *The Fourth Book of Lessons for the Use of Schools* (Montreal, 1845), 211.

5. See David A. Rausch, *Zionism within Early American Fundamentalism, 1878–1918* (New York and Toronto: Edwin Mellen Press, 1979), 83-146.

6. Ibid., 106, 153; Montreal *Daily Witness*, 12 February 1898.

7. Albert E. Thompson, "The Capture of Jerusalem," in *Light on Prophecy: A Coordinated, Constructive Teaching, Being the Proceedings and Addresses at the Philadelphia Prophetic Conference, May 28-30, 1918* (New York: Christian Herald Bible House, 1918), 152-53, quoted in D. A. Rausch (above, n.5), p. 119.

8. See, for example, this author's "Divergent Paths: Early Zionism in Canada and the United States," *Jewish Social Studies* 44 (Spring 1982): 159-83; and "The Americanization of Canadian Zionism," in *Contemporary Jewry: Studies in Honor of Moshe Davis*, ed. Geoffrey Wigoder (Jerusalem: Institute of Contemporary Jewry, Hebrew University, 1984), 129-58.

9. Leon Goldman, "History of Zionism in Canada," in *The Jew in Canada*, ed. Arthur Daniel Hart (Toronto and Montreal: Jewish Publications, 1926), 305; Louis Rasminsky, ed., *Hadassah Jubilee*, (Toronto: Hadassah, 1928), 150; *The 100th Anniversary Souvenir of Jewish Emancipation in Canada and the Fiftieth Anniversary of the Jew in the West, 1832-1932* (Winnipeg: Israelite Press, 1932), 40; Esther Waterman, ed., *Golden Jubilee: Canadian Hadassah WIZO, 1917-1967* (Montreal: Eagle Publishing Co., 1967), 27.

10. Transcription of handwritten note by Henrietta Szold, 192[?], Henrietta Szold Archive, Central Zionist Archives, Jerusalem (hereafter: CZA), File A125/20. In "The Americanization of Canadian Zionism" (above, n.8), this author mistakenly wrote of the warm relations between American Hadassah and Canadian Hadassah–WIZO. At the time, the note cited herein, as well as other comments of Henrietta Szold in private letters, had not come to light. Sources for the earlier mistaken judgment are those cited above in note 9, which ignore the disagreement for obvious reasons.

11. See Hertzel Fishman, *American Protestantism and a Jewish State* (Detroit: Wayne State University Press, 1973), 64-70.

12. Arthur W. Roebuck, *The Roebuck Story* (Don Mills, Ontario: T. H. Best Printing Co., 1963), 129-30, 142, 150; *The Canadian Who's Who*, vol. 11 (Toronto: University of Toronto Press, 1969), 946.

13. A. W. Roebuck (above, n.12), 159, 162-63.

14. "Twenty-Fourth Canadian Zionist Convention Official Report of Proceedings at Toronto," *Canadian Zionist* 1, no. 10 (February 1935): 5-10; "Sir Ellsworth Flavelle Opens Palestine Exhibit," *Canadian Zionist* 14, no. 5 (June 1947): 5; Irving Abella and Harold Troper, *None Is Too Many: Canada and the Jews of Europe, 1933-1948* (Toronto: Lester & Orpen Dennys, 1983), 183; Zachariah Kay, *Canada and Palestine* (Jerusalem: Israel Universities Press, 1978), 84-87, 100, 117-21, 147. See also Roebuck's series of articles on Israel in the Toronto *Star*, between October and December 1955.

15. For a discussion of Holy Land symbols applied to the United States, see Perry Miller, *The New England Mind*, vol. 2, *From Colony to Province* (Cambridge, Mass.: Harvard University Press, 1955). See also M. Davis, "Spiritual History" (above, n.2).

16. Adolphus Mordecai Hart [Hampden], *The Impending Crisis* (New York: n.p., 1855), 4.

17. Carl Berger, *The Sense of Power* (Toronto and Buffalo: University of Toronto Press, 1970), 171-72.

18. "The Year 5667," *Jewish Chronicle* (London), 6 September 1907, p. 11.

19. Richard S. Lambert, *For the Time Is at Hand* (London: Andrew Melrose, [1947]), 95.

20. Molly Lyons Bar-David, *My Promised Land* (New York: G. P. Putnam, 1953), 139. See also Michael Brown, "A Paradoxical Relationship: American Jews and Zionism," in *An American Historian: Essays to Honor Selig Adler*, ed. Milton Plesur (Buffalo: State University of New York at Buffalo, 1980), 89-92.

21. See Z. Kay (above, n.14), pp. 43-45.

22. *The Canadian Who's Who*, vol. 4 (Toronto: University of Toronto Press, [1948]), 82; *Canadian Zionist* 2, no. 1 (March 1935): 12.

23. *Who's Who in Canada, 1934-35* (Toronto: International Press, 1935), 272; A. W. Roebuck (above, n.12), pp. 162-63.

24. John Buchan, *Memory, Hold the Door* (Toronto: Musson Book Co., 1940), 226.

25. "Zionist News, Lord Tweedsmuir Expresses Unabated Interest in Zionism," *Canadian Zionist* 3, no. 7 (December 1936): 58; "Lord Tweedsmuir Receives Mr. Jaffe," *Canadian Zionist* 6, no. 1 (April 1938): 174; "Canadian Zionists Mourn Viceroy's Passing," *Canadian Zionist* 7, no. 5 (February 1940): 1; Bernard Joseph, Montreal, letter to Dr. Chaim Weizmann, London, 26 January 1938, in CZA (see above, n.10). See also Z. Kay (above, n.14), pp. 64-65.

26. Yitzhak Eleazari-Volcani [A. Zioni], "From Travelling Abroad," *HaPo'el Ha-Za'ir*, 8 October 1920 (Hebrew). See also Cecil Roth, *The Nephew of the Almighty: An Experimental Account of the Life and Aftermath of Richard Brothers, R.N.* (London: E. Goldston, 1933); R. S. Lambert (above, n.19); Henry Wentworth Monk, *A Simple Interpretation of the Revelation Together with Three Lectures Lately Delivered in Canada and the United States* (London: Tallant and Co., [1852]); Albert M. Hyamson, s.v. "Anglo-Israelitism," in *Encyclopedia of Religion and Ethics* (Edinburgh: Clark, 1908); William H. Poole, *Anglo-Israel; or, The Saxon Race Proved to be the Lost Tribes of Israel, In Nine Lectures* (Toronto: William Briggs, 1889).

27. See Charles Freshman, *The Jews and the Israelites* (Toronto: A Dredge, 1870), 453-54; Manitoba *Free Press*, as quoted in Samuel Joseph, *History of the Baron de Hirsch Fund* (Philadelphia: printed for Baron de Hirsch Fund by Jewish Publication Society, 1935), 362; Rev. J. W. Beaumont, *Judaea for the Jews* (London, Ontario, and Toronto: Bart Rawlinson and B.A. Taylor, 1876).

28. "Literary Notices," *New Dominion Monthly* (June 1876): extracts (June, December, 1876).

29. Mary Ellen Ross, *The Legend of the Holy Stone* (Montreal, 1878), 461.

30. *Palestine Exploration Fund Quarterly Statement*, 1871-78; [Walter Besant], *Our Work in Palestine* (Toronto: Stevenson, 1873). On Draper, Hagarty, Ryerson, and Allan, see George Maclean Rose, ed., *A Cyclopaedia of Canadian Biography*, (Toronto: Rose Publishing Co., 1886), 166, 173-74, 575-78, 90-91. On the Palestine Exploration Fund, see Neil Asher Silberman, *Digging for God and Country* (New York: Alfred A. Knopf, 1982).

31. "An Inspiration to Zionists," editorial, *Canadian Zionist*, 13 December 1940 (at various intervals published weekly). See also Michael Brown, *Jew or Juif: Jews, French Canadians, and Anglo-Canadians, 1759-1914* (Philadelphia: Jewish Publication Society, 1987), 55, 176-77.

32. On Sebag-Montefiore's service in the Holy Land, see Col. J. H. Patterson, Plymouth, personal letter to Vladimir Jabotinsky, London, 23 October 1917, in Jabotinsky

Archive, Jabotinsky Institute, Tel Aviv, File 1917; and Mordecai Ben Hillel HaCohen, *Milhemet Ha'Amim* 5 (Jerusalem 1920, Hebrew), 34. On Bernard Joseph, see Goldie Yosef, *Ir VeEm* (Jerusalem: Reuven Maas, 1979, Hebrew); and *Canadian Zionist* 5, no. 9 (February 1938): 136. On Canadians in the Jewish Legion, see Vladimir Jabotinsky, *The Story of the Jewish Legion*, trans. Samuel Katz (New York: B. Ackerman, 1945); Leon Cheifetz, "Canada's Contribution to the Jewish Legion," *Bulletin* of the Veterans of the Jewish Legion, May 1976; and Z. Kay (above, n.14), pp. 46-53.

33. In 1907, two government ministers had assured the Canadian Zionists, meeting in convention in Ottawa, that "Zionism had the support of the [Dominion] Government." See *Report of the Proceedings of the Convention of the Federation of Zionist Societies in Canada* (Montreal, 1907). See also Z. Kay (above, n.14), pp. 40-41.

34. See David J. Bercuson, *Canada and the Birth of Israel: A Study in Canadian Foreign Policy* (Toronto: University of Toronto Press, 1985), 14-53; Z. Kay (above, n.14), pp. 7-114.

35. Cf. Ben Dunkelman, *Dual Allegiance: An Autobiography* (Scarborough, Ontario: New American Library, 1978), 13.

36. Quoted in L. Goldman (above, n.9), p. 302.

37. "The Jubilee Forest," November 1935.

38. David Eisen, *Diary of a Medical Student* ([Toronto]: Canadian Jewish Congress, 1974), 13-14.

39. Quoted in "United Palestine Appeal Broadcast Stirs Canadian Jewry," *Canadian Zionist* 1, no. 3 (May 1934): 1-2.

40. H. W. Monk (above, n.26); *Canadian Zionist* (June 1947).

41. "Status of Dominion Idea for Palestine," Toronto *Daily Star*, 13 February 1935; "Jewish State for Palestine Urged," Montreal *Gazette*, 11 February 1935; "Palestine—A Jewish Dominion," *Canadian Zionist* 9, no. 2 (10 October 1941): 4; M. L. Bar-David (above, n.20), p. 279.

42. Frère Joseph A. l'Archévêque, *Vers la Terre Sainte* (Montreal, 1911), 175-76.

43. Marian Keith was the pen name of Mary Esther Miller MacGregor (1867–1961), wife of the Rev. Donald Campbell MacGregor, a Presbyterian minister. She authored a number of works of light fiction as well as evangelical romances very popular in their day. See below, note 45.

44. J. Bell Forsyth [a Canadian], *A Few Months in the East; or, A Glimpse of the Red, the Dead, and the Black Seas* (Quebec: John Lovell, 1861), 77-81.

45. Mary Esther Miller MacGregor [Marian Keith], *Under the Grey Olives* (Toronto: McClelland and Stewart, 1927), 81-83, 145.

46. The account of Hout's trip, originally published in *La Semaine Religieuse de Québec*, is quoted in David Rome, *Clouds in the Thirties: On Antisemitism in Canada, 1929-1939* (Montreal: Canadian Jewish Archives, 1977), 20-22.

47. See Werner Cohn, "English and French Canadian Public Opinion on Jews and Israel: Some Poll Data," *Canadian Ethnic Studies* 11 (1979): 31-48; Irving Abella and Paul Sniderman, "Stubborn Stereotypes," Toronto *Globe and Mail*, 9 April 1988.

48. On Canadian Zionism, see the sources in note 8 above; also Harold M. Waller, "Canada," in *Zionism in Transition*, ed. Moshe Davis (New York: Arno Press, 1980), 111-20. On Jews in Canada, see I. Abella and H. Troper (above, n.14); M. Brown (above n.31); Morton Weinfeld, William Shaffir, and Irwin Cotler, eds., *The Canadian Jewish Mosaic*, (Toronto: John Wiley and Sons, 1981).

Comment

Abraham J. Karp

On May 28, 1773, it being the first day of Shavuot, the Jews of Newport, Rhode Island gathered in their synagogue to celebrate the Festival. Joining them at worship were the leading citizens of that city and colony. The Reverend Ezra Stiles, then minister of the Second Congregational Church—later president of Yale University—records in his diary some of the distinguished men present, among them Governor Wantan and Judges Oliver and Achmuty of the Colony's highest court.

What caused the Jews to invite their Christian neighbors, and what caused their neighbors to accept the invitation was the presence at the synagogue of Rabbi Haim Isaac Carigal of "the city of Hebron, near Jerusalem, in the Holy Land." The rabbi, an emissary from the Jews of the Holy Land to their co-religionists in the New World, delivered a sermon on "The Salvation of Israel," spoke for forty-seven minutes in "Spanish" (Ladino?), but, as Stiles reports, kept the audience—perhaps six of whom understood the language he spoke in—in rapt attention as they listened to the exotically garbed preacher. What had brought Jews and Christians together that day was a shared reverence for the Holy Land; what kept their attention was the vicarious experience of being in physical proximity to that sacred soil, through the presence of a native and religious representative of that hallowed Land. The sermon was translated into English and—against the expressed wishes of the preacher—published as a memento of the occasion when a community, divided by creed, was united by a common veneration—a veneration of the Holy Land.

Sixty years later, another emissary from the Holy Land, Rabbi Enoch Zundel of Jerusalem, came to New York, seeking aid for the Jews in the ancient homeland from their brethren in the New World. He carried with him a letter from the rabbis of Jerusalem addressed to Mordecai M. Noah. The letter, it is interesting to note, was translated from Hebrew into English by the Christian Hebraist, W. L. Roy, and it was published in the *New York Christian Intelligencer*, together with an account of a meeting of Rabbi Zundel with the leading clergymen of New York. The emissary told his eager audience of "Jerusalem, the holy city, and the condition of the Jews there." The article quotes Zundel's plea to the ministers assembled and through them to America: "You did much for the Greeks; and will you not admit, even as Christians, lovers of the Old Testament patriarchs and prophets, that you owe at least as much, nay, much more, to *us Jews*?"

This appeal did not fall on deaf ears. Four ministers volunteered to form a committee to receive any funds "which benevolent Christians may condescend to give." A memento of Zundel's visit remains, a published portrait of him, wrapped in *tallit*, wearing a turban-like head covering, holding an open book. The portrait was offered for sale on his departure.

For American Jews and Christians in the nineteenth century, the Holy Land was both memory and destiny; for Jews, the ancient and future homeland; for Christians, the land of patriarchs and prophets, and of the birth, ministry, and passion of the Savior, and the site of his Second Advent. We need add that America was a Protestant Bible-reading nation (no Rome to compete with Jerusalem) whose Puritan tradition gave great prominence to the Old Testament, which made for a very special affinity for the Holy Land. It was upon this base that Professor Moshe Davis and his co-workers, Professors Robert T. Handy and Selig Adler, began to build their America–Holy Land Project.

The five chapters in this section afford us a fine review of the state of America–Holy Land scholarship, past, present, and future. Each is quite different, yet they form an integrated whole.

Robert Handy's is a straightforward account of the beginnings and development of the project in size and scope. From a small gathering of interested scholars and students at New York's Union Theological Seminary who conceptualized the subject in 1970, it expanded to the 1975 colloquia at the National Archives in Washington, D.C., where the rich holdings in archival depositories were identified and described, and the 1983 gathering that added descriptions and sampling of materials in British and Turkish holdings. This was followed by the 1987 Scholars Conference in Jerusalem, which internationalized the scope of the endeavor through reports on work being done in Iberoamerica, France, Germany, and England. It is of interest to note that the traditional geographic expansion of culture westward from Europe to America is here reversed. Scholarly work initiated in America has spawned interest and creativity on the European continent.

David Klatzker's study calls attention to pilgrimages, the American Christian expression of interest in and veneration for the Holy Land. He touches upon a variety of motivations for the pilgrimages ranging from the purely religious to those bordering on the recreational. But in all, the lure of the Holy Land was dominant. His account is effective in that it arouses our desire to get to the original, to the published volumes, many of which were reprinted as one of the first ventures of the America–Holy Land project. Klatzker's is a fine, scholarly account; however, he does not include major works by Holy Land travelers who did more than a few weeks' touring. These include, for example, missionary-physician J. T. Barclay's *The City of the Great King* (Philadelphia, 1857); *Palestine, Past, Present and Future* (Philadelphia, 1859), by the Reverend Henry S. Osborn, who describes himself as "Prof. Natural Science in Roanoke College, Salem, Va., Member of the American Scientific Association, and Hon. Member of Malta (Mediterranean) Scientific Institute"; and *Incidents of Travel in Egypt, Arabia Petraea, and the Holy Land* (New York, 1837), by an American, John L. Stephens, which in the two years following its initial publication went through ten editions.

Gershon Greenberg's Hegelian construct of the subject at hand is historically intriguing and pedagogically effective. His conceptual organization of the material gives it an intellectual structure that imposes a unity on a diversity of source material and challenges the creative imagination of the serious student. Its focus is essentially the Jewish perspective, but the Christian approach is adequately presented—as it is in his volume *Holy Land and Religious America*, which promises to be the needed textbook on the subject. Greenberg's argument that America–Holy Land Studies be located within Religious Studies is well taken, as his charted "dialectical journey through American religious history" demonstrates.

Here and there, one does want to raise the question of evaluation. For instance, are Felsenthal, Levias, and Fineshreiber really the best exemplars of those "who begin to alter Reform's monolithic non-Zionist stance"? Felsenthal, certainly; but Levias, although a member of the faculty of Hebrew Union College and associated with Reform for a decade, was never really a part of that movement; and Fineshreiber will go down in Zionist history as one of the founding and leading members of the anti-Zionist American Council for Judaism. Would not Gustav Gottheil, rabbi of New York's Temple Emanuel who was a vice-president of the Federation of American Zionists, and Max Heller, Reform rabbi in New Orleans who was an honorary president of the Zionist Organization of America, serve as better examples?

Michael Brown's fine chapter is useful for its overview of Holy Land literature and important for the distinction he draws between the place of the Holy Land concept in American and Canadian national ideology. The reasons he gives for the differences are on target: America's self-image as the new Zion, a claim Canada never made; the geopolitical fact that the United States early viewed itself as a major power, hence was rightfully involved in the affairs of other parts of the world, the Near East among them—a status Canada never attained in reality or even in aspiration; and the Canadian desire as a new nation to seek roots in Britain, while young America sought them in the Holy Land. Brown offers the kind of insight that should be employed in the expanded concept of Holy Land Studies launched at the Jerusalem Conference.

In her excellent review chapter, Deborah Dash Moore reminds us of the truism that the future always builds on the past. We must add that special skills are needed to retrieve the past and that among these is a specialized knowledge of language. For our purposes, for example, the Hebrew required is the Hebrew of the nineteenth century, that of the Haskalah and of written rabbinic discourse. The Yiddish of the Old Yishuv will also be required, with mastery of a whole glossary of words and phrases peculiar to the place, time, and way of life of that rather cosmopolitan community.

Moore's suggestion that our attention should be drawn to architecture is most pertinent. May I commend two American architects from Zanesville, Ohio? Jacob Schumacher and his family moved from Zanesville, Ohio in the 1860s to join the German Templer colony in Haifa. He was its architect; a manuscript map of that German American colony is in the Library of Congress. His son Gottlieb, born in Zanesville, worked out of Haifa as an architect and builder until 1918, constructing roads, bridges, and even some Jewish settlements. He was also the author of a number of books on the Holy Land.

Moore's pointing to the frontier theme echoes Brandeis' view of the similarity of the American frontier experience and Jewish colonization, of the *halutzim* and the pioneers who built America as brothers in national and spiritual adventure. Her thoughtful and promising suggestions may well be used to determine the agenda for the next stages of America–Holy Land Studies.

One is heartened by the thoughtful work of Klatzker, Greenberg, and Brown, and by the challenging project of Moore. It bodes well for the future of America–Holy Land Studies.

PART II
IBEROAMERICA

Chapter 7

The Concept of the Holy Land in Iberoamerica

Leonardo Senkman

The pervasive influence of the Holy Land idea can be traced throughout the cultural history of Iberoamerica. During the colonial period, Iberoamerica was *Judenrein* from a legal point of view, and the Catholic Church was integral to the new societies. The concept of the Holy Land was, nonetheless, present in various transformations. In the fluid atmosphere of Latin Catholicism, where the line between the Church and the independent states was blurred and overlapping jurisdiction persisted, the Jews continued to be viewed as a foreign element that could not be assimilated; but paradoxically, the concept of the Holy Land was an inherent part of the civilization in the new Latin American republics. Notwithstanding the fact that the social norms of cultural pluralism were never completely accepted, the secular nation-states in Latin America during the second half of the nineteenth and the early twentieth centuries curiously accommodated veneration for the biblical tradition linked to the Holy Land idea along with their parochial *crisol de razas* (racial melting pot) outlook and acceptance of mixed India-European populations.

Therefore, tracing the Holy Land concept in Iberoamerica must be part of a broader study of its civilization. The encounter between the concept and the Spanish and Portuguese Catholic civilization in Latin America extends over a long period of time and touches upon many variables. It is suggested that the study include: (1) The earliest formulations in colonial times, during the conquest and the evangelization of Iberoamerica, through an eschatological and utopian dimension; (2) Biblical motifs and their linkage to the Holy Land (Old and New Testament) in modern Latin American culture; (3) Jewish Restoration and support for the Zionist endeavor; (4) Latin American Jewish attachment to the Holy

Land/Eretz Israel, in terms of literary creation and personal settlement. It should be noted that such a comprehensive study has yet to be undertaken.

THE HOLY LAND IDEA IN THE ESCHATOLOGICAL THOUGHT OF COLONIAL LATIN AMERICA

From the very discovery of the New World, the concept of the Holy Land was part of the encounter with its civilization. Johen Phelan has demonstrated the messianism of Christopher Columbus, as expressed through several frequently reiterated notions.[1]

During the third voyage, Columbus formulated a theory according to which the Earthly Paradise was situated in South America. The four rivers named in Genesis—of which he managed to see only the mouth of the Orinoco—formed a Land of Grace, in the center of which was a protuberance like the small end of a pear. Indeed, the notion of America as the Earthly Paradise is, according to Mario Góngora's study, the origin of the earliest utopian theories.[2]

Of more frequent occurrence in the writings of Columbus is the crusading impulse of the restoration and rebuilding of the Holy House in Jerusalem. On December 26, 1492 he noted that with the profits of his voyage, Jerusalem could be reconquered in three years. In 1498 he bequeathed money in a will, to be deposited in the Bank of St. George in Genoa, to be used for the liberation of Jerusalem. In his letter of 1501 or 1502 to Ferdinand and Isabella, he made an impassioned defense of the visionary outlook based mainly on the Prophets and other biblical sources, as compared with study and discourse—which, he said, profited him nothing.

The idea that the end-of-days is imminent finds particularly emphatic expression in the writings of Columbus. He displays zeal to restore Jerusalem as the center of Christendom. Jerusalem would be the venue for the eschatological events described in the Apocalypse, for the prophecies of the bliss and glory of the Holy City to which the Old Testament so often refers, as well as for the struggles against the antichrist and the final triumph of God that the New Testament foretells. Columbus believed that the kings of Spain had been summoned by God to reconquer Jerusalem, basing his idea on the "Book of the Prophecies"—especially on a saying of Joaquim di Fiore, which he repeated to the Catholic sovereigns in 1492, and which he quoted in the letter of 1501 or 1502 concerning Spain and Jerusalem.[3]

One problem raised by the discovery of America was that of the origin of the American Indian population. The intellectual curiosity aroused by exposure to American Indian cultures, and the need to reconcile them in some way with traditionally accepted historical and biblical beliefs, produced ambitious schemes seeking to explain the spreading to the Americas of the people described in the Old Testament. The canonical and apocryphal books of the Bible, in addition to Greek and native Indian accounts, were the main sources for the various theories about the origin of the Indians. Numerous scholars of the nineteenth and twentieth centuries contributed to this long-drawn-out controversy. In addition to Góngora, Lee E. Huddelston has described the development of the controversy before the beginning of the eighteenth century.[4]

The most complete inventory of these theories is found in the chronicle entitled *Orígines de los Indios del Nevo Mundo e Indias Occidentales*, published in 1607 by the Dominician Gregorio Garcia; his own attitude was completely eclectic. Garcia quoted a vast number of authorities and expounded and analyzed each of the theories about the alleged origins of the Latin American aboriginal population: Carthaginian origins; Jewish origins; colonization from the biblical land of Ophir; the Platonic myth of Atlantis; the possibilities of colonization by the Greeks, Phoenicians, Chinese, or Tartars.[5]

Of these theories, the most important in any consideration of American eschatological schemes and utopias, according to Mario Góngora, is undoubtedly that of attributing the Indians to Hebrew origin—if only because, in the early seventeenth century when Garcia was writing, this theory was the most widely held among the Spaniards in the West Indies. As soon as it was discovered that the natives of Yucatan practiced circumcision, the name of the area was connected with the biblical Joktan, and observers emphasized numerous real or supposed analogies based on character, ceremonials, customs, dress, infant sacrifice, and so forth, which were held to apply to the American Indians in general.

The origin of the population was attributed to the migration of the Ten Tribes of Israel who were carried off as captives to Assyria and never returned to their homeland. Instead, they crossed the Euphrates and reached Assareth, whence they would return at the end-of-days according to the fourth Book of Esdras. This apocryphal account enjoyed great authority among the Jews of later periods and among the Christians in northern Europe because of its connection with the eschatological belief in the return of the Children of Israel to the Holy Land. In 1567 it was accepted by Johannes Fredericus Lumnius, the commentator on the Apocalypse, and by the French cosmographer Gilbert Genebrard. This theory was also expounded by the Mexican chroniclers Juan Tover, Juan Suarez de Peralta, and Diego Durán in the 1570s.[6]

The theory of the Jewish origin of the American peoples gave rise to the apocalyptic conclusions, for it implied that the Indians were God's people and that their conversion heralded the consummation of all things. To such thinkers as Jerónimo de Mendieta, the prophecy of the return in Esdras 4, considered in association with St. Paul's prediction of the restoration of Israel within the Church, provided the most authoritative confirmation of the hopes he placed in the natives of the New Spain. On the other hand, in the view of the Dominican Diego Durán, the punishments with which God so often threatened His people in the Old Testament on account of their idolatry were now being meted out in the shape of the epidemics, which since the Conquest had befallen the descendants of that people in the New World.

The Franciscan missionaries are another source of eschatological notions regarding the New World. This subject has been investigated in great detail by modern historians such as J. L. Phelan and M. Bataillon. The latter has pointed out the traces of Joachim of Fiore's ideas among the French Franciscans who set off in 1516 to evangelize the mainland of South America. This is most apparent in Martín de Valencia, a monk from the province of Extremadura who belonged to a movement of poor evangelists founded, along the lines of so many others in that same Order, at the beginning of the sixteenth century. Martín de Valencia was the leader of the twelve missionaries who went to Mexico at the request of Cortés. He undoubtedly influenced the latter's Fourth Letter, in which the Conquistador asked Charles V to establish a monastic Church of poverty rather than one with bishops and prelates, as being more suitable for the mission territories.[7]

Against this background of eschatological theories and enthusiasm over the prospect of the final conversion of the peoples of the New World—a process that some Franciscans clearly considered to be a task appropriate to the end-of-days—one finds Holy Land motifs. Motolinia (Fray Toribio de Benavente), the best known representative of the first generation of Franciscans in Mexico, drew a historical analogy between the ten plagues of Egypt and the "grievous plagues" of the New World: death, epidemics, heavy labor in the mines, and work on the building of the great Spanish city of Mexico (*Historia de los Indios de la Nueva España* [1546], Chap. 14). Jerónimo de Mendieta had compared with Moses the character of Hernan Cortés the Conquistador, who opened the doors to the new Christendom for the missionaries.

The idea of a "New Church," as expressed in the writings of Martín de Valencia, Motolinia, and above all, Mendieta, was a concept similar to that of a monastic and spiritual church that would resemble the Primitive Church described in the Acts of the Apostles; it included many motifs connected to the Holy Land. As Phelan has emphasized, Mendieta's outlook is not like Motolinia's idyllic optimism relating to an idealization of the natural state of man. Mendieta ends his book with the appalling demographic catastrophe that befell the Indians, and he concludes in a tone of lamentation. He looks on death as a relief for the natives from their labors and as punishment for the Spaniards. In Mendieta's view, the "golden age" of the missions came to an end after the 1560s; he attributed their decadence to the covetousness of the Spaniards, which was principally manifested by the *repartimientos* (assignment of native Indians to forced labor) and their devastating consequences.

In 1576 R. P. Fray Bernardino de Sahagun, one of the foremost chroniclers of the conquest of Mexico, made some important observations concerning the successive journeying of the Church. It had spread from Palestine to Asia, Africa, Germany, and the rest of Europe, a large part of which had now been lost to the Faith, with Spain and Italy having been saved; from there it had crossed the ocean to the West Indies.[8]

The Franciscan Gonzalo Tenorio, a native of Quito, was an example of a form of chiliasm with a specifically American bias, which gave Spain a central role in eschatological speculations. In Tenorio's view, Spain is the New Israel because of its orthodoxy and devotion; but of late it, too, had shown weakness. The divine vocation of Spain, at the end-of-days, would be to announce "the Gospel of the Kingdom." The messianic mission of Spain, therefore, rested in the Indies.[9]

One of the most fascinating outcomes of the encounter between Hebrew culture during the sixteenth century and the growing interest in the recently discovered New World was the translation into Hebrew of the famous chronicle about the conquest of Mexico and the Indies written by Francisco Lopez de Gómara. In 1566, Yoseph ben Yeoshua Hacoen, descendant of exiles from Spain, a well-known translator into Hebrew of books of the Renaissance period, translated a brief version of two chronicles of Gómara, *Sefer HaIndia Hachadasha Ha-Sefaradit VehaPiru* and *Sefer Francisco Corteiz*. Both manuscripts are located in the Columbia University Library and are still unpublished. In addition to their historical interest, the texts represent a valuable source reflecting Jewish curiosity about the New World, in terms of the Renaissance and humanistic component that characterizes the intellectual outlook of Yoseph ben Yeoshua Hacoen.[10]

America did not occupy a prominent place in the eschatological theories of eighteenth-century thinkers and theologians. The exiled Chilean Jesuit Manuel Lacunza (whose Hebrew-Marrano name was Yeoshaphat ben Ezra) lived in Italy and London and widely propagated the chiliastic theme at the end of the eighteenth and the beginning of the nineteenth century, in his book *La Venida del Mesias en Gloria y Majestad* (Puebla, Mex.: Oficina de Gobierno, 1821). He may justly be regarded as one of the most significant Chilean religious thinkers and as a forerunner of Zionism, on account of the profundity and logical consistency of his scriptural exegesis and the place of the Holy Land in his eschatological fervor.[11] The Argentinian general Manuel Belgrano was deeply influenced by Lacunza and helped the book to be published in 1816 in London. He himself demonstrated his knowledge of the history of the "Old Israel" in his letter to Gral San Martín, sent from Santiago del Estero in April 1814, where he alluded to "the generals of the people of Israel."[12]

BIBLICAL MOTIFS IN EARLY LATIN AMERICAN LITERATURE

The influence of the Hebrew Scriptures continued to be pervasive during the period of Latin American independence. Two significant writers who played crucial roles in the creation of their nation-states provide good examples of this influence.

During the early period of Argentinian independence, a young poet, José Rivera Indarte (born in Córdoba in 1814), was one of the most severe critics of the tyrannical regime of Juan Manuel de Rosas. After his forced exile to Montevideo, Rivera Indarte continued his campaign, writing his poems under the suggestive title of *Melodias Hebraicas*. Influenced by European romanticism, he and other anti-Rosas writers such as Florencia Varela, Esteban Etcheverria,

José Mármol, and Juan Cruz Varela, used literature as a political weapon in their fight against dictatorship. Strongly inspired by the poetic books of the Hebrew Scriptures, his *Melodias Hebraicas* deal with several well-known biblical figures such as Belshazzar, Samson, and Absalom. He interpreted the prophetic passages of Elijah and Samson as symbols of the future of Argentina, and he reached the conclusion that the Rosas regime would collapse, just like those nations that subjugated the Old Israel. Not only did he take Lord Byron's title "Hebrew Melodies" for his book, but he imitated the latter's work "Belshazzar" in his attempt to draw a parallel between the fate of the king of Babylonia and that of Rosas. For Rivera Indarte, the heroes of the Bible were profound symbols, and the history of Israel was a source for learning the principles of justice and the need to battle tyranny and oppression.[13]

In the Empire of Brazil, the playwright Domingos José Gonçalves de Magalhães published his tragedy *Antonio José ou O Poeta e a Inquisição* in 1839. The play had been performed the previous year. It was inspired by the life and death of a Brazilian-born Jew, Antonio José da Silva, who was tried and condemned by the Inquisition to be burned at the stake in Portugal. Gonçalves de Magalhães held that his play had a "national theme." One of the founders of the Brazilian theater, Magalhães decided to focus on a Luso-Brazilian hero—a Jew in the writer's fictional tragedy, but a New Christian in the historical situation of seventeenth-century Brazil—in order to establish the independent national theater in his country at a time of transition from the regency to the government of Emperor Don Pedro II. Biblical ideas of justice, primarily the Mosaic Law and its images, pervade the tragedy in the romantic liberal tradition characteristic of the entire work of Magalhães, both dramatic and poetic. It is possible to hear biblical stirrings in the dramatic dialogue between Antonio José and Frey Gil in the fifth act of the play, where the author attempts to effect a *sui generis* reconciliation and rapprochement between the religious world of the Mosaic Law and that of the Law of Christ.[14]

CONTEMPORARY LATIN AMERICAN LITERATURE AND THE BIBLE

Motifs of the Holy Land and the renaissance of the Jewish homeland are apparent in several works by outstanding Latin American writers and poets. But in contrast to the pilgrimage literature, which constitutes a fruitful source for documenting the involvement of individuals from North America in the Holy Land, these writers were not Catholic pilgrims inspired by religious doctrine, but literati with deep cultural roots in the biblical tradition. The founders of modernism in Latin American poetry, like Ruben Darío and José Martí, did not travel to the Holy Land to report about their experiences, as did North American authors like Herman Melville and Mark Twain. The biblical episodes and images found in some poems by Latin American writers were inspired more by lyrical and esthetic insights than by Christian devotion. A relevant example is the poetry and prose of the Chilean Nobel Prize–winner Gabriela Mistral, who wrote an exciting and impassioned account of her personal relationship to the Holy Land by way of the Bible.[15]

Immediately after the creation of the State of Israel, a flow of Latin American writers began to visit that country. A long list of books, pamphlets, articles, and poems, written after their visits, expressed the fascination and deep linkage between the Iberoamerican intelligentsia and Israel. A cultural link was formed between Jerusalem and Iberoamerica. Latin American writers began to be translated into Hebrew, and Israeli poets and authors were translated into Spanish and Portuguese.[16] It is significant that three of the eleven prestigious Jerusalem Prizes awarded to date have been given to Jorge Luis Borges, Pedro Vargas Llosa, and Octavio Paz.

Jorge Luis Borges is perhaps the primary writer whose attachment to the Jewish and biblical tradition makes him a paradigm of the profound link between modern Latin American literature and the spiritual concept of the Holy Land. By his own testimony, Borges states that he may well have entered literature by way of the *ru'ah ha-kodesh* (Holy Spirit). This is not to say that he holds this concept as a religious tenet. Borges begins to elucidate what these words mean when he responds to a question about the impact of the Bible on him. "All countries have produced fine writing, but I wonder who invented the idea that all writing came from the *Holy Ghost.* . . . After all, you don't find in other literatures that kind of thing. . . . They believed in the Spirit. They believed that the writer was a kind of scribe, transcribing."[17]

What strikes Borges most in relation to Scripture is the traditional view of the writer not as creator, but as amanuensis; not as originator, but as transmitter of something that comes from outside him, from beyond. The Hebrew Bible provides the basis for Borges' belief in the theory of verbal inspiration, which deemphasized the notion of a text springing spontaneously from the author and rooted primarily in his inner self. Edna Aizenberg, who has studied the influence of the Bible on Borges' theory of writing, points to the key phrase in his explanation of the poetics applied to the Bible, "write by dictation and impersonal secretaries," as his description of the residue of the Holy Spirit idea in his work. The regnant approach to Scripture provided Borges with an antecedent for a dictated, impersonal literature. Carried to its ultimate consequences, this literature became anti-romantic, humanized, at once classic and modern. According to the theory of verbal inspiration, Borges notes that God dictates what he wants to say, word for word.[18] As Borges explains it, the Bible, which is characterized by multiplicity—many books, many writers, a plural name—was considered a unitary work, *pluribus unum*, because it ultimately had one Author: the *ru'ah ha-kodesh*. Borges discovers the oldest esthetics of the Bible—that of impersonal secretaries who take dictation—which became the newest esthetics in contemporary literature. And this is not the only area where Borges finds the modern in the ancient Bible. His innovative, contemporary writings have another biblical forerunner: the anonymous author of the Book of Job.

The Book of Job, which he knew from childhood, always was one of Borges' favorites. He numbered it among the world's literary masterpieces, alluded to it repeatedly in essays and conversations, included certain of its motifs in his works, and made it one of the topics of his lectures.[19] Borges has a special predilection for this scriptural tale because, as Edna Aizenberg explains it, the account of the God-fearing man from the Land of Uz who suffers without sinning provides the theme and the technique with which he created his literature. Indeed, one can extrapolate from the Book of Job the basic conceptual and poetic propositions that give form to Borges' fictional cosmos.[20]

According to Borges, his first visit to the living reality of Israel was the culmination of a lifelong fascination with the heritage of Judaism and the Bible. He wrote:

> Early in 1969, invited by the Israeli government, I spent ten very exciting days in Tel Aviv and Jerusalem. I brought home the conviction of having been in the oldest and the youngest of nations, of having come from a very living, vigilant land to a half-asleep nook of the world. Since my Genevan days, I had always been interested in Jewish culture, thinking of it as an integral element of our so-called Eastern civilization, and during the Israeli-Arab war of a few years back I found myself taking immediate sides. While the outcome was still uncertain, I wrote a poem on the battle. A week later, I wrote another on the victory.[21]

The Jewish state was fascinating to Borges because it embodied both a continuity with a timeless tradition and a contemporization of that tradition. But if Borges was impressed by the Jewish state as the land where Jewish history is both confirmed and changed, in the poem "Israel, 1969," inspired by his first visit and published just a few months after his return home, it is the change—Israel as discontinuity with the Judaic tradition—that concerns him. Together with the image of Israel as the oldest of nations, its language as the "Language of Paradise" of the West's venerable text, Israel seems to Borges a negation of one persistent feature of the Jewish condition: diaspora and all that it meant. Borges was accustomed to depict and describe the Jewish condition as one of nostalgia and exile, generally devoid of insolence and courage; the direct contact with Israel suggested a modified definition of *lo hebreo* (the Jew). His support of Israel reached a climax in June 1967, at the outbreak of the Six Day War. At that time, his concern for what he saw as the threat to Israel's existence found its strongest expression in a poem, "A Israel".[22] Through its verses he once more emphasized the connection between the people of Israel and the sacred Book that is the fountainhead of Western civilization, and he speculated on his own possible Jewish ancestry. When Israel turned out to be the victor in the war, Borges again expressed his feelings in poetry. This second poem, entitled simply "Israel," had as its main theme the tenacity of the Jew to live on despite persecution.

The State of Israel, then, rounded out and enlarged Borges' fascination with *lo hebreo* in several ways. First, Israel served as a living expression of the Judaic tradition; second, by confronting the author with the antithesis of the cerebral wanderer he admired, Israel modified his vision of the Jews. Finally, Israel, as the Jewish state existing under the threat of destruction, was for Borges one more moment in the cyclical battle between Jew and anti-Jew.

THE HOLY LAND IN THE WORKS OF JEWISH LATIN AMERICAN WRITERS

The preoccupation with the process of acculturation and integration, and the concern with identity, are predominant among the traits characterizing Jewish Latin American writings in Spanish and Portuguese. Countries like Argentina, Uruguay, Brazil, and Chile, long considered the melting pot of South America with their Spanish, Italian, German, and English immigrant mix, also have a less recognized but equally significant Jewish ethnic population. Whereas most other countries of Indo-America turned to their indigenous roots for inspiration, Argentina in particular tended to depict the problems of its largely European immigrant strains and traditions.

The lengthy process of acculturation was experienced and expressed by a talented group of immigrant Jewish writers in Argentina: Alberto Gerchunoff, Samuel Eichelbaum, and Cesar Tiempo. New loyalties to the country demanded assimilation as one of the civic virtues. New and invigorating myths replaced those of previous generations. Jewish traditions began to be modified: The desire to be an Argentinian, a man with a history that is inscribed in the very soil that he learned to work, forged visions that were rooted in the initial ecstasy of the newcomers.

During the first stage of the process of acculturation to Argentina, writers like Gerchunoff described the country in quasi-messianic terms. In idealizing Argentina as the Promised Land, Gerchunoff drew upon images and scenes from the Bible. In *The Jewish Gauchos*, his masterpiece, the generally brief sketches of Jewish life in the new farming communities of the Jewish Colonization Association (JCA) provide a composite picture of Jews who had found their homeland in Argentina. In their hymns of praise, the Passover *Haggadah* was joined to the Argentine national anthem.

Alongside the strong determination to become part of a national entity, other poets like Carlos M. Grünberg (*Mester de Judería*) and Lazaro Liacho (*Sionidas desde las Pampas*) were inspired by Holy Land motifs. Their new citizenship and sense of gratitude and loyalty to their new country did not signal the abandonment of previous traditions and the love for Zion. On the contrary, their poems and works provide a legitimate equilibrium between both loyalties and loves.[23]

In recent years, however, the descendants of Jewish immigrants have not proven to be as self-indulgent with regard to their integration both as Jews and as Argentinians. Confronting history with reality, tradition with immediate needs, and Latin American and Jewish interests with the more encompassing issues of nationalism, revolutionary and imperialistic struggles, the new generations have encountered a complex and entangling web of concerns that did not lend themselves to unidirectional or clearcut solutions.

Two worlds appear to strive for the attention of these new generations of Jewish writers and, eventually, for their participation: the world of Latin America and, at the same time, the world of a conscious Jew and a proud Zionist. If only subliminally, their inherent difference from the rest of the population demands an approach to history and tradition that questions the meaning of certain rites, seeks to derive a lesson from the all-too-easily forgotten events of World War II and the Holocaust, and—above all—relates to the creation and existence of the State of Israel. The two worlds that vie for the attention of these writers involve, in fact, two languages, two calendars, two traditions, two cultures. Two civilizations, with their respective codes, signal different messages to those who have to opt for one or strive to integrate some elements of each into a more global concept of self-identification and of one's role in society. Israel, as a source for Jewish identification, has entered this world of the new generation of writers born in Latin America.

It is not by chance that we find the Jewish writers who have lived or studied in Israel more deeply attached to the Jewish state as a source of inspiration. The Argentinian Mario Satz wrote poems and novels about the mystery and enchantment of Jerusalem in kabbalistic terms: *Sol* (1976), *Luna* (1977), *Poética de la Cabala* (1982), and comments and translation of *Sefer HaBahir* (1985). Ricardo Feierstein wrote an incisive novel, *El Caramelo Descompuesto* (1979), about the utopian way of life of the kibbutz vis-à-vis the search for socialism and the New Left ideas of the Jewish intellectuals of Latin America during the 1970s. The Peruvian writer Isaac Goldemberg, who spent a year in a kibbutz, wrote a dramatic account of the existential itinerary of one of the main characters in his novel *Tiempo al Tiempo* (1984). The Mexican Jewish writer Esther Seligson has embraced biblical themes, Jewish philosophy, and kabbalistic motifs in her short stories and, principally, in her novel *La Morada en el Tiempo* (1984). Seligson spent one year studying Mishnah and Kabbalah in Jerusalem.

The Six Day War influenced a select group of Argentinian writers who were shocked by the possibility of the destruction of Israel. Their response was expressed in several important books: *Refugiados: Crónica de un Palestino*, by Marcos Aguinis (1967); *Ser Judío*, by Leon Rozitchner (1968); and *Etiquetas a los Hombres*, by Bernardo Verbitzky (1969).[24] The increasingly deep attraction to Israel led some Latin American Jewish writers to set up in 1985 the International Association of Jewish Writers in Spanish and Portuguese Languages. The association has over 100 members.[25]

LATIN AMERICAN SUPPORT FOR JEWISH RESTORATION IN THE HOLY LAND

The campaign for Jewish restoration in the Holy Land was supported by public opinion and many governments in Latin America from the very beginning of the Zionist endeavor. As early as 1917, on the occasion of the Balfour Declaration, a warm wave of solidarity and sympathy spread throughout the Latin American countries. Recent research has demonstrated the scope and meaning of the impact of the Balfour Declaration on Argentinian public opinion and on the Zionist Federation there.[26]

In the Latin American republics, the cause of Jewish Restoration was supported not only politically, by public figures, but culturally and intellectually as well. In 1929, the recently established Hebrew University of Jerusalem drew the attention and support of a range of Argentinian intellectuals, such as Horacio Quiroga, and the nationalist writer Leopoldo Lugones, who was the first honorary chairman of the Argentinian Friends of the Hebrew University and who headed the editorial board of the Spanish journal *Cuadernos de Oriente y Occidente*, published in 1927.[27]

During the late 1930s, a distinguished group of intellectuals and public personalities in Argentina endorsed the aims of the Argentinian Republic Chair at the Hebrew University, established by the local Friends of the Hebrew University of Jerusalem. The former president of the Republic, Dr. Marcelo T. de Alvear, expressed his spiritual attachment to Jewish Restoration in the Holy Land when he stated:

> There is something strangely suggestive in this singular endeavor for the colors of one of the youngest nations in the world to be seen presiding over a tribune of science erected by the efforts of an ancient people, thousands of years old, that today arises from its ashes to invite free men of all the world to voice their thoughts and their faith from the new University, built on the site of the home of their forefathers in the Holy Land.[28]

On the occasion of the convening of the First Latin American Zionist Congress (Montevideo, March 1945), pro-Zionist views and support were voiced by prominent personalities in the realm of literature, politics, government, journalism, and academe. Among them were José Pedroni, Arturi Capdevilla, Roberto Giusti, and Julio A. Noble from Argentina; Gabriel Gonzalez Videla, Natalio Berman, and B. Troncoso from Chile; Augusto Turenne and A. Guani from Uruguay; the presidents of Ecuador and Costa Rica; the foreign ministers of Paraguay and Bolivia; and senators from Peru.[29]

The cause of the Jewish state was supported by the more progressive elements in Latin America prior to 1947. The region's foremost advocates of Jewish statehood included Guatemala's Jorge Garcia Granados and President Juan Jose Arevalo; Mexico's Vicente Lombardo Toledano and muralist Diego Rivera; Argentina's socialist politician Enrique Dickmann; and Uruguay's Rodriguez Fabregát. Other important personalities such as Germán Arciniegas, Eduardo Santos, Baldomero Sanín Cano of Colombia, and Humberto Alvarez, Rene Silva Espejo, and Juvenal Hernandez of Chile, gave full support to the Partition Resolution in November 1947. Their vote was crucial at the United Nations, for the Latin American states made up more than one third of the two-thirds majority needed to secure the passage of the UN resolution approving the partition of Palestine. Thirteen countries voted in favor, six abstained, and only one was against.[30]

Prior to 1944, Argentinian journalist Rufino Marín had conducted an interesting survey of Latin American public opinion regarding the need to consider the idea of a Jewish state once the war would be over. The results of this poll were published in his book, *Lo que piensa América del problema Judío*. In its pages it is possible to find a broad range of different views voiced by prominent personalities, such as Ruben Darío, the famous Nicaraguan poet; Gabriel del Mazo, Argentinian politician and academic; Ruben Figuerola, member of parliament for the State of Guerrero, Mexico, and director of the *Movimiento Campesino*; Rafael Franco, former president of Paraguay; Argentinian former president Agustín P. Justo; and Cuban ambassador Ramiro Hernandez Portela.[31]

The Jewish Agency's policy of promoting the creation of pro-Palestine committees in each of the Latin American republics was a way of awakening and nurturing interest and support for the Zionist cause among non-Jews during the years 1943–1946. The first Comité Pro-Palestina Hebrea was formed in Costa Rica, under the presidency of Joaquín Garcia Monge; the last was the Comité Pro-Palestina Hebrea in Buenos Aires, established in 1946. Similar committees also existed in Chile, Uruguay, Brazil, Colombia, Guatemala, Cuba, and Mexico. Their primary objectives were to cultivate pro-Zionist public opinion throughout the region, and to secure in any way possible, specific positive instructions from each of the Latin American governments in the event the Palestine issue was debated at the United Nations. Some pro-Palestine committees played a role in that endeavor—notably those of Paraguay, Uruguay, and Colombia—by enlisting sympathetic politicians, intellectuals, and journalists for the cause of a Jewish State.[32] Jewish Agency officials in Argentina, such as Abraham Mibashan, succeeded in enlisting the support of distinguished members of parliament, such as E. Dickmann; and thanks to the effort of Natan Bistritzky, the Jewish National Fund's representative in Latin America, prestigious intellectuals in Chile, Peru, and other countries were enlisted as well. In Argentina, cultural contacts were established through the good offices of Alberto Gerchunoff, who wrote for *La Nación*. He won the support of a number of Argentinian personalities who forwarded a message to the World Christian Conference for Palestine, in which the distinguished signatories expressed the belief that "the establishment of a Jewish state in Palestine represents an act of historical justice." Headed by three former Conservative government foreign ministers—Nobel Peace Prize-winner Carlos Saavedra Lamas, José María Cantilo, and Adolfo Bioy—the statement was second-best to Argentina's participation at the conference.

These pro-Palestine committees differed from similar groups in the United States in the fact that in Latin America they did not have to be sponsored by nor addressed to a Christian public. While the North American groups functioned under the umbrella of the American Christian Palestine Committee, the Latin

American Comités Pro-Palestina Hebrea were not associated with any religious group and expressed a cultural rather than a religious dimension. Their members were drawn from a variety of political forces in Latin America. In Argentina, for example, when the committee was finally formed, the executive presidency was entrusted to Leandro Benitez Piríz, a former Radical Party member who had converted to Peronism and was close to Argentina's vice-president. As a balance, the poet Arturo Capdevila, and the conservative politician Tomás Amadeo, were asked to serve as honorary presidents. The three vice-presidents were Prof. Ernesto Nelson, a government supporter, *La Prensa* editor Adolfo Lanus of the opposition, and Socialist leader Américo Ghioldi. The secretariat was composed of two active Peronistas, congressmen Luis Zara and Jerónimo Peralta. Finally, the list of members included majority bloc parliamentarians John William Cooke, Cipriano Reyes, José V. Tesorieri, and Roberto Decker.[33]

The Argentine committees' activities seeking to publicize the history and aims of political Zionism included commemorations of the anniversaries of the Balfour Declaration, the British Mandate, and the first World Zionist Congress. It also circulated several publications, among which one should note Jerónimo Peralta's pamphlet, *The Jewish Question*, which was distributed in Argentina and the neighboring countries. Piríz and Zara also helped enlist majority bloc congressmen to sponsor a pro-Zionist parliamentary initiative (which was unsuccessful) and facilitated contacts between the Jewish Agency representative and Argentine diplomats. Piríz participated in the delegation of Latin American Pro-Palestine Committee leaders who presented a memorandum in favor of Jewish statehood to the foreign ministers attending an international conference in Petropolis, Brazil. Alberto Gerchunoff, the well-known Jewish intellectual of Argentina, was sent on behalf of the Pro-Palestine Committee to enlist other prestigious writers and to seek the sympathy and support of the molders of Latin American public opinion, especially those whose anti-Nazi wartime record made them the natural allies of the local Jewish community, long before the question of Jewish statehood reached the United Nations.[34]

Similar organizational activities were carried out by other pro-Palestine committees, such as that of Columbia, whose government finally abstained in the UN vote in November 1947. That committee coordinated all the work throughout the northern sector of Latin America. The prestigious intellectual Baldomero Sanín Cano was its president; its members included Eduardo Santos, editor of Bogotá's *El Tiempo* newspaper; the Conservative Congressman Villegas, editor of *El Siglo*; the distinguished writer Germán Arciniegas; and Dr. José Chavez. The future president of Colombia, Alberto Lleras Camargo, addressed the first meeting of the Comité Pro-Palestina Hebrea.[35]

LATIN AMERICAN–JEWISH SETTLEMENT IN ISRAEL

Jews from Latin America began to settle in Palestine as early as the 1920s. In the following decades, despite the difficulty of obtaining immigration certificates from the British mandatory authorities and the outbreak of World War II, immigration to and pioneering settlement in the Holy Land gained impetus as a result of the Zionist enterprise. In the pre-State period and through the late 1950s, Zionist pioneering idealism was the principal motivating force behind immigration. Most of the Latin American Jews settled in the kibbutzim; they had been members of the various Youth and Hehalutz movements in Argentina, Uruguay, Brazil, Chile, Cuba, Costa Rica, and Venezuela.[36] The crucial role played by the Latin American pioneering movement in the settlement of Eretz Israel was officially recognized at the First Latin American Zionist Congress, held in Montevideo (March 10–15, 1945). On behalf of the Central Bureau for Zionism in Latin America, it adopted a resolution: "To devote preferential attention to the Zionist youth movement, especially to its role of developing *halutzim*, which must be considered one of the most important Zionist goals in America."[37]

NOTES

1. Johen L. Phelan, *The Millennial Kingdom of the Franciscans in New Spain* (Berkeley: University of California Press, 1970).

2. Mario Góngora, *Studies in the Colonial History of Spanish America* (Cambridge: Cambridge University Press, 1975), 20. Góngora's study is an important contribution to the spiritual history of colonial Hispano-America.

3. Ibid., 208. "Columbus was influenced by the prophecy attributed to the *Pseudo-Methodius*, written in the Eastern Empire around the seventh century and republished many times after being first printed at Cologne in 1475. According to this, a victorious monarch would subdue the Muslims, reign happily in Jerusalem, finally lay down his Crown and submit to the Cross, and this would be the signal for the immediate coming of the Antichrist and his brief reign of iniquity."

4. Lee Eldridge Huddleston, *Origins of the American Indians: European Concepts 1492–1729* (Austin: University of Texas Press, 1965). See also M. Góngora (above, n.2), pp. 205-20.

5. José Durand, "Peru y Ophir en Garcilaso Ynca, el Jesuita Pineda y Gregorio Garcia," *Historica* 3, no. 2 (1979): 35-50.

6. L. E. Huddleston (above, n.4), 34.

7. Marcel Bataillon, *Evangélisme et Millénarisme au Nouveau Monde* (Paris: Colloque de Strassbourg, May 9–11, 1957), cited in M. Góngora (above, n.2).

8. Pedro Borges, O.F., "El sentido transcendente del Descubrimiento y Conversion de las Yndias" (1956), cited in M. Góngora (above, n.2), 211.

9. Antonio Eguiluz, O.F., "Fray Gonzalo Tenorio y sus teorias escatológicas-providencialistas sobre las Yndias," *Missionalia Hispanica* 48 (1959): 26-39.

10. The manuscript in the Columbia University Library consists of translations Hacoen made of two chronicles of Lopez de Gómara: *HaIndia Hachadasha*, pp. 72-231, and *Sefer Francisco Corteiz*, pp. 177-297. Lopez de Gómara was secretary to Cortés, and in 1552 he published *História de las Indias y Conquista de Mexico*. See Raphael Weinberg, "Yoseph ben Yeoshua Hacoen and his book Metzib Guevuloth Amim," *Sinai* 12 (August-September 1973, Hebrew): 4-31.

11. Mario Góngora, *Aspectos de la Ilustración Católica en el pensamiento y la vida*

eclesiástica chilena, 1770–1814 (Santiago, Chile: Universidad Católica, 1957).

12. See the influence of Lacunza's book on the history of fundamentalism, in Ernest Sandeen, *The Roots of Fundamentalism: British and American Millenarianism, 1880–1930* (Chicago: Chicago University Press, 1970). Although Lacunza's book was banned in 1824 by the Index—a clerical commission of inquiry for the purpose of censorship in Chile and other Spanish-American countries—its influence was important among intellectuals who did not refrain from reading it. The Argentinian writer and politician Domingo F. Sarmiento wrote in his *Recuerdos de Provincia* that his uncle, Fray Pascual, recommended Lacunza's book. See Lazaro Schallman, "El judaísmo y los judíos a través de las letras Argentinas," *Comentario* 48 (1966): 113-15; Abel Cháneton, *Un precursor de Sarmiento y otros ensayos históriscos* (Buenos Aires: Gleizer, 1934), 121; and Antonio Portnoy, "El Gral, Belgrano y la venida del Mesías," *Judaica* 57 (1938): 119-21.

13. See *Poesías de José Rivera Indarte, y biografía del autor escrita por el coronel de artilleria D. Bartolomé Mitre*, vol. 1 (Buenos Aires: Imprenta de Mayo, 1853); and Antonio Portnoy, "Las Melodias Hebraicas de Rivera Indarte: un cantor de las glorias de Israel en la época de Rosas," *Judaica* 59-61 (1938): 247-50.

14. Kathe Windmuller, *O Judeu no Teatro Romántico Brasileiro, Una revisão da tragedia de Gonsalves de Magalhães, Antonio José ou O Poeta e a Inquisicão* (São Paulo: Universidade de São Paulo, Centro de Estudios Judaicos, 1984), 1-60.

15. See Gabriela Mistral, "Mi experiencia con la Biblia," *Chile escribe a Israel* (Santiago, Chile: Andrés Bello, 1982), 97-102. On the attitude of Mistral toward the Jewish religion, see Marta Taylor, *Sensibilidad religiosa de Gabriela Mistral* (Madrid: Gredos, 1972), 86-87.

16. Ramón Diaz, ed., *Poesía Hebrea Moderna* (Madrid: Aguilar, 1970); and *Poesía de Israel*, ed., trans. Cecilia Meireles (Rio: Civilização Brasilera, 1962).

17. Edna Aizenberg, *The Aleph Weaver: Biblical, Kabbalistic and Judaic Elements in Borges* (New York: Scripta Humanista, 1984), 76.

18. Jorge L. Borges, "Una vindicación de la Cabala," in *Obras Completas* (Buenos Aires: Emece, 1976), 2111.

19. Motifs from Job appear in "Deutsches Requiem," ibid., 576; "Everything and Nothing," ibid., 804; see also Jorge Borges and Margarita Guerrero, *El libro de los seres imaginarios* (Buenos Aires: Kier, 1976), 39-40, 137. Allusions to the Book of Job can be found in the essays "Examen de matáforas," in *Inquisiciones* (Buenos Aires: Emece, 1980), 74; "La adjetivacion," in *El Tamaño de mi esperanza* (Buenos Aires: Proa, 1926), 51-52; and "Sobre los clásicos," in *Obras Completas* (Buenos Aires: Emece, 1974), 773.

20. E. Aizenberg (above, n.17), 78-83.

21. Ibid., 60-61.

22. *Davar* 112 (January-March 1967): 3.

23. Carlos M. Grünberg, *Mester de Judería* (Buenos Aires: Argos, 1940) and *Junto a un río de Babel* (Buenos Aires: Acervo Cultural, 1965); Lazaro Liacho, *Sionidas desde las Pampas, y Sonata Judía de Nueva York* (Buenos Aires: Candelabro, 1969).

24. See my analysis of these writers in *Identidad Judía en la Literatura Argentina* (Buenos Aires: Pardés, 1983), chap. 11.

25. The Jerusalem-based Central Institute for Cultural Relations between Israel, Iberoamerica, Spain, and Portugal took the initiative to organize the new International Association of Jewish Writers in Spanish and Portuguese Languages.

26. Victor Mirelman, "Zionist Activities in Argentina from the Balfour Declaration

to 1930," in *Studies in the History of Zionism* (Jerusalem: Hasifriya Hazionit, 1976, Hebrew), 212–14. For the following years until 1945, see Silvia Schenkolewski, "The Relationships between the Zionist Movements and the Jewish Community in Argentina, 1935–1943," *Zionism* 11 (1986, Hebrew): 296-332.

27. *Cuadernos de Oriente y Occidente* appeared only twice during 1927, under the editorship of Samuel Glusberg. It published the writings of a wide range of Argentinian writers who supported The Hebrew University of Jerusalem. Among them were Horacio Quiroga, Leopoldo Lugones, and Ezequiel Martinez Estrada, who were on the editorial board of the journal.

28. See Leon Kibrik, ed., *Fundación Catedra República Argentina en la Universidad Hebrea de Jerusalém* (Buenos Aires: Leon Kibrik, 1940).

29. *Primér Congreso Sionista Latinoamericano, Informe General* (Buenos Aires: Consejo Central Sionista Argentina [CCSA], 1946), 41-72.

30. Edy Kaufman, Yoram Shapira, and Yoel Barromi, *Israel–Latin American Relations* (New Brunswick, N.J.: Transaction Books, ca. 1979), 23; Nathaniel Lorch, "Latin America and Israel," *Jerusalem Quarterly* 22 (Winter 1982): 41.

31. See Rufino Marín, *Lo que piensa America del problema Judío* (Buenos Aires: Editorial America, 1944), 167-225.

32. Moshe Tov, *El Murmullo de Israel: Historial Diplomático* (Jerusalem: Semana, 1983); Oral history conducted in the autumn of 1979, Institute of Contemporary Jewry, Oral History Division, The Hebrew University. See also the first chapter of the diplomatic account of Jacob Tzur, the first Israeli ambassador in Argentina and Uruguay, *Cartas Credenciales, No. 4* (Jerusalem: Semana, 1983), 19-37.

33. Ignacio Klich, "Argentina, the Arab World, and the Partition of Palestine" (Ph.D. diss. in progress, St. Antony College, Oxford University).

34. Ibid.

35. M. Tov (above, n.32).

36. See Donald L. Herman, *The Latin American Community of Israel* (New York: Praeger, 1984), chap. 2; Moshe Sicron, *Immigration to Israel from Latin America* (Tel Aviv: Tel Aviv University, 1974); Florinda Goldberg and Josef Rosen, eds., *Los Latinoamericanos en Israel* (Buenos Aires: Contexto, 1988), 18-43.

37. *Primér Congreso Sionista* (above, n.29), 21.

CARAVAN OF THE EXPEDITION

Caravan of W. F. Lynch and naval crew; en route from Acco to Tiberias.

Source: William F. Lynch, *Narrative of the United States Expeditions to the River Jordan* (Philadelphia: Lea & Blanchard, 1849), p. 147.

Rolla Floyd.

An Independent American, who has had more experience as a Tourist Agent than any other man living in the Holy Land, has a home for visitors to the
Holy City. House, and Camp, ready at short Notice,
for from one to a hundred persons, beautifully situated outside the City Walls, in an olive grove. He will
give information gratis. Satisfaction guaranteed.
Charges moderate.

ADDRESS:— ROLLA FLOYD.
JERUSALEM.
Palestine.
Telegraphic Address :— FLOYD, JERUSALEM.

ROLLA FLOYD, & Co.,

American Tourist Agency,

having had more than 20 years' experience with Tourists in the
Orient, wish to inform the public that they have he has

CARRIAGES and HORSES always ready to
convey Passengers from

JAFFA TO JERUSALEM

We have the best dragomans in the country, regularly employed.

FIRST-CLASS HOTEL ACCOMMODATION PROVIDED.

At Jaffa, *Hotel Palestine*—Ramleh, *Hotel d'Italie*—In the
Valley of Ajalon, half-way to Jerusalem, *Hotel Jonas*,—Jerusalem, *Hotel Feil*, and *Jerusalem Hotel*—Hebron, *Hotel Hebron*,
(the only Hotel there)—Damascus, *Hotel Dimitri*—Baalbec,
Hotel Victoria, and at Beyrout, *New Hotel*.

He can furnish tickets from Beyrout to DAMASCUS and BAAL-
BEC by Diligence, special carriages, or by saddle-horse.

He has the largest and the best stock of camping imple-
ments in the country, and convey passengers singly, or in companies to any number to all parts of PALESTINE, SYRIA, EAST of
the JORDAN, the HAURAN, PALMYRA, and the DESERT.

Charges moderate.

PERFECT SATISFACTION GUARANTEED.

Address :—

ROLLA FLOYD,
JAFFA,
PALESTINE.

Announcement of Rolla Floyd American Tourist Agency, Jaffa.

Source: Helen Palmer Parsons, ed., *Letters from Palestine: 1868–1912, Written
by Rolla Floyd* (Dexter, Me.: Helen Palmer Parsons, 1981), p. 136. Courtesy of
Helen V. Parsons.

Rolla Floyd with family and friends in garden for tea.

Source: Helen Palmer Parsons, ed., *Letters from Palestine: 1868–1912, Written by Rolla Floyd* (Dexter, Me.: Helen Palmer Parsons, 1981), p. 126. Courtesy of Helen V. Parsons.

"At Ease," Canadian Soldiers of the Jewish Legion resting with friends near Petach Tikvah during World War I.

Source: From private collection of Prof. Michael Brown. Courtesy of Prof. Michael Brown.

Alliance Isráelite Universalle School in Tel Aviv, established in 1890s.

Source: Simon Schwarzfuchs, *The Alliance in Mediterranean Communities in the 19th Century*. (Jerusalem: Misgav Yerushalayim, 1987, Hebrew), facing p. 84. Courtesy of Misgav Yerushalayim.

Carmelite Monastery on Mount Carmel, built by French Catholics during the years 1875–1880.

Source: Louis Charles Lortet, *La Syria d'Aujourd'hui* (Paris: Hachette & Cie, 1884), p. 173.

Evangelical Church at Waldheim, a Holy Land settlement in the Lower Galilee, built in 1915.

Source: Private collection of Dr. Yossi Artzi, 1987. Courtesy of Dr. Yossi Ben-Artzi, Haifa.

Talitha Kumi Girls School, established by Germans in Jerusalem in 1868

Source: Private collection of Dr. Yossi Artzi, University of Haifa. Courtesy of Dr. Yossi Ben-Artzi, Haifa.

Augusta Victoria convalescent home and hostel on Mount Scopus, dedicated to the Queen of Germany, in 1910.

Source: A fund-raising postcard circulated at beginning of the 1900s. Private collection of Haim Goren (Haifa). From the collection of Mr. Haim Goren.

Scottish Hospital on the Sea of Galilee, established by the Scottish Mission at Tiberias in 1894.

Source: W. P. Livingston, *A Galilee Doctor, the Life of Dr. Torrance of Tiberias* (London: Hodder & Stoughton, 1925), p. 176.

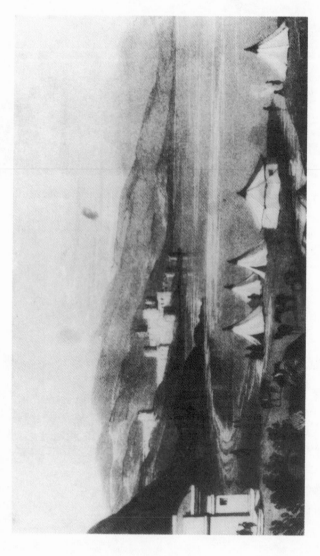

View of Tiberias. Etching by Lord Egerton during a tour in 1840.

Source: Lady Harriet Catherine Egerton, *Journal of a Tour in the Holy Land* (London: Harrison, 1841), p. 72.

PART III

WESTERN EUROPE

Chapter 8

France–Holy Land Studies: Teaching and Research

Catherine Nicault

INTRODUCTION

The chronological range of this subject is immense, much broader than for America–Holy Land relations, which began in the seventeenth century. For France, along with other West European countries, study should commence at the beginning of the Middle Ages, when this country emerged in the Christian West as a state-entity. In particular, the Crusades constitute a significant period in relations between France and the Holy Land.

The suggestions included in this chapter are not intended to cover the entire chronological range. Since the group responsible for this chapter comprised historians of the contemporary period, a political scientist, a sociologist, and a linguist, its analysis is limited to those fields of study and periods with which the group is familiar—namely, the nineteenth and twentieth centuries, or more precisely, from the Napoleonic period to the creation of the State of Israel in 1948. However, the linguistic and cultural relations between France and the Holy Land are considered over a longer period.

That said, the relations between France and the Holy Land offer a rich field of research. The wealth of subjects for study proposed here, according to a thematic classification, points to the existence of considerable lacunae. The movement of people between the two countries is conceivably a first approach. In any event, it offers an initial source to delve more deeply into various aspects of the subject. Such preliminary studies do not present serious methodological difficulties.

THE FRENCH IN THE HOLY LAND

A distinction should be made between the French who settled for a long period, or permanently, in the Holy Land, and those who were only passing through.

Few French lived in Palestine during the period being considered—no more than some 200 before 1914.[1] Unlike Germany, France did not possess Christian agricultural settlements enabling it to swell its numbers in the Holy Land, and unlike Russia, it had no Jewish immigrants there. French citizens in Palestine were limited to consular personnel, the few employees of the French banking and railway companies, members of the Catholic missions, the leaders of the *Alliance Israélite Universelle* schools, and Jews of Algerian origin. It is important to learn more about this population and their institutions. We can define their sphere of influence, for example, by measuring the extent of consular protection (in particular of the North Africans) and the number of pupils who attended the Alliance schools and the missions.

With regard to the protection of Latin Christians by France, it would be useful to know its precise implementation, and the extent to which other European powers such as Italy—or Russia, protector of the Orthodox Christians—succeeded in defining their fields of activity in the nineteenth century. There is also much to be gained by studying the role of the consuls general who served in Jerusalem;[2] and by defining more accurately the French imprint on pupils in the French religious schools. Their education once completed, did they tend to leave their native land? If so, the schools as a means of French influence in the Holy Land would not have had quite the value with which they were credited.

During the nineteenth century, the Holy Land received many visitors, among them a fair number of French—beginning with Bonaparte's troops! For the most part they were pilgrims and tourists, with a smaller number of politicians and journalists. A study of these journeys, the expectations of the visitors and the impressions they brought back, would make it possible to define what motivated their permanent interest in the country.

Who were the soldiers and scientists who took part in the 1799 campaign in Syria? How did their encounter with the Holy Land take place? What impressions were drawn in France from their adventure? Does a link exist between the memories of this campaign in the Orient and the romantic voyages that were to follow?

With regard to pilgrimages, we have some knowledge of the work of the *Frères Assomptionnistes* prior to 1914,[3] but it is not comprehensive. Nor has any study been made of the image of the Holy Land retained by these pious faithful, even though a substantial popular pilgrim literature does exist.[4]

Jewish travelers constitute another category of visitors. It would be interesting to follow in the footsteps of Albert Cohn, later a close associate of Baron Edmond de Rothschild, another regular visitor to Palestine. Edmond Fleg, Chief Rabbi Israel Lévi, André Spire, and Sylvain Lévi should also be studied in this context.

The attraction that the Holy Land held for the French tourist highlights the social elite's conception of its cultural roots there. For this privileged class, Palestine was in fact a high point of organized tours, generally marking an interval between visits to Italy, Greece, Turkey, and Egypt—clearly a return to the sources of pagan and Judeo-Christian antiquity. Did these trips also enable the travelers to observe the contemporary upheavals that were taking place in the Holy Land? Or did they come away only with an impression of ancient Palestine? These cultural concerns also played a role in the visits made in the 1920s and 1930s by French political leaders;[5] from then on, they also took an interest in developments in the Jewish National Home. Similar interest was shown by renowned journalists sent to Palestine by leading Paris newspapers.[6] The frequency of such visits, the events that gave rise to them, and the reputation of the special correspondents serve as a barometer of the interest shown by the French press in current events in Palestine.

PALESTINIAN JEWS IN FRANCE

Some Jews of the Holy Land found their way to France. Apart from emissaries sent to collect funds for the Orthodox community, and Zionist propagandists, France opened its doors to young Palestinian Jews who wished to study there; to former pupils of the Alliance schools in Palestine; to *halutzim* forced temporarily to leave the country then in the grip of an economic crisis;[7] as well as to those who had been disappointed by Zionism and who wished to settle in France. These groups should be studied.

LINGUISTIC AND CULTURAL RELATIONS

At the end of the nineteenth and beginning of the twentieth century, French diplomacy encouraged the spread of the French language as an effective means of influence in the world at large. In Palestine, first the dissemination of French and then its preservation during the period of the Mandate took a great deal of effort. Yet we know little about the exact place occupied by the French language in the Holy Land. In the final analysis, were the missions or the Alliance more effective in spreading the language? What efforts did the French government make to encourage the teaching of French in the educational system and, after 1925, at the Hebrew University of Jerusalem?

The place of the study of Hebrew in France should, in our opinion, also be taken into consideration. If the interest shown in such study is primarily of a biblical nature, then the attraction of the Holy Land is not alien to it. The monks of the Middle Ages studied Hebrew in a theological perspective, yet Pierre Dubois, a thirteenth-century cleric, also considered it a means by which Christendom could take possession of the Holy Land. This interest seems to have become more pronounced during the Renaissance period; however, we know more of the return to Greek and Roman sources during that era than we do of the no less real return to Hebrew sources. When the Collège Royal, the future

Collège de France, was founded around 1530, Hebrew was part of its curriculum. Humanists saw in the rediscovery of the original biblical text an opportunity to counter the Sorbonne and its scholastic teaching. Some even considered Hebrew as the first human language and, therefore, as a perfect tongue. This field is only beginning to be explored and deserves greater attention.[8]

For the later period, with which we are particularly concerned, more should be known about the teaching of classical Hebrew in Protestant, rabbinical, and possibly in Catholic, seminaries, as well as at the Collège de France. An analysis should be made of the successive titles given to the "Chair of Hebrew" there, a list of those who held it, and the causes for its lapse in various periods. A study of the teaching of modern Hebrew in France, where Eliezer ben Yehuda— in 1881 a student at the Ecole Normale d'Instituteurs (Teachers' College) of the Alliance in Paris—began to use Hebrew as his everyday language, also appears essential, but it is likely to be more difficult to carry out. Apart from the Ecole des Langues Orientales,[9] modern Hebrew is taught by short-lived associations, often Zionist inspired, which have limited budgets and produce meager results.

The theme of cultural exchanges offers broader perspectives. Israeli enthusiasm for archaeology is well known, as is the contribution made to Palestinian archaeology by the Ecole Biblique de Jérusalem. French archaeologists participated in the early digs in Palestine in the mid-nineteenth century. Prominent among them was Paul-Emile Botta (1802–1870), who at one time was French consul there.[10] This tradition continued through the period between the two World Wars.

The Holy Land was an important source of inspiration for French painters and engravers. Beginning in the Middle Ages, religious painting increasingly depicted imaginary biblical landscapes. The tradition was carried on in the seventeenth century, as shown in Nicolas Poussin's *Ruth et Boaz*,[11] and through the nineteenth century with *Le Cantique des Cantiques* by Gustave Moreau[12] and *La Lutte de Jacob avec l'Ange* by Eugène Delacroix.[13] Contemporaries of the latter two artists imagined the Holy Land in far more epic and fantastic forms than those with which Gustave Doré endowed it in his famous illustrations for the Bible (1864). Romantic and Orientalist painters continued in this vein, although it remained somewhat secondary in their works: Baron Antoine Gros (*Bonaparte visitant les pestiférés de Jaffa*, 1804, the Louvre) and Delacroix (*La bataille de Nazareth*) illustrated the main episodes of the 1799 campaign without ever having visited the Holy Land. The Orientalists appear to have preferred a rich, almost Byzantine vision of ancient Judea, of which *Salomé dansant devant Hérode* by Gustave Moreau is a good example.[14] One could probably find extensions of this approach among the French pre-Raphaelites, like Odilon Redon and Puvis de Chavannes.

The inspiration that French artists have drawn from biblical and Holy Land sources requires further investigation. In music one can point to Arthur Honnegar's oratorio *Le roi David* (1924) and opera *Judith* (1926), and to the opera *David* (1952–1953) by Darius Milhaud, another member of the Group of Six formed in 1918. A broader consideration of this area is called for.

The nineteenth century was the century of travel; photographs and sketches from life were fashionable. Maxime du Camp, Flaubert's companion on his trip to the Orient, left a considerable collection of negatives of images of Palestine around 1850.[15] Painters also went there in search of inspiration. Conversely, in the 1920s and 1930s, "Palestinians" like Feder exhibited regularly in Paris and illustrated travel accounts with original engravings.[16] It would be instructive to study what image of the Holy Land was thereby conveyed to the French public.

The romantic movement greatly developed the literary genre of the travel narrative. In an upsurge of religiosity and sentimentalism, renowned writers took the road to Palestine and left accounts of their stay. *L'Itinéraire de Paris à Jérusalem* by Chateaubriand (1811) and *Le voyage en Orient* by Lamartine (1835) are the best known. Thus, books became the basis of a literary tradition illustrated notably by Gustave Flaubert (*Voyages*, posthumous), Pierre Loti (*Jérusalem* in 1895 and *La Galilée* in 1896), and Joseph Kessel (*Terre d'amour*, 1927). A series of lesser-known authors also published in the press travel narratives of a high literary standard.[17] Other scholars should continue in the path of Claude Vigée, who has already devoted some of his works to these romantic journeys.

The theme of the Holy Land is not absent from the theater and the French novel. In the dramatic genre, it is worth recalling that Corneille, and more so Racine (*Bérénice, Esther, Athalie*), drew on subjects from Jewish history; but they do not seem to have had many imitators. Alexandre Dumas *fils* (*La femme de Claude*, 1873), Maurice Donnay (*Le retour de Jérusalem*, 1904), and other less well-known authors drew inspiration from the Jewish renaissance in contemporary Palestine. Paul Claudel's play *Tête d'or* could be related to our theme.

Where the novel is concerned, the Holy Land has given rise only to mediocre works—the *Siona* series, popular novels set in Palestine, certain works by the Tharaud brothers, the work of Myriam Harry, and *Le puits de Jacob* by Pierre Benoît (1925). At the beginning of the century, neither Edmond Fleg nor Emile Zola succeeded in creating the "Zionist" novel of which each had dreamed. To these must be added such Orientalist writers as Louis Massignon, a Christian Arabist who retained a constant interest in the Holy Land and Jewish culture.[18]

Conversely, what influence did France exert upon the literature of the Jewish community in Palestine? In particular, a study of the "Canaanite" movement revolving around the poet and novelist Yonathan Ratosh, which was centered in Paris between the two World Wars, would be of great interest.

IDEOLOGICAL AND POLITICAL INTERRELATIONSHIPS

Many of the Jewish and non-Jewish precursors of Zionism were Frenchmen, and the subject deserves to be examined in depth. For example, was Bonaparte one of Zionism's precursors? A study devoted solely to the Saint-Simon group would be justified, for they seem to have greatly influenced certain French Jews, such as Adolphe Crémieux.

Above all, France is the country where Herzl was living at the time he was developing his ideas for *The Jewish State*. Zionist historians and Herzl's biographers have frequently emphasized this relationship, pointing to the role played by the Dreyfus affair in the crystallization of his ideas on the "Jewish problem." However, the four years Herzl spent in Paris remain to be studied, in order to determine the precise influence of the French political ambiance on his formulation of the Jewish problem, his conception of the state to be created, and the functioning of the Zionist movement.

Still in connection with Zionism, except for the pre-1914 period, little is known about the views held by the great French political groups.[19] A study of the press, publications, and even newsreels of the 1930–1948 period can provide a rich source of data.

The development of the kibbutzim as a unique aspect of practical Zionism gave rise to varying reactions in France: open hostility from the right toward these "Communist settlements," and a favorable and admiring reaction from the left, notably on the part of the Protestant economist Charles Gide (1847–1932), who visited the kibbutzim and made them known in France.[20]

Also to be investigated are relations between political parties in France and in Jewish Palestine; research into the ties between the Zionist socialists and the French socialists seems essential. The subject is vast and the sources scattered. The biographical approach appears to be an effective way of tackling it, and indeed, a study of Marc Jarblum, a French Zionist, is presently being undertaken.[21] Biographies of many other personalities should prove fruitful. The Zionist convictions of Léon Blum and his role as mediator among the Jews of Palestine, the Zionist movement, and France have not yet been adequately clarified. Anatole de Monzie (1876–1947), difficult to place politically but a longtime avowed friend of Zionism, is also an apt subject. Other personalities to be studied are Marius Moutet and Jean Longuet.

The ties between the Revisionist movement and France deserve a closer look. Ze'ev Jabotinsky, who lived in Paris between the two World Wars, had solid supporters within the small French Zionist circles. He certainly influenced the literary groups of Russian- and Yiddish-speaking Jews, such as the Canaanite movement mentioned above, as well as the poet David Knout.[22] The influence of Italian fascism as a paradigm on Jabotinsky has often been emphasized. But did not the extreme right-wing movements that posed a threat to the French Republic in the 1930s also play a part? It would be useful, too, to understand the attraction Jabotinsky had for a significant number of Parisian Zionists, and the consequences this had on the French Zionist movement before World War II.

Finally, one should study the connection that existed from 1945 to 1948 between the right-wing parties, first and foremost the Gaullists of the *Rassemblement du Peuple Français*, and the extreme Zionist groups such as the Irgun and the Stern group.[23] What was the origin of these relationships, and what concrete form did they take? It seems urgent to undertake such a study while some of the principal protagonists, such as Jacque Soustelle, can still be interviewed.

ECONOMIC AND DIPLOMATIC TIES

Napoleonic studies have not made much of Bonaparte's great oriental campaign, part of his dream to achieve the greatness of Caesar or Alexander. What was the Holy Land's place in this romantic ideal? What meaning, what aim, did he attribute to his stay there in 1799? The answers must be sought not only in the available texts but also in the works that the Emperor commissioned from official artists to commemorate the campaign—paintings, engravings, medals, and so forth. The subject should be studied also from the viewpoint of the local inhabitants.

Since the Second Empire, the protection of the Holy Places has always been considered by the French authorities—albeit anti-clerical—to be a means of exerting diplomatic influence. What successive forms did this interest take? How did such concern interfere with government policy toward the Vatican which, following the separation of Church and State in France in 1905, tended to favor Italian aims? In the 1920s, there was talk of creating an international commission of control with the framework of the League of Nations. Political rivalries, principally between France (which sought to preside over the commission) and Great Britain (the Mandatory power) finally prevented its creation.[24]

Further research should also be undertaken regarding the place of Palestine and its attendant problems—Capitulations, missions, growth of the Jewish population, Zionism, rise of French imperialism—in French-Ottoman relations from 1880 until about 1914. But this cannot be defined properly unless a picture is drawn of the struggles for influence in the Holy Land in which France, England, Germany, Italy, and Russia were engaged. Only partial studies exist at present.[25]

Studies on France–Holy Land relations during the Fourth and Fifth Republics are more numerous. However, these were written by journalists and/or political scientists who did not have access to French diplomatic archives sealed for the post-1945 period. Paradoxically, no works exist on relations between France and Palestine, or between France and Zionism, in the interwars period of 1917–1948, for which archival records are available. Research should be undertaken in the Levant, in France, and in North Africa—and not solely from the French point of view. The attitude of the Zionist Organization toward France from 1897 to 1948 would be a fascinating theme of study.

Studies have been made of the British view of the diplomatic and military events that, as a result of World War I, led to establishment of the British Mandate over Palestine, long coveted by its French ally. The French point of view has not yet been documented.[26] How did the French authorities react to the Balfour Declaration? Had they themselves established a policy concerning Zionism? Did they realize that their interests in Palestine were in jeopardy? How did they attempt to parry British ambitions? Works devoted to the *mésentente cordiale* existing between France and Great Britain in the 1920s cover the disagreements concerning Germany, Turkey, or Syria, but they omit the problems raised by the proximity of the French Mandatory power in Lebanon and Syria, and British-mandated Palestine. During the demarcation of the common border and throughout the first half of the 1920s, tension ran high; but of this little is known. The situation was complicated by the existence of a third party—namely, the Zionists of the Jewish National Home. Their attitude toward France, at first very close to that of London, later tended to distance itself somewhat from the British line.

Economic ties in two areas should also be examined: (1) specific economic relations that were established between the French Mandates over Syria and Lebanon, and Palestine,[27] and (2) commercial and possibly technical exchanges between France and Ottoman Palestine. A study of the ties between Marseille and Palestine offers a particularly interesting topic. One might also seek to define more precisely France's role in the economic development of the Holy Land through the Alliance Israélite Universelle and its investments in the railway companies and the Messageries Maritimes, the only company offering regular transportation service to Jaffa during the Ottoman period.

Certain groups worked toward strengthening the political, cultural, and economic ties between France and Palestine. The *Ligue des Amis Français du Sionisme*, and the *Comité France-Palestine*, which was founded in 1925 and tried, *inter alia*, to set up a Franco-Palestinian Chamber of Commerce, could be profitably examined.

THE JEWS OF FRANCE AND THE HOLY LAND

Historians of assimilation have placed greater emphasis on the process of Jewish integration into France than on the relations maintained by French Jews with the Holy Land. They have, of course, noted the increasing coolness of this relationship, and the purely symbolic interpretation given to such religious themes as the return to Jerusalem. However, if for assimilated Jews the Promised Land is no more than a symbol, if they equated the Promised Land with France, what were the successive shifts through which this evolution took place? Rabbinical writings are an indispensable source from which one can derive an analysis of the terms used to denote Palestine in various periods: Zion, Eretz Israel, the Promised Land, and the Holy Land.[28]

Even when assimilation had reached its peak, not all French Jews had lost interest in Palestine. French Jewry is fond of recalling the role played by some of its members in the renewal of the Jewish community there in the nineteenth century, even before the birth of modern Zionism. However, the pro-Palestine tendency within French Jewry that inspired this undertaking is still only partially known. Several biographies exist of Edmond de Rothschild, and one of Adolphe Crémieux is soon to appear, but other members of the movement deserve the same attention. For example, Charles Netter, the founder of Mikveh Israel, and above all Zadoc Kahn, who—through his ties with Rothschild, the Lovers of Zion group, and the Zionists—stood at the hub of relations between the Holy Land and the Jews of France at the turn of the century.[29] Also to be studied are the French Jewish organizations that sought to promote the love of Zion. Such groups existed from the pre-Zionist period until World War II, although they attracted few members and survived only with difficulty. Research into organized Zionism in France and the attitude of French Jewry toward that movement can also be carried out on a regional basis; the attitudes of the Jews of Alsace-Lorraine toward Zionism is a fine subject.

The relationship between French Jewry and Zionism has given rise to much debate but insufficient research. An institutional study of the movement is only at its beginnings. It is fairly well documented for the pre-1914 period, and initial studies of the Zionist groups are appearing for the period between the wars,[30] but much still remains to be done in this field. More extensive use of the Yiddish Zionist press can be particularly helpful. Current interest in the Jewish Resistance during World War II has given rise to studies focusing on the role played by certain Zionist groups within this Resistance, but a comprehensive study is still awaited.[31] Extension of the examination of these relationships over a relatively longer period would permit an appraisal of the often stressed but little analyzed turnabout of French Jewry in its attitude toward Zionism following the upheavals of the war and the revelation of the Nazi genocide.

A complete appraisal of the attitude of the French Jewish community to Zionism and Palestine should also include data on French Jewish *aliyah*. Whereas quantitative studies of this kind exist for the Jews of North Africa who migrated to Israel, similar analysis of the Jews of France has long been neglected. This work should be accompanied by a study of the specific characteristics of this immigration. From which regions of France did these immigrants come? Were they members of youth movements, and did they have any special preparation? What proportion among them chose kibbutz life? Did many of them take a new Hebrew name? Such an inquiry obviously demands an extremely critical analysis of the sources, including oral testimony, the use of which is always somewhat sensitive.[32]

FRENCH CHRISTIANS AND THE HOLY LAND

The creation of the State of Israel in 1948 raised two questions in the Christian world. What political significance was to be granted to the emergence of a Jewish State? Was this historic event of religious import for the Christian conscience? Contradictory replies to these questions were advanced within Catholicism and Protestantism. But if the creation of the State provoked an increasingly firm response on the part of French Christian circles, it did not lessen its interest in the Holy Land. It is hardly surprising that French Christians, also citizens of the "eldest daughter of the Church," have constantly sought to make their presence in Palestine felt.

In the nineteenth and twentieth centuries, French Christians established this relationship mainly through pilgrimages and concern for the Holy Places. Given the French ambition to be guardian of the Holy Places—a religious issue with numerous diplomatic, political, and even military aspects—France was considered, at least until 1905, to be the unofficial protector of the interests of the Latin Christians. The policy pursued by the French in Palestine greatly pleased Catholic public opinion, which was less than satisfied with the religious policy followed in France itself. At the end of the nineteenth century, then, Palestine appeared to be a privileged place where religious Frenchmen saw their beliefs reconciled with their patriotism, since, like the secular Republic, they hoped that Palestine would one day become French territory. This convergence of interests deserves greater emphasis.

The support given by the French authorities also explains the relative prosperity of the numerous French Catholic convents, missions, and churches in the sites holy to Christianity (Bethlehem, Nazareth, Jerusalem); a complete list of these institutions should be made. Also important to study would be the activity of certain religious orders such as the Congrégation de Notre Dame de Sion,[33] the Franciscans (who have held the title "Custodians of the Holy Land" since 1333), the Salesian Fathers, the White Fathers (Church of St. Anne), and the Dominicans (Ecole Biblique and Ecole d'Archéologie Biblique). What institutional and financial ties linked the Church of France with these various institutions in the Holy Land? What was the nature of the relations between these institutions and the French authorities in Palestine, in particular the consuls? What kinds of contacts existed between them, the Christian institutions of other nationalities or rites, the various Christian communities (Greek Orthodox, Greek Catholic), and the Jews and Muslims? All these are subjects to be investigated.

Another avenue to be explored could be the attitude shown by French Catholic and Protestant public opinion toward Palestine. Building upon existing studies of the pre-1914 period, there is clearly need to examine the religious press following the Balfour Declaration and later during the establishment of the Jewish National Home. There are undoubtedly many more points of contact between French Protestants and the Zionist movement—empathy between minorities, pro-Dreyfus militancy, joint participation in secular or socialist struggles, the use of Hebrew by pastors studying the Old Testament, and so forth. Does all this point to ties of a different kind with the Holy Land, and a different evaluation of the Zionist phenomenon?

Here again, the biographical method could prove useful. It could be applied to leading members of liberal Catholicism (Charles Montalembert), of social Catholicism (Marc Sangnier, Albert de Mun), or of fundamentalism (Louis Veillot). Among the Protestants we have already noted Charles Gide as an interesting figure to examine. It would be most desirable to have a study of the attitudes toward Palestine and Zionism of André Siegfried, a prominent French political scientist.

CONCLUSION

A review of the connections between France and the Holy Land, and the many avenues for research to which it gives rise, reveals relationships different from those that link America to the Holy Land. The studies published on the latter subject throw into relief the depth of spiritual and cultural ties as opposed to political involvement—with the exception of the part played by the United States in the birth of the State of Israel and afterwards. The relations between France and the Holy Land as considered within the chronological and thematic limits mentioned are ties of a more practical nature, more highly developed and more regular, although they remain modest in scope. Political and diplomatic ambitions are constantly present within the framework of the Middle East problem, although they are not deemed essential by the French authorities. Spiritual ties are certainly less widespread.

Given the state of Jewish studies in France, is it realistic to offer so many directions for study? We are cautiously optimistic. The past decade has witnessed a revival of the study of Jewish civilization in France; such subjects could now find a place in university curricula. A growing number of departments for Hebrew studies have a broad conception of their field of interest, going beyond theological and linguistic courses to touch on culture and history. In addition, many of the topics suggested here can find a place in research units that are not specifically Jewish, such as political science, French literature, comparative literature, and international relations. Experience has shown that general historical publications welcome papers on Jewish themes related to Jews and Judaism.

NOTES

This chapter was written in cooperation with Professor André Kaspi (Sorbonne), Professor Claude Tapia (Université de Tours), Sophie Kessler-Mesguich (Ecole des Hautes Etudes du Judaïsme, Paris), and Alain Dieckhoff (Conseil National de la Recherche Scientifique, Paris). I am grateful to Mr. A. Dieckhoff for his helpful suggestions.

1. Jacques Thobie, *Intérêts et impérialisme français dans l'empire ottoman (1895–1914)* (Paris: Publications de la Sorbonne, 1977), 817.

2. The French consulate in Jerusalem was opened at the end of 1842; the first consul to be appointed there was Count Gabriel de Lantivy. See Maurice Degor, "Les créations de postes diplomatiques et consulaires françaises de 1815 à 1870," *Revue d'Histoire Diplomatique*, 100ᵉ année, 1–2 (1986): 25-64; René Neuville, *Heurts et malheurs des consuls de France à Jérusalém aux 17e, 18e, et 19e siècles* (Jerusalem: [n.p.], 1947–1948).

3. Pierre Sorlin, *La croix et les juifs, 1880–1899: contribution à l'histoire de l'antisémitisme contemporain* (Paris: B. Grasset, 1967), 345; Catherine Nicault, La France

et le sionisme (1896–1914) (Ph.D. diss., Sorbonne, 1985), vol. 1, pp. 306-10.

4. C. Nicault (above, n.3), pp. 311-15. The subject catalogue (1894–1925) of the Bibliothèque Nationale in Paris lists more than sixty titles.

5. Philippe Berthelot, Secretary General of the Quai d'Orsay, had intended to visit Syria, Lebanon, and Palestine early in 1926. A translation of his statements to *Doar Hayom* of 16 February 1926 was sent to Paris by the French consul in Jerusalem, Gaston Maugras (Ministère des Affaires Etrangères [MAE], Levant-Palestine, vol. 29, dispatch dated 22 February 1926). Apparently this visit did not take place; see Jean-Luc Barré, *Le Seigneur-Chat, Philippe Berthelot, 1866–1934* (Paris: Plon, 1988).

6. Joseph Kessel was sent by *Le Journal* in 1926, and Albert Londres by *Excelsior* in 1929.

7. A note dated 8 December 1926 by Louis Canet, in charge of religious affairs and Jewish questions at the Quai d'Orsay, mentioned, for example, a request made by André Spire on behalf of fifteen *halutzim* who were forced to come to France because of unemployment (MAE, Levant-Palestine, vol. 29, p. 86).

8. Sophie Kessler-Mesguich is preparing a thesis entitled "Les études hébraïques en France du 16e au 18e siècles: grammaires et enseignement."

9. The Chair of Modern Hebrew was created there in 1926–1927 through the efforts of the Comité France-Palestine, which was established in 1925.

10. Paul-Emile Botta is best known in the history of archaeology for his excavations in Mesopotamia.

11. The Louvre, 1660–1664.

12. The Dijon Museum, 1853.

13. Chapelle des Saint-Agnes in the Saint Sulpice Church in Paris, 1861.

14. Cabinet des dessins, the Louvre, 1876.

15. Maxime du Camp (1822–1894) recalled his apprenticeship with a photographer in preparation for this journey in his *Souvenirs littéraires* (Paris: Hachette, 1882–1883). In 1852 he published an album entitled *Egypte, Nubie, Palestine et Syrie: dessins photographiques recueillis pendant les années 1849, 1850 et 1851* (Paris: Gide et J. Bundry, 1852). This is the first book to be illustrated with photographs.

16. See, for example, Pierre Bonardi, *Le retour à Jérusalém, avec 64 dessins inédits de Feder* (Paris: Andre Delpeuch, 1927).

17. Louis Bertrand, "L'enchantement de la mer Morte" and "En Gedi," *La Revue des Deux Mondes* (1 May 1910): 129 and (1 June 1910): 575; also André Chevrillon, "En Judée," *Le Revue des deux Mondes* (15 March 1893): 292; le Marquis de Voguë, "Jérusalem, hier et aujourd'hui, notes de voyage", *Le Correspondant* (25 June 1911): 1041; and others. The primary source material for this study appears in Jean-Claude Berchet's anthology, *Le voyage en Orient, anthologie des voyageurs français dans le Levant au 19e siècle* (Paris: Robert Laffont, 1985). Interesting elements are also found in Shalev Ginossar's study, *Voyage littéraire en Terre Promise* (Paris-Geneva: Champion, Slatkine, 1986).

18. Massignon appears to have visited Jerusalem twenty-eight times, the first of which was in 1917 with General Allenby. See Dominique Bourel, "Six lettres de Louis Massignon à Martin Buber," *Pardés* 2 (1985): 173-81.

19. C. Nicault (above, n.3).

20. Charles Gide came to Palestine in 1925 to attend the opening ceremonies of The Hebrew University of Jerusalem. It was then that he discovered the kibbutzim. An advocate of cooperation, defined as a compromise between capitalism and collectivism,

Gide sponsored cooperatives for production and distribution in the Languedoc region, under Protestant management.

21. Philippe Boukara is preparing a dissertation entitled ''Marc Jarblum, sioniste français (1887–1972): socialisme et politique juive.''

22. Ruth Rishin of the University of California at Berkeley is at present working on the life and work of David Knout, who played an important role in the Jewish Resistance in France during the Nazi occupation.

23. These ties are noted in André Kaspi, ''La France et la reconnaissance de l'Etat d'Israël (mai 1948-janvier 1949),'' *Enjeux et puissance: pour une histoire des relations internationales au 20e siècle: mélanges en l'honneur de Jean-Baptiste Duroselle* (Paris: Publications de la Sorbonne, 1986), 319-29. Regarding the relationship between political parties in France and in Palestine, see David Lazar, *L'opinion française et la naissance de l'Etat d'Israël, 1945–1949* (Paris: Calmann-Levy, 1972); Jacques Derogy, *Histoire de l'exodus: la loi de retour* (Paris: Fayard, 1969).

24. Francois Delpech, ''Les chrétiens et la Terre Sainte: suggestions pour une meilleure approche du problème de Jérusalem,'' *Sur les juifs, études d'histoire contemporaine* (Lyon: Presses Universitaires de Lyon, 1983), 391-471.

25. J. Thobie (above, n.1); C. Nicault (above, n.3); Sergio I. Minerbi, *L'Italie et la Palestine, 1914–1920* (Paris: Presses Universitaires de France, 1970); Isaiah Friedman, *Germany, Turkey and Zionism, 1897–1918* (Oxford: Clarendon Press, 1977); Rashid I. Khalidi, *British Policy toward Syria and Palestine, 1906–1914* (London: Ithaca Press, 1980).

26. C. Andrew and Kanya-Forstner, ''La France à la recherche de la Syrie intégrale, 1914–1920,'' *Relations Internationales* 19 (Autumn 1979): 263-78.

27. There was a Palestinian booth at the Exposition Universelle held in May 1937 in Paris.

28. Jean-Marc Chouraqui is at present preparing a thesis on nineteenth century rabbinical writings (University of Aix-en-Provence).

29. Antoine Halff is preparing a thesis on Zadoc Kahn, under the direction of Professor François Furet (Ecole des Hautes Etudes en Sciences Sociales, Paris) entitled ''Aux origines françaises du sionisme: le grand rabbin Zadoc Kahn.''

30. See C. Nicault (above, n.3); Nelly Las, ''Les juifs de France et le sionisme de l'Affaire Dreyfus à la seconde guerre mondiale (1896–1939)'' (Ph.D. diss., Israel, 1985).

31. See Renée Poznansky, ''La Résistance juive en France,'' *Revue d'Histoire de la Seconde Guerre mondiale et des conflits contemporains* 137 (January 1985): 3-32; Lucien Lazare, *La résistance juive en France* (Paris: Stock, 1987).

32. Doris Bensimon-Donath (Professor, University of Caen and INALCO, France) studies the French *aliyah* in her *Les juifs de France et leur relations avec Israël, 1945–1988* (Paris: L'Harmattan, 1989).

33. François Delpech has already made a general study of this congregation: ''Notre Dame de Sion et les juifs. Réflexions sur le Père Théodore Ratisbonne et sur l'évolution de la Congrégation de Notre Dame de Sion depuis les origines,'' in *Sur les juifs* (above, n.24), 321-71.

Chapter 9

French Archives as a Source for the Study of France–Holy Land Relations

Ran Aaronsohn

French archives are a little-known but rich source for the study of France–Holy Land relations. Relevant material is housed in four types of archival repositories: Public institutional archives; Jewish institutional archives; Christian institutional archives; and private collections.

Public Institutional Archives. These include *Les Archives Nationales Françaises*, *La Bibliothèque Nationale*, *L'Institut de France* (collections of the National Academy of Arts and Sciences), *Les Archives du Ministère des Affaires Etrangères*, *Les Chambres de Commerce* throughout France (particularly the one in Marseilles), and regional archives of the Départements (administrative units of government).

Jewish Institutional Archives. Among these are archives of the *Alliance Israélite Universelle*, *Le Consistoire Central in Paris*, and records of the local and regional Jewish communities throughout France, such as those of Alsace: *Consistoire d'Haguenau*, *Consistoire de Strasbourg*, and so on.

Christian Institutional Archives. Especially important are those of French Catholic religious orders that were active in Palestine. Among these are the *Pères de l'Assomption*, *Dominicains*, *Franciscains*, *Soeurs de St. Josef*, *Filles de Charité*, and *Soeurs de Sion*.

Private Collections. These are held by descendants of individuals or families who were involved in some way with Palestine (e.g., the collection of Mme.

This analysis is based on a survey begun in the 1980/81 academic year (while studying at the Université de Paris IV—Sorbonne) and completed during another visit in 1986. I would like to express thanks to the Ministère des Sciences and the Attaché Culturale in Israel for supporting the research.

Levi-Schied, located in Biarritz), or they are collections with no family or other connection to the Holy Land.

From the point of view of accessibility, the four types of archives may be categorized in two main groups: Public and Jewish institutional archives; and Christian institutional archives and private collections.

Public and Jewish Institutional Archives. Most of the relevant material is located in Paris. Much of the material is organized in record groups, or in collections that document the activities of various government or other public bodies, and of Jewish organizations. In government archives there are, as well, collections of personal papers of individuals who served France in a public or private capacity in connection with the Holy Land.

Christian Institutional Archives and Private Collections. In those instances where collections are systematized, material is generally arranged by topic. Relevant material is interspersed with other information on a particular subject. Whereas the institutional archives are generally located in Paris, private collections are scattered throughout France.

The following samples, culled from three important government and Jewish institutional archives, concern France–Holy Land relations in the last quarter of the nineteenth century. Information in parentheses pertains to box or folder location. This chapter does not pretend to provide a complete picture of the relevant material housed in France, or even a representative sample of it. It is aimed at presenting the character of chosen archives and some types of primary sources housed there, as a basis for research on the relationship between France and the Holy Land.

ARCHIVES NATIONALES FRANÇAISES

Among the many relevant collections are the following: *Ministère de Commerce et Industrie*, *Ministère de Cultures*, and Archives of the House of Rothschild. The first and second consist of government records, the third of private papers.

Ministère de Commerce et Industrie. Included are commercial reports of consuls in Jaffa (1863–1904) and Jerusalem (1870–1891), and of vice-consuls in Haifa (1893–1906). Among the latter is a thirty-page annual report on commercial and maritime activities in Haifa (1892), which lists imports and exports by product and country. France, surpassed only by Turkey, was the second largest source of imports through Haifa port. The major item was clothing; animal hides and roof tiles were among other products imported. France was also the prime market for exports from this port. During 1892, more than 50 percent of the products shipped from Haifa (valued at 1,890,000 francs) were destined for delivery there. The principal export, sesame seeds, was sent almost exclusively to France.

Appendix 1 provides a summary, in translation, of this report, typical of many sent regularly to the ministry.

Ministère de Cultures. Here there are a considerable number of documents relating to visits of travelers, pilgrims, and missionaries to Palestine (1876–1891). Included are lists of pilgrims to the Holy Land (March 1883 through June 1884) arranged according to place of residence in France, and a list of the thirty-three missionary-envoys to Palestine in the summer of 1886 (various documents, Box F19/3136).

Archives of the House of Rothschild (one collection). This is the only Rothschild collection accessible to researchers (under specific conditions, and upon the approval of the Rothschild family). There is substantial documentation of the family's widespread business affairs. They had no business connections with the Holy Land, but there is extensive information about the philanthropic activities of the Rothschilds on behalf of the Jewish urban communities in Eretz Israel, particularly in Jerusalem and Hebron. A major beneficiary was the Rothschild Hospital, funded by donations sent by the family through an intermediary, the Jerusalem banker Yaacov Valero. Several large one-time transfers were made, such as one totalling 180,000 francs in 1886, probably to acquire land for the construction of the new hospital to be built outside the Old City walls on the Street of the Prophets (Frères Rothschild, 132AQ/16L10, 26L17).

ARCHIVES DU MINISTERE DES AFFAIRES ETRANGERES (MAE)

Included are reports and correspondence of French consuls in Jerusalem, consuls and vice-consuls in Jaffa and Haifa, and consular agents in Safed and Tiberias. Also included are dispatches of general consuls in Beirut and Damascus whose sphere of responsibility included northern portions of Palestine, in accordance with the administrative structure of the Ottoman Empire. These records have been grouped in sections: Correspondance Consulaire et Commerciale; Correspondance Politique et Commerciale; Archives Diplomatiques Rapatriées de Beyrouth; and Correspondance Politique.

Correspondance Consulaire et Commerciale (CCC). One example is a volume of reports by consuls in Jaffa (1887–1897). It contains a comprehensive report forty-three pages in length on the economic situation in Palestine. This report provides detailed information, *inter alia*, on maritime commerce (imports and exports moving through the port of Jaffa), domestic transportation (the Jaffa-Jerusalem railway), and various agricultural projects (CCC Jaffa 1887–1897, *sans numéro*, 30.6.1896).

Appendix 3 provides data about agricultural products exported from Haifa, selected from another detailed document written by the consul general of France in Beirut.

Correspondance Politique et Commerciale (CPC). In this collection there are twelve volumes relating to Palestine in the 1880s. Among many other items, these document the construction of French religious institutions in the Holy Land, such as the church at Abu Ghosh, the Sainte Anne Church, and the Terra Sancta compound in Jerusalem, including maps, sketches, and photographs (CPC Jérusalem 16, 1886; 18, 1888; 23, 1897; various pages).

There are reports pertaining to French educational institutions in Palestine and neighboring regions that include information about each of the schools established by the French, with maps showing their location (CPC Beyrouth 31, 1888; 38, 1894; Jerusalem 23, 1891). There is correspondence concerning financial aid given by the French government to each of the institutions—a total of 104,108 francs to twenty-two schools (CPC Jérusalem 23, 1891), a detailed list of Western powers' educational institutions in the Galilee, and so on.

Appendix 2 consists of part of a report concerning those institutions that relate to Jewish schools (CPC Beyrouth 31, 1888).

The collection is also a source for information about topics including the following: health and medical conditions in Palestine; postal and transportation services; competition between representatives of France and other European powers (with particular reference to the Holy Places); the attitude of the Ottoman authorities toward Jewish immigration and settlement in Palestine, and toward foreigners in general (incorporating the French reaction).

Archives Diplomatiques Rapatriées de Beyrouth (located in Nantes). This small collection includes correspondence between the vice-consul in Haifa and consular agents in Safed and Tiberias, and with the general consuls in Beirut to whom they were responsible. Contents relate particularly to the protection of the rights and property of French citizens in the north of Palestine. These were generally local, resident Jews, Muslims, and Christians (mostly of Algerian origin) who held French citizenship or enjoyed French protection. The consular agents in Safed, who were members of the Abo family, were Algerian Jews. Documents in this collection are in Hebrew and Arabic as well as French (Caiffa, *sans numéro*, 1882–1890; Saffed et Tiberiade, *sans numéro*, 1882–1890).

Correspondance Politique (CP). This collection, in a group of files entitled "Nouvelle Série, Turquie-Politique Intérieure," contains essential information about France–Holy Land relationships in the late nineteenth century and on the eve of World War I. The files entitled "N.S. Turquie–Palestine, Dossier Général" (volumes 129 to 135) include consular correspondence dealing with every subject of interest to French policy in late Ottoman Palestine (Capitulations, protection of Christians, Jewish immigration, French officials' attitude toward Alliance schools and Baron's colonies, etc.). The following files (volumes 136 to 138) entitled "N.S. Turquie–Sionisme" deal essentially with Zionism as opposed to French cultural influence in the whole eastern Mediterranean area, with some important information on Palestine scattered through them, too.

ARCHIVES CENTRALES DE L'ALLIANCE ISRAELITE UNIVERSELLE (AIU)

Of special interest in these archives are documents relating to Jewish interests in the Holy Land, particularly the development of AIU educational institutions in Eretz Israel, which were supported and administered from headquarters in Paris. At the end of the nineteenth century these included schools in Haifa, Jerusalem, and Mikveh Israel near Jaffa.

There is extensive correspondence with Shmuel Hirsch, principal of the Mikveh Israel agricultural school from 1879 to 1891 (Series Israel XXXVIII), which includes information about subjects such as banking services, agriculture, and Jewish immigration. There is also material dealing with the establishment of the colonies (*moshavot*) of the First Aliyah, and communications between Baron Edmond de Rothschild, who supported the new Jewish settlement movement, and the Alliance, many of whose staff in Eretz Israel were in his employ.

There is a report on agricultural conditions in Mikveh Israel in 1883, giving details about the experimental export of wine and oranges to Paris through agents in Marseilles and Lyon, and the import of "oranges d'été" through Nice (E 120/b, 26.3.1884). Interesting, too, is the correspondence regarding the drilling of wells in the Jaffa region, between a French hydraulic engineer located in Paris and a Jew from Palestine who studied with him there, as well as with the employees of Baron de Rothschild and members of the Jewish settlements in Eretz Israel (E120/f, 17.1.1888, 24.3.1888, 30.10.1888). There is also information concerning two Jews from Palestine who studied wine-making in Bordeaux under a subsidy from the AIU, and about a French barrel-maker who was sent by Baron de Rothschild to Rishon Le-Zion, the location of the first modern winery in Palestine (E120/g, 25.12.1889).

SUMMARY

The French archives, like any other sources of material for research, have their advantages and disadvantages. The public archives listed in this chapter are selective by definition: They normally focus on specific targets. The fact that the documents therein were written mostly by outside observers of Palestine should be kept in mind. The documents of the Foreign Ministry—perhaps the most important collection—deal with macro-issues: mostly with international commerce, but to some extent with domestic trade or the economic activity of the local population. Concerning the educational institutions, for instance, we learn only about matters that serve French interests, not about the students themselves. Thus, the image, interesting and vivid as it is, does not provide the whole picture.

All are selected examples of archival material from a vast, virtually untapped lode in French repositories. A comprehensive survey of these repositories and other research institutions, both in France and Israel, would lead to identification and evaluation of relevant groups of records and individual documents. Such an effort can provide a basis for research projects and university study of France–Holy Land relations.

APPENDIX 1

Vice-Consul of France in Haifa, 1.10.1893
Report on Commercial and Maritime Trade in Haifa, 1892 (Summary)

Imports through the Haifa Port
The total value of imported goods arriving in Haifa in 1892 was 2,140,000 francs. The main import was clothing, followed, in decreasing order, by building lumber, rice, indigo, woven cloth and materials, and metal utensils.

Other than Turkey and regions of the Ottoman Empire, the country providing most imports was France, which directly shipped clothing, hides, and roof tiles (in order of economic importance). If, however, one takes into consideration imports that reached Haifa indirectly, via Beirut and ports in Egypt, imports from Austria exceeded those from France.

Exports through the Haifa Port
The total value of exported goods in 1892 was 1,890,000 francs. The primary destination of over 50 percent of all exports from Haifa was France. The value of the goods shipped to France was more than three times the value of those shipped to Turkey, and seven times the value of goods exported to England or Italy. The primary export, sesame, was shipped almost entirely to France. The second most important export was wheat, exported mainly to Turkey and Italy. Other agricultural products were exported in small quantities.

Trade in Haifa and the Region
In 1892, 280 ships docked at the Haifa port, averaging 600 tons per ship. (Details of maritime shipping in various categories are given in tables attached to the report.)

There are no paved roads, despite the fact that the number of pilgrims would argue for the construction of roads to handle carriages. Under these circumstances, in the good (dry) season, the trip from Haifa to Acre takes two hours; to Nazareth, six hours; and to Jaffa, about eighteen hours of riding. . . . About three years ago, an Englishman, Mr. Pilling, tried to construct railroad tracks from Haifa, through Acre, to Damascus, and to build a port in Haifa; work on the port was barely undertaken, and only ten kilometers of the railroad tracks were laid . . .

Source: Archives Nationales–Ministère de Commerce et Industrie, F12/7193: Caiffa (1883–1906), 30 pp.

APPENDIX 2
Les Écoles des Colonies Juives et le Consulat Français
(partie du rapport sur les établissements scolaires)

"Les Israélites ont en Syrie des écoles purement hébreïques où l'enseignement est spécial. Elles portent le nom de Talmud Torah. A Beyrouth 350 élèves les fréquentent; á Damas elles comptent 650 enfants.

Aux environs de Nazareth, M. Edmond de Rothschild a fondé une colonie israélite qui porte le nom de Zammarin. Il y a là des juifs de toutes les nations. A leur tête se trouve un français qui a reclamé pour sa colonie la protection française. Nous n'avons pu la lui donner officiellement, mais je lui viens officiellement en aide. Une ou deux écoles ont été ouvertes à Zammarin, mais je les crois entretenues par M. de Rothschild. Je ne parle pas des centres israélites tels que Saffed où nombre de petites écoles rudimentaires ont été ouvertes depuis plusieurs années."

Source: Archives de Ministère des Affaires Etrangères, CPC Turquie-Beyrouth 31 (Janvier-Juin 1888), pp. 223 bis–224.

APPENDIX 3
Consul Générale de France à Beyrouth, 22.5.1889
Rapport sur la situation économique, pour l'année 1888 (data choisi)

Produit Exporté	Quantités (kgs) Acre	Haifa	Valeurs (frs.) Acre	Haifa	Destinations Principales
Blé	41,160,000	13,729,000	5,214,420	1,708,140	Italie
Sésames	2,900,000	?	?	?	France (Marseille)
Maïs	2,100,000	—	210,000	—	Algérie
Orge	1,667,504	—	152,410	—	Angleterre, Turquie
Fèves	660,000	—	80,520	—	Angleterre
Pois chiches	262,500	—	34,912	—	Turquie, Angleterre
Lentilles	158,000	—	15,770	—	France (Marseille)
Racines	?	—	?	—	Amerique

Source: Archives du Ministè des Affaires Etrangères—CCC
Beyrouth 10 (1889), pp. 159–170

Chapter 10

France and the Holy Land: Introducing the Subject in French Universities

Sophie Kessler-Mesguich

The France-Holy Land nexus is a two-term expression. But a third element should be added: the *religious* (Jewish or Christian) value attached to the concept of Holy Land or Eretz Israel. Reference to library files, thesis topics, and university course titles shows that generally these three terms are thought of in pairs. From the Jewish perspective, the stress is laid on the dual topics of France and (French) Judaism. The reason for this is without doubt the special history of Jews in France: Emancipation and assimilation are the prime factors that have determined a specifically French-Jewish identity. Thus, a great deal of work has been done on the "internal" development of French Jewry, while in the area of France–Holy Land (Palestine, Israel) relations, the study is primarily sociological, such as how Israel is perceived by French Jews, or the role of French Jews in Zionism. However, when the France–Holy Land relationship has actually been explored, this has often been from a Christian point of view (i.e., as a location where Christ lived), while the third term has been ignored. Initially, therefore, we should adopt the broadest possible approach without excluding any of the areas, and only later should we select more restricted subjects according to the context in which they are to be addressed, such as Jewish or general teaching.

In this chapter, we shall deal with three main issues: Teaching and research possibilities within existing academic structures; suggestions for the integration of Jewish studies in French universities; and special topics for the study of France and the Holy Land.

JEWISH STUDIES IN FRENCH UNIVERSITIES

A survey of the curricula of various Hebrew studies departments indicates that apparently there are no special courses on France-Israel relations, although they might be dealt with in seminars at the masters or doctoral level. Thus, an important potential exists here, particularly as a Chair in Contemporary Jewish History has just been established at Aix-en-Provence. Specific proposals for teaching and research topics developed during International Center workshops could be passed on to the departments concerned. For example, there might be a masters seminar on France and the Holy Land, bringing together students working within different historical periods. The exchange of various points of view makes possible a wide-ranging approach to the topic.

As has already been said, France–Holy Land studies should not be confined within the boundaries of Jewish or Hebrew courses. On the contrary, it can perfectly well be included in Teaching and Research Units (Unités de Formation et de Recherche—UFR) that have no fundamental connection with Judaism: Literature (French writers and the Holy Land), history (French policy on the Holy Land relative to the whole of the Middle East), philosophy (e.g., problematic aspects of exile, of the concept of land). However, this very process of integration generates certain problems, linked on the one hand to the specific structure of French universities, and on the other hand to the place to which Jewish Civilization studies should aspire within these universities. Before considering the methodological and analytical aspects of our topic, we need first to consider the more general problem of ethnic studies and their position in the educational structure.

CURRENT DEVELOPMENT

Many para-universities and other centers for study are currently being established. In 1984, for example, the Paris Jewish Studies Center (le Centre Rashi) together with the University of Paris 1 introduced a university diploma in Jewish studies, *Diplôme universitaire d'études juives* (DUEJ). The curriculum defines as its goal to provide "in a strictly scientific spirit general and specific education, to impart knowledge of Judaism and encourage research in the field." This original approach, the first involving cooperation between a Jewish institution and a university, requires eight "general" credits to be taken from the various subjects taught at Paris 1 (history, geography, philosophy, ancient or modern languages, social sciences) and twelve "specific" credits relating to various Jewish areas and taught at le Centre Rashi (for example, modern Hebrew, biblical exegesis, introduction to the Talmud, Jewish medieval and contemporary history and thought). After overcoming the initial difficulties that are inevitable in a new venture, this program is now moving along smoothly.

Various other study possibilities have been created in Paris. The University of Paris 4 (Sorbonne) now has its own *Centre d'études juives* (Jewish Studies

Center), which provides several seminars and lectures related to Jewish art, literature, and civilization, including the Jewish languages (Hebrew, Judeo-Spanish, Yiddish). In 1986, the *Fonds Social juif unifié* (FSJU) together with the *Fonds d'investissement pour l'éducation* (FIPE) set up a Community University for Young Leadership. This is a purely private initiative, but the choice of the term "university" is a revealing one. The *Alliance Israélite* also organizes a series of seminars. Jewish education is thus currently endeavoring to model itself along university lines, adopting the rigorous and scientific standards required by such an approach.

In the field of research, the *Institut national des langues et civilisations orientales* (INALCO) in 1986 set up an *Ecole des hautes études de judaïsme* (whose very title alludes to the most prestigious French institutes of higher education). The aim of this School of Higher Jewish Studies is to "promote on the highest level the teaching, research, and development of Hebrew and Jewish studies." Students in these areas can attend a range of seminars (philosophy, history, sociology of Judaism, educational sciences applied to Judaism, Jewish languages) that will allow them to acquire more in-depth knowledge in a particular area.

In addition to these initiatives on the university level, there are other indications of broader interest in a scientific approach to Judaism. French translations are being produced of the Midrash, kabbalistic texts, and the writings of great Jewish thinkers of the past.[1] A number of German Jewish philosophical works, previously unknown to the French public, have been appearing.[2] Publications in 1986 included a scholarly introduction to Talmud studies,[3] and a philosophical work.[4] Major works on Kabbalah have also appeared,[5] and a paperback series on Jewish thought has been prepared for the general public.[6] Finally, several scientific and cultural journals are appearing. Apart from the scholarly *Revue des Etudes Juives*, which dates back to the last century and is read mainly in learned circles, there are *Yod* (which concentrates on Hebrew languages and literature), *Pardés* (philosophy and history), *Les Nouveau Cahiers* (all aspects of Jewish culture), and *Traces* (focusing on Diaspora Jewry).

"ETHNIC STUDIES" AND MINORITY CULTURES

This growth in Jewish studies raises the question of the position of such studies. At a juncture where nothing is more fashionable than the concept of cultural minorities, what should be the place of Judaism?

It is commonly said that French universities are Jacobinic and centralist in nature. However, recent years have witnessed in France, as in other countries of Europe, growing recognition of the value of minority languages and cultures— all in the cause of the right to be different. In this spirit, in October 1981 the European Parliament adopted a resolution recommending the various states "to authorize everywhere the teaching of the literature and history of the communities concerned" (i.e., those whose culture is considered a "minority" one within a given national community).

In France, the February 1982 Giordan Report, presented to the Ministry of Cultural Affairs under the title "Cultural Democracy and the Right to be Different," argues for respecting linguistic and cultural differences. This report classifies the Jewish community with "non-territorial linguistic and cultural minorities" such as the Gypsies and Armenians, as opposed to "territorial" minorities (Basques, Bretons, Occitanians). However, the Jewish situation is ambiguous: Should the stress be laid on its existence as a cultural minority, or on its universalism? Integration in universities would certainly differ according to the option selected. The Giordan Report takes account of this issue when it states: "It must not be forgotten that these various linguistic anchors (Yiddish, Judeo-Spanish, Judeo-Arabic, Hebrew) are not exclusive of the recognition of a *Jewish cultural identity expressed through the medium of the French language*" (emphasis added). Given what already exists, what strategy should be adopted in order to encourage growth in this area?

INTEGRATING THE SUBJECT IN THE FRENCH UNIVERSITY SYSTEM

First, it should be stressed that Hebrew and Jewish studies have only recently been introduced into French universities. The numbers of such departments have increased thanks to the efforts of Professor René-Samuel Sirat, Chief Rabbi of France from 1980 to 1987, and Head of the INALCO Hebrew studies department. Fifteen years ago, it was not easy to find academic advisors for research on Jewish subjects (the same still holds true for certain universities, particularly in philosophy departments). Today, apart from the two Paris universities (Paris 3 and 4) that have complete Hebrew courses, there are many credit courses—and this is what interests us—with Jewish content located in other departments. For example, the English department of Paris 8 offers credit courses on the American Jewish novel, while Paris 7, through the Jewish-American Study Center, offers credit courses in Yiddish and Jewish history. Outside Paris, the universities of Lille, Lyon, and Strasbourg prepare students for the university diploma in Jewish studies and a B.A. in Hebrew (and sometimes also for teaching and Ph.D. examinations). However, many other universities include Hebrew and Jewish history in their history, French, and modern languages departments. Section 4 (historical and philological studies) of the *Ecole pratique des hautes études* (EPHE) offers high-level courses in Hebrew and Aramaic, comparative Semitic studies, and medieval Hebrew paleography; Section 5 (religious studies) has three chairs in Judaism: Talmudic and Rabbinic, Hellenistic and Roman, Medieval and Modern.

In the area of Jewish history, we noted previously the establishment of a Chair at the University of Aix-en-Provence, as an example of the teaching vitality to which we referred. Another noteworthy item is the existence of an *Association pour la recherche sur l'histoire contemporaine des juifs* (RHICOJ), set up by a group of young historians and researchers who have organized a symposium and contributed to a Jewish history textbook for use in schools and universities.

Thus, there are three different approaches:(1) University-style teaching given in a "private" center, as in the case of the *Centre universitaire d'études juives* (CUEJ); (2) university departments of Hebrew studies; and (3) credit courses in Jewish subjects that are integrated into "general" departments. The DUEJ, the *modus operandi* of which has been described already, is an original combination, possibly to be placed in the third category. Growth is particularly likely in the area of such "hybrid" courses. Let us consider the example of philosophy. There is no Chair of Jewish philosophy or Jewish thought in any general philosophy and research unit in France. In other words, philosophy students can complete their entire course without having any contact whatsoever with medieval or modern Jewish thought. This deficiency could be corrected through close association between a Jewish studies center and a university, because then options could be offered that would allow an introduction to Jewish thought to be included in general philosophy studies.

From this vantage, the topic of France and the Holy Land, precisely because of its wide scope, could usefully be the subject of research in many spheres, thereby encouraging the training of academic staff who are not specialists in Judaism but who are interested in acquiring knowledge in this area. The advantage of such a development is that it takes account at one and the same time of Jewish specificity and of integration into universities, thus avoiding the "ghetto" effect—which sometimes threatens Jewish teaching and which current developments are striving to counter.

What conclusions can be drawn from this brief review of Jewish studies in France? The framework encourages us to be relatively optimistic; today, solid yet flexible structures exist almost everywhere. At crisis-racked universities, which feel out of step with the needs of today's world and are querying their future, when the humanities are being increasingly dropped by students who feel that they offer uncertain employment possibilities (apart from teaching), vigilance must be maintained to ensure the requisite standard of quality and scholarship. In the light of this state of affairs, and of the general framework of Jewish studies in France, we must now analyze the topic before us and seek to identify all its possibilities.

SOURCES AND ANALYSIS OF TERMS

Sources

There are many scattered sources dealing with relations between France and the Holy Land. Some have already been classified and studied; many of them are still unpublished. Clearly, such sources can gradually be organized and analyzed as topics of research at the masters and doctoral levels. The following categories can be identified: the press, archives, rabbinical sermons, literature, and the arts.

The press, Jewish and non-Jewish. This is definitely a prime research tool for historians and researchers in the area of relations between France and Palestine prior to 1948. There are two works, for example, that use the press as their material (and similar methods could be extended to other periods): David Lazar, *L'opinion française et la naissance de l'Etat d'Israël 1945–1949*; Jean-William Lapierre, *L'information sur l'Etat d'Israël dans les grands quotidiens français en 1958.*[7] Possibly more than any other source, the press reflects public opinion and its fluctuations. For example, in 1960, a special issue of *Le Figaro*, printed in both French and Hebrew (a technical feat at the time), gave an enthusiastic presentation of the young state's achievements and potential in all areas. More recently, stress has been laid on the influence of the media upon French public reaction to the Lebanon War.

Archives. These are scattered throughout France (*Archives Nationales, Alliance Israélite, Commission française des archives juives*, and other repositories) and Israel. In order to research an issue such as relations between French Socialists and Zionists, it would be necessary to carry out a systematic study of the archives of the political parties and major trade unions in both countries. This would shed interesting light on a little-researched area in Zionist history.

Rabbinical sermons. These are clearly a mine of information on French Jews' perception of the Holy Land, on both the religious and political level; university research on this issue is currently being carried out.

Literature. This is a vast field. Throughout the nineteenth century the *"journey to the Orient"* (with biblical echoes as a special feature of travels in Palestine) was a basic reference, as shown by the extensive anthology of Jean Claude Berchet, entitled *Le voyage en Orient.*[8]

The arts. Palestine has been a major area of inspiration for painters, engravers, and photographers. A variety of sources exist, which should be examined and studied systematically.

Analysis of Terms

Holy Land. Each of the French designations of this area, which is simultaneously geographical, symbolic, and religious, has a precise significance and cannot be used interchangeably. In English one may use *Holy Land*, but in France *Terre Sainte* has a specifically Christian connotation. It is the use of the adjective *saint* (holy) that provides this coloring: *la sainte Bible, l'Ecriture sainte* (and particularly *les saintes Ecritures*) are also Christian expressions. (A French language *histoire sainte* textbook for ''Israelite youth'' was once published, but at a time when the term ''temple'' was used in French for ''synagogue.'') It should be noted that in French the term *terre sainte* (lower case) designates ''sanctified ground, consecrated for the burial of the faithful''—(Littré), that is, a sanctified cemetery (or a church). The 1690 Furetiére Dictionary, which reproduces this definition, adds: "above all else, the name *Holy Land* is given to Palestine, and *holy city* to Jerusalem, because there God worked the mysteries of our redemption." The Robert Dictionary (1985, new edition) gives the following definition of Holy Land: "where Christ lived, according to the Gospels."

If we wish to highlight further the implications of this expression, we must contrast it with others. The term "Palestine" has two different accepted meanings: either historic/geographic (in particular to designate ancient times) or highly political. The political meaning has in fact varied over time, as can be seen from the fact that in 1925 the France-Palestine Committee was Zionist! From 1948 on, "Israel" emerges, designating the State (while continuing to designate the Jewish People by metonymy). More rarely, the term "Zion" is found (with Jewish or Christian religious connotations, or with political connotation in Zionist texts).

All of these terms have complex interrelations, which should be analyzed. An interesting exercise would be to trace the development in these terms (Holy Land → Palestine → Israel) through library "subject" indexes. The French National Library (which generally acts as a model for the others) used the key word "Holy Land" until 1925, and then replaced it altogether with "Palestine" and "Israel."

In a society where religious values are important, the expression "Holy Land" has a symbolic power of evocation. This becomes clear in the narratives of nineteenth-century travelers. Chateaubriand was "filled with fear and awe" when he saw the Carmel:

> I was about to set foot on the land of miracles, of the sources of the most sublime poetry, the site of, even humanly speaking, the greatest event to have ever changed the face of the world, that is to say the coming of the Messiah; I was about to land on these shores, which had been visited before me by Godfrey of Bouillon, Raimon de Saint-Gilles. . . . and this Saint Louis, whose virtues were admired by the Infidels.[9]

The reason for this extensive quotation is that it demonstrates the two basic elements subsumed in the expression "Holy Land"—the Christian faith, and the Crusades. However, as French society has become increasingly secular, the expression has naturally lost its force; in current usage, it is practically used only by travel agencies offering trips "in the footsteps of Jesus."

France. While the term "Holy Land" creates semantic problems, the concept of "France" requires clarification of a more historical nature. The Middle Ages (above all, the period of the Crusades) is an important chapter on its own in the study of France–Holy Land relations; this would perhaps be best dealt with in another study, in light of the special scholarly fields involved. We would, however, stress the importance of this period, from both the political (recovery of the holy places) and religious/symbolic points of view.

Having said this, clearly the richest period for our topic is that from the time of Napoleon I to modern times, with its many links between France and Palestine in the political, diplomatic, economic, religious, and cultural spheres. Before commenting on these points, it should be noted that we essentially considered the expression France *and* the Holy Land from the French perspective. However, it is most instructive (as Catherine Nicault has emphasized) occasionally to reverse directions and see what contribution Palestine has made to France in all these areas.

(1) A separate political analysis should be prepared of French territorial ambitions in the region (from the time of Bonaparte to that of the Syrian/Lebanese Mandate) and their influence on the Zionist movement.

(2) France has played an important economic role in the region, initially as a Mandatory power, and then by investing in Palestine proper. With reference to the contemporary period (after 1948), an economist could study Franco-Israeli economic relationships, as affected by the political situation (embargoes, Arab boycotts, etc.)

(3) From the (Christian) religious point of view, France has a physical presence in the Holy Land in the form of numerous missions or churches. Here, too, change has occurred in French policy; for example, the question of the Holy Places is to some extent contingent upon Church-State relations. From the sociological point of view, it would be interesting to conduct surveys of Catholics and Protestants visiting the Holy Land today. Having come there to return to the founts of their faith and gaze upon the landscape of the Bible, what have they seen of contemporary Israel, and what for them is the relationship between these two images?

(4) Finally, in the area of cultural exchanges, the immediate reference is to the fundamental role played by *l'Ecole biblique de Jérusalem*, particularly in the archaeological sphere. Herein lie interesting research possibilities.

As has been seen, there are many aspects to "France" as a concept; thus, depending on the aspect selected, a variety of research projects can be carried out. However, as indicated, we must not ignore the Holy Land perspective. Any reaction or attitude may generate a not-insignificant reaction in its wake. Characteristic of France–Holy Land relations is the fact that the elements we have identified for analytical purposes are inextricably linked, in contrast to the relationships with other countries that have less marked affective and symbolic connotations. In our topic, political, economic, religious, and cultural aspects have been intertwined throughout the ages. This is a point which must be kept in mind, whatever the particular research (or teaching) topic.

FRENCH JEWS AND THE HOLY LAND

A distinction must be made between this more specific relationship and the more general one discussed previously. Here, too, the approach to the subject will vary over different time periods. For the Middle Ages, a study is required of the presence and perception of the Land of Israel in rabbinical texts. French medieval Judaism came to full maturity in the eleventh and twelfth centuries (particularly in Champagne) and has left us a large body of literature (chronicles, *responsa*). It would be important to investigate whether French Jewish communities, which were fairly well structured from the eleventh century on, had a different relationship with the Holy Land than did, for example, the communities of the Rhineland. Medieval Jewish texts should also be studied to find out the reaction of French rabbis to Crusader undertakings.

French Jewry's relationship with the Holy Land can also be analyzed in economic terms; emissaries from Eretz Israel made periodic fund-raising visits to Jewish communities. This research could be part of a more general work on the development of the French Jewish community.

As of the nineteenth century, the approach would be more political and sociological in nature. Research will have to take account of Emancipation and its consequences (in terms of Zionism and the migration of French Jews to Eretz Israel). The question of dual loyalty has often been raised since the founding of the State of Israel. Systematic study of this issue, as presented in the press, might give a clearer idea of French public opinion as well as the attitude of Jews to this question. Similarly, sociologists and political analysts tend to refer to the "Jewish vote" because of French Jewry's ties with Israel. This concept could be examined in a political science study.

Our topic also has a literary aspect. This is a very rich area because in the nineteenth century, as mentioned, the "journey to the Orient" played a very special role (initiation, rite of passage, return to the sources—Athens and Jerusalem) under the influence of the Romantics. A study can be made of the specific nature of the Holy Land in literature (Palestine and French writers), with an attempt to see how it differs in the imaginary sphere from other aspects of what is called the "Orient," a geographical region that is not clearly defined but is also a coded system of representation (see Berchet's work cited earlier). Another approach might be a comparative literature survey: How do French travelers perceive the Holy Land?

The history of art would also be a possible research field; there are many pictorial, photographic, and film representations of the Holy Land. These portray a complete imaginary social and religious world (see Catherine Nicault's Chapter 8 for examples).

SUMMARY

As stressed at the outset, an attempt has been made to cover a wide variety of possible approaches, in the light of work already carried out in this area. The field is extremely broad and should undoubtedly be studied in depth. Some of these proposals may remain in the realm of theory due to insufficient source material. Some are primarily research topics, while others are more suitable for teaching; some can easily be included in general education (e.g., history, general and comparative literature, history of art, political science), while others would be more suitable for Hebrew and Jewish studies departments. In such cases, the suggestions are a starting point for more detailed analysis, which must also keep more immediate and long-term goals in mind.

NOTES

1. The Verdier publishing house, in particular, is publishing both traditional texts (such as Midrash, Talmud, Zohar, Maimonides) and contemporary essays (philosophy) in the collection called "Les dix paroles."

2. Cf. the translations of Maurice-Reuben Hayoun, in charge of the Patrimaine (Heritage) series at the Cerf publishing house.

3. Herman-Leberecht Strack and Günter Stemberger, *Introduction au Talmud et au Midrash*, trans. and adapt., M. R. Hayoun (Paris: Cerf, 1986).

4. Marc-Alain Ouaknine, *Le livre brûlé*, lire le Talmud (Paris: Lieu commun, 1986).

5. Cf. Haim Zafrani, *Kabbale, vie mystique et magie* (Paris: Maisonneuve et Larose, 1986); and an anthology of kabbalistic texts, Alexander Safran, *Sagesse de la Kabbale* (Paris: Stock, 1986).

6. Armand Abécassis, *La pensée juive*, vols. 1 and 2 (Paris: Le livre de poche, 1987); vol. 3 (1989). Cf. also the numerous publications of the Presences du Judaïsme series of the Albin Michel publishing house.

7. D. Lazar, *L'opinion française et la naissance de l'Etat d'Israël 1945–1949* (Paris: Calmann-Laévy, 1972); J. W. Lapierre, *L'information sur l'Etat d'Israël dans les grands quotidiens français en 1958* (Paris: Centre national de la recherche scientifique publications, 1969).

8. J. C. Berchet, *Le voyage en Orient* (Paris: Robert Laffont, 1985).

9. Chateaubriand, François Auguste Rene (Vicomte de), *Itinéraire de Paris à Jérusalem et de Jérusalem à Paris* (Limoges: E. Amdant, 1876), pt. 3.

Comment

André Kaspi

From the chapters of Catherine Nicault, Ran Aaronsohn, and Sophie Kessler-Mesguich, it is evident that in the field of Holy Land Studies, French researchers are behind their American, British, and German colleagues. The excellent reports presented at the Workshop on Western Societies and the Holy Land, held in Jerusalem in 1988, reflected the depth of research in various European countries and the weakness of French studies. What are some possible explanations for this?

It is difficult to propose definite answers, but some hypotheses may be suggested. French historians, for example, created a school for the history of international relations, originally activated by Pierre Renouvin and later by Jean-Baptiste Duroselle. The school produced numerous original works: French relations with Germany, Russia, Italy, the Ottoman Empire, the United States, and Africa were carefully analyzed, clarified on the basis of archival material, and placed within a broad framework that included economic, political, military, and cultural relations. These works were published and have served as a base for in-depth studies, which continue to inspire deeper examination. Still, entire sectors of research remain untouched. Little has been written on French ties with Central and Eastern Europe, or with more remote areas such as Latin America and Oceania. Some pioneering studies demonstrate the path that young research workers will undoubtedly follow in the future.

So far, research into the Middle East and, more particularly, regarding Israel has been limited. The theme is potentially rich. However, existing studies give the impression that this field of research is barren. Nonetheless, in the consciousness of every Frenchman of whatever religion or background, whether author, painter, or traveler, the Near East holds a choice and time-honored place. There is a mine of information about this area that begs to be explored.

First, research candidates are paralyzed by the constraints of vocabulary. Should the term "Holy Land" be employed? This would too easily confirm the Catholic heritage that considers—as we are reminded by Sophie Kessler-Mesguich—that to follow the steps of Jesus means to walk across the "Holy Land." In contrast to the English expression, the two words in French, *"Terre Sainte,"* are laden with Christian connotations, whereas the expression "Eretz Israel" evokes a Jewish resonance.

The term "Palestine" has been employed during specific periods. In the period considered contemporary by French historians, Palestine was one of the Ottoman Empire's provinces or, between the two World Wars, the object of political claims—and therefore it took on a polemical significance. Here, then, is a region to which the French are profoundly attached by the weight of cultural, religious, and spiritual references, but they do not know how to call it without giving it a label. Instead of entering the arena to confront this difficulty, they tend to neglect the very source of their spirituality and seek other horizons for their research.

A second explanation involves methodology—the unavoidable need for a multidisciplinary approach. For example, French scholars who participated in the Jerusalem Workshop included historians, a sociologist, a political scientist, and a linguist. The research program proposed by Catherine Nicault strengthens the conviction that without the joint efforts of diverse specialized fields, it will be impossible to undertake serious and systematic studies. History, for example, offers a method and state of mind; it serves as a basis for analysis. Sociology, political science, and economics add variety and profundity. Above all, the study of the languages of the region is indispensable. There are other disciplines as well without which research is circumscribed. The creation of work teams is therefore unavoidable.

Research in France, however, is too often partitioned: Historians associate with other historians, sociologists with other sociologists, and linguists with other linguists. Joint projects are still rare. In the area under discussion, these exceptions must become the rule. For example, should a researcher wish to evaluate the relations between France and the Holy Land on the eve of World War II, he will, of course, have to start by investigating what the French people of that period were thinking and feeling. This would require special attention to the formation of mentalities and of culture, providing detailed collective presentations illustrating French-Turkish, French-Syrian, French-Lebanese, French-Palestinian, and other relations. After this, it would be necessary to trace economic, political, and diplomatic ties between France and the Holy Land, and to follow the interaction between these areas—a complex panorama that is far more intricate than French-Italian or French-American relations. This underlines the complexity of the task.

Finally, it must be acknowledged that French researchers have evidently left the subject to the theologians, simply because they have had the false impression that France plays a minor role in this region of the world—and that it is more promising to study Africa, where France was a colonial power; Western Europe, where France concentrates her diplomatic action; or North America, with which France has enjoyed privileged relations for centuries. It is curious that France, which considers itself the guardian of Lebanese Christians, which intervened in their favor during the Second Empire and continues to recall the period when it could respond effectively, has not sufficiently studied its role regarding the Maronites, nor its relations—conflicting or friendly—with Syria. Does France feel that despite everything, it was and still is largely a minor power in the Middle East? This would not conform with past or present international realities. Whatever the reason may be, it is important that the French realize that they are bound by history, culture, and their national interests to this region of the world.

In conclusion, I would like to propose that every project director initiate broad inquiries, assign research subjects, and encourage students to work in this area. It would be even better if joint undertakings by scholars, research centers, and universities were created, in order to stimulate an academic area that is seriously impoverished in France. Only through a partnership of energies and abilities will research be stimulated. It will be up to the teams to define a program, recruit those who will be charged with executing it, and supervise the quality of the research undertaken. In a word, the work will be collective or it will not be at all.

What is needed is a center of studies on the relations between France and the Holy Land, directed by a scientific council. Such an enterprise should be binational, engaging France and Israel, strengthening the ties that unite the two countries, without losing sight of the fundamental interests of academic research. Under these conditions, it will be possible to invest this field of study with the full vigor it deserves.

Chapter 11

The German Protestant Network in the Holy Land

Erich Geldbach

BACKGROUND

The nineteenth century has been described by the late Kenneth Scott Latourette of Yale University as the great century of the expansion of Christianity.[1] The Protestant churches finally began to realize that the "church" is more than an organization within the boundaries of a small territory; it is an apostolic church— that is, it has a mission to fulfill. The idea that the church is catholic, that is, universal, was never abandoned by the Roman Catholic Church, neither when the East-West split occurred in the eleventh century, nor after the introduction of various Reformation and post-Reformation churches in the Western tradition.

When Protestant leaders began to grasp the idea that the Church's mission was to spread the gospel throughout the world, they established a variety of missionary societies, church agencies, and para-church organizations to fulfill the Great Commission. It is, therefore, not surprising that the Protestants also directed their attention to the Holy Land, and especially to Jerusalem.

For decades, in fact for centuries, German Protestants had recognized the importance of Jerusalem: "Jerusalem, thou city on a hill: wilt God I were in thee."[2] This hymn by Johann Matthäus Meyfart (1590–1642), at one time professor at Jena, was often sung in Protestant church services. But Jerusalem was thought to be a heavenly place. The "city on the hill" had been totally spiritualized as a city beyond the human sphere. As Meyfart expressed it, the human heart must depart from this world in order to reach the gates of eternity and to sing the pure hallelujah for ever more, accompanied by instruments and choirs immeasurable. Jerusalem was thought of as God's dwelling place, where He reigned and where the believers would one day join the angelic hosts in eternal praise of Him who had created heaven and earth. Within this conceptual frame, Jerusalem and the Holy Land had no relevance as geographic entities. Practical theology and church organization were in a different sphere.

Within the new missionary movement, however, things began to change radically. This shift is particularly evident in relation to a group outside the accepted theological norm and the established church. In 1854, a meeting was held of "Templers" who wanted to emigrate to the Holy Land. When the Interior Minister of Würtemberg inquired why he had not been warned of such agitation, his civil servants replied that they had mistakenly thought of the heavenly Jerusalem. They had read the spiritualized concept to which they were accustomed into the historical frame that the Templers considered real.[3]

The efforts of the missions were understood as part of eschatology. Certain "signs of the times" could be observed; a number of passages from Holy Scripture seemed to indicate that these signs could be understood to mean that the end-of-days was close at hand. Johann Albrecht Bengel (1687–1752), a spokesman for the movement of Pietism, read the Book of Revelation, the last book of the Christian Bible, as a prophetic vision of the various stages of church history. By comparing the events told in the holy book with events in history and with those presently taking place, Bengel concluded that the end-of-days was to be at Easter 1836; his grandchildren were going to be eyewitnesses of this long-awaited event. He had computed the different numbers of the Book of Revelation, the Book of Daniel, and other biblical books, and he meticulously applied the laws of mathematics to reach his conclusion.[4]

The French Revolution, Napoleon's rise to power, and his sweeping victories in Europe seemed to underline Bengel's predictions. Was not the antichrist to come from the West? The conjunction of political events was reason enough for the Orthodox Czar Alexander of Russia, the Roman Catholic Emperor Franz Joseph of Austria, and the Protestant Prussian King Friedrich Wilhelm III to unite in a Holy Alliance against the apocalyptic beast.[5] The eschatological ideas of Bengel had been kept alive by Philipp Matthäus Hahn, Johann Heinrich Jung-Stilling, and others, and they were transmitted to the czar by Juliane Freifrau von Krüdener (whom, incidently, Goethe had much ridiculed).

Many Protestants who went to the Holy Land spent their childhood in this heated eschatological-apocalyptic atmosphere. Even after Pietism had been replaced as a dominant movement in the church, a constant Pietist undercurrent persisted. In Bengel's immediate surroundings, in Württemberg and southern Germany in particular, there was a strong influence of Pietism. It surfaced in the early nineteenth century as the *Erweckungsbewegung*—the Awakening Movement. A similar movement flourished at about the same time in the United States.

THE AWAKENING MOVEMENT

The members of the "awakening" had a strong commitment to spreading the gospel at home and abroad. They were willing to contribute time, money, talent, and even their lives to this task. Missionary zeal was motivated by two reasons. One was the burning desire to save souls during this last time span of grace. Soon there would be no opportunity left for poor sinners—including Jews—to repent and be converted. The second reason was to help usher in the Kingdom of God. The sooner the elect from the nations were gathered, the sooner Christ would appear in all his glory to establish the Kingdom. This eschatological idea moved awakened Christians to undertake a tremendous number of missionary efforts in many parts of the world, and particularly in the Holy Land—for, as history would soon come to an end and Christ would soon come again, Christians began to think about where he was going to appear. It took little imagination to assume that history would end where the *Heilsgeschichte*, the history of salvation for Jews and Gentiles, had its origin. Holy history would come to a conclusion in the Holy Land. Holy history provoked the thought of holy geography; *Heilsgeschichte* and *Heilsgeographie* go hand in hand. Thus, the Holy Land and the Holy City gained importance in the eyes of awakened Christians.

Other German Christians who emerged from the Pietist-awakening tradition but developed a different theological rationale for being in the Holy Land were the Templers. They were considered to be religious fanatics or extremists by "normal" church standards. They shared the eschatological approach of the awakened Christians, but they were not part of the established church and were thus able to follow their own insights without organizational restraints.

German Protestants who went to the Holy Land were deeply influenced by the movement of the awakening and its underlying awareness that the final stage of historical development was close at hand. This gave all their endeavors a sense of urgency. It must be noted that these marginal groups did not represent German Protestantism as a whole, but they were much more active and committed than the rest. Nor did these groups constitute a typical cross-section of the Protestant population in Germany. Many missionary activities in the Holy Land were directed from Switzerland, especially from Basel; nationality was of only secondary importance to the awakened Christians. Contrary to a widespread assumption that Christian missionary work goes hand-in-hand with the building of national colonial empires, it must be noted here that the first loyalty of the awakened Christians was not to a nation, but to their Lord and to those organizations that they perceived to be vessels or channels of their Lord. However, they wanted to be *deutsch-evangelisch*.[6] Many resisted the idea of merging with the Anglicans. Although they would freely associate with "evangelical" Anglicans, they had little regard for the place Anglicans traditionally ascribed to the apostolic succession of bishops. Nor did they understand why the office of a bishop was considered to be a necessary mark of a true church. The socio-economic background of many German Protestants who came to the Holy Land, and their theological education—if, indeed, they had received such an education—suggests that their theology was simple, unsophisticated, and perhaps naively biblicistic in outlook.

GERMANS IN THE HOLY LAND

The Germans in the Holy Land fall into several categories. Some went to settle there permanently; they emigrated in order to live and die in the Holy Land. The Templers are a good example of this first group. Others went to serve in various capacities, with the tacit understanding that in the course of their service they could face death, but that they may be able to go "back home" some day; the craftsmen-missionaries from St. Chrischona are an example.

A third group of Germans were in the Holy Land on temporary duty, in the diplomatic service or representing the established church for a limited period of time. Yet other Germans went to the Holy Land as adventurous tourists or with certain goals in mind: Geographers wanted to look at the topography; scholarly theologians tried to find biblical sites or gather information that would help understand the Bible; archaeologists searched for remains of bygone cultures. Among the theologians one also finds some who came to the Holy Land as pilgrims. Even Protestants, who usually do not believe in holy places or shrines, went on pilgrimages to visit the places where Jesus had lived and preached.

Interest in the Holy Land and pilgrimage to its sites could have two different effects upon Protestant theologians. It might reinforce the faith of a visitor who came to the Holy Land as a committed Christian, saw the holy places, and felt reassured. To walk the paths that the Lord had once walked was an uplifting experience; the truth of the word of God and of holy history was experienced. For example, when Friedrich Adolph Strauss approached Jerusalem for the first time, he was reminded of Psalms 120 to 134, the Songs of Ascent, and he saw the world in springtime colors. When he perceived the skyline of Jerusalem from the distance, he was so deeply moved that tears began to flow:

> "I am unworthy of all grace and faithfulness that thou, O Lord, hast granted me, thy servant"—thus it rang in my heart ever more cheerfully. My Savior's redeeming eyes had looked at these hills. On these paths the sound of his footsteps was heard. Here the City which he looked at and wept over. There the place of the cross where the most terrible sin of humanity and where the abounding grace of God was revealed.[7]

Such experience had the additional effect of making the visitor aware of the grim difference between the idealized Holy Land or Holy City and the devastating living conditions of real people in the holy places. This experience, both positive and negative, usually left a lasting imprint on visitors. They became actively involved in seeking to improve conditions in the Holy Land after they had returned to Germany. Strauss, for example, became secretary of the *Jerusalemverein*, which was organized in 1852 in Berlin, and he served in that capacity for three decades.

On the other hand, an encounter with the Holy Land sometimes led to a demythologizing of the scriptural reports or records, and an erosion of the individual's theological system or faith. For example, after Friedrich Naumann visited the Holy Land, he felt compelled to reevaluate and reorganize his entire theology.[8] Subsequently he went into politics.

THE ANGLO-PRUSSIAN BISHOPRIC AND C.C.J. BUNSEN

The establishment of the joint Anglo-Prussian Bishopric of St. James in 1841 can be considered a turning point in the relation of German Protestants to the Holy Land, although individual Germans had been there before—most of them as missionaries in the service of English church societies. Perhaps it is not an exaggeration to contend that with the joint English Prussian religious venture the city of Jerusalem entered the age of modernity. New York theologian Edward Robinson, who visited Jerusalem in 1838 and again in 1852, noted that the Anglo-Prussian Bishopric and other institutions that were related to the Church of St. James in one way or another were prominent signs of change for the better.[9]

Why was the Bishopric established? If the political and military situation is put aside at this point, the available sources indicate that it was the former head of the Prussian legation to the Holy See, Christian Carl Josias Bunsen, who first conceived the idea.[10] His diplomatic career at the Holy See had come to an end in the course of what is called the *Kölner Wirren*. Prussia had acquired the so-called Rhine provinces at the Vienna Congress after the Napoleonic wars. Thus, Roman Catholic territories were added to the otherwise overwhelmingly Protestant state. How to deal with mixed marriages became a tense issue. The Prussian government forcefully deposed the Archbishop of Cologne because he followed the Vatican instruction and refused to comply with new civil regulations on mixed marriages. Bunsen became a *persona non grata* in Rome and was transferred to a diplomatic post in Switzerland.

However, Bunsen was a close friend of the crown prince, who came to the throne as Friedrich Wilhelm IV in 1840. In 1822 and again in 1828, Friedrich Wilhelm had visited Rome, and Bunsen had served as his personal tour guide. Thus, an intimate bond developed between the two; it lasted even after Bunsen fell into disfavor with the Prussian administration. (Indeed, the last signature of Friedrich Wilhelm IV, before a stroke paralyzed him, conferred a title of nobility upon Bunsen.[11]) Bunsen must have conveyed the idea of a Bishopric to the crown prince.

In April 1841, the newly crowned Friedrich Wilhelm IV called Bunsen to Berlin-Potsdam to give him special instructions. He was to go as the king's personal envoy to London, where he arrived in July. His mission was to negotiate the Jerusalem Bishopric with the government of Her Majesty, and with the Archbishop of Canterbury and the Bishop of London. To the consternation of almost everyone—especially John Henry Newman and the Tractarians—his mission was a success. Bunsen, who had married Frances Weddington in 1817 in

Rome and therefore had family ties with English society, presented himself wherever he was as a vibrant personality, a pious family man, and at the same time, a compelling intellectual with an astounding range of scholarly interests.

Bunsen's Jerusalem plan was broached earlier, in December 1838, when he was in England and discussed it with Lord Ashley. Ashley was the leader of the evangelical wing of the Church of England, a movement that was similar in piety and theological outlook to the awakening movement on the Continent. Bunsen confessed that his idea of a Bishopric also received impetus when he learned about Christian Friedrich Spittler's plan to send a colony of Protestant missionaries from the *Missionshaus* in Basel to the Holy Land.[12] In the person of Bunsen the two movements—one within the Church of England and the other within continental Protestantism—joined forces.

Bunsen's motives were varied. First, he sought to hold the Roman Catholic Church in check. By internationalizing both the Church of England and the Prussian Church he hoped to create a sense of universality or catholicity in both churches. True catholicity, he argued, does not deny national independence. The Bishopric in Jerusalem, the beginning of a worldwide Protestant community, was to be a demonstration against the Roman Catholic Church insofar that a harmonious interaction of both catholicity and nationality might be achieved.[13] The true church of the future would display both characteristics; the national character of each church would be held in check by the universal approach, while the catholicity of the Protestant community would not do away with national characteristics of each church. Bunsen had no doubt that the American missionaries in the Holy Land would eventually be part of the new arrangement and add to the universality of the endeavor.[14]

Second, in order for the gospel to take deep roots on Mt. Zion, from where the message of salvation had emerged, there must be *one apostolic church*. Therefore, the two Protestant churches of England and Prussia must form an alliance: "The two Protestant sister churches must over the Savior's grave clasp hands in an eternal alliance."[15] Bunsen foresaw a network of Bishoprics in Nazareth, Bethlehem, and other places.

Third, the union of the sister churches had another goal—to prove a place for the Jews. The union could not do without a Jewish dimension. The Protestant congregations were to be missionary in orientation and composed of natives and foreigners, Jews and Gentiles. Thus, when the Jewish convert, Dr. Michael Salomon Alexander, was consecrated and sent to the Holy City, Bunsen concluded that if with God's help the work would prosper, the beginning of the restoration of Israel would be accomplished.[16]

Bunsen's concern for the restoration of Israel coincided with similar ideas of Friedrich Wilhelm IV. In a letter of August 26, 1841, the Prussian king informed his envoy that the reestablishment of the Jewish People and the reuniting of the Church in the apostolic succession were of his innermost dreams. That these hopes were politically unrealistic was conceded by the king. Yet he thought that it was the task of kings to provide institutions and then wait to see if they would be used by God to further His will. The Jerusalem Bishopric was such an institution, which at the same time was to secure an equal status for Protestantism among the churches of the Orient and to prevent many different and separated Protestant churches from settling in the Holy Land and thus be a *grässliches Argernis* (a monstrous irritation or stumbling block) for Turks, Jews, and Oriental Christians alike. Finally, the Bishopric might, in time to come, serve as the center of *Judenchristen* (Christian Jews) and as a center for a "greater union of different Protestant confessions."[17] What Bunsen had been able to accomplish in England appeared to be providential to the Prussian king. He was particularly intrigued *"wie der Gedanke für Israel aufgefasst und in dem Plan als Grund und Zweck verwebt ist"*—how the thought for Israel is conceived and woven into the plan as its basis and purpose. For this the king would like "to prostrate myself in the dust before God how everything has worked together so providentially."[18]

The London Society for Promoting Christianity amongst the Jews (LJS) had acquired a piece of land in Jerusalem. It was Dr. Alexander McCaul, one of the outstanding leaders of the society, who on September 25, 1839 communicated to Bunsen the idea of turning Jerusalem into a "free city" under the joint protection of the Christian powers of Europe.[19] Bunsen entertained this idea for a while, but he concluded that it was England's mission to be the sole protector of Christians in the Holy Land. Political and military events, in conjunction with Ibrahim Pasha's victory in the decisive battle near Nezib, had prompted England, Russia, Austria, and Prussia to sign the quadruple alliance on July 15, 1840 to rescue the Sultan in Constantinople. Bunsen regarded this situation as a God-given historical moment that demanded action on the part of England. The "signs of a restoration of Zion" are evident, as Bunsen wrote to Lord Ashley on August 3, 1840, and he continued:

> Is it not providential that the fate of the Holy Land has been placed in the hands of England at the very moment when the Lord, whose blessed feet touched that holy ground, is worshiped by believers in the English tongue and according to the liturgy of the English Church on Mt. Zion, when learned Jews and Rabbis unite their songs of praise in their own language with that of England's Christian sons?[20]

Bunsen suggested that an English factory be built on the coast so that resources would be made available to the Jews: "For the Jewish inhabitants of Jerusalem must not go on begging as they have done all the 1800 years."

Lord Ashley summed up his own and Bunsen's activities when he sent Bunsen his picture and wrote underneath that both men had worked "through God's grace, for the strengthening of evangelical truth, the well-being of Israel, and the expansion of the Kingdom of our blessed Lord."[21]

Fourth, Bunsen's ideas went far beyond a future Protestant community or the restoration of Israel and the well-being of Jews in the Holy Land. He also had political aims in mind for England and Prussia. As Bunsen negotiated with the primate of the Church of England and with the Bishop of London, in whose jurisdiction lay the administration of Anglican churches in countries or territories overseas, and as he communicated with leaders of the evangelical and broad wings of the Church of England, he exerted great influence and was able to repel the attempts of the Tractarians or the High Church party to lead the Church of England back to Rome.[22] In England, Bunsen's anti-Catholic tendency directed the attention of the English bishops and the English public to continental Protestantism rather than to Rome.

In Prussia, on the other hand, Bunsen displayed an anti-Russian tendency. Russia, for him, was politically as anti-liberal and arch-conservative, if not reactionary, in its monarchical absolutism as Rome was religiously an obstacle to progress. Bunsen's encounter with the English Parliament and with leaders of various political factions led him to believe that the natural political ally of Prussia was not czarist Russia, as the Holy Alliance suggested, but democratic England. His policy was to align Prussia with England and, by doing so, to strike a blow at his anti-liberal, conservative enemies. In both cases Bunsen succeeded momentarily, but he failed in the long run.

Newman left the Church of England as a direct result of Bunsen's activities and joined the Roman Catholic Church, where he eventually became a cardinal. The Roman hierarchy was thus re-introduced in England, and the Catholic Church again became a factor in the religious life there. In Prussia, Bunsen had no power base of his own other than the king; only his personal intimacy with Friedrich Wilhelm IV prevented his early downfall. He served as Prussian envoy to the Court of St. James from 1842 to 1854, at which time the conservative "Kamarilla" (cabal) prevailed, and Bunsen resigned from his diplomatic post.

Fifth, Bunsen had a lively interest in liturgy. He devised the liturgy for the Protestant services in the Prussian legation in Rome. Not even the Italian Waldensians were allowed to conduct services in Rome and so, for years, the Prussian legation was the only place in the city where a Protestant worship service was held.

Thus, many Protestants of different nationalities, especially visitors from England and the United States, would gather on Sundays in the Prussian legation, thereby expanding the number of individuals with whom Bunsen was acquainted.[23] Bunsen also devised the liturgy for the Jerusalem church, and wrote to his wife, "[so] from the Capital in Rome to Mount Zion in Jerusalem that which is dearest to my heart could be saved."[24]

Sixth, in the final analysis, all of Bunsen's motives find their explanation in the eschatological expectation he shared with many awakened Christians. Bunsen believed in God-given historical opportunities and the duty of politicians to act and provide the means for God's will to be done. The church that would eventually emerge from the Jerusalem Bishopric would be the church "which would meet the Savior at his second coming."[25] This eschatological outlook united the awakened Christians on the Continent, the evangelical party in the Church of England, and Bunsen, a diplomat of importance, who saw the footprints of God in history.

The first bishop of the joint Bishopric, Dr. Alexander, assumed his post in 1842. His untimely death only four years later required the Prussian king to name a successor. Upon Bunsen's recommendation he chose Swiss-born Samuel Gobat, who was the Bishopric's influential leader for more than three decades, until 1879. Under his supervision a number of missionary and charitable efforts were launched.

THE PROTESTANT "NETWORK"

Many of the German Protestants who worked for the Holy Land were closely related (see chart). Samuel Gobat, a graduate of the Missionshaus in Basel, was a lifelong friend of its head, Christian Friedrich Spittler. Gobat married Maria Zeller, a daughter of Christian Heinrich Zeller who headed another of Spittler's endeavors, the orphans' school in Beuggen. The couple's fifth child, Dora Gobat, married Heinrich Rappard, who for many years was the "Inspektor" of St. Chrischona, still another of Spittler's projects. C. F. A. Steinkopf,[26] who for fifty years served as pastor of the German-speaking church in London, was closely associated with Spittler's *Deutsche Christentumsgesellschaft*,[27] the Missionshaus in Basel, and the St. Chrischona mission school near Basel. Steinkopf displayed great interest in missionary work, and both Gobat and Bunsen faithfully attended his church services.

Spittler's interest in the Holy Land had first been kindled by the reports of pious and learned Gotthilf Heinrich von Schubert of Munich, who traveled to the Holy Land in 1836–1837.[28] He asked Spittler to consider sending missionaries there. Spittler had apparently thought of doing this immediately, but it was only ten years later that he dispatched two young, committed graduates from St. Chrischona. Throughout Spittler's life, the Jerusalem project remained his "favorite child."[29]

In 1854 one of Spittler's most intimate friends, Johann Ludwig Schneller, arrived in the Holy Land together with his wife. The Schneller family provides another vivid example of close ties to the Holy Land. Ludwig, the second son of Johann Ludwig Schneller, succeeded his father in the leadership position of the Syrian Orphanage and began to build churches in Hebron, Beit Jala, and Bethlehem. He married Catharina Tischendorf, whose father had named her in honor of St. Catherine's Cloister where he had discovered the *Codex Sinaiticus*. Constantin Tischendorf's son Paul served until 1899 as German consul in Jerusalem.

In the 1850s a German-speaking congregation began to gather in Jerusalem. A Dane by the name of Hans (John) Nicolayson, a German-speaking missionary who had been in the Holy Land under the auspices of the English Church Missionary Society, served as its first pastor. He was succeeded by Rev. Valentiner, whom Friedrich Wilhelm IV sent to Jerusalem. In 1852 a Jerusalemverein (association) was organized in Berlin to support the German missionary projects financially and otherwise. Its first secretary was Friedrich Adolph Strauss, who in 1846 had returned from a two-year pilgrimage to the Holy Land and other countries. The president of the Jerusalemverein was Wilhelm Hoffmann who served until his death in 1875.

Hoffmann's family was intricately involved in Protestant projects. His father was a leader in the Awakening Movement who became mayor of a new Pietist settlement called "Kornthal" in 1817. The king of Württemberg, fearing that some of his best farmers would emigrate to Russia for religious reasons, had granted a statute of independence from the established church to the village of Kornthal. Wilhelm Hoffmann, before accepting the position of court preacher in Berlin in 1852, had served for eleven years as inspector of missions in Spittler's Basel Missionshaus. His son Carl came to Jerusalem in 1866 as successor to Rev. Valentiner; and his brother Christoph, founder and main organizer of the *Tempelgesellschaft*, had been inspector at St. Chrischona from 1853 to 1855.

This short list of prominent names is presented to demonstrate how closely Protestants who were interested in the Holy Land were intertwined either by family relationships or by a common understanding of the gospel in the Pietist awakening tradition. Similar familial patterns may be found in other religious renewal movements as well. In this case, the believers had been instructed all their lives to treat each other as sisters or brothers; even after a split occurred, as was the case with the Tempelgesellschaft, communications were not severed completely.

An extensive network emerged as a result of the efforts to renew Christianity at home and spread the light abroad. Although the awakened Christians liked to refer to themselves as "the quiet of the land," they had access to people in high places, even to the king of Prussia himself.

If the Jerusalem Bishopric may be considered to be a turning point in the history of the Holy Land, it is quite remarkable that Samuel Gobat and the eschatological readings of the Prophets were involved, in some fashion, in the political conditions surrounding the establishment of this institution. In the winter of 1827–1828, Gobat was in Alexandria to await clearance to travel to Abyssinia. As a close friend of Boghos Bey, the first minister of Mohammed Ali, Gobat spent several evenings with the minister, staying up past midnight to read Holy Scripture together. One evening Boghos Bey and Gobat discovered in the Prophets that the Turkish government would soon be destroyed. Gobat reports:

> I looked at these prophecies of Holy Scripture with theological eyes, remembering that with the King of Kings a thousand years is like one day. Boghos Bey considered the matter with political eyes that focusses on man's rather than God's work. The Pascha and he regarded Egypt as totally different from Turkey. . . . After I had left Alexandria, I never thought much about this incident. But when I returned from Abyssinia for the first time again in 1833, I visited Boghos Bey. As soon as he

The German–Holy Land Network

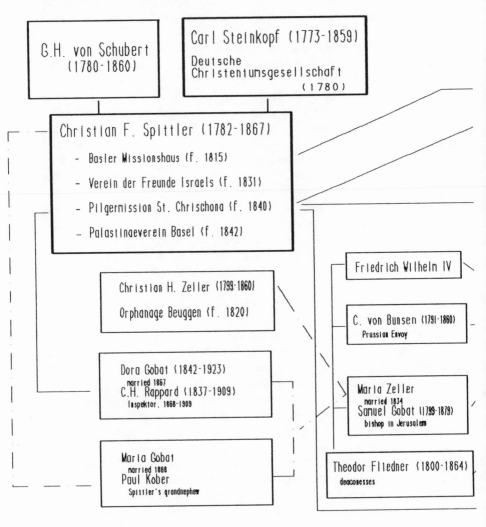

G.H. von Schubert (1780-1860)

Carl Steinkopf (1773-1859)
Deutsche Christentumsgesellschaft (1780)

Christian F. Spittler (1782-1867)
- Basler Missionshaus (f. 1815)
- Verein der Freunde Israels (f. 1831)
- Pilgermission St. Chrischona (f. 1840)
- Palastinaeverein Basel (f. 1842)

Christian H. Zeller (1799-1860)
Orphanage Beuggen (f. 1820)

Dora Gobat (1842-1923)
married 1867
C.H. Rappard (1837-1909)
Inspektor, 1868-1909

Maria Gobat
married 1868
Paul Kober
Spittler's grandnephew

Friedrich Wilhelm IV

C. von Bunsen (1791-1860)
Prussian Envoy

Maria Zeller
married 1834
Samuel Gobat (1799-1879)
bishop in Jerusalem

Theodor Fliedner (1800-1864)
deaconesses

KEY

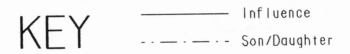

——————— Influence

· · — · — · · Son/Daughter

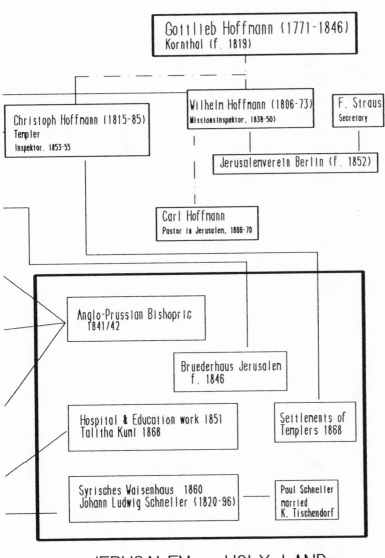

Gottlieb Hoffmann (1771-1846)
Kornthal (f. 1819)

Wilhelm Hoffmann (1806-73)
Missionsinspektor. 1839-50)

F. Straus
Secretary

Christoph Hoffmann (1815-85)
Templer
Inspektor. 1853-55

Jerusalemverein Berlin (f. 1852)

Carl Hoffmann
Pastor in Jerusalen. 1866-70

Anglo-Prussian Bishopric
1841/42

Bruederhaus Jerusalen
f. 1846

Hospital & Education work 1851
Talitha Kumi 1868

Settlements of
Templers 1868

Syrisches Waisenhaus 1860
Johann Ludwig Schneller (1820-96)

Paul Schneller
married
K. Tischendorf

JERUSALEM - HOLY LAND

heard that I was at the door, he came, smiled and said: "Do you remember that evening when we studied the prophecies together? A few days later I related our findings to the Pascha, Mohammed Ali, who went with me through the prophecies again and then made the decision to attack the Ottoman Empire. This was the beginning of our occupation of Syria."[30]

Gobat comments that thus a small spark may ignite a great fire.

The military and political interpretation of the prophecies had serious consequences. The Egyptian forces nearly brought about the total collapse of the Turkish Empire. The Turks then tried to reorganize their system of government and administration as well as their military forces. In 1839 the Sultan felt strong enough to attack the Egyptians and recapture the areas that had been occupied by Egypt; when he lost the decisive battle near Nezib, the European powers came to his rescue. In return, they demanded certain rights in Palestine, among them the right to establish consulates and the Bishopric in Jerusalem.

When Gobat was consecrated bishop, the sermon preached during the service was based on Isaiah 62:1: "For Zion's sake will I not hold my peace, and for Jerusalem's sake I will not rest, until the righteousness thereof go forth as brightness, and the salvation thereof as a lamp that burneth." This verse sums up what the Protestants who went to the Holy Land were trying to achieve. They were convinced that for centuries the Land had been under a curse (even the Jews would say that), that it was in every respect backward, and that it was the task of Protestant Christianity to let the light of the gospel shine so that true civilization would uplift the living conditions, the civil administration, and the attitudes of the people toward each other. Thus, eventually, the true worship of God would be introduced into the Land. Whether the activities would be directed toward Arabs, Jews, Oriental Christians or fellow-countrymen, of Roman Catholic or of no religious persuasion, did not matter. The only concern was to spread the gospel of brightness and keep the lamp burning.

THE BRÜDERHAUS

The model for much of the Protestant activities in the Holy Land was initially the Pietist settlement of Kornthal. Spittler wanted to establish such a colony in the Holy Land, and Bunsen favored this. He foresaw that the plan to set up a Christian colony would be attractive to thousands of young people, of whom the very best could be selected; only the best were good enough.[31]

As it turned out, however, the beginnings were very modest indeed. Only two young men, Ferdinand Palmer and Conrad Schick, went out to set up a *Brüderhaus*. Prospects were not very good; an earlier group of Germans from Wuppertal—another center of Pietist awakening tradition—had failed to establish a colony. Two more Chrischona brothers, Samuel Müller and Heinrich Baldensperger, were sent to Jerusalem in 1848. Although the brothers tried to work in their craft, teach some schoolchildren, and provide lodgings for European visitors, the project disintegrated. Gradually all except Müller left the Brüderhaus to work in various capacities for Bishop Gobat. Schick was head of the "House of Industry" before moving on to become an architect (*Baurat*) with outstanding achievements to his credit. "Talitha Kumi" and other major projects in the Holy Land were designed and built by him.

In 1854 and again in 1860, Spittler sent more Chrischona brothers to Jerusalem. Some traveled on to Abyssinia to continue Gobat's former work and to expand it by establishing a network of missionary outposts from Alexandria to Abyssinia, the so-called *Apostelstrasse* and the *Prophetenstrasse*. Johann Ludwig Schneller and his wife arrived in Jerusalem with the 1854 group. He was supposed to be the *Hausvater* of the Brüderhaus, as he had held such a position in St. Chrischona. However, Schneller acquired a piece of land in 1855 outside the city wall where he built a house for his family. Spittler sensed that the future of the Brüderhaus was in jeopardy, and in 1857 he invited Christian businessmen to invest in a company in Jerusalem. The company flourished, especially after Hermann Loewenthal and Johannes Frutiger took over its leadership.[32]

In 1860, Christians were persecuted in Lebanon and Damascus, and Schneller began to build an orphanage for Christian children; it gradually severed its ties with the *Pilgermission* and developed into an independent organization. Upon Johann Ludwig Schneller's death in 1896, his sons Theodor and Ludwig took over the leadership. When Theodor retired in 1928, his oldest son Hermann succeeded him.

When Gobat was in London to be consecrated Bishop of the Jerusalem Bishopric, Theodor Fliedner was also in the British capital to install four deaconesses as nurses in the newly established German hospital at Dalston. Gobat and Fliedner met in the home of the Prussian envoy Bunsen, at which time Gobat expressed his hope that in the future, deaconesses might also serve in Jerusalem.[33] In 1850, Gobat sent word that two deaconesses were urgently needed to cope with an epidemic. After consulting with King Friedrich Wilhelm IV, Fliedner decided to double the number and sent four sisters, two trained as nurses and two as teachers. Fliedner accompanied them on their trip to the Holy City, arriving in April 1851. A few weeks later a small hospital was opened and a school was started. In 1868, a new building was erected by Conrad Schick. It was called "Talitha Kumi," as it was to be a means to awaken the daughters of Zion from their spiritual death.

German Protestants were active in Jerusalem, Bethlehem, Beit Jala, Hebron, Haifa, Jaffa, and other places. Their main concern was in the area of *diakonia*: to care for the sick and the orphans, to educate and instruct children in a craft, and to provide rooms for visitors to the Holy Land. The emphasis on education may be interpreted as a typical Protestant approach. By way of contrast, it may be said that even in the nineteenth century, an Orthodox Christian or a Roman Catholic in the Orient did not need to know how to read or write. Attending mass was most important, and there the priest would act on behalf of the faithful. In Protestantism, however, and especially in the tradition of the awakening, personal commitment and personal devotion were required. The latter required a person to be able to read because the Bible was the center of one's life, certainly one's devotional life. The personal reading of God's word and the active participation in Bible study groups presupposed literacy. Thus, educational facilities were necessary to fulfill the missionary function of spreading the word. In addition, a person was to be educated so that he or she could be self-supporting and live a responsible life. Begging was considered an act beyond proper Christian behavior. Hence the Protestant missionaries tried to teach the children under their care a craft so that they could support themselves.

CHRISTIAN HOFFMANN AND THE TEMPELGESELLSCHAFT

The main organizer of the Tempelgesellschaft, Christian Hoffmann, had been elected in 1848 to the National Assembly, which convened in Frankfurt/Main, running successfully against the famous skeptic Dr. David Friedrich Strauss. However, Hoffmann soon became disillusioned with the discussions in Frankfurt and resigned before the conservative forces put an end to the German-style revolution. Nonetheless, his political experiences left a lasting impression on him, particularly the idea that the present forms of Christianity, whether Protestant or Roman Catholic, no longer provided a viable frame of reference for society and its development. Something new needed to be created.

Hoffmann felt that a renewal would only come from concentrating on the Kingdom of God. That kingdom was actually not bound to any geographic place, but Hoffmann felt that the Holy Land was the natural place for the kingdom to take initial form, if only because the prophets—including Jesus—had lived and spoken there. But Hoffmann also knew that the Orient was too weak and too uncivilized to initiate a renewal. For him the Turks, despite all rhetoric to the contrary, were still barbarians and hostile to culture.[34] The Orient needed outside help for its own renewal before it, in turn, might be an influence for renewal in other parts of the world.

That help must take the religious history of the Orient into consideration, but at the same time freedom for spiritual development must be ensured. Neither liberal political ideas, Protestantism, nor Roman Catholicism could, in Hoffmann's view, achieve this goal. Liberalism appeared devoid of a religious base and too many prejudices prevailed in both Roman Catholicism and Protestantism. A new form of Christianity was what the Orient might rightly demand from the Occident. Hoffmann did not maintain that the Tempelgesellschaft and its colonies in the Holy Land were the realization of that new form of Christianity. But he was convinced that the Tempelgesellschaft knew the task and attempted to fulfill it. The Templer, therefore, deserved the attention of all well-meaning people in the Occident.

The renewal of the Orient would have far-reaching implications for the Occident. Nothing less was at stake than the question of whether Christianity could remain the basis for culture of European nations and, indeed, for all mankind, or whether other competing ideas would take over. The Occident, as Hoffmann saw it, was exposed to a number of competing ideas such as extreme nationalism, "infidelity à la Strauss," the philosophy of the subconscious, materialism, Darwinism, or Socialism, and the churches were too weak to respond to these challenges.

But it was clear to Hoffmann that a decision was pending for or against Christianity and that a decision could not be expected from the State. Were the State to yield to the non-Christian forces, it would obviously turn anti-Christian. Were the State, on the other hand, to declare itself to be Christian, then its citizens or subjects would accept Christianity only because it was the law of the land. That, however, would create bigotry and would also be anti-Christian. The consequence of these deliberations is evident: Where there is no consensus among the citizens of a State as to the *Geltung*, the common application of Christianity, the State has no other option than to be neutral.[35]

Hoffmann wrestled with the issue of how a state is supposed to behave when it is faced with competing value systems. What stance should a state take when a pluralism of *Weltanschauungen* divides the population? Hoffmann's answer brought him close to a free-church approach: The separation of state and church is a necessary political expression in such a situation. But the separation is only the beginning of the real battle between Christianity and anti-Christianity. In Hoffmann's view, the latter also included popery and Jesuits, for they suppress ideas and coerce people.[36] Protestantism, however, is weak, and the complete disintegration of *kirchlichen Protestantismus* is only a question of time.[37]

As neither Roman Catholicism nor Protestantism represented true Christianity, Hoffmann remained with the question of how to realize the Kingdom of God on earth. For an answer, he went back into holy history and concluded that at all times people need symbols of hope. Moses led God's people out of Egypt and gave them the commandments; Christianity was based on the resurrection of Jesus Christ, which enabled his disciples to envision the future Kingdom of God and to wrestle with its enemies. Thus, Hoffmann sought something that would kindle the people's imagination, so that Europe might be rescued from the dangers of either Jesuit Rome or the socialist or philosophical forms of atheism.

For Hoffmann, such a sign of hope was the revitalization of the Orient, uplifting it from backwardness, decay, and poverty to the level of human dignity. He referred to these developments as a "peaceful crusade." Like the crusaders of the Middle Ages he wanted to conquer the Holy Land, but by peaceful and spiritual means. Hoffmann was convinced that the reestablishment of culture— what he called the "building-up of the spiritual temple in Jerusalem"—had far-reaching repercussions. That temple was to be both the sign of, and the means to, a restitution of true and pure Christianity in the Occident as well.

Numerical considerations were dismissed by Hoffmann. After all, Christianity developed from tiny beginnings and spread from the Orient to the four corners of the earth. Could the Tempelgesellschaft not be the core or nucleus of a new form of true Christianity? For this reason the spiritual aim of the Tempelgesellschaft—as carried out through its programs of planting congregations, its leadership role, worship services, and educational efforts—must remain the first priority. Seek ye first the Kingdom of God, and all the rest—commerce, industry, agriculture, science, and the fine arts—will be added.[38]

The Holy Land would thus not be the recipient of benevolence or the target of missionary endeavors alone. With vital help from the Occident it would assume, once again, its role as a geographic entity from which religious and cultural innovations would guide the future of world history: *ex oriente lux.*

THEMES FOR FUTURE RESEARCH

Hoffmann deserves a closer look. His development may be more complex than has so far been assumed. That he was a religious outcast does not mean that scholars should not direct their attention to him or to others in the Hoffmann camp—for example, Georg David Hardegg[39] or Christoph Paulus. The close association between the leadership of the Tempelgesellschaft and the Alliance Israélite Universelle, and the *Alliance Universelle de l'Ordre et de la Civilization* of Henry Dunant, the founder of the Red Cross, should also be explored.[40]

The different accounts of people who journeyed to the Holy Land need to be freshly examined. This may begin with Swiss-born Johann Ludwig Burckhardt (Lausanne, 1784) who had studied in Göttingen and set out to explore the Holy Land and adjacent areas. His accounts were first published in London; in 1824 they were edited in German by theologian Wilhelm Gesenius of Halle University.[41] Gotthilf Heinrich von Schubert's three-volume account of his journey is said to be a literary masterpiece.[42] Moritz Busch used for his book *A Pilgrimage to Jerusalem* the subtitle *Pictures without a Halo.*[43] What kind of criticism is implied here? The director of the Lutheran Leipzig Mission, Karl Graul, reported his experiences from a strictly Lutheran point of view and as a mission strategist.[44] Books were written by Friedrich Liebetrut[45] and Eduard Ohnesorge.[46] The latter's diary was edited by Wilhelm Hoffmann of Potsdam-Berlin (another example of the Holy Land network). The reformed pastor E. W. Schulz published his account of a journey in 1851; in it, he makes reference to a group of pious people from the Wuppertal region.[47]

The Steinbeck brothers from Hamburg, Thiede and his wife from Neukirchen, Müller from Barmen, and Steinborn from Elberfeld are subjects for study. German craftsmen and journeymen who traveled to the Holy Land in search of employment and who were sometimes conspicuous because of their behavior are also suitable subjects.

Many aspects of military and diplomatic involvement of Germans in the Holy Land have not been fully researched. Schulz, the first Prussian consul in Jerusalem, and some of his successors were devout church people as well as good diplomats. One of Bunsen's close associates, H. Abeken, should also be researched.[48]

A constant flow of new information about the Holy Land found its way to the public in new journals.[49] A survey of these journals should include theological journals as well. They all need to be reviewed for references to developments in the Holy Land. Similarly, daily papers should be checked to find such references.

Tourist guidebooks, like those of Friedrich Graf von Schack and Fürst Chlodwig Hohenlohe, may also contribute to our knowledge.

Finally, the activities of churches, church groups, or individual church people require further study. A few examples would be Dr. Barth of Calw and his Calwer *Missionsblatt*, the Moravian activities among the lepers in the Holy Land, Fliedner's deaconesses,[50] the Spittler network,[51] and various associations like *Palästinaverein Basel* (founded in 1842), *Jerusalemverein Berlin* (founded in 1852), *Deutsches Palästinawerk*, *Evangelischer Verein für das Syrische Waisenhaus*, *Jerusalemstiftung*, and the *Evangelischer Zweig des Johanniterordens*.

NOTES

1. Kenneth S. Latourette, *History of the Expansion of Christianity*, 7 vols. (New York: Harper, 1937–1945), cf. particularly vols. 4-6, *The Great Century*.

2. Hymn 320 in the *Evangelisches Kirchengesangbuch*.

3. Alex Carmel, *Die Siedlungen der württembergischen Templer in Palästina 1868–1918* (Stuttgart: W. Kohlhammer, 1973), 12.

4. See Ernst Benz, "Johann Albrecht Bengel und die Philosophie des deutschen Idealismus," *Deutsche Vierteljahresschrift für Literaturwissenschaft und Geistesgeschichte* 27 (1953): 528-54; Friedrich Groth, *Die "Wiederbringung aller Dinge" im württembergischen Pietismus*, Arbeiten zur Geschichte des Pietismus 21 (Göttingen: Vandenhoek und Ruprecht, 1984).

5. Cf. Ernst Benz, "Die abendländische Sendung der östlich-orthodoxen Kirche. Die russische Kirche und das abendländische Christentum im Zeitalter der Heiligen Allianz," *Abhandlungen der Akademie der Wissenschaften und der Literatur Mainz* 8 (1950).

6. Letter from Ferdinand Palmer to Christian Friedrich Spittler, cited in Alex Carmel, *Christen als Pioniere im Heiligen Land* (Basel: F. Reinhardt, 1981), 136. Concerning Spittler, see p. 55.

7. Friedrich A. Strauss, *Sinai und Gogatha, Reise in das Morgenland*, 3d ed. (Berlin: Jonas Verlagsbuchhandlung, 1850), 202.

8. Friedrich Naumann, *Asia* (Berlin-Schöneberg: Verlag der "Hilfe," 1900), 102-20.

9. Peter Gradenwitz, ed., *Das Heilige Land in Augenzeugenberichten* (Munich: Deutscher Taschenbuchverlag, 1984), 125.

10. Christian Carl Josias Freiherr von Bunsen, *Aus seinen Briefen und nach eigener Erinnerung geschildert von seiner Witwe, Deutsche Ausgabe, durch neue Mitteilungen vermehrt von Friedrich Nippold*, vol. 2 (Leipzig: F. A. Brockhaus, 1869), 171. For a detailed study, cf. Kurt Schmidt-Clausen, *Vorweggenommene Einheit: Die Gründung des*

Bistums Jerusalems im Jahre 1841 (Berlin/Hamburg: Lutherisches Verlagshaus, 1965), 85-118.

11. C. Bunsen, ibid., vol. 3 (1871), 507.

12. C. Bunsen (above, n.10), p. 196.

13. Ibid., 173.

14. For Bunsen's ideas on church reform, cf. my article, "Reform der Kirche. Bemerkungen zum Kirchenbegriff Christian Carl Josias Bunsens," *Zeitschrift für Religions— und Geistesgeschichte* 27 (1975): 153-65.

15. C. Bunsen (above, n.10), p. 199.

16. Ibid., 171.

17. Leopold von Ranke, ed., *Aus dem Briefwechsel Friederich Wilhelms IV mit Bunsen* (Leipzig: Duncker and Hümblot, 1873), 94f.

18. Ibid., 95.

19. Cited in K. Schmidt-Clausen (above, n.10), p. 89.

20. C. Bunsen (above, n.10), p. 151.

21. Ibid., 190.

22. Ibid.; the "broad wing" is the liberal branch of the Church of England.

23. For details, cf. Robert Preyer, "Bunsen and the Anglo-American Literary Community in Rome," in *Der gelehrte Diplomat*, ed. Erich Geldbach (Leiden: E. J. Brill, 1980), 35-44.

24. C. Bunsen (above, n.10), p. 188.

25. A. J. C. Hare as quoted by K. Schmidt-Clausen (above, n.10), p. 97.

26. Winfried Eisenblätter, "Carl Friedrich Adolph Steinkopf (1773–1859)" (Ph.D. diss., Zurich, 1967).

27. The yearbook *Pietismus und Neuzeit* 7 (1981) was dedicated to the "Deutsche Christentumsgesellschaft." Cf. also Ernest Staehelin, *Die Christentumsgesellschaft in der Zeit der Aufklärung und der beginnenden Erwachung* (Basel: Friedrich Reinhardt Verlag, 1970); and his *Die Christentumsgesellschaft in der Zeit von der Erweckung bis zur Gegenwart* (Basel: Friedrich Reinhardt Verlag, 1974).

28. Gotthilf H. von Schubert, *Reise in das Morgenland in den Jahren 1836 und 1837*, 3 vols. (Erlangen: J. J. Palm and E. Enke, 1838/39).

29. A. Carmel (above, n.6), p. 93.

30. *Samuel Gobat—Evangelischer Bischof in Jerusalem, Sein Leben und Wirken meist nach seinen eigenen Aufzeichnungen* (Basel: Verlag von C. F. Spittler, 1884), 116-19.

31. C. Bunsen (above, n.10), p. 199.

32. Alex Carmel, "Der Bankier Johannes Frutiger und seine Zeitgenossen," *Pietismus und Neuzeit* 11 (1985): 139-58.

33. Theodor Fliedner, *Reisen in das heilige Land* (Dusseldorf: H. Voss, 1858), 163.

34. Christoph Hoffmann, *Occident und Orient* (Stuttgart: Steinkopf, 1875), 252.

35. Ibid., 262.

36. Ibid., 269.

37. Ibid., 267.

38. Ibid., 271.

39. Gottlob David Sandel, *Georg David Hardegg. Revolutionär, Mitbegründer und Vorsteher der Deutschen Tempelgesellschaft, 1812–1879*, Lebensbilder aus Schwaben und Franken 9 (Stuttgart: Kohlhammer Verlag, 1963), 350-73.

40. Cf. Alfred Quellmalz, "Henry Dunant und seine evangelische Freunde In Schwa-

ben und im Elsass,'' *Blätter für württembergische Kirchengeschichte* 63 (1963): 166-227.

41. Johann L. Burckhardt, *Reisen in Syrien, Palästina und der Gegend des Berges Sinai*, ed. Wilhelm Gesenius (Weimar: Gr. S. priv. Landes-Industrie-Comptoir, 1824).

42. G. H. von Schubert (above, n.28).

43. Moritz Busch, *Eine Wallfahrt nach Jerusalem, Bilder ohne Heiligenschein*, 2 vols. (Leipzig: F. A. Brockhaus, 1863).

44. Karl Graul, *Reise nach Ostindien über Palästina und Egypten von Juli 1849 bis April 1853* (Leipzig: Dörffling und Franke, 1854).

45. Friedrich Liebetrut, *Reise nach dem Morgenlande, insonderheit nach Jerusalem und dem heiligen Lande*, 2d ed. (Hamburg: Agentur des Rauhen Hauses, 1858).

46. Eduard Ohnesorge, *Der Zions-Pilger. Tagebuch auf der Reise nach Jerusalem*, ed. Wilhelm Hoffmann (Berlin: O. Kritz, 1858).

47. E. W. Schulz, *Reise in das gelobte Land im Jahre 1851*, 2d ed. (Mühlheim/Ruhr, 1859).

48. Cf. H. Abeken, *Babylon und Jerusalem* (n.p., 1851).

49. For example, *Neueste Nachrichten aus dem Morgenlande; Sammlungen.*

50. *Berichte über die Diakonissenstationen im Morgenland (1851–   ).*

51. For example, Baldensperger's diaries, letters, and numerous archival materials.

Chapter 12

Sources for Germany–Holy Land Studies in the Late Ottoman Period: German Libraries and Archives

Haim Goren

The Israel State Archives holds one of the major collections on the subject of Germany–Holy Land relations; namely, remains of the German consular files from Jerusalem, Haifa, and Jaffa (1838–1939). This material has served as the basis for several studies and undoubtedly will continue to be consulted by scholars and students. However, despite the qualitative and quantitative importance of this collection, it cannot serve as a sole basis for research, even for topics included in its files. The scholar must turn to the extensive material in libraries and archives scattered throughout East and West Germany, only a fraction of which has been studied and analyzed.

This survey presents selected examples of the different types of archives and libraries containing material dealing with specific aspects of the broad spectrum of Germany–Holy Land relations. It delineates the diversity of the material, as well as problems of accessibility. Reference books listed at the end of this chapter are useful guides to the location of material.

STATE ARCHIVES

These are generally well-organized, comprehensive archives of ministries and other governmental agencies that functioned in the individual states prior to and after the formation of the Second Reich (1871). Some are located in cities that have served as capitals: Berlin (Prussia and later Germany), Stuttgart (Württemburg), Munich (Bavaria), and Bonn. Other archives have been transferred to Koblenz and Freiburg.[1]

Politisches Archiv des Auswärtigen Amtes, Bonn

This archive contains the files of the German Foreign Ministry since 1867, the year of the founding of the North German Confederation. The catalogue of these files, compiled in England where the Foreign Ministry documents were transferred after World War II, is titled *A Catalogue of Files and Microfilms of the German Foreign Ministry Archives 1867–1920* (1959). Alex Carmel notes that this collection contains more material on Eretz Israel under Ottoman rule than any other archive in the Federal Republic of Germany. A large portion of the files are grouped under the heading "Turkey," whose reference is I.A.B.q. The following are examples of the material available:

No. 33:Disputes over holy sites in Palestine

No. 105:The protest of the Russian government against [German] General Consul von Alten in Jerusalem

No. 126:Protection of Christians in the Holy Land

No. 140:Christian-Muslim strife in Haifa

No. 175:A series of files on the general subject of "Christians in Turkey" including, *inter alia*,
    a. Catholics
    d. Protestants (three files)
    e. Holy sites, including a plan for the renewal of the Kingdom of Jerusalem under Catholic rule (two files)
    g. The Cenaculum and the Dormition (twelve files)

Other files include:

I.A.A.S. 36: The visit of His Excellency the Crown Prince to the East and to the opening of the Suez Canal

Preussen 1, Nr. 4v: His Royal Majesty's trip to Athens and Turkey, beginning 1 August 1898; His Majesty's trip to the East (twelve files).

Bundesarchiv—Militärarchiv, Freiburg i. Br.
(Military Archives, etc.)

In 1967 the military records in the West German State Archives were transferred from Koblenz to Freiburg. Most of the material relating to the Holy Land is located in the naval files, under the general reference RM. The archive and its files are catalogued according to the various naval branches. The following are examples of relevant files from various sections:

RM 1: The Imperial Admiralty

RM 1/v:

No. 1876: Protection of Germans in foreign countries by dispatch of German warships. A long series of files arranged according to ships' names. Knowledge of the name of the ship and the date of its docking at one of the local harbors in Palestine facilitates retrieval of relevant records. Alex Carmel cites the report of Korwetten Kapitain Graf von Hacke as an example of the quality of the material, and adds that he was unable to find a report of similar quality and scope in any of the documents of the political archives of the Foreign Ministry in Bonn.

No. 2351: Preparations for the transfer of Prussian troops assigned to Syria, August–December 1860

Nos. 2364–2369: Dispatch of warships to the Mediterranean

RM 5: Naval headquarters 1899–1919

RM 5/v:

Nos. 2320–2323: The war between Germany and Russia, France, and England; The Turkish War; The Campaign against the Suez Canal and Egypt

Nos. 3862–3863: Operations on the Turkish coast

RM 38, 39, 40, 41 contain extensive material on German military activity during World War I.

Hauptstaatsarchiv Stuttgart (The Central Archive of Württemberg)

Most of the material concerning the Holy Land in this archive relates to the formation and organization of *Die Tempelgesellschaft* (Temple Society) in the kingdom of Württemberg and its subsequent settlement in Palestine. The majority of this material is found in two sections: (1) Kabinettsakten IV, E 14 (1585) (Sekten und Schwärmer 1818–1887); and (2) Akten des Königl. Ministeriums der auswärtigen Angelegenheiten E 46/48.

The Stuttgart authorities closely followed the founding and development of the Temple Society. Consequently, they devoted much space to Palestine and its environs in their correspondence with and about this society, which had fulfilled its stated goal of settlement in the Holy Land. Alex Carmel and Paul Sauer's studies of the Templers relied heavily on this material.[2] Additional material in the same blocs deals with scholars from Württemberg in the East as well as other topics, such as the founding of the *Erlöser Kirche* (German Church of the Redeemer) in Jerusalem.

Zentrales Staatsarchiv der Deutsche Demokratische Republik (DDR), Dienststelle Merseburg

As noted previously, the documents in the Foreign Ministry archives in Bonn date only from 1867. The State Archives at Merseburg cover the period prior to that year, and they were believed to contain rich source material on Prussia-Holy Land relations, a supposition borne out by Christiane Schütz's recent doctoral thesis.[3] Among the documents she cited are the following:

2.4.1. Abt. 1, Nr. 12570–12573:

Foreign Ministry correspondence concerning the construction of a church for the joint English-Prussian Bishopric in Jerusalem, from Kaiser Friedrich Wilhelm IV, among others.

Rep. 76-III, Sekt. 1, Abt. XVIII, Generalia 110a, Bd. III:

A file concerning the Jerusalem Bishopric.

Rep. 151 I.C., Nr. 8413:

Finance Ministry correspondence regarding the establishment of institutions for the Bishopric and the Evangelical community in Jerusalem.

CHURCH ARCHIVES

Evangelisches Zentralarchiv in West Berlin

This is an umbrella organization for the various evangelical churches in West Germany. It is relatively easy to locate a large quantity of archival material relating to the activities of various branches and organizations of these churches in the Holy Land, beginning with the 1830s. The first well-documented topic is the foundation of the joint English-Prussian Bishopric in 1841. The material on the *Evangelischer Jerusalemsverein* and *das Deutsche Evangelische Institut für Altertumsforschung des Heiligen Landes zu Jerusalem* is outstanding. Other files are devoted to evangelical communities and institutions in the Holy Land. Most of the material is filed in sections 5, 7, 55, 56.

Bestand 5: Covers church activity outside Germany. The relevant files for our subject are under the heading "Asiatic Turkey." For example:

No. 2000 (Asiatic Turkey 6e): The Evangelical Bishopric in Jerusalem, December 1841–August 1889

Nos. 1969–1970 (Asiatic Turkey 12): The church affairs of the German evangelical community in Jaffa, June 1864–May 1925

Bestand 7: Evangelischer Oberkirchenrat

Nos. 410–414: His Excellency Kaiser Wilhelm II's trip to Jerusalem for the dedication of the Erlöser Kirche

Nos. 3906–3908: *Berliner Jerusalemsverein* (The Jerusalem Association in Berlin)

Nos. 5934–5937: *Die Deutsche Evangelische Stiftung für* . . . (The German Evangelical Foundation for Antiquity Research of the Holy Land)

Bestand 55: All the files are devoted to the founding of Das Deutsche Evangelische Institut für Altertumsforschung des Heiligen Landes in Jerusalem.

Bestand 56: Evangelischer Jerusalemsverein; files devoted to communities and institutions in the Holy Land. They include material on the construction of the Muristan section in Jerusalem and the founding of the Erlöser Kirche (C 1–3), the cemetery (C 4), and various institutions (all of section D).

Historisches Archiv des Erzbistums Köln

This church archive is devoted to the activity of Catholic Germany in the Holy Land. The archbishop of Köln extended his patronage to societies functioning on behalf of and in the Holy Land. The documents are concentrated in three files in CR 22.11. Files nos. 1, 2, and 7 are devoted to the German Catholic societies mentioned previously, to the Knights of the Holy Sepulcher, and to German Catholic interests during World War I.

CENTERS OF SOCIETIES ACTIVE IN THE HOLY LAND

Die Tempelgesellschaft

The Templer headquarters are currently located in a suburb of Stuttgart. Its leadership has seen to the collection and cataloguing of all available documents and memoirs of members who lived in the Holy Land. As a result, the archives are rich in documents, maps, and personal journals. In addition, it houses all the volumes of the society's periodical, *Die Warte des Tempels*, published since 1845, which contains a vast amount of material relating to the Holy Land. Alex Carmel notes that its weekly reports on events in Palestine are the most reliable and comprehensive consecutive source for the activities of the German settlers there.

Evangelischer Jerusalemsverein

The modest library and archives are located in the headquarters of the *Berliner Missionswerk*. The archives contain files on the Anglican Bishopric and the evangelical community in Jerusalem, the girls' school Talitha Kumi, and the Syrian (Schneller) Orphanage. The library has almost complete sets of the various periodicals of the society, of which the most important is *Neuste Nachrichten aus den Morgenlande*.

Deutscher Verein vom Heiligen Lande

Founded in 1895 as the successor to prior Catholic societies, it oversaw most of the German Catholic activity in the Holy Land. Its headquarters and library are located in Köln. However, most of the library and essentially all of its archives were destroyed during World War II. This is an example of one of the major problems affecting research in Germany.

GERMAN SCIENTIFIC SOCIETIES ACTIVE IN PALESTINE AND THE EAST

Die Deutscher morgenländische Gesellschaft

Founded in 1845, the purpose of this society was to promote broad scientific studies of Asia. Its headquarters were located in Halle and Leipzig. Its library and archives are presently in Halle a/S in the German Democratic Republic. The catalogues for the East German archives (see list of reference books at the end of this chapter) indicate the preservation of substantial material on the activity of various prominent scientists, including H. Guthe, J. H. Gadow, J. G. Wetz-stein, and others.

Die [Königliche] Bayerische Akademie der Wissenschaften

The headquarters of this still active scientific body are located in Munich. The academy houses the library and archives as well. The archives contain the personal files of the member scientists, including reports and letters concerning their expeditions; for example, the expedition to the East initiated by G. J. von Schubert in the 1830s. The library houses all the academy's publications. The volumes of the *Abhandlungen* and the *Sitzungsberichte* contain scattered reports on studies of the Holy Land; these are relatively accessible through the detailed indexes.

Das Gustaf Dalman Institut für biblische Landes und Altertumskunde, Griefswald

In 1902, Gustaf Dalman founded, in Jerusalem, *Das Deutsche Evangelische Institut für Altertumsforschung des Heiligen Landes zu Jerusalem*, which he headed until the outbreak of World War I. During the war he joined the theological faculty at Griefswald (in East Germany), and in 1919 he founded a still functioning institute there, parallel to the one in Jerusalem. The institute has preserved substantial material on the activities and research of Dalman, A. Alt (Dalman's replacement in Jerusalem), and others.

PRIVATE ARCHIVES AND COLLECTIONS

Some of the estates belonging to this category are still in private hands, while others have been transferred to public institutions. Apparently, there is still much material waiting to be uncovered, and from time to time new significant material is revealed. The scope of these collections is usually narrow. I limit myself to a few examples.

W. L. Janssen (1830–1900), whose papers are the property of his relatives in Aachen. Janssen founded, headed, and guided many of the Catholic societies active in the Holy Land. His papers include extensive correspondence with his representatives in Palestine, as well as church and political bodies in Germany. This material served, for example, as the basis for a study of the Catholic aspects of Kaiser Wilhelm II's visit to the Holy Land.

J. Zeller (1830–1902), Bishop Samuel Gobat's son-in-law, served as a member of the Anglican Mission in Palestine from 1856 to 1901, working primarily in Nazareth and Jerusalem. A great deal of material about him and his work was collected by his relative, Liesel Reichle-Zeller, in conjunction with the family foundation *Martinszeller Verband e.V. Stuttgart.*

H. Renard of Köln, an architect, designed two of the monumental German buildings in Jerusalem—the Dormition Church and Abbey on Mount Zion and St. Paul's Hospice opposite the Damascus Gate. His papers are stored in the *Historisches Archiv der Stadt Köln*, under Abt. 4: Nachlass Renard. They include plans for his buildings as well as sketches and pictures of buildings, graves, and architectural features of Jerusalem. Dr. Edina Meyer utilized this material for her article on the Dormition that appeared in *Architectura* 1984.

J. Frutiger (1836–1899) of Basel arrived in Jerusalem in 1858 and lived and worked there for more than thirty years. He was known mainly as a dynamic banker, and as one of the heads of the German evangelical community in Jerusalem. His descendants have preserved his and his wife's diaries, as well as other documents connected with the family's activities in Jerusalem. His grandson made copies available to Alex Carmel, who utilized them for an article summarizing Frutiger's activities, in the process of shedding new light on life in Palestine in the last decades of the nineteenth century.[4]

CENTRAL LIBRARIES

Material on Germany–Holy Land relations is available in many libraries throughout Germany, but it is difficult to point to a particular library specializing in the subject in its entirety. Certain libraries focus on specific aspects, such as theology, geography, or biblical archaeology. I have elected to describe two of the largest libraries, which contain a variety of material—archives, travel literature, contemporaneous studies, periodicals, newspapers, maps, and current research.

Staatsbibliothek Preussischer Kulturbesitz, West Berlin

Berlin, capital of Prussia and all of Germany, naturally served as a center of Germany–Holy Land activity. It played a leading role in policy-making, in church, mission, and evangelical activities, in research, and in other areas as well. Its library rivals that of Munich for the title of "the largest library in Germany." No serious scholar of Germany–Holy Land relations can ignore it. The relevant material is located in the various branches of the general library, as well as in special divisions: the East, cartography, and manuscripts.

G. H. Degering's three-volume work (see list of reference books at the end of this chapter) serves as the basis for locating the considerable archival material in the manuscript division, but the card catalogue in that division should be consulted as well. The manuscript division contains the papers of German travelers and scholars, and documents related primarily to Berlin researchers, both those active in the region and those who studied the area from Germany. These documents are mainly classified in the reference group "Ms. Germ. Quart." Among the outstanding personalities represented here are J. G. Wetzstein, R. Röricht, and C. Ritter.

The main library's collection of periodicals and newspapers, some of them rare, is of great value to the scholar of Germany–Holy Land relations. It houses the numerous publications of the Berlin Academy of Sciences, which included (thanks largely to C. Ritter) extensive coverage of Palestine, and progress reports on various research projects. For example, we find there a complete set of the daily (later, weekly) *Das Ausland*, which devoted considerable attention to the Holy Land.

Berlin houses other libraries that can help the scholar. These include the main library of the Free University, as well as its geography division; the library of the Berlin Geographical Society; and the libraries of two theological seminaries— *Diakonisches Werk des Evang. Kirche in Deutschland* and *Kirchliche Hochschule*.

Bayerische Staatsbibliothek, München

This huge library, like its sister library in Berlin, has an extensive repository of material for the scholar on various aspects of Germany–Holy Land relations.

The manuscript division houses the papers of many Bavarians involved with Palestine in various capacities. K. Dach's book (see list of reference books at the end of this chapter) serves as an initial guide for location of the material. Among the more significant collections for our topic are those of G. H. von Schubert and J. N. Sepp.

Much additional material is available in the collections of the cartography and Oriental divisions. The main library's collection of all types of literature dealing with the Holy Land is truly outstanding. However, two difficulties hamper the interested reader: (1) the catalogue available to the public dates only from 1911, and (2) even if the scholar consults the comprehensive catalogue for the entire library, many books, especially those dealing with our topic (among them rare travelers' accounts), were destroyed during World War II.

Nevertheless, the library contains extensive material. One way of locating it is to search drawers W35 (Palestine) and W58 (pilgrimages and journeys to Palestine, 1600–1800). The library also houses one of the important collections of Bavarian periodicals and newspapers, among them the *Allgemeine Zeitung*, which appeared alternately in Augsburg and Munich, and published many articles and reports from and about the Holy Land.

NOTES

1. Alex Carmel, "Documentary Material in Austrian and German Archives Relating to Palestine during the Period of Ottoman Rule," in *Studies on Palestine during the*

Ottoman Period, ed. Moshe Maoz (Jerusalem: Magnes Press, 1975), 568-77; idem, "Historical Sources on the History of Eretz Israel during the Ottoman Period in Archives in Austria and Germany," *Cathedra* 1 (September 1976, Hebrew): 157-91.

2. Alex Carmel, *German Settlement in Palestine during the Later Periods of Turkish Rule: Political, Local and International Problems* (Jerusalem: Israel Oriental Society, The Hebrew University, 1973, Hebrew); Paul Sauer, *Uns Rief das Heilige Land: Die Tempelgesellschaft im Wandel der Zeit* (Stuttgart: K. Theiss Verlag, 1985).

3. Christiane B. H. Schütz, "Preussen in Jerusalem (1800–1861): Karl Friedrich Schinkels Entwurf der Grabeskirche und die Jerusalempläne Friedrich Wilhelms IV" (Inauguraldissertastion zur Erlangung der Doktorwürde, vorgelegt der Philosophischen Fakultät der Rheinischen Friedrich-Wilhelms-Universität zu Bonn, Berlin, 1986).

4. Alex Carmel, "The Diaries of Johannes and Maria Frutiger," *Cathedra* 48 (June 1988, Hebrew): 49-72.

REFERENCE BOOKS

Archiv in deutschsprachigen Raum (Minerva Handbücher). 2 vols. Berlin and New York, 1974.

Archive und Archivare in der Bundesrepublik Deutschland, Osterreich und Schweiz. Munich, 1986.

Verzeichnis der Schriftlichen Nachlässe in deutschen Archiven und Bibliotheken:

Band 1: *Die Nachlässe in den deutschen Archiven (mit Ergänzungen aus anderen Beständen).* Ed. Wolfgang Amadeus Mommsen. Teil I: *Einleitung und Verzeichnis.* Boppard am Rhein, 1971. Teil II: Boppard am Rhein, 1983.

Band 2: *Die Nachlässe in den Bibliotheken der Bundesrepublik Deutschland.* Ed. Ludwig Denecke. 2. Auflage, völlig neu bearbeitet von T. Brandis. Boppard am Rhein, 1981.

Gelehrten-und Schriftstellernachlässe in der Bibliotheken der Deutschen Demokratischen Republik:

Teil 1: *Die Nachlässe in den wissenschaftlichen Allgemeinbibliotheken.* Ed. Ruth Unger. Berlin, 1959.

Teil 2: *Die Nachlässe in wissenschaftlichen Instituten und Museen und in den allgemeinbildenen Bibliotheken.* Ed. H. Lüfling und Ruth Unger. Berlin, 1968.

Teil 3: *Nachträge, Ergänzungen, Register.* Ed. H. Lüfling und H. Wolf. Berlin, 1971.

Dache, K. *Die schriftlichen Nachlässe in der Bayerischen Staatsbibliothek München.* Wiesbaden, 1970.

Degering, Hermann, ed. *Kurzes Verzeichnis der germanischen Handschriften der preussischen Staatsbibliothek.* I. Die Handschriften in Folioformat. II. Die Handschriften in Quatroformat. III. Die Handschriften in Okatavformat und Register. Graz: Akademische Druck- und Verlagsamt, 1970.

Chapter 13

Germany–Holy Land Studies: A Conceptual Framework

Yossi Ben-Artzi

Research on Germany–Holy Land relations has been confined mainly to individual in-depth studies covering particular topics. In the main, these studies are limited to a specific academic discipline or to a related area, but they do not examine the subjects in total context. For example, Mordechai Eliav has devoted his attention to the connections between the Jewish community in Palestine and various German agencies, both Jewish and non-Jewish, such as philanthropic societies and the German diplomatic corps.[1] In his studies, events and processes governing Germany–Holy Land relations are examined from the perspective of Jewish history.

Germany–Holy Land interaction is examined from a Zionist viewpoint by Isaiah Friedman. He incorporates this approach into a broader treatment of the complex relationships in Palestine under Ottoman rule.[2] Alex Carmel writes from the perspective of Christian activity, particularly by Protestants, as developed by such groups as the Templers or by individuals.[3] While Palestine is the focal point for Carmel, his work, by its very nature, examines the background of individuals or groups under study, but always against the broader context of nineteenth-century developments. Thus, he synthesizes German Protestant activity in particular, in both political events and in the development of the country.

Other shorter papers, published in Israel and in Germany, analyze the various actors—Jews, Christians, religious and social groups—and the political and diplomatic factors in the wide spectrum of Germany–Holy Land history. This variegated activity calls for a shared conceptual framework.

My approach is based on the following propositions:

1. Germany–Holy Land relations represent a complex network of various fields of activity; no single in-depth study of a particular aspect illuminates it fully. Understanding this rich texture requires an interdisciplinary approach.

2. Research studies, both those rooted in a particular discipline as well as those based on an interdisciplinary approach, together enhance the scope and depth of the field.

3. The direction of inquiry may be lateral (from Germany to the Holy Land, or the opposite) or bilateral (combined relationships and interrelationships).

4. The relevant time span for the conceptual framework encompasses the modern era. For the present it should terminate at the outbreak of World War I.

5. Our goals may be advanced through cooperation among scholars in different countries, by encouragement of instruction and research at advanced university levels, and through academic publications.

The wide spectrum of Germany–Holy Land relations cannot be attributed to the initiative or planning of any specific agency motivated by special interests. Nonetheless, certain aspects in that relationship were the result of preferred policies of groups and individuals whose goals were the strengthening of such ties. Spittler's mission, the Templer settlement plans, the dispatch of emissaries to study conditions in Palestine prior to initiating projects,[4] as well as diplomatic initiatives, all illustrate the contention that the nature of Germany–Holy Land relations must be examined in a total context.

The entire phenomenon is to be viewed in its widest perspective, even if at times there seems to be no apparent connection between its components. For example, examination of German diplomatic activity would not shed light on its geographic, cultural, or economic effects, unless they too were studied, both individually and with regard to their place within the total system. No one scholar is capable of analyzing all these aspects in depth, although he may mention them or refer the reader to bibliographical material. This complexity is the basis of our conceptual framework and determines its research topics as well.

RESEARCH TOPICS

To date, most research has been located within the discipline of history. Although the studies dealt with different subjects, they are all the work of historians: Historical processes and phenomena are central to these studies, which are essentially descriptive and chronological in nature.

History remains a central motif in all the topics suggested in the following sections, but some require, in addition, analysis from cognate disciplines.

Geographical Influences and Phenomena

The growing number of historical geographers illustrates the thriving connection between history and geography. There are groups of academicians in many countries, including Germany and Israel, who define themselves as historical geographers. This development enables the expansion of research on Germany–Holy Land relations to include the physical landscape.

Any activity with practical implications leaves its mark on the physical environment, faithfully expressing contemporaneous aspirations, ideas, and experiences of individuals and agencies. Historical geography facilitates comprehension of the physical landscape of the past (and its remains in the present) by describing the *realia* of the past with the aid of historical sources. It should be noted that even a historian like Alex Carmel, who studies the political and religious activities of German groups in the Holy Land, finds himself unable to ignore the physical results of their activities. However, lacking geographical or architectural training, Carmel presents tentative conclusions, thus leaving the task of analyzing his findings to others.[5] Many groups left their mark on the physical landscape of the Holy Land. For example, Templers established settlements; missionary societies built public buildings, schools, hospitals, and churches. Future research can be expanded to include changes in the physical landscape of the Holy Land as a result of the activities of German groups, both Jewish and Gentile.

Specific areas for future research could include rural settlement, urban settlement, immigration, and communications and transportation. Aspects of these areas include:

1. Rural settlement (in its broad sense): Founding of settlements, land purchases, construction of housing, type of economy.

2. Urban settlement: Changes in the construction, nature, and characteristics of cities in Palestine.

3. Immigration as a central factor in the creation of Germany–Holy Land ties: Dimensions and characteristics; influence on the landscape; points of origin; and types of belongings brought to Palestine.

4. Communications and transportation: Communications between Palestine and Europe in general, and Germany in particular; the nature of German activity in these areas, and its relationship with other countries involved in mail and telegraph services, and in marine and land transport.

Economic Aspects

Activity on the part of various groups, mainly in Palestine and to a lesser degree in Germany, should be examined in conjunction with the geographical factors mentioned previously. Three areas should be explored: (1) commerce, import, and export; (2) industry and crafts; and (3) agriculture.

Commerce, Import, and Export. Commercial corporations and firms introduced many innovations that transformed the local markets. The firm of Spittler and Co., with branches in Jerusalem and Jaffa, was mentioned in articles by Carmel[6] and Sinno;[7] a detailed study of its operations and contribution to the economy of Palestine has yet to be undertaken. The Templer settlers Breisch and Dück owned the largest shops in the country, which imported lumber, iron, kerosene, and other basic commodities. They served as trustees for banks and monetary transactions, and they also dealt in tourism and transportation. The little that is known about them and other entrepreneurs only touches upon the daily life in Palestine. If their business transactions and initiatives, financial records, and so forth were uncovered, our knowledge would be greatly enhanced.

Industry and Crafts. Settlers of German descent played a major role in the introduction of modern manufacturing and industry into Palestine. The exact nature of the role of the German companies that shipped machinery, tools, ploughs, motors, and other equipment has yet to be determined. Best known of these entrepreneurs are the Wagner Brothers of Jaffa who cast metal, and the Struve family which produced olive oil and by-products in Haifa. There were German metal-workers, carpenters, wagonmakers, and other craftsmen who employed modern machinery and advanced methods. Apart from the fact of their existence, little is known about the nature of their products or their contact with and influence on the local population. The accidental discovery of the archives of a Haifa family of carpenters, the Haars, sheds new light on their business methods and customers and, thus, on our understanding of the relationships between Jews, Germans, and Arabs in that city.

Agriculture. N. Talman has recently begun a basic study of the agricultural activities of the Templers. Beyond Carmel's work, and an earlier study by Karl Imberger,[8] this obvious field of inquiry lies fallow. Talman's research will undoubtedly illuminate important aspects of the development of Palestine, as well as relations between German settlers and Jewish and Arab farmers.

Art and Architecture

Art is another academic discipline that should be explored in the study and evaluation of Germany–Holy Land relations in the nineteenth century. The work of many artists and artisans has been overlooked and remains unknown to the general public. Such was the fate of Gustav Bauernfeind, whose paintings of Palestine are first being evaluated eighty years after his death.

Drawing, painting, and sculpture, as well as crafts, developed alongside German political, religious, and settlement activities. These expressions require study by art historians, experts in the trends and forces at work in Europe and Germany during the nineteenth century.

Architecture is another relevant discipline for research. German professionals participated in all stages of planning, surveying, and construction in urban and rural settlements. Their building activities were extensive, due to the large number of German settlers and agencies active in the Holy Land. A thorough survey of buildings constructed by Germans, now in progress, assumes the existence of no fewer than one thousand such structures in nineteenth-century Palestine.[9] Germans also built agricultural settlements; urban suburbs; and health, education, welfare, and religious institutions—all under the guidance of professionals, some achieving fame, others remaining anonymous. These professionals were active both in Germany and in Palestine, and they were German-trained for the most part. Toward the end of this period, German Jews also began to build within the Jewish community in Palestine.

Some major figures and building projects have been studied. Conrad Schick is well known through Carmel's articles,[10] as is Gottlieb Schumacher. However, the architectural contributions of figures such as Theodor Sandel and his son Benjamin, Ernst Voigt, and others have not been researched. German Jews like J. Treidel, a surveyor, and A. Berwald left their mark within the Jewish sphere, but little is known about their method of work. Well-known German edifices like the Church of the Dormition[11] and the Augusta Victoria complex[12] have been studied; but many other building projects, located mainly in Jerusalem and partly in the Galilee and the Coastal Plain, await historical and architectural analysis.

Biographies

Studies of personalities like Schick, Spittler, Fliedner, Frutiger, Gobat, and others hint at the historical riches available through biographical investigation of figures involved in various fields of endeavor affecting Palestine. Biography reflects the actual landscape of the country during the subject's lifetime. The daily activities of these individuals, their personal relationships, and the groups with whom they were in contact shed light on historical and geographical processes.

Little attention has been devoted to Jewish figures of German origin active in Eretz Israel, in both the old and new Yishuv. Well-known scholars and public figures such as Yehoseph Schwarz and Arthur Ruppin, as well as lesser-known personalities such as Elias Auerbach, David Trietsch, Otto Warburg, Paul Nathan, Willy Bambus, and Zelig Suskin await thorough study.

Scientific Studies

Haim Goren's doctoral thesis is devoted to German scientific studies of nineteenth-century Palestine. Such writings, both comprehensive and local in nature, were undertaken by scholars and research institutes and appeared in journals and professional literature, contributing to knowledge of the Holy Land and its characteristics. These studies should be collected, and the role of German scholarship with regard to Palestine should be assessed.

Literature and Journalism

Journalism and *belles lettres* are an important tool for regional studies; just as Hebrew literature from the First Aliyah illuminates its period, so, too, German material on Palestine, whether originating there or in Germany, should be collected and studied. Journalism certainly constitutes an important research tool, both for the information it contains and for its reflection of the atmosphere of its time. Both the Hebrew and German press served as major conduits of information between Palestine and Germany.

DIRECTIONS

What is the optimal and most realistic way of widening the scope of the informational framework for the study of Germany–Holy Land relations?

At present, the *Jahrbuch des Instituts für Deutsche Geschichte*, published in Tel Aviv, is the only forum for studies on Germany–Holy Land relations. It covers a portion of the areas mentioned above and deals with the modern era and political processes as well.

Promotion of academic studies of Germany–Holy Land relations, both in Israel and Germany, is an essential goal. Research topics will subsequently serve as subjects for courses. Academic study in this field today takes place mainly at the masters and doctoral level; nonetheless, undergraduate courses should be offered as well, in order to attract interested students at an early stage. Basic knowledge of geography, and an acquaintance with archival and bibliographical material, should be acquired early in the course of study.

The bilateral nature of the subject lends itself to joint courses and, at the very least, to tours and meetings among students with shared interests from both countries—in addition, of course, to the vital need for ongoing exchange among scholars.

NOTES

1. Mordechai Eliav, *Love of Zion and Men of Hod: German Jewry and the Settlement of Eretz-Israel in the 19th Century* (Tel Aviv: HaKibbutz Hameuchad, 1971, Hebrew); *The Jews of Palestine in German Policy: Selected Documents from the Archives of the German Consulate, 1842–1914* (Tel Aviv: HaKibbutz Hameuchad, 1973, Hebrew and German).

2. Isaiah Friedman, *Germany, Turkey and Zionism 1897–1918* (Oxford: Clarendon Press, 1977).

3. Alex Carmel, *Die Siedlungen der württembergischen Templer in Palästina, 1868–1918* (Stuttgart: W. Kohlhammer, 1973); "Der Missionar Theodor Fliedner als Pioneer deutscher Palästina-Arbeit," *Jahrbuch des Instituts für Deutsche Geschichte* 14 (1985): 191-220.

4. Haim Goren, "German Catholic Activity in Palestine, 1838–1910" (M.A. thesis, The Hebrew University of Jerusalem, 1986, Hebrew), 25-28.

5. Yossi Ben-Artzi, *The Jewish Colony in the Landscape of Eretz Israel, 1882–1914* (Jerusalem: Yad Itzhak Ben-Zvi, 1988, Hebrew), 79-96.

6. Alex Carmel, "Christian Friedrich Spittlers Beitrag zum Wiederaufbau Palästinas im 19 Jahrhundert," *Pietismus und Neuzeit* 7 (1981): 147-79.

7. Abdul-Raouf Sinno, *Deutsche Interessen in Syrien und Palästina 1841–1898* (West Berlin: Baalbek, 1982), 148.

8. Karl Imberger, *Die deutschen landwirtschaftlichen Kolonien in Palästina* (Ohrlingen: F. Rau, 1938).

9. "Deutsche Bauten in Palästina," Field Survey, 1985–1988 (in preparation).

10. Alex Carmel, "Wie es zu Conrad Schick nach Jerusalem kam," *Zeitschrift des deutschen Palästina-Vereins* 99 (1983): 204-18.

11. E. Meir, "Die Dormition auf dem Berg Zion in Jerusalem . . . ," *Architectura* (1984): 149-70.

12. Christiane B. H. Schütz, Preussen (1800–1861): Karl Friedrich Schenkels Entwurf der Grabeskirche und die Jerusalempläne Friedrich Wilhelms IV (Ph.D. diss., Friedrich Wilhelm's University of Bonn, Berlin, 1986).

Chapter 14

Research into German Christian Contributions to the Rebuilding of Eretz Israel: A Personal Record

Alex Carmel

Yehoshua Ben-Arieh's first book, *The Rediscovery of the Land of Israel in the Nineteenth Century* (1970), was a significant breakthrough in the study of the Christian contribution to the development of the Holy Land in the last century. A few Israeli scholars had previously touched upon one or another facet of Christian activity, but they had focused mainly on the Jewish contribution to the rebuilding of the Land. Ben-Arieh's book made evident the importance of re-search into Christian activities within the framework of the historical geography of Palestine.[1]

Research into the German contribution to the development of Palestine was particularly problematic in the political sense. When Uriel Heyd convinced me, in the mid-1960s, to utilize my knowledge of German to write my doctoral thesis on the Templer settlements in Palestine at the close of the Ottoman rule, I found myself in an almost completely neglected field—undoubtedly due in part to the language difficulty. Yet the Germans were by far the largest Christian element then active in Palestine: Among 5,000 Christians of European (or American) origin who lived in Palestine in 1914, about 3,000 were German (including some 2,200 Swabian settlers), a decisive component in every sense, to which serious attention should be paid.

About twenty-five years have passed since I first set foot in the national and church archives in Germany (and in Basel) that contain material touching upon Palestine.[2] In most of those institutions—about two dozen collections, some of which Haim Goren describes in Chapter 12—I received superb assistance in my research. However, in several archives, particularly those of the missionary societies that were formerly active in Palestine but had ceased their activities or limited them to the Arab population, I initially encountered a rather reserved response. It soon became apparent that a Jew coming from Israel for the legitimate scholarly purpose of uncovering documents that were considered, a hundred or a hundred and fifty years ago, to be extremely restricted—and which, in part, reveal bitter conflicts and intrigues among the Christians—is not always a welcome guest. Furthermore, since the mission in the nineteenth century frequently focused particularly on the Jews (although it failed completely) and because this subject is still a sensitive topic in Israel, leading to violence from time to time, the missionary societies suspect the innocence of the visitor from Israel or fear that problems may arise from what they see as "snooping" into their documents. In addition, at times there are political reservations regarding Israel, for missionary activity in the past—and to this very day—has been carried out primarily among the Arab population. Moreover, with the intensification of the Israel-Arab conflict, the missions tend to identify with the Arab point of view. As a result, my work at first met with some difficulties.

Pertinent sources are preserved within a narrow group of individuals associated with the *Palästina Deutsche*, many of whom (and, of course, their descendants) retain mutual ties and coordinate information about publications dealing with them. I believe that with the publication of my work in the German language, most of them have been convinced that my research into the activities of the German Christians is free of "political accounting" and is objective. No doubt helpful is the fact that my book on the Templers was published by the (national) Association for the Study of the History of Württemberg, and my study of missionary pilgrims appeared as a publication of the Theological Faculty of the University of Basle,[3] two clearly academic institutions that certainly cannot be suspected of bias. As a result, two of my students, Yossi Ben-Artzi and Haim Goren, who have recently been in Germany to study the activities of the German Christians in Palestine, have experienced a measure of trust even among those elements that in the 1960s had considerable reservations about me.

In light of this, it is important to emphasize the benefits that will accrue from cooperation with German scholars in this field. Erich Geldbach's contribution to this volume is a good example of the usefulness of joint German-Israeli research. An initial exchange of views in this regard took place in Jerusalem in the summer of 1987, in the Germany–Holy Land sessions within a seminar on Western Societies and the Holy Land, sponsored by the International Center for University Teaching of Jewish Civilization.

In the autumn of 1987, a parallel institute was established at the University of Haifa, together with the Gottlieb Schumacher Chair for the Study of the Christian Contribution to the Rebuilding of Palestine in the Nineteenth Century. Financial support for the institute and chair has been forthcoming from the Research Office of Baden-Württemberg and the Daimler-Benz Company, both located in Stuttgart, the capital of the former Württemberg principality, the homeland of the Swabians. The German contribution to the development of Palestine in the nineteenth century is of sufficient importance for both the Germans and the Israelis to be equally interested in encouraging its study in their universities. It may be anticipated that the cooperation now being planned between the institute in Haifa and the International Center for University Teaching of Jewish Civilization in Jerusalem will bear fruit in this area of research.

NOTES

1. Credit should also be given to my late teacher, Uriel Heyd, for similar pioneering work in the area of Middle Eastern Studies. Heyd recognized the importance of studying Palestine during the Turkish period, and his first work, *Dahir al-Amr, the Governor of Galilee in the Eighteenth Century* (Jerusalem: Rubin Mass, 1942, Hebrew), served as a guide for many students who began to plow "foreign fields" (from the Jewish point of view, of course) in the history of this land.

2. The major collections are listed in my article "Documentary Material in Austrian and German Archives relating to Palestine during the Period of Ottoman Rule," in *Studies on Palestine during the Ottoman Period*, ed. M. Ma'oz (Jerusalem: Magnes, 1975), 568-77.

3. *Die Siedlungen der württembergischer Templer in Palästina 1868–1918* (Stuttgart, 1973); *Christen als Pioniere im Heiligen Land* (Basel: Friedrich Reinhardt Verlag, 1981).

Comment

Franklin H. Littell

The developing discussion on Germany and the Holy Land represents significant widening of the research and publication that began with the subject of America and the Holy Land. As the early research reports indicate, despite the serious archival and library losses in German cities during World War II, a vast quantity of German primary sources remains largely untapped. We may also assume that when the Turkish archives become more accessible, the decades of close political and commercial cooperation between the German states and the Ottoman Empire, and between Germany and the Turkish Republic, will add greatly to the resources available for study of Germany and the Holy Land.

So far, the opening of the research/discussion in this area has spotlighted a factor that is also important for America–Holy Land Studies—namely, the prominence of the religious motif. Erich Geldbach's paper (like the presentations by Alex Carmel and Christiane Schütz at the first meeting of the *Arbeitsgemeinschaft: Deutschland und das heilige Land*, 24–25 March 1988 in Bensheim) points to the fascination with the Holy Land among religious circles in Germany.

Two Germany–Holy Land initiatives were prominent, quite different in style although remarkably influenced by similar eschatological assumptions. First in political significance was the establishment of the Jerusalem Bishopric as a joint effort of the Old Prussian Union Church and the Church of England. The idea was launched by C. C. J. Bunsen, confidant of King Friedrich Wilhelm IV of Prussia. As an ecclesiastical undertaking it reflected not only early ecumenical vision, but also the hope of forestalling the advance of Roman Catholic influence.

In England, the Jerusalem church outpost appealed to the evangelical wing of the established church, which was influenced as they were by Pietism and revolted as they were by the Tractarians. In the German states it appealed to those children of latter-day Pietism—largely fruits of the *Erweckungsbewegungen*—who were still within the established churches, as well as to the generation of the early German Free Church movements. As an ecclesiastical strategy, it anticipated by a generation the bitter struggle between state policy and Ultramontanism in Bismark's time (the *Kulturkampf*).

The second major religious impulse was more popular in nature, involving hundreds of emigrants to the Holy Land and thousands of fatherland supporters of their work there. The Tempelgesellschaft of Württemberg, land of Pietist impulses, was the most noteworthy of these movements. The work of the Templer colonies in Jaffa, Jerusalem, and Haifa lasted a century and was very important to the beginnings of scientific agriculture and small industry in the Holy Land.

The Templers had close cooperative relations with other Pietist movements and colonies in Germany and in German-speaking Switzerland. In fact, an amazing network of persons and institutions linked several of the most famous centers of awakened Christianity in nineteenth-century German states. The roll call of family names and place names includes some of the most famous missionary and social Christian leadership of the era: Schneller, Fliedner, Hoffman, Kornthal, St. Chrischona.

Among the Pietist groups the belief circulated that the return of the Jews to the land of their fathers would be among the signs indicating an imminent consummation to this history (after all, only a *Zwischenstadium*), a consummation signaled by the Return of the Lord Jesus and the establishment of His Kingdom. The return of the Jews to the Holy Land ranked with great wars and revolutions, plagues, and other tribulations as a sign of the closing of the age—although in contrast, the return of the Jews would be an occasion of joyful excitement among the remnant of faithful Christians. When Christ returned, He would, of course, make His appearance in His homeland; and some of the Pietists in the Holy Land settled there in order to be on the scene on that great morning of the New Day initiating the New Era.

The Zionist Pietists viewed their Jewish neighbors in the Promised Land, poor as they were, as evidence of God's continuing faithfulness to all of His promises. A generation later they welcomed the immigrants of the First Aliyah as an exciting pledge of the dramatic events soon to occur.

AMERICAN PARALLELS

Because of the flexibility and fluidity of American denominational formations, it is possible to trace the impact of Zionist thought upon Christian ecclesiastical structures. Major denominations in America can be divided rather neatly by how they stand on Jewish survival, a restored Jewish state, and Hebrew Christian missions. The established churches of Britain and Europe do not yield such typological interpretation, since their ballast is located elsewhere.

Pietist movements, both within the larger churches and the separatist groups, have been an important part of American Protestant history. Some, like the Moravians, were present long before the founding of the American republic. While the Moravians remained within the religious establishment in Europe, in the New World they became a separate denomination. In their first century they were one of the most world-minded of Christian movements, with missionaries seeking "the first fruits of the nations" from India to Labrador to the Gold Coast. However, attention to Jerusalem, although important in their understanding of the last things, was spiritualized. The Jerusalem component in the "heartfelt" and "spiritual" Christianity of the Moravians was usually the "heavenly Jerusalem."

The orientation of other Pietist movements that flowered in America, such as the separatist Brethren churches and the communitarians of Zoar, Amana, Bethel, and others was similar. Their members were simple farmers, and the earthly Jerusalem was far from them in the early decades of the nineteenth century.

Distance and primitive traveling conditions did not, however, dampen the zeal of the Mormons for the Holy Land. One of the most remarkable religious movements to develop out of Puritanism, and one of the most powerful as well as unique communities in the American religious rainbow, the Mormons are to this day among the most devoted and consistent advocates of Zion and the Zionist state.

The prophet himself, Joseph Smith Jr., sent to Jerusalem one of the earliest messengers to go forth from the infant movement. When Orson Hyde stood on the Mount of Olives in October 1841, he offered a prayer for the Land, for the ingathering of the people, and for an eventual restored Jewish state. Smith's vision called for the building of a Temple north of Independence, Missouri for the people of the church in the new world, paralleled by the rebuilding of the Temple for the people of the first covenant (the Jews). His vision of the future did not include Christian conversionism directed toward Jews.

The Mormons remain adventists, and it is significant that the larger branch has established an educational unit for its young people, an overseas unit of Brigham Young University, near The Hebrew University of Jerusalem. A committee of the smaller branch is working on the reconstruction of buildings of the Adams Colony in Jaffa.

After savage persecution in the nineteenth century, which led most Mormons to seek refuge in the territories beyond what was then the United States, that movement has become an exceedingly wealthy and politically powerful community. They have some of the most extensive archives and family histories of any church in the world, and their interest in the Jewish people and in Israel should make their scholars readily accessible for collaborative work on the theme of America and the Holy Land.

Apart from a few hundred German Mormons recruited since World War II, the only German movement with a comparable aversion to Hebrew Christian missions and a Zionist orientation would be the Plymouth Brethren. This movement, founded in England and America by John Nelson Darby (1800–1882), has been the fertile source of a Christian theology in which Jewish survival and ingathering are cardinal principles. The dispensationalism of Darby has—through the Niagara Bible Prophecy Conferences, the Scofield Reference Bible, and the founding of dozens of Bible colleges—become a major influence within several mainline Protestant denominations in America.

These two movements call for much greater attention than they have yet received from students of religion. Dr. Geldbach's monograph on Darby, published in German (Wuppertal: 3rd ed., 1975), is of use to American and English scholars who are drawn to study this most underrated of influential Christian teachers of the last hundred years.

Study of Darby's influence in the churches of England, Europe, and North America, and on Holy Land Studies, indicates the need for cooperative international scholarship, which has become the order of the day.

PART IV
GREAT BRITAIN

Chapter 15

Britain and the Holy Land: 1830–1914

Vivian D. Lipman

"This country of Palestine belongs to *you* and *me*, it is essentially ours. . . . It is the land towards which we turn as the fountain of our hopes; it is the land to which we may look with as true a patriotism as we do this dear old England of ours, which we love so much." Thus William Thomson, Archbishop of York, in opening the foundation meeting of the Palestine Exploration Fund in London, June 22, 1865, expressed the relationship of Britain to the Holy Land as one of virtual identification.[1] Thomson's language may be regarded as hyperbolical, but it does represent something of the feelings of a sincere British Christian toward the Holy Land, nurtured not only by study of Scripture but by the long association between Britain and the Holy Land. This relationship was so long-standing and complex that one can refer to only some of the aspects—from the period of the Crusades and earlier, through the influence of the Land of the Bible on English literature and religious thought (which in the seventeenth century was at times overwhelming), to the political, economic, and cultural concerns of the nineteenth century and later.

If we seek to study this relationship, it is reasonable to look to the highly successful America–Holy Land Studies Project as an exemplar. However, the British attachment has been of longer duration and includes aspects not found in America's relationship to the Holy Land. I therefore begin by considering one period—the nineteenth and twentieth centuries—and focusing attention on the British presence in Palestine during that period. I have published elsewhere an account of the America–Holy Land relationship over the same period, as reflected in British archival sources.[2]

Palestine in the early nineteenth century was a remote, neglected part of the

Ottoman Empire, not even an administrative entity but divided between two or three separate administrative jurisdictions.[3] Jerusalem was, until the middle of the century at least, a provincial, unsanitary town of a few thousand inhabitants, remote from the main lines of communication, in a countryside rarely free from banditry and subject to occasional insurrection. It was only with the opening of a carriage road in 1868—the railway did not arrive till 1892—that Jerusalem became readily accessible from Jaffa and the outside world.

The non-Islamic subjects of the Ottoman Empire were divided by religion into more or less autonomous communities. Each community or *millet* managed its own religious and cultural affairs under its religious leadership, and the latter was responsible to the authorities for the payment of taxes. This was modified by the system of Capitulations, which granted consuls of foreign states jurisdiction over the citizens of their countries and over protected persons. These arrangements, originating in treaties made between the medieval Italian city-states and the Byzantine Empire, were later written into treaties between the Ottoman Empire and Western states, although they were formally enacted by decrees of the Sublime Porte. Proceedings against subjects, or protected persons, of a Western state could be undertaken only in that state's consular court, unless the state, as was common during the nineteenth century, agreed to allow part of the process to take place in the Ottoman courts. The status of a protected person—and even more, naturalization—was highly prized by members of the minority communities in the Ottoman Empire, because of the immunity such status conferred from the jurisdiction, at times even from the taxes, of the Ottoman authorities.[4]

BRITISH INTERESTS

Britain was the first power to open a consulate in Jerusalem, in 1838, with the appointment of William Tanner Young as vice-consul (subsequently consul). France, Prussia, and Sardinia appointed consuls in 1843, Austro-Hungary in 1849, and Spain in 1854. The Russian consul in Jerusalem (at first a rabbi was appointed consular agent) was responsible to the Russian consulate-general in Beirut. There had previously been British consular agents in Jaffa, who were responsible to their consuls in Acre and Beirut.[5]

As a major international power, Great Britain was interested in the affairs of the region. For instance, she intervened in 1840 to help Turkey drive out the Egyptians, who, although nominally part of the Ottoman Empire, had from 1832 to 1840 forcibly occupied Syria and Palestine. Britain also aided Turkey, a major participant in the Crimean War which originated in a dispute over the Holy Places in Jerusalem. The British ambassador to the Porte, Sir Stratford Canning (later Lord Stratford de Redcliffe), exercised a decisive influence over the policies of the Ottoman Empire during his periods of service at Constantinople (1808–1814; 1826–1827; 1832; 1842–1858).[6] The area of the Holy Land was of strategic interest to Britain as it occupied a vital position on the route to India and the East, an importance not lessened by the opening of the Suez Canal in 1869.

British interests in the Holy Land in the nineteenth century were religious and cultural as well as political and economic. From the end of the eighteenth century, there was immense pressure from the Evangelicals in Britain for missionary activity both at home and abroad. In Britain it led in 1809 to the foundation of the London Society for Promoting Christianity among the Jews (usually called the London Jews' Society, or LJS). The LJS turned its attention in the 1820s to conversion of the Jews in Europe and elsewhere, including the Holy Land, where its first permanent emissary was a Dane, John Nicolayson.[7] He arrived in Jerusalem in 1826 but left in a general exodus of missionaries in 1828, because of unsettled conditions. Returning in 1831, he set up a permanent mission in 1833. The 1830s, with Egyptian rule in Palestine and Syria, was a period more favorable for missionaries. Mehemet Ali, the ruler of Egypt, was anxious to make a good impression on Western opinion, particularly upon Britain (which then supported him), and he ordered relaxation of the restrictions on resident Christians and Jews, and on foreign missionaries and visitors.

A more general missionary body, the Church Missionary Society (CMS) founded in 1799, had already dispatched emissaries to the Holy Land. Its object was "to propagate the gospel among the heathen." A strictly Church of England organization, founded by Evangelicals of the "Clapham Sect," it was not as enthusiastically or widely supported in its early days as was the LJS. There was some scepticism about its prospects of success, especially as the object of its activities in the Ottoman Empire would be the Muslims, co-religionists of an arbitrary ruling power. The CMS did not engage in permanent activities in the Holy Land until mid-century.[8] From the 1840s, the Church of Scotland was also active in missionary work in the Holy Land, particularly in the Galilee. In addition to major organizations, individuals like Lewis Way[9] or the banker Henry Drummond (who financed the journeys of the convert traveler and missionary, Joseph Wolff),[10] were also pioneers in missionary activity.

Complementing the missionary work was the British and Foreign Bible Society, whose aim was to spread the Bible (both Old and New Testaments) to a wide readership. The Bible Society's task was to translate the Bible into as many languages as possible, and to sell it inexpensively or distribute it free of charge through a network of depots and salesmen. In its emphasis on the text of the Bible, to the exclusion of the traditional interpretations of the Roman Catholic Church, the Bible Society reflected the evangelical tradition and aroused the opposition of the Roman Catholic hierarchy.

In the Holy Land, and particularly in Jerusalem, there was a great variety of faiths. The majority population was Muslim, but there were various kinds of Christians—Greek Orthodox, Roman Catholic, Uniate churches of orthodox rite but in communion with Rome (notably the Greek Catholics or Melchites), Armenians, as well as very small groups like the Copts or Ethiopians. The Muslims enjoyed predominance, being of the faith of the ruling power; the Greek Orthodox had longstanding monastic and other institutions and enjoyed the patronage of the Russian Empire, which sent increasing numbers of pilgrims to the Holy Land; the Roman Catholics or Latins claimed the traditional custody of the Holy Places and were backed by the French government. The British, as a Protestant power, found no adherents among the native population but sought to protect the Jews. The instructions to W. T. Young, the first British consul, from Lord Palmerston included a duty "to afford protection to the Jews generally."[11] The appointment of Young, and his special injunction in relation to the Jews, was largely due to the influence of the philanthropist, statesman, and Evangelical, Lord Shaftesbury, who served as Foreign Secretary from 1830 to 1841 and from 1846 to 1851.[12]

THE ANGLO-PRUSSIAN BISHOPRIC

Lord Shaftesbury was also instrumental in the foundation of another center of British influence in the Holy Land, the Bishopric.[13] The LJS wanted an English church in the Holy Land, a mission under episcopal authority, and a center where the missionaries could receive both adults and children for instruction. The Bishopric was the result of an agreement between Great Britain and Prussia, whose monarch Frederick William IV was intensely interested in spreading the gospel. Britain and Prussia agreed to share the cost and to make appointments alternately. This Anglican-Lutheran joint operation aroused the opposition of the Catholics in Britain, because it involved a measure of union with the Protestant Lutheran Church, which was non-episcopal. It was this joint Bishopric which finally destroyed John Newman's faith in the Anglican Church.[14]

The Bishopric was aimed primarily at the conversion of the Jews; according to his mandate, the Bishop was not to interfere with the Muslim or Christian subjects of the Porte. Even regarding the evangelization of Jews, the Bishop, although not inhibited from seeking to convert them if they were Ottoman subjects, would not have the protection of the British consul in so doing. As a symbol of the direction of the mission, the first holder of the Bishopric was a converted Prussian Jew, Michael Solomon Alexander, a former minister of the Jewish congregation in Plymouth, England. Alexander's "letter commendatory" stipulated that "his chief missionary care will be directed to the conversion of the Jews, to their protection, and to their useful employment."[15]

The Bishopric soon founded three main institutions: a training center for Jewish converts, a "school of industry" (a hostel for training converts in construction work), and an "inquirers' home" for accommodating prospective adult converts. In 1845, Colonel Rose, the consul-general in Beirut, raised the question of an Anglican church for Jerusalem. A *firman* was obtained from the Sublime Porte by Stratford de Redcliffe, but its implementation was obstructed by the local administration in Jerusalem. Eventually it had to give way, but it persisted in regarding Christ Church, near the Jaffa Gate, as a consular chapel, which had the effect of emphasizing the links between the British political and religious presence in the city.[16]

In 1845, Consul Young's term of office ended, and Bishop Alexander died. Their successors who arrived in 1846 were destined to stay longer and to make a more lasting impact on the British presence in Jerusalem. The new consul, James Finn, was accompanied by his wife Elizabeth Ann, daughter of the missionary James McCaul.[17] They were a forceful couple and were soon in conflict with the new Bishop, Samuel Gobat, who was nominated by the King of Prussia. Gobat was a French-speaking Swiss, who had been a CMS missionary in Ethiopia.

During his tenure, 1846–1879, Gobat changed the main direction of the Bishopric from the conversion of the Jews to Christianity, to the conversion of the native Christians—mainly Greek Orthodox—to Protestantism. The underlying argument for this move was that while the conversion of the Muslims was the ultimate objective, this was clearly impossible under the current circumstances of Muslim rule; but when it should become possible at some future date, the most suitable to undertake the process would be their fellow Arabs, the native Christians. These, however, would first have to be converted to the correct form of Christian belief, which was Protestant. Logically, this argument should have applied to the Latin Christians as well. But these, with their effective Church discipline and the long-standing relations of their hierarchy with Ottoman authorities, were too hard a nut to crack. Gobat, and the CMS missionaries whom he brought back in force to the Holy Land, seem to have left the Latin Christians pretty well alone. The CMS established a permanent mission in 1851 under F. A. Klein (like Gobat, a French-speaking Swiss), with Charles Sandreczki, a German-speaking Pole and former Catholic, as lay secretary. With the aid of the CMS (to whom he later entrusted most of his institutions), Gobat built up a chain of schools and other services for the Christian Arab population. This tended to create the appearance of an "English party" among the native population, akin to the association of the local Greek Orthodox with Russia and the local Roman Catholics with France. There was even a belief—which the Foreign Office took steps to quash—that joining the Church of England in some way might confer British protection.

The work of Gobat and the CMS aroused opposition on several fronts. The Russians and French helped the Orthodox and Latin Churches to increase their efforts among the native Christians. In Britain there was strong opposition to the Bishopric within the Church of England, because of sympathy with the Greek Orthodox. The Muslims sometimes reacted with violence, as at Nablus in 1853, when Gobat had the church bells rung to celebrate the Turkish decree conferring on Christians, as subjects of the Ottoman Empire, equal rights with Muslims. The LJS felt that the Bishopric, originally constituted to foster their efforts, now was indifferent to their cause.[18]

James Finn

The British consul James Finn, aided—if not spurred—by his wife, was hyperactive; the archives of the Foreign Office show almost daily dispatches from him, either to London or to his senior consul in Constantinople. (As a "political" consul he was entitled to write directly to London.) The Finns were particularly concerned with the position of the Jews; although their overt posture was to help the Jews by providing employment or protection without expecting conversion, in view of the Finns' conversionist antecedents, there may have been some such hope at the back of their minds. Partly because of this, partly because of the Finns' authoritarian attitudes, they gradually became suspect in the eyes of many of the Jerusalem Jewish leaders. However, when Finn was ultimately removed, the Ashkenazi rabbis submitted a testimonial on his behalf to Queen Victoria.

Sir Moses Montefiore also became increasingly suspicious of Finn's attempt to exercise power over the Jews of Jerusalem; the fear of conversionism—however long-term and remote in Finn's case—was always present. The activities of Montefiore cannot be omitted in considering the overall impact of British interest in the Holy Land. There was a certain ambivalence in his relations with Finn; he relied on Finn, as he did on British diplomatic envoys and consuls throughout his field of operations, for local political support and intervention with the authorities. Finn, on his part, saw in Montefiore's projects for relief and employment an extension of British influence in the area, as a counter to the French. For instance, he saw Montefiore's provision of medical attention and ideas for a hospital as an answer to French initiatives implemented by Albert Cohn on behalf of the French Rothschilds.[19]

Finn's activities made Britain the leading force in Jerusalem in the 1850s, a period in which Britain's aid to Turkey in the Crimean War naturally enhanced her authority in the Ottoman Empire. This was also the period of Ottoman reforms, or the *Tanzimat*, which began with the Hatti-Sherif of Gulhane in 1839 and was continued by the Hatti-Humayun of 1856. These reforms were aimed notably at improving the position of the minorities, but there was also modernization of the administration, army, and education. This period, until early in the reign of Abdul Hamid II, was a favorable one for Western influence in general and particularly for Britain.

Finn's quarrels in the 1850s with Bishop Gobat and with Dr. Macgowan of the LJS (themselves at odds with Gobat and the CMS) tended to fragment the British residents in Jerusalem into three parties. Finn was a dedicated worker for his causes; he never took a holiday in seventeen years of service in Jerusalem. But his tendency to quarrel with nearly everyone, and the debts that he incurred in using his own funds for projects of relief and employment for the Jews of Jerusalem, led to his bankruptcy and recall in 1862.[20] His successor, Noel Temple Moore, adopted a much lower profile.[21] His dispatches were less frequent, his interventions less dramatic, and he was on better terms with the other Britons in Jerusalem.

Finn had taken advantage of a decision by the Foreign Office in 1849 to grant British protection to Russian Jews, whose own government had refused to continue its protection (because they had failed to return to Russia to re-register), and he offered that special status freely. In the 1870s, when many of those originally granted protection had died, it was decided to limit the privilege to those who were descendants of British persons, and the registers were checked. Ultimately, those under fifty years of age were given five years notice that their inherited protection would expire on 1 January 1890; on that date the majority of the Russian Jews, 1,456 in number, lost British protection.[22]

If British political influence was less obtrusive after Finn's departure, it was reinforced in the cultural sphere by the formation in 1865 of the Palestine Exploration Fund (PEF). This organization had a committee representative of all Christian opinion in Britain, and two leading Jews as well—Moses Montefiore and Lionel de Rothschild. While inspired by the religious associations of the Holy Land, the PEF stressed the need for a purely scientific approach to the study of the country's archaeology, geography, geology, and natural history.[23]

After Gobat's death, the Prussians withdrew support from the Bishopric, which they regarded as having too much of a British character; the Lutheran clergy were in any case unwilling to accept re-ordination from an Anglican bishop. Gobat was succeeded by Joseph Barclay, formerly in charge of the LJS in Jerusalem; however, he died after a short period in office. In 1887 Barclay was succeeded by George Francis Popham Blyth, who remained in office until 1914. Blyth's mandate was entirely different from that of Gobat. He did not seek to build up an Anglican constituency by conversion from the Eastern churches, but he sought to act as an envoy from the Church of England to them. He was, in fact, welcomed by the Greek Orthodox as an ally against the Roman Catholics, who had revived and extended their activities (as had the Eastern Orthodox) in response to the Protestant missionary work of Gobat and the CMS. Meanwhile, even the LJS had modified its work to provide more educational and medical services rather then to proselytize directly.

Blyth did not want to be dependent on the CMS, like Gobat, or on the LJS, like Alexander and Barclay. The "Jerusalem and the East Mission" was founded in 1889 to provide direct support and work under the Bishop's control. Blyth developed his own network of institutions: a training college for native clergy and teachers, an orphanage, schools for boys and girls. His policy was not to have separate schools for Jews, Christians, and Muslims, but to teach pupils from different backgrounds in the same schools, using the English language as a unifying factor. Conversion to Anglicanism was not required for entry to the schools, and at least as far as Christians and Muslims were concerned, the schools were not used for proselytization; they therefore achieved considerable prestige among the local Arab population. Blyth built up his own clerical and lay staff, and in 1898 St. George's was consecrated as a collegiate church for the diocese.[24]

BRITISH-TURKISH RELATIONS

After about 1880, there was a change in British policy toward the Ottoman Empire. Previously, British policy had been directed toward bolstering the Empire as a defense against Russia. Now the emphasis was on staking a claim for areas of British influence or even direct control, once the Ottoman Empire had broken up. A beginning had been made with Britain's takeover of Cyprus under the treaty of Berlin of 1878, and with the occupation of Egypt at the time of the revolt by Ali Pasha in 1882.

Turkish perceptions of British power, and of Western influence generally, also changed. On the one hand, there was growing German influence, marked locally in Palestine by the founding of the Templer and similar colonies, and the prestigious visit of Kaiser Wilhelm II to Jerusalem in 1898. After 1883 the Turkish army was trained by a German military mission under von der Goltz, and the foundations were laid for the alliance of Turkey with the Central Powers. Turkish nationalist sentiment grew, with consequent resentment of the activities and privileges of foreigners on Turkish territory. For instance, in 1880, thirty Protestant schools were closed, arousing the protests of the missionaries who expressed their disapprobation to the American Minister in Constantinople; the latter received only limited support from his British and German colleagues.

From the early 1890s, the Sublime Porte took a negative attitude toward Jewish settlement in Palestine; by 1887 Jewish visitors to the Holy Land were limited to a one month's "pilgrimage," which was extended to three months after British protests in respect of British subjects. The regulation was re-imposed in 1901. While administrative inefficiency and corruption prevented these regulations from constituting a complete ban on Jewish immigration, they—and restrictions on land purchase by foreigners—are evidence of the growing feeling against foreign influence in the Ottoman Empire. This attitude was reinforced after the Young Turks came to power in 1908. The unilateral Turkish abrogation of the Capitulations system in 1913 was the culmination of a policy aimed at ending the old relationship with Western powers, under which an antiquated government was forced to tolerate foreign intervention and jurisdiction within its own territories.[25]

Nevertheless, in less than a century, British activity in the Holy Land had built up a continuing political presence in the form of the Jerusalem consulate; a Bishopric, and representation of various other missionary bodies with a collegiate church and a long-established Anglican church; a school system in Jerusalem and other towns and villages, in which English was the language of instruction; and various medical institutions, including the ophthalmic hospital founded in 1882 by the British branch of the Order of St. John of Jerusalem. A segment of the native Arab population was linked to the Church of England in worship, and a much wider sector was permanently influenced by education in British schools. In the cultural field, the foundation of the PEF in 1865 provided a major learned society, which funded professional surveys of Jerusalem and subsequently of the whole of the country west of the Jordan—an enduring contribution—and instituted an ongoing program of archaeological research and excavation.

British travelers to Palestine grew in numbers in the nineteenth century. From the 1860s, Thomas Cook organized the flow of tourists, which was greatly increased by the opening of the railway from Jaffa to Jerusalem in 1892; the number of British tourists passing through Jaffa increased from 802 in 1890 to 1,305 in 1897. Less information is available on British trade with the Holy Land. The available evidence suggests a drop in British exports to Palestine in the second half of the century, as the trade was too limited and unprofitable to attract English agents. There was an increasing export of oranges to Britain and, at the end of the century, a noticeable export trade in barley from the Negev for the British brewing industry. The second half of the nineteenth century witnessed an increase in the tonnage of British shipping using the port of Jaffa—from 4,346 tons in 1862 to 184,616 in 1897; these figures do not include the Khedivial Mail Line ships from Egypt which shortly thereafter transferred to the British flag (see item PRO FO 195/2062). The economic relationship between Britain and the Holy Land up to 1914 has been little explored and deserves further study.[26]

ARCHIVAL SOURCES

The archival sources for the study of Britain and the Holy Land are too vast to be discussed here. To some extent these sources are outlined in Appendices 2b (which deals with the Public Record Office), 2c, and 2d to my chapter "America–Holy Land Material in British Archives" in *With Eyes Toward Zion–II*, edited by Moshe Davis. There are brief descriptions of the archives of the Palestine Exploration Fund and of a number of Christian religious bodies (British and Foreign Bible Society, Church Missionary Society, Church's Ministry among the Jews–London Jews Society, Jerusalem and the East Mission, Lambeth Palace Archives) in volume 4 of *Guide to America–Holy Land Studies, 1620–1948*, edited by Menahem Kaufman and Mira Levine. The *Guide* contains descriptions of a number of personal archives, but these are only a few of an infinitely greater number, because only those that contain material about Americans were included. The National Register of Archives in Chancery Lane, London, itemizes over 20,000 collections of archives in Britain, and a fair number of these must contain material relevant to British–Holy Land relations.

Noel Matthews and M. Doreen Wainwright, *A Guide to Manuscripts and Documents in the British Isles relating to the Middle East and North Africa*, ed. J. D. Pearson (Oxford: Oxford University Press, 1980), has references to Palestine on approximately 140 of its more than 400 pages, although some of these relate to events after 1914. The entries vary from brief but comprehensive statements such as "Public Record Office Foreign Office General Correspondence, FO 78 Turkey 1780–1905, 5490 volumes," to more detailed catalogues of archival collections—for example, taken at random, "Two letters from William Holman Hunt in Jerusalem to Ford Madox Brown, on the identification of Emmaus, artistic matters, and the situation in Palestine, 1 Oct. 1876 and 23–5 Jan. 1887" in the British Library (Add. Mss 38794, ff. 224–31). It is clear that Matthews and Wainwright will provide a mine of information for archive searchers on British–Holy Land relations, but because of the disparity in the entries it cannot serve as a guide in the same way that the *Guide to America–Holy Land Studies* can for America–Holy Land relations.

Britain and Palestine 1914–1948, compiled by Philip Jones and published for the British Academy by Oxford University Press (Oxford, 1979), also includes pre-1914 papers of those who continued their activity in relation to Palestine from 1914 to 1948. It includes details of personal papers, with short biographical notes; records of selected organizations and societies, with descriptions of these institutions as well as of their archives; the contents of official archives in Britain (notably the Public Record Office, with lists of files); notes on archives in Israel, Arab countries, and the United States; and a guide to selected libraries and record offices in Britain. It is thus a full handbook and guide for the 1914–1948 period, but it only marginally covers the earlier period, although many of the biographies and descriptions of organizations relate to individuals and bodies active before 1914.

NOTES

1. Report of Proceedings of a Public Meeting, held in Willis' Rooms, St. James', on Friday, 22 June 1865, p. 3. William Thomson (1819–1890) became Bishop of Gloucester, then Bristol, in 1861, and Archbishop of York in 1862. See *Dictionary of National Biography*, vol. 19 (1900; reprint, Oxford University Press, 1922).

2. V. D. Lipman, ''America–Holy Land Material in British Archives, 1820–1930,'' in *With Eyes Toward Zion–II*, ed. Moshe Davis (New York: Praeger, 1986).

3. Moshe Ma'oz, *Ottoman Reform in Syria and Palestine, 1840–61* (Oxford: Oxford University Press, 1968).

4. For a general summary of ''Capitulations,'' see Georg Schwarzenberger in *Chamber's Encyclopaedia*, vol. 3 (London: George Newnes, 1959), 87-88; for Palestine, see Frank E. Manuel, *Realities of American Palestine Relations* (Washington: Public Affairs Press, 1949).

5. Arnold Blumberg, ed., *A View from Jerusalem 1849–1858: The Consular Diary of James and Elizabeth Finn* (London and Toronto: Associated University Presses, 1980).

6. Stratford Canning, 1st Viscount Stratford de Redcliffe (1786–1880), served in the British embassy in Constantinople from 1808 to 1814 and was ambassador from 1826 to 1827, in 1832, and from 1842 to 1858. He was created a viscount in 1852.

7. John Nicolayson was active in Jerusalem from 1823 until his death in 1856. A Dane by birth, he became a British protected person in 1847. See A. Blumberg (above, n.5), pp. 61-62.

8. See *The Church Missionary Society in Palestine* (London: CMS, 1891).

9. For an account of Lewis Way, see James Parkes, ''Lewis Way and His Times,'' *Transactions of the Jewish Historical Society of England* 20 (1959–1961): 189–201; hereafter cited as *Trans JHSE*.

10. Joseph Wolff (1792–1862), a Bavarian convert from Judaism to, successively, Roman Catholicism and the Church of England, undertook many missionary journeys to Asia, Africa, and Europe. He named his son, the diplomat and politician Henry Drummond-Wolff, after his banker patron.

11. Albert M. Hyamson, *The British Consulate*, vol. 1 (London: E. Goldston, 1934), 2.

12. Henry John Temple, 3rd Viscount Palmerston (an Irish peerage that allowed him to sit in the House of Commons), was later Prime Minister, 1855–1858, 1859–1865.

13. Antony Ashley Cooper, 7th Earl of Shaftesbury (1801–1885), reformer and philanthropist, was a member of Parliament from 1826 to 1851 (as Lord Ashley); he was the son-in-law of the second wife of Lord Palmerston, the leading influence on British foreign policy of the period.

14. See R. W. Greaves, "The Jerusalem Bishopric, 1841," *English Historical Review* (July 1949): 328-52.

15. Michael Solomon Alexander (1799–1845) was born in Germany and came to England in 1820, where he served as reader and ritual slaughterer in Norwich, Nottingham, and Plymouth until his conversion to Christianity in 1825. He became a Christian clergyman and served as a London Jews' Society missionary. From 1832 to 1841, he was professor of Hebrew at King's College, London. Appointed the first Anglican bishop in Jerusalem in 1841, he was also responsible for Anglican interests in Syria, Iraq, Abyssinia, and Egypt, where he died.

16. See Abdul L. Tibawi, *British Interests in Palestine 1800–1901* (Oxford: Oxford University Press, 1961).

17. James Finn (1806–1872) was consul in Jerusalem from 1845 to 1862. For his previous career, see Beth-Zion Lask Abrahams, "James Finn," *Trans JHSE* 27 (1978–1980): 40-51.

18. For the conflict between Gobat and the LJS, see especially A. L. Tibawi (above, n.16), pp. 89-112.

19. Considerable literature on Moses Montefiore and the Holy Land is listed on pp. 73-114 of Ruth Goldschmidt-Lehmann, *Sir Moses Montefiore, Bart., F.R.S., 1784–1885: A Bibliography* (Jerusalem: Misgav Yerushalayim, 1984). See also articles in *Cathedra* 33 (October 1984, Hebrew).

20. For the end of Finn's consulate, see especially A. Blumberg (above, n.5), pp. 312-21.

21. Noel Temple Moore CMG (1833–1903) had been at the British consulate in Beirut from 1851 to 1860. After serving as consul in Jerusalem from 1862 to 1890, he was consul-general in Tripoli from 1890 to 1894.

22. See A. M. Hyamson (above, n.11), vol. 2 (1941), pp. 349-80, 451.

23. See my paper on the origins of the Palestine Exploration Fund, in *PEQ,* 120 (1988).

24. A. L. Tibawi (above, n.16), pp. 251ff.

25. A. M. Hyamson (above, n.11), vol. 1, pp. l-liv, and related documents arranged chronologically in vol. 2.

26. Some preliminary material on trade is given at the end of the References below.

REFERENCES

In addition to the sources quoted in the chapter, the following works, mainly secondary and in English, may be helpful. The object has been to cite general works that contain references to additional sources, rather than biographies of individuals or monographs.

Political

Friedman, I. "Palestine and Protection of Jews in Palestine 1839–1851." *Jewish Social Studies* 30 (1968): 23-41.

Vereté, Mayir. "Why was a British Consulate Established in Jerusalem?" *English Historical Review* (April 1970): 317-43.

Tenenbaum, Mark. "British Consulate in Jerusalem 1850–90." *Cathedra* 5 (1978, Hebrew): 83-108.

Christian Religious

Gidney, William T. *History of the London Society for Promoting Christianity amongst the Jews, from 1809 to 1908.* London: LJS, 1908.

Goodall, N. *A History of the London Missionary Society.* London: Oxford University Press, 1954.

Greaves, R. W. "The Jerusalem Bishopric 1841." *English Historical Review* (July 1949): 328-52.

Sapir, Shaul. "Historical Sources relating to Anglican Missionary Societies in Jerusalem and Palestine." *Cathedra* 19 (April 1981, Hebrew): 155-70.

Morgenstern, Arieh. "The Perushim, The London Missionary Society and the Opening of the British Consulate in Jerusalem." *Shalem* 5 (1987): 115-37.

Restorationism

Kobler, Franz. *The Vision Was There; A History of the British Movement for the Restoration of the Jews to Palestine.* London: Lincolns-Prager, 1956.

Bentwich, Norman and Margery, and John M. Shaftesley. "Forerunners of Zionism in the Victorian Era." In *Remember the Days*, edited by John M. Shaftesley. London: Jewish Historical Society of England, ca. 1966.

Vereté, Mayir. "Restoration of the Jews in English Protestant Thought." *Middle East Studies* (1972): 3-50.

Finestein, Israel. "Early and Middle 19th-Century British Opinion on the Restoration of the Jews to Palestine: Contrasts with America."

Kochan, Lionel E. "Jewish Restoration to Zion: Christian Attitudes in Britain in the Late 19th and Early 20th Centuries." This and Finestein in *With Eyes Toward Zion– II*, edited by Moshe Davis. New York: Praeger, 1986.

Montefiore

Parfitt, Tudor. "Sir Moses Montefiore and Palestine." In *Sir Moses Montefiore, A Symposium*, edited by Vivian D. Lipman. Oxford: Oxford Centre for Postgraduate Hebrew Studies and Jewish Historical Society of England, 1982.

Cathedra 33 (October 1984, Hebrew): Kark, Ruth. "Agricultural Land and Montefiore's Second Visit," pp. 55-92. Kedem, Menachem. "George Gawler," pp. 93-106. Morgenstern, Arieh. "The First Jewish Hospital in Jerusalem," pp 107-24. Verbin, Mordechai. "Y. M. Pines and the Montefiore Testimonial Fund," pp. 125-48. Bartal, Israel. "Montefiore and Eretz Israel," pp. 149-60.

Schischa, A. "The Sage of 1855." In *The Century of Moses Montefiore*, edited by Vivian D. Lipman. Oxford: Oxford University Press, 1985.

Davis, Moshe. *Sir Moses Montefiore: American Jewry's Ideal*. Pamphlet Series, no. 4. Cincinnati: American Jewish Archives, 1985.

Archaeology, Travel

Watson, Sir Charles M. *Fifty Years Work in the Holy Land: A Record and a Summary 1865–1915*. London: PEF, 1915.

Kirk, M. E. "Short History of Palestine Excavation." *PEQ* 44 (1902): 131.

Elath, Eliahu. "Condor Reignier Conder." *PEQ* (January-June 1965): 21-41.

Hopkins, Ian W. S. "Captain MacGregor and the Exploration of Upper Jordan." *PEQ* (1983): 55-59.

Ben-Arieh, Yehoshua. "19th Century Western Travel Literature to Israel." *Cathedra* 40 (July 1986, Hebrew): 159-88.

Economic Relations

There is no full study, but see Gerber, Haim. "Modernization in Nineteenth-Century Palestine: The Role of Foreign Trade." *Middle East Studies* (1982): 250-64.

Trade reports from British consuls appear in the following volumes in the Public Record Office: FO 78/803 (1849); 839 (1850); 1537 (1860); 1874 (1865); 2297 (1873); 3341 (1881); 3421 (1882); 4218 (1887); 4294 (1890); FO 195/2062 (1899); 2255 (1907).

Chapter 16

British–Holy Land Archaeology: Nineteenth-Century Sources

Rupert L. Chapman

The discovery of ancient Palestine is a two-fold task, which involves both surface exploration and excavation. The technique and methods employed by both types of archaeological work have improved immeasurably since the beginning of scientific exploration in 1838, and of excavation in 1851. This first phase came to a close with the beginning of scientific excavation in 1890. The second phase, which lasted until the outbreak of the War in 1914, was, as we shall see, a period of collection and publication of material, which was not dated or classified with sufficient accuracy to make it of much value to the historian. During the third phase, since the close of the War scientific method in the archaeology of Palestine has improved so remarkably, and the amount of work accomplished has so increased that archaeological data which were quite meaningless now yield important historical information.[1]

W. F. Albright

The title of this article raises three important questions of definition: "British," "archaeology," and "nineteenth century." To begin with the last of these, British archaeological explorations in the Holy Land began in the immediate aftermath of the defeat of Napoleon at Acre, with the work of Edward Daniel Clarke in 1801. The end of the period, however, presents a problem. Technically, the end of the nineteenth-century occurred on January 1, 1901. The year 1901, however, is significant only as the year in which Dr. Conrad Schick died. The actual end of nineteenth-century British archaeology in the Holy Land came in August 1914, with the outbreak of World War I. When work resumed, not only had most of the *dramatis personae* changed, but the very structure of archaeology itself, as a field of study, both in the Holy Land and elsewhere, had been fundamentally altered.

The next term we must consider is "British." Normally, we would consider as British archaeology only that carried out by British archaeologists. Yet from the beginning, the main British archaeological organization in the Holy Land, the Palestine Exploration Fund (PEF), employed scholars who were not British. We need only mention Prof. Charles Clermont-Ganneau, a French diplomat; Dr. Gottlieb Schumacher, a German engineer; Dr. Conrad Schick, a German architect; and Dr. Frederick J. Bliss, an American scholar. Even today the PEF has been known to employ "the odd American." For the purposes of this chapter, I regard as British archaeology all the work carried out under the major financial and organizational sponsorship of British organizations.

Finally, there is the definition of the term "archaeology." Many definitions have been offered, no one of which is completely satisfactory, simply because of the complexity and breadth of archaeology as a field of study. I suggest that archaeology is the study of human behavior in the past through the study of artifacts and the associations between them. This is deliberately vague, for to be too precise would be to exclude parts of the field that should be included. Other aspects will emerge in subsequent sections of this essay.

This chapter is not a history of the work of British archaeologists in the Holy Land in the nineteenth century in the sense of listing the archaeologists and the discoveries they made. The major facts regarding what was done and by whom have been presented many times; I would draw particular attention to Sir Charles Watson's *Fifty Years Work in the Holy Land* (1915), which covers precisely this period. The purely archaeological significance of the work done in this period for our present understanding of the ancient Near East is, of course, continually being reassessed; this, however, is not a part of the history of archaeology, but of the profession of archaeology itself.

In this chapter, I discuss first the context of British archaeology in the Holy Land, particularly the motivations for it. Then I look at the two major periods into which it may be divided and consider the method, theory, and aims of those working in each of these periods. I also hope, by means of quotations and references, to place the study of British archaeology in the Holy Land in the nineteenth century firmly within the context of the study of the general history of archaeology. I indicate some of the sources, particularly the archival sources, that may furnish a basis for future studies of this subject.

THE CONTEXT

Political Context[2]

Generally speaking, the political context for the initial period is set within the rise of the second British Empire, following the loss of the American colonies in 1781 and the crisis of the Napoleonic War. The end of this period in 1815 saw the beginning of general European expansion and imperialist competition.

Within Britain this was a period of considerable change, which led, at times, to great upheaval, and in a few cases even to large scale rioting and local turmoil. We may mention here the Chartist Movement of the 1820s, the Great Reform Act of 1832, the Reform Acts of 1867 and 1884, and the shift of power from the House of Lords to the House of Commons as exemplified in the appearance after 1868 of a majority of Prime Ministers from the Commons.[3]

Within the Near East the geopolitical situation was quite remarkably reminiscent of conditions there in the thirteenth century B.C.E., with the Ottoman Empire and the Egyptian empire of Muhammad 'Ali battling for possession of the Levant, and an increasing amount of intrusive Western influence. This parallel extends even to the prior economic decay and depopulation of the country and to the peasant revolt of 1834. The second half of the century saw the increasing penetration and domination of the area by the various European powers (Britain, France, Germany, Russia) using as their means the time-honored system of "Capitulations," and the simultaneous decline of the Ottoman authority over Palestine. This period also saw the first manifestations of the rise of the Arab nationalist movement.[4]

Economic Context

In the early nineteenth century the world economy was undergoing radical change. For the most part it was an agriculture-based, pre-industrial system. The British economy, however, was in the throes of a revolution that led to political, religious, intellectual, and social changes. This revolution was the shift from an agricultural to an industrial base. The Industrial Revolution created new wealth on an unheard-of scale, wealth that quickly began to be channeled into a multitude of scientific research endeavors that had hitherto been economically impracticable. One of these was the exploration of the Holy Land. It also created an unprecedented need for both sources of raw materials and export markets for manufactured goods, especially cloth; this led to increased British interest in the Ottoman Empires. A secondary requirement created by the Industrial Revolution was the need for short, secure lines of communication and supply/transport between Britain and her raw materials and markets. Hence the intense British interest in Egypt.[5]

The effects of endemic diseases, especially plague, malaria, typhoid, and cholera, led to depopulation. Deforestation of unterraced hills, with the neglect of existing terraces, led to erosion and an increase in marshland in low-lying areas with substantial rainfall, and deserts in areas of marginal rainfall. This in combination with many factors—the decline of the central administrations of Turkey and Egypt, corruption of the local officials, inequities of the tax system and the increasingly uncompetitive position of the handicraft production of the Near East in relation to the developing industrial production of the West European countries, especially Great Britain—conspired to produce a massive economic decline in the Near Eastern economy. This is reflected in the descriptions of the desolate state of the Holy Land by the early explorers. Gradually, in the course of the century, as Western influence in the Holy Land increased, so did the inflow of capital. The general economic condition improved accordingly, but only at the expense of an increasing loss of political control by Istanbul.[6]

Religious Context

The religious context of British archaeology in the Holy Land is equally complex. Within Britain, the eighteenth century had been a period of surpassing dullness and complacency, after the upheavals of the seventeenth century. This contentment was profoundly shaken by the secularist challenges of prerevolutionary and revolutionary France. It was further shaken by the Methodist movement of John and Charles Wesley, and again by the secularism of the European revolutions of 1848. These led to the rise of both the "Evangelicals" and the "High Church" or "Anglo-Catholic" party, which arose out of the Tractarian or "Oxford Movement" led by John Henry Newman, within the Church of England. The greatest shocks were yet to come, however. These were administered by the publication of Darwin's *On the Origin of Species* in 1859 and by the rise of the Tübingen school of biblical criticism. These challenges created an unprecedented need to establish the historical accuracy of the Bible, as a means of defending its theological accuracy. That the one was neither necessary nor sufficient to establish the other was a point alien to the intellectual climate of the day—and is still not totally comprehended. Within Britain, the nineteenth century also saw the Catholic Emancipation in 1829 and the Jewish Emancipation in mid-century. The increased freedom for the Jewish community in Britain in this period was partly a result of the rise of the Jewish banking and finance houses, and partly due to the increasing approval of religious toleration.[7]

Within the Near East the eighteenth century saw the rise of the Wahabis in Arabia, followed by a general Islamic revival in the nineteenth century. These developments affected the local situation in which the early explorers, antiquaries, and archaeologists worked. Starting with Napoleon's appeal to the Christians during his invasion of Syria, and increasingly—following the use by Ibrahim, son of Muhammad 'Ali, of Christian troops under Bashir Shihab to put down a rebellion of the Druze in 1837—the interests of the various religious communities were perceived as conflicting, and the result was violence between them. Intercommunal strife was sometimes exacerbated, deliberately or otherwise, by European powers in pursuit of their own ends. The activities of Western Christian missionaries and the increasing demands of the native Christian population, and the challenge of secularists within the Turkish and Arab populations, also led to a religious reaction on the part of the Islamic majority population.[8]

Intellectual Context

The intellectual context of British archaeology in the Holy Land in the nineteenth century is perhaps the most exciting aspect of all. The seventeenth and eighteenth centuries had seen unprecedented developments in British philosophy, expressed in the work of Hobbes, Locke, and Hume. This period also saw the appearance of Newton's work in physics, the developments of Priestley and Boyle in chemistry, and Malthus' *Essay on the Principle of Population*. In 1848 John Stuart Mill published his *Principles of Political Economy*. In 1859 came the publication of Darwin's *On the Origin of Species*. From the 1850s on, the monumental works of Herbert Spencer began to appear. In this period, too, lie the origins of modern anthropology, in the works of Edward B. Tylor in England and Lewis Henry Morgan in the United States. In short, after centuries when theology and the Church were supreme, a new intellectual freedom—indeed, revolution—was under way. There was an intellectual ferment in Britain with few parallels in the whole of human history. This was only a part of the general intellectual climate of Europe of this period, with developments similar to those in Britain occurring in virtually every country.[9]

In this period archaeology developed, initially in Denmark, out of antiquarianism. There was a general increase of interest in the past, expressed in research focused on many lands quite unconnected with the Bible and/or imperialism. The development of British archaeology in the Holy Land sprang from this context, as well as from those previously discussed. It is, however, interesting to note that few, if any, of the pioneers of British archaeology in the Holy Land had any background in the archaeology of Britain. The general teaching of Latin and Greek, and the interest in classical archaeology—which at that time consisted primarily of art history and art criticism—meant that most had a background in these areas. Many also came from classical philology, and from theology and/ or biblical studies. Hence, British archaeology in the Holy Land, like its American counterpart, must be seen as having developed independently of other regional archaeologies. This independent development led to a rather parochial view of archaeology in the Holy Land, which in some cases has gone so far as to see it as a discipline separate from general archaeology. This view has persisted, to the detriment of Levantine archaeology, until recently, although not within British archaeology in the Holy Land.[10]

Social Context

The nineteenth century was a period of unprecedented social change, brought about by the Industrial Revolution, resulting in a completely new type of social structure, which David Thomson has called "the social service state."[11] With this came a new ideology, with new values, explicit and implicit; in particular, a new status for science and technology, and for academic knowledge generally.

It was within this social context that general archaeology and the regional sub-discipline of Levantine archaeology arose.

The social context of British archaeology in the Holy Land is particularly interesting. No one has, to my knowledge, carried out a study of the early British explorers and archaeologists in social terms comparable to the study of Danish archaeology by K. Kristiansen. In this respect an analysis of the lists of those invited to take part in founding the Palestine Exploration Fund, those who accepted, and the subsequent lists of committee members and subscribers would be revealing. It would also be of considerable interest to study the backgrounds of the early archaeologists and contributors of articles to the *Quarterly*. I suspect that two groups would be strongly represented on all of these lists. The most numerous would be members of the new and rising middle class—ranging from skilled artisans to university-educated professionals—who were in the forefront of the drive for better education in every field of learning. Second would be the newly wealthy industrialists. The older aristocracy certainly took part in the work of the PEF, but they were, almost by definition, fewer in number. A proper study of this subject would unquestionably be rewarding.[12]

Each of these categories would constitute a field of research in itself; each and all of them relate directly to the study of the subject of this chapter.

THE EARLY PERIOD OF STUDY

The Antiquarian, or Fact-Gathering, Period

The first period in the work of the British in the Holy Land was not strictly speaking archaeological, but antiquarian. The distinction between antiquarianism and archaeology is somewhat difficult to define; it is in part a difference of emphasis. One should note that the intellectual structure of this stage of British archaeology in the Holy Land is found in many other regional archaeologies and, indeed, in many other disciplines. It would seem useful, therefore, to consider some of the studies that have focused on this stage elsewhere.

David L. Clark has referred to this as the period of "Consciousness":

> Consciousness is perhaps achieved when the discipline is named and largely defined by specifying its raw material and by pragmatic practice—archaeology is what archaeologists do. Thenceforth, the practitioners are linked within an arbitrary but common partition of reality, sharing intuitive procedures and tacit understandings, whilst teaching by imitation and correction in the craft style.[13]

Lewis R. Binford has referred to this as the "Relic and Monument Period."[14] He has emphasized that in this period large quantities of facts were gathered concerning "relics," which I have referred to as "artefacts mobiliers," and "monuments," which I have referred to as "artefacts fixes."[15] "But the context of the finds was not well documented."[16] Binford's analysis reveals the lack of a concept of association, and of taxonomic and chronological frameworks within which to place the facts, and of a generally agreed underlying intellectual framework—what Thomas S. Kuhn has called a "paradigm."[17]

Kuhn has provided what is probably the best description of this stage:

> In the absence of a paradigm or some candidate for paradigm, all of the facts that could possibly pertain to the development of a given science are likely to seem equally relevant. As a result, early fact-gathering is a far more nearly random activity than the one that subsequent scientific development makes familiar. Furthermore, in the absence of a reason for seeking some particular form of more recondite information, early fact-gathering is usually restricted to the wealth of data that lie ready to hand. The resulting pool of facts contains those accessible to casual observation and experiment together with some of the more esoteric data retrievable from established crafts like medicine, calendar making, and metallurgy. Because the crafts are one readily accessible source of facts that could not have been casually discovered, technology has often played a vital role in the emergence of a new science.[18]

Kuhn goes on to point out that while this has been an essential stage in the development of a number of disciplines, the result is "a morass." It produces a mass of facts, some later to be shown important and others irrelevant, some quickly explained and others whose complexity renders them difficult to understand for a considerable period.

Finally, Gordon R. Willey and Jeremy A. Sabloff have referred to this as the "Classificatory-Descriptive Period" and described it as follows:

> The principal focus of the new period was on the description of archaeological materials, especially architecture and monuments, and rudimentary classification of these materials. Throughout the period, archaeologists struggled to make archaeology into a systematic scientific discipline. They did not succeed, but they laid the foundations for many of the achievements of the twentieth century.[19]

In this period the artifacts and monuments were studied largely as objects illustrative of historical documents. Although the aim was, as today, to learn more about the past, the artifacts and monuments were not seen as sources of information in and of themselves, independent of the historical record. In this sense the scholars of this period were more akin to the modern expert on antiques, who may dispose of an immense amount of esoteric information on a class of antiquities, such as pottery, but who brings that information to bear on the study of the pottery itself, rather than attempting to use pottery to study wider aspects of the history of the people who made and/or used the pottery, as the archaeologist does.

Palestine Exploration Fund

Between 1801 and 1865, the history of British archaeology in the Holy Land is the history of the more or less systematic exploratory efforts of individuals. By the 1850s it was clear that an organized effort was required to ensure proper funding and a systematic formulation of questions concerning the Holy Land and search for answers. The chief event of this period was the foundation of the Palestine Exploration Fund in 1865. This was the immediate result of the travels of Dean Arthur P. Stanley in the country in 1852 and 1862, his subsequent involvement of George (later, Sir George) Grove in preparing the list of place-names identifying the biblical sites in the country, and from Grove's involvement in the compilation of Sir William Smith's *A Dictionary of the Bible*. Grove, who was to be the driving force behind the foundation of the Fund, was made acutely aware at this time of the need for an accurate map of the Holy Land. Grove brought this problem, plus the lack of a proper water supply for Jerusalem, to the attention of Baroness Burdett-Coutts, who gave £500 for a survey of the city, in order to enable such a supply to be provided. The success of this survey encouraged Grove to attempt "to establish a society for the scientific exploration of Palestine," which led, on May 12, 1865, to the foundation of the PEF.[20]

From the beginning, the PEF operated on the basis of three principles:

1. That whatever was undertaken should be carried out on scientific principles.
2. That the Society should, as a body, abstain from controversy.
3. That it should not be started, nor should it be conducted, as a religious society.[21]

In pursuance of the first two principles the PEF hired the best available surveyors, officers and men of the Royal Engineers (responsible for the Ordnance Survey in Britain until a few years ago). The second principle embodies the idea of a pure, Baconian, inductivism, which was quickly found to be unworkable in practice.[22] The third principle was also of fundamental importance. It aimed not so much at religious neutrality as at complete religious inclusion. In pursuit of this aim, invitations to join the Committee of the PEF were issued at the beginning not only to all of the various factions within the Church of England, but to leading Nonconformists, Catholics, and Jews. In part, of course, these invitations were issued to individuals who had an interest in the Holy Land and who might make a financial contribution to the proposed work of the Fund, such as the aged Sir Moses Montefiore, but it is clear that it was also very much desired to obtain a completely ecumenical representation on the Committee.

While the original motivation for the work of the PEF was primarily the investigation of biblical history, that of the earliest explorers, Sir Charles Wilson, Sir Charles Warren, and others, was initially to do the job they were being paid for. Yet, having begun to work in the Holy Land, most of these people continued their involvement to the end of their lives. Both individually and collectively, they seem very quickly to have transcended their initial motivations and to have become fascinated by the archaeology of the Holy Land as a field of study with an intrinsic interest of its own, apart from the biblical connection—although their interest in this connection always remained very strong. One aspect that needs further investigation in this and later periods is the religious affiliation of the archaeologists. It seems very likely that the pattern will be closer to that of the United States, with the majority being Protestant Christians, rather than that of France, where the majority were Dominican priests. There does not appear to be a substantial Jewish involvement, and it would be interesting to explore the reasons for this; if indeed it is true, they must lie in factors external to archaeology itself.

For this period, the archives of the PEF contain a wealth of material, the earliest of which are the minute books of the Jerusalem Literary Society from 1849, along with a number of other papers associated with this organization. From the period immediately preceding the foundation of the Fund, the archives contain the papers of the Jerusalem Water Relief Society and of Wilson's Ordnance Survey of Jerusalem, including a number of the manuscript maps. The papers and plans of the survey of Jerusalem that Warren prepared for the PEF are, of course, well represented.

One of the most important sections of the PEF's archive consists of the surviving administrative documents of the Survey of Western Palestine (some 434 documents) and the surviving field reports of the officers who carried out the Survey: Stewart—14 documents, Drake—93 documents, Conder—563 documents (not counting microfilm copies of Conder's letters to his family, the originals of which are now in the Hebrew University of Jerusalem), Kitchener— 82 documents, Clermont-Ganneau—32 documents. In addition, there are miscellaneous letters of Kitchener (38 documents), Warren (11 documents), and Wilson (14 documents); the papers of the Palestine Pilgrims' Text Society, the Syrian Improvement Committee, the Sinai Survey of 1868–1869, Edward H. Palmer's Expedition to the Desert of the Exodus of 1869–1870, and concerning the murder of Professor Palmer and his companions in 1882. The Survey of the Wady Arabah in 1883–1884, and the Survey of Eastern Palestine are also well represented. Another important set of documents consists of the papers of Dr. Conrad Schick—277 documents—many of which are articles, plans, and so forth that were never fully, or even partially, published, and Dr. Gottlieb Schumacher—115 documents. An interesting document of a colorful nineteenth-century traveler is the sketchbook of John ("Rob Roy") Macgregor, who belongs to a category of travelers additional to those listed by David Klatzker—namely, "British eccentrics" (see chapter 5).

CONFLICTING RESEARCH PROGRAMS

Archaeology as History: Petrie's Research Strategy and Program

It has long been recognized that the publication of Sir W. M. Flinders Petrie's report on his excavations at Tell el Hesy opened a new period in the archaeology of the Holy Land. It is, however, essential to recognize that it did *not* also close an old one. Antiquarian research (as defined previously) continues, and will always do so, in British archaeology in the Holy Land as well as in work carried out by scholars of all nationalities and in all other subdisciplines of archaeology; there is no reason why this should not be so. The difference now is that the study of the objects as subjects of interest in their own right is subordinated to the broader aims of archaeology as a discipline. In particular, the facts garnered concerning individual artifacts and artifact types are now utilized not simply to illustrate the known historical record, but to learn about aspects of the past not mentioned therein, and/or to check the accuracy of that record as presently received and understood. One of the most important aspects of this shift from antiquarianism to archaeology is the dramatic improvement in the recording of the context of the finds and the increased interest in the study of the associations between finds, that is, the study of which artifact types are sometimes, always, or never found together in primary association.[23]

It is interesting to examine Petrie's achievement in the light of the philosophy of disciplines. Kuhn begins his study of *The Structure of Scientific Revolutions* by defining "normal science":

> In this essay, "normal science" means research firmly based upon one or more past scientific achievements, achievements that some particular scientific community acknowledges for a time as supplying the foundation for its further practice. . . . Aristotle's *Physics*, Ptolemy's *Almagest*, Newton's *Principia* and *Opticks*, Franklin's *Electricity*, Lavoisier's *Chemistry*, and Lyell's *Geology*—these and many other works served for a time implicitly to define the legitimate problems and methods of a research field for succeeding generations of practitioners. They were able to do so because they shared two essential characteristics. Their achievement was sufficiently unprecedented to attract an enduring group of adherents away from competing modes of scientific activity. Simultaneously, it was sufficiently open-ended to leave all sorts of problems for the redefined group of practitioners to resolve.[24]

Clearly, Petrie's *Tell el Hesy* was such a paradigmatic work, that is, it established a new research strategy. While Tell el Hesy was far from being the first tell ever excavated, Petrie's report on it resulted from Schliemann's work at Troy, and it introduced into Levantine archaeology the new conceptual framework for understanding the nature of the tells that form so prominent a feature of the Near Eastern archaeological landscape. Unfortunately, at this stage Petrie does not appear to have recognized the significance of empirical stratigraphy, since all his finds at Hesy are recorded using vague horizontal locations and height above sea level. For this reason it must be said that although his Hesy report does identify eleven "cities," it does not offer a usable methodology for the stratigraphic separation of the occupation phases of these structures. It did, however, provide a taxonomic framework for the classification of the material, especially the pottery, and a chronometric system by means of which the assemblages of recovered artifacts could be dated. Petrie calibrated this system with a high degree of success by means of a technique he invented, namely, cross-dating, using Egyptian material found at Hesy and Levantine material found in Egypt. At the same time, Petrie's single season of excavations, and his typically telegraphic site report, clearly did not exhaust the possibilities of any of the lines of investigation that he had opened. Hence, it possessed both essential characteristics of a paradigmatic work. Moreover, in choosing to study the topics he did, Petrie also provided a research program.[25]

But Petrie's research program never achieved complete acceptance. This also is a normal characteristic of the development of disciplines. Clarke has called this the phase of *self-consciousness* and has described it as characterized by

> contentious efforts to cope with the growing quantity of archaeological observations by explicit but debated procedures and the querulous definition of concepts and classifications. [In this phase] . . . it is no longer possible either to teach or to learn the vast body of data and complex procedures by rote. Instead, classes of data and approaches are treated in terms of alternative models and rival paradigms; inevitably, the comparison of classes introduces counting and measuring which in turn entails a modest amount of mathematical and statistical methods and concepts. . . . This process is also marked by the emergence of competitive individualism and authority, since the individual's living depends on the reputation he achieves as a focus in the media or by innovation and intensive work in a specialist field. The politics and sociology of the disciplinary environment increasingly develop this "authoritarian" state in which each expert has a specialist territory such that criticisms of territorial observations are treated as attacks upon personalities. This gradually becomes a seriously counterproductive vestige of a formerly valuable disciplinary adaptation by means of which authorities mutually repelled one another into dispersed territories, thus effectively deploying the few specialists over the growing body of data.[26]

The result of this process is an increasing degree of specialization within research programs differentiated, in the case of archaeology, along regional, chronological, topical (e.g., ceramics, architecture, cultural ecology, etc.), or methodological lines, until the point is reached when the general discipline, archaeology, "hardly exists as one subject at all." It has also been called the "Artifact and Assemblage Period," and the "Classificatory-Historical Period," emphasizing "The Concern with Chronology."[27]

At almost exactly the same time that Petrie's research program began to find adherents, a second research program developed, partly arising from Petrie's work. This research program will be examined in subsequent sections of this chapter; within its parameters the first four syntheses of the archaeology of the Holy Land—three of which were British—were written.

The PEF's archives contain a wealth of material relating to the work done under Petrie's research program, in particular, Petrie's own field reports (30 documents). These do not include the field records; the latter were found, apparently by the late Father John Matthers, in the Petrie Museum at University College, London (copies are available on microfiche). The archives also contain Bliss' correspondence and reports on his work at Tell el Hesy, Jerusalem, Tell Zakariya, Tell es Safi, Tell ej-Judeidah, and Tell Sandahannah (342 documents). Of particular interest are the field notebooks of R. A. S. Macalister for Tell Zakariya, Tell es Safi, and Tel ej-Judeidah [PEF/BLISS/151/1–2]. The field records of Bliss' excavations at Tell el Hesy are not included in the PEF's archives, and a search for them at the American University in Beirut and the National Museum in Istanbul by the late Father John Matthers failed to locate them.[28]

From this period also come the reports and correspondence of W. E. Jennings Bramly, the papers of the Reverend J. E. Hanauer, the papers of Professor T. Hayter-Lewis, and the papers—including correspondence from Capt. Stewart F. Newcombe, C. Leonard Woolley, and Thomas E. Lawrence—of the "Wilderness of Zin" Survey of 1914. It is perhaps worth noting here that these papers reveal quite clearly that the involvement of Woolley and Lawrence in this expedition was an unplanned accident, a matter of convenience arranged by Sir Frederick Kenyon of the British Museum, and not in response to any instructions from Hogarth, contrary to the theory of Philip Knightley and Colin Simpson.[29]

Archaeology as Ethnography: Vincent and Macalister

The first synthesis of the archaeology of the Holy Land appeared in 1907. While this synthesis, Vincent's *Canaan*, was French and not British, it was very influential and was written within a research program that, although short-lived, could boast four additional syntheses, all of them British, before it was abandoned. These other syntheses were Macalister's *Gezer I-III*, *A Century of Excavation in Palestine*, *A History of Civilization in Palestine*, and Handcock's *Archaeology of the Holy Land*.[30]

While Macalister's *Gezer* was technically a site report, it was unlike any that had preceded it in the British archaeology of the Holy Land; nor, indeed, was it like any that succeeded it. Rather than presenting the data and then the excavator's analytical conclusions, Macalister presented a synthesis of his conclusions illustrated by the excavated evidence. This alone would not be sufficient to constitute a separate research program. The programmatic distinction between the work of Macalister as well as of Vincent and Handcock, and that of Petrie and his successors, is that the aim of the former in their analysis, and the synthetic result, was not the production of a narrative history written on the basis of the archaeological evidence, with or without the support of historical documents. The goal was the production of an ethnographic account of the ancient peoples; that is, a description of their way of life, based on the excavated remains plus observations of the way of life of the contemporary Palestinian peasants. Binford has referred to this as "middle range research." That this was the case is clear, not only from the arrangements of Vincent's, Macalister's, and Handcock's volumes, but also from the opening sentence of Handcock's preface: "The writer's object in this volume is to give some account of the arts, crafts, manners, and customs of the inhabitants of Palestine from the earliest times down to the Roman period." Interestingly, this approach is not so far removed from that of, for example, Colin Renfrew.[31]

At the turn of the century, however, neither the stratigraphic nor the post-excavation analytical concepts and methods were capable of successfully pursuing this goal. In the hands of excavators such as Macalister, there was still too little attention to the precise context of the finds: "The exact spot in the mound where any ordinary object chanced to lie is not generally of great importance; thus, so long as we know the date at which a certain type of knife was used, it does not much matter, as a rule, in which of the houses it was discovered." Moreover, the concept of the sub-assemblage was not yet developed. The definition of this concept may be derived from Clarke's "assemblage," if the latter is taken as a stratigraphic phase at a specific site. With this proviso, I would define a sub-assemblage as an associated set of contemporary artifact-types from one particular activity area within a single assemblage. Although George A. Reisner had introduced the full modern concept in 1908, the fact that his work was not published until 1924 meant that other scholars were not able to take advantage of this great advance until after World War I when Fisher introduced a primitive version of the concept as the traditional "locus."[32]

While Macalister was particularly interested in the observation of the "manners and customs" of the local Palestinian villagers, and while he made the uniformitarian assumption that in the "unchanging East" the ways of the modern villagers were identical to those of their remote ancestors, he—and all of the other ethnographers of that and later periods—failed to connect, in an adequate and logically secure fashion, observable patterns of spatial distribution among associated contemporary artifacts to patterns of actual human behavior. Nor was the intellectual climate ready for this conceptual leap. Economic and social history were largely developments of the future, and British archaeology in the Holy Land was derived mainly from classical archaeology, biblical studies, theology, and linguistics, rather than from history or anthropology.

It must also be said that Macalister's own attitude may have had a good deal to do with the demise of his research program. Reading Macalister's work is quite difficult today. His syntheses are interlarded with long passages expressing open contempt for the local villagers, the Turks, both officials and otherwise, the Americans (especially American tourists), the Jewish colonists, and the inhabitants of Palestine from the Lower Paleolithic on. The only good thing that Macalister can find to say about Islam is that it has abolished drunkenness. Indeed, one can quickly reach the point of wondering why, given his complete contempt for the ancient and modern people of the area, he took up the study of the archaeology of Palestine in the first place. In any event, it seems highly likely that the particular form of his synthesis—which, like that of his contemporaries involved in the study of North American archaeology, consisted of a set of completely ahistorical descriptions of various aspects of the cultures concerned—was dictated largely by his contempt for the local population. This is clearly borne out by his repeated attribution of all progress in the ancient and modern Levant to outside influence.[33]

Macalister's works make it abundantly clear that he regarded the population of the Levant as having been, from the beginning, incapable of progress. It is but a small step from this assumption to the hypothesis that there has been no progress and, hence, to the presentation of a completely ahistorical picture of the successive cultures of the "unchanging East." He did, of course, admit trivial modifications, particularly in ceramic types, but even this was attributed to outside influence or imitation of past models. His perception of the archaeology of the Levant must be seen as a hindrance to further progress and deeper understanding; its nullification was one of the greatest contributions of W. F. Albright.

Macalister was an amazingly active correspondent; his papers in the archives constitute a block of no fewer than 419 documents. These do not, unfortunately, include any surviving field records from his excavations at Gezer, and an inquiry as to whether these survived in the archives of the University of Dublin revealed that they were not there either.[34]

Archaeology as Taxonomy: The Unadopted "Three Ages" Research Strategy and Program

By the time Petrie's *Tell el Hesy* was published in 1891, a research strategy and program known as the "Three Ages" system had been virtually universally accepted in Western Europe since the 1850s. It was given its definitive form between 1860 and 1900 by Gabriel de Mortillet and Oscar Montelius, so that it is sometimes also referred to as the "Montelian research strategy." That Petrie was well aware of this is beyond question, because he provided a statement outlining why he rejected the Three Ages system. He shared this rejection with his great contemporary, Sir Arthur Evans, whose Minoan terminology and seriation were based on the stratified material from Knossos, and not on the concept of a sequence of stone, bronze, and iron "ages." Petrie's influence was such that for more than twenty years British archaeologists in the Holy Land, almost alone among British archaeologists, held out against the Three Ages system.[35]

It is particularly interesting that this system was not accepted by the practitioners of the Vincent-Macalister research program, either. Yet as far as I can determine, Macalister was the first person to use the Three Ages system, in essentially its modern sense, to classify the Palestinian material; he was later to describe it as "the corner-stone of modern archaeology."[36]

Petrie gives the following reason for rejecting the Three Ages system:

A couple of generations ago there were laid down the main subdivisions of successive ages of stone, bronze, and iron; and then the division of the stone age into palaeolithic and neolithic. After that followed the separation of palaeolithic into four main periods in France, more or less applicable to other lands. Further definition was yet found to be necessary, and the neolithic and bronze ages were marked off into many classes, which had to be distinguished by the names of places where they were first found; and thus we reach a multitude of names, such as Mycenaean, Hallstattian, the period of La Tene, etc. Such a piecemeal plan is well enough for a beginning; but it is not capable of exact definition, it is cumbersome, and it does not express the relation of one period to another.[37]

He then goes on to propose that the material should first be placed in chronological order by the purely objective means of mathematical seriation, a technique that he invented and called "sequence dating." While it is true that in this respect Petrie's thinking and his actual work in the pre-dynastic Egyptian cemeteries anticipated the thinking of later scholars such as David L. Clarke and Stanley South, it is also true that recent developments, notably the analysis of empirical stratigraphy and the invention of radiometric dating methods, have provided a more logically sound basis for the seriation of the excavated material.[38]

Postscript: The Triumph of the Three Ages Research Program

By the time work could be resumed in the Holy Land after World War I, much had changed. Most of the *dramatis personae* were different: There was a different political administration—the British Mandate Authority—administering different antiquities laws; and archaeologists, British and non-British, were at last operating under a single research program—the Three Ages system. That this was the case, however, was not completely clear until 1922, when the now famous meeting took place in Jerusalem at which the British, French, and Americans agreed on a common terminology. The acceptance of the Three Ages system terminology signaled acceptance of the research program created by Christian Thomsen in 1836 and modified into its definitive form by de Mortillet and Montelius, about which I have written elsewhere.[39]

Since that time only two limited changes of research strategy have taken place in British archaeology in the Holy Land, both in the realm of stratigraphic analysis. The first was the introduction by Fisher of the recording and reporting of finds in traditional "loci," a necessary refinement of the methodology introduced at Tell el Hesy by Petrie. The significance of the locus for the refinement of ceramic seriation was immediately recognized, and it was applied with decisive effect by Albright in the reports of his excavations at Tell Beit Mirsim. The potential contribution of this kind of spatial data to the cultural analysis of the excavated material was, however, less clearly recognized, in part because of the conceptual limitations inherent in the Three Ages system itself, and in part because of the isolation of Levantine archaeology from anthropology (except in the person of Albright), and from other subdisciplines of archaeology, such as European prehistory, in which Childe, in particular, did much work along these lines.

The second change was the re-introduction by Dame Kathleen M. Kenyon of the techniques of observation, excavation, and recording of empirical stratigraphy first introduced by Reisner. Unfortunately, Kenyon failed to recognize the significance for cultural analysis of the distributional data of archaeological materials, and she published her finds from Jericho only by stratigraphic phases. In this respect her work is a retrograde step, especially as the distributional details could only have been recovered from the markings on the actual shards—only a handful of which, arranged in type series, have been retained.[40]

Given the developments in general archaeology during the last thirty years, it is possible that we may soon see another shift of research strategy, this time affecting the analysis of excavated material in cultural terms, to rival the magnitude of that caused by the publication of *Tell el Hesy*. In any event, it is essential, if we are to properly appreciate the work of our predecessors of whatever nationality, to understand all those aspects of their world and work that I have attempted to sketch in this chapter. For this purpose the pre-1918 archival material of the PEF, which has now been conserved, catalogued, guarded, and filed, is vital, as is a proper analytical framework within which to synthesize this material.[41]

NOTES

1. William F. Albright, *The Archaeology of Palestine and the Bible*, The Richards Lectures Delivered at the University of Virginia (New York: Fleming H. Revell Co., 1932), 17–18.

2. The major sources are the archives of Britain, Turkey, and the Holy Land. One might also consider the unpublished correspondence in the Palestine Exploration Fund (PEF) archives, and the records of the Turkish courts, now located in Jerusalem. See Moshe Ma'oz, *Studies on Palestine during the Ottoman Period* (Jerusalem: Magnes Press, 1975), 517-82.

3. David Thomson, *England in the Nineteenth Century (1815–1914)*, The Pelican History of England, vol. 8 (Harmondsworth, Middlesex: Penguin Books, 1950), 12, 32, 44, 83-87, 238-39.

4. Yehoshua Ben-Arieh, *The Rediscovery of the Holy Land in the Nineteenth Century* (Jerusalem and Detroit: Magnes Press and Wayne State University Press, 1979), 68; Norman K. Gottwald, *The Tribes of Yahweh: A Sociology of the Religion of Liberated Israel 1250–1050 B.C.E.* (London: SCM Press, 1979); George D. Mendenhall, "The Hebrew Conquest of Palestine," *Biblical Archaeologist* 25 (1962): 66-87; *The Tenth Generation: The Origins of the Biblical Tradition* (Baltimore: Johns Hopkins University Press, 1973); "Social Organization in Early Israel," in *Magnalia Dei: The Mighty Acts of God: Essays on the Bible and Archaeology, in Memory of G. Ernest Wright*, ed. F. M. Cross, W. E. Lemke, and P. D. Miller, Jr., (Garden City, N. Y.: Doubleday & Co., 1976), 132-61; Sarah Searight, *The British in the Middle East* (London: East-West Publications, 1979), 17; Abdul L. Tibawi, *A Modern History of Syria including Lebanon and Palestine* (London: Macmillan, 1969), 29, 32, 63-206, 259.

5. D. Thomson (above, n.3), pp. 82-83, 138; George M. Trevelyan, *English Social History: A Survey of Six Centuries Chaucer to Queen Victoria* (London: Reprint Society,

1948); A. L. Tibawi (above, n.4), p. 86; S. Searight (above, n.4), pp. 151-70.

6. A. L. Tibawi (above, n.4), pp. 77, 177; Y. Ben-Arieh (above, n.4); S. Searight (above, n.4); A. L. Tibawi, *British Interest in Palestine 1800–1901; A Study of Religious and Educational Enterprise* (Oxford: Oxford University Press, 1961), 126-27, 213.

7. Gerald R. Cragg, *The Church and the Age of Reason 1648–1789*, The Pelican History of the Church, vol. 4 (Harmondsworth, Middlesex: Penguin Books, 1971), 33-34, 49-55, 112-33; D. Thomson (above, n.3), p. 60; A. L. Tibawi (above, n.6), p. 183; D. Thomson (above, n.3), p. 61; A. L. Tibawi (above, n.4), p. 133; G. R. Trevelyan (above, n.5), pp. 357-60, 398-99.

8. A. L. Tibawi (above, n.4), pp. 39, 79, 170-72, 181-85.

9. Marvin Harris, *The Rise of Anthropological Theory* (London: Routledge & Kegan Paul, 1968).

10. Glyn E. Daniel, *A Hundred and Fifty Years of Archaeology* (London: Duckworth, 1975).

11. D. Thomson (above, n.3), pp. 135-36.

12. K. Kristiansen, "A Social History of Danish Archaeology (1800–1975)," *Towards a History of Archaeology*; Being the Papers Read at the First Conference on the History of Archaeology in Aarhus, 29 August–2 September, 1978, ed. G. E. Daniel (London: Thames & Hudson, 1981), pp. 20-44; D. Thomson (above, n.3), pp. 45, 50, 115, 135, 138, 146, 175.

13. David L. Clarke, "Archaeology: The Loss of Innocence," in *Analytical Archaeologist: Collected Papers of David L. Clarke*, edited by his colleagues (London: Academic Press, 1979), 83-103. (Originally in *Antiquity* 47 [1973]: 6-18, 83.)

14. Lewis R. Binford, *Bones: Ancient Men and Modern Myths, Studies in Archaeology* (London: Academic Press, 1981), 4-6; idem, *In Pursuit of the Past* (London: Thames & Hudson, 1983), 80-84.

15. R. L. Chapman, "Excavation Techniques and Recording Systems: A Theoretical Study," *Palestine Exploration Quarterly* (*PEQ*) 118th Year (1986): 5-26.

16. L. R. Binford (above, n.14, 1981), p. 80.

17. Thomas S. Kuhn, *The Structure of Scientific Revolutions*, 2d ed. (Chicago: University of Chicago Press, 1970), 10-11; L. R. Binford, (above, n.14, 1981), pp. 23-25; M. Harris, *Cultural Materialism: The Struggle for a Science of Culture* (New York: Random House, 1979), 26.

18. T. S. Kuhn (above, n.17), pp. 15-16.

19. Gordon R. Willey and Jeremy A. Sabloff, *A History of American Archaeology*, 2d ed. (San Francisco: W. H. Freeman & Co., 1980), 34; B. G. Trigger, *Time and Traditions: Essays in Archaeological Interpretation* (Edinburgh: Edinburgh University Press, 1978), 59, 61, 80.

20. Dean Arthur P. Stanley, *Sinai and Palestine: In Connection with Their History*, 5th ed. (London: John Murray, 1858), xi; Sir William Smith, *A Dictionary of the Bible: Comprising its Antiquities, Biography, Geography, and Natural History*, 3 vols. (London: John Murray, 1863); Sir Charles M. Watson, *Fifty Years Work in the Holy Land: A Record and a Summary* (London: PEF, 1915), 14-15, 17.

21. C. M. Watson (above, n.20), p. 18.

22. M. Harris (above, n.17), pp. 6-7; C. M. Watson (above, n.20), p. 19.

23. Sir W. M. Flinders Petrie, *Tell el Hesy (Lachish)* (London: PEF, 1891); W. F. Albright (above, n.1), pp. 17-18; R. L. Chapman (above, n.15), p. 9.

24. T. S. Kuhn (above, n.17), p. 10.

25. W. M. F. Petrie (above, n. 23), pp. 21-29; S. N. Kramer, *The Sumerians: Their History, Culture, and Character* (Chicago: University of Chicago Press, 1963), 8–9, 15; Heinrich Schliemann, *Troy and Its Remains* (London: 1875); idem, *Ilios, The City and Country of the Trojans* (London: 1880); idem, *Troja: Results of the Latest Researches and Discoveries on the Site of Homer's Troy* (London: 1884); W. F. Albright, *From the Stone Age to Christianity: Monotheism and the Historical Process* (Baltimore: Johns Hopkins Press, 1940), 3; idem, *The Archaeology of Palestine: A Survey of the Ancient Peoples and Cultures of the Holy Land* (Harmondsworth, Middlesex; Penguin Books, 1949), 29; R. L. Chapman (above, n.15), p. 21.

26. D. L. Clarke (above, n.13), pp. 83, 84.

27. T. S. Kuhn (above, n.17), pp. 10-22; L. R. Binford (above, n.14, 1981), pp. 6-20; idem, (above, n.14, 1983), pp. 84-87; G. R. Willey and J. A. Sabloff (above, n.19), p. 83.

28. Verbal communication from the late Father John Matthers.

29. P. Knightley, and C. Simpson, *The Secret Lives of Lawrence of Arabia* (London: Panther, 1971), 55-57.

30. Le Père Hughes Vincent, *Canaan d'après l'exploration récente* (Paris: Librarie Victor Lecoffre, 1907); R. A. S. Macalister, *The Excavation of Gezer 1902–1905 and 1907–1909*, vol. 1 (London: PEF, 1911), vol. 2 (1912), vol. 3 (1912); idem, *A History of Civilization in Palestine*, Cambridge Manuals of Science and Literature (Cambridge: University Press, 1912); idem, *A Century of Excavation in Palestine* (London: Religious Tract Society, 1925), 2d ed. (1930); Percy S. P. Handcock, *Archaeology of the Holy Land* (London: T. Fisher Unwin, 1916).

31. L. R. Binford (above, n.14, 1981), pp. 21-31; idem, *Working at Archaeology: Studies in Archaeology* (London: Academic Press, 1983), 10, 18-19, footnote 5; P. S. P. Handcock (above, n.30), p. 7; Colin Renfrew, *The Emergence of Civilization: The Cyclades and the Aegean in the Third Millennium B.C.* (London: Macmillan & Co., 1972).

32. R. A. S. Macalister (above, n.30, 1911), p. ix; D. L. Clarke, *Analytical Archaeology*, 2d ed. (London: Methuen & Co., 1978), fig. 49 and pp. 245-46; G. A. Reisner, Clarence S. Fisher, and David G. Lyon, *Harvard Excavations at Samaria (1908–1910)* (Cambridge, Mass.: Harvard University Press, 1924), 36–42; G. Ernest Wright, "Archaeological Method in Palestine: An American Interpretation," in *Eretz-Israel: Archaeological, Historical and Geographical Studies*, vol. 7 (W. F. Albright Volume), ed. A. Malamat (Jerusalem: Israel Exploration Society, 1969), 120–23; R. L. Chapman (above, n.15), pp. 10-14; Philip J. King, *American Archaeology in the Mideast: A History of the American Schools of Oriental Research* (Philadelphia: American Schools of Oriental Research [ASOR], 1983), 76-77.

33. R. A. S. Macalister, *Gezer*, vol. 2 (above, n.30), p. v; Bruce G. Trigger, *Time and Traditions: Essays in Archaeological Interpretation* (Edinburgh: Edinburgh University Press, 1978), 87–88; R. A. S. Macalister, *Gezer*, vol. 3 (above, n.30), pp. 31-32, 58-59; idem, *Century of Excavation* (above, n.30), pp. 56, 210-16, 241.

34. Verbal communication from Dr. B. S. J. Isserlin.

35. B. G. Trigger, *Gordon Childe: Revolutions in Archaeology* (London: Thames & Hudson, 1980), 25; G. E. Daniel, *The Three Ages: An Essay on Archaeological Method* (Cambridge: Cambridge University Press, 1943); idem, *A Hundred Years of Archaeology* (London: Gerald Duckworth & Co., 1950); idem, *A Hundred and Fifty Years of Archaeology* (London: Gerald Duckworth & Co., 1975), 149–51, 190–95; *Towards a History*

of Archaeology, Being the Papers Read at the First Conference on the History of Archaeology in Aarhus, 29 August–2 September 1978, ed. G. E. Daniel (London: Thames & Hudson, 1981); Sir W. M. Flinders Petrie, *Methods and Aims in Archaeology* (London: Macmillan & Co., 1904), 127.

36. Unpubished letter to Sir Charles Wilson in 1902 (PEF/MAC/89); Macalister, as quoted in Daniel, *A Hundred and Fifty Years* (above, n. 35), p. 51.

37. W. M. F. Petrie (above, n.35), pp. 127-30.

38. D. L. Clarke, *Analytical Archaeology* (London: Methuen & Co., 1968); Stanley South, *Method and Theory in Historical Archeology* (New York: Academic Press, 1977).

39. R. L. Chapman, "The Three Ages Revisted: A Critical Study of Levantine Usage," Part I, *PEQ*, 121st Year (July-December, 1989), Part 2, *PEQ*, 122d Year (January-June, 1990).

40. P. J. King (above, n.32), pp. 76-77; W. F. Albright, *The Excavation of Tell Beit Mirsim Volume 1: The Pottery of the First Three Campaigns*, *ASOR Annual*, vol. 12 (New Haven: ASOR, 1932); idem, "The Excavation of Tell Beit Mirsim 1A. The Bronze Age Pottery of the Fourth Campaign," *ASOR Annual*, vol. 13 (1933): 55-128; *The Excavation of Tell Beit Mirsim Volume 2: The Bronze Age*, *ASOR Annual*, vol. 17 (1938); idem, *The Excavation of Tell Beit Mirsim Volume 3: The Iron Age*, *ASOR Annual*, vol. 21-22 (1943); R. L. Chapman (above, n.39); B. G. Trigger (above, n.35); G. E. Wright (above, n.32); K. M. Kenyon, *Excavations at Jericho, Volume Three: The Architecture and Stratigraphy of the Tell* (London: British School of Archaeology in Jerusalem [BSAJ], 1981); idem, *Excavations at Jericho, Volume Four: The Pottery Type Series and Other Finds* (London: BSAJ, 1982); idem, *Excavations at Jericho, Volume Five: The Pottery Phases of the Tell and Other Finds* (London: BSAJ, 1983).

41. A set of catalogues containing summaries of the contents of virtually every document is available.

Chapter 17

British Opinion and the Holy Land in the Nineteenth Century: Personalities and Further Themes

Israel Finestein

Interest in the history and geography of the Holy Land was evident at many levels in nineteenth-century British society. It emerged from an ancient and sustained interest in the Bible, an interest that was not confined to the membership of the Established Church. Indeed, it was more marked, direct, and personal among many members of the dissenting bodies—long before they acquired the general appellation of Nonconformists. The Calvinist element in these groups accentuated their sense of attachment to the Old Testament and their intellectual and emotional ties with Restorationist ideas.

In the major provincial cities, dissenting circles derived much strength from a combination of the personal success often enjoyed by the practitioners of economic individualism, and the inner comfort they felt as practitioners of religious individualism. This enjoyment of both material and spiritual well-being was part of the social milieu in the newly expanded commercial and industrial urban areas and ports outside London.

Their success seemed to them the fruits of moral zeal and proof of moral worth. They had a profound sense of accountability and providential design, and they drew special inspiration from the Old Testament. Expressions of religious zeal, based upon interpretations of the Bible, influenced public opinion.

Local newspapers flourished, usually espousing partisan positions; their editors were almost as influential in affecting local opinion as were the headmasters of the larger provincial schools, some of whom were *litterateurs* whose works were read nationally. The relationship of such views to the public positions of local members of Parliament would be a fruitful topic for investigation.

Evangelical opinion, both inside and outside the Church of England, derived guidance from the Bible and inspiration with respect to social policy, national aspiration, and personal codes of conduct. The hallmark of Evangelicalism was moral fervor and personal responsibility. The abolition of the slave trade (in 1806) and of slavery in the British Empire (in 1833) sprang from moral imperatives as eloquent as those that directed responsible citizens to seek improvements in education, the legal system, and labor conditions.

What were the prevailing opinions concerning Jews, Judaism, and the Holy Land in the principal provincial centers in the first half of the century? The conversion of the Jews was a desideratum, difficult though such a task was acknowledged to be. So, too, a need was felt to weigh the current meaning of the original "chosenness" of the Jews and to consider whether the dramatic and rapid changes of the period might carry messianic portents bearing upon the fate of the Jews, and the possibly related fate of the Holy Land. These considerations attracted attention even outside the Church of England. Their impact upon leading public figures, both lay and clerical, deserves to be examined in terms of public and private attitudes toward Jews, Judaism, and Restorationism. What prompted some leading clerics of the Church of England to show greater interest in the Holy Land than did others? Was conversion of the Jews always seen as the precondition to any kind of restoration to the Holy Land?

SCOTLAND

Scotland requires separate study. There, the importance of Calvinism (through Presbyterianism and Congregationalism) in national life was stronger than elsewhere in Britain, and a sense of compact Scottish nationality added a further dimension to the interest in the Jewish national condition. Furthermore, popular education was better developed in Scotland than in England and provided greater intellectual content to the study of the Bible.

New College, Edinburgh, was the divinity school of the Free Church community of Scotland. That community was a highly influential and well-organized "separatist" segment of Scottish Christianity. There was a marked emphasis in the Free Church upon the significance of the Old Testament, and a greater degree of individual and congregational independence, but these nuances distinguishing it from the Presbyterian Church of Scotland did not detract from their common Calvinism.

The methods and substance of biblical study and presentation that were developed at New College influenced the study of the Hebrew language and extended biblical and theological inquiry at Oxford and Cambridge. The immediate and long-term influence of New College upon attitudes toward Jewish history and toward prophecy, within learned circles as well as popular opinion, would be a fruitful subject of study.

Beginning in 1843, John Duncan served for twenty years as Professor of Hebrew and Oriental Languages at New College. He was succeeded by Andrew Bruce Davidson, the noted Hebraist and theologian who held the post until his death in 1902. Davidson's special field was the language and theology of the

Hebrew Bible. Like Henry Hart Milman, his older contemporary in England, Davidson sought to present—although from a different standpoint—the actors in the Hebrew Bible as participants in a live historical process and to expound their language in ways they would have understood. His annotated editions of books of the Prophets reveal his attachment to the Hebrew Bible as literature having contemporary significance in matters of private practice and public policy.

Davidson's illustrious pupil, Sir George Adam Smith, visited Palestine on a series of occasions, twice touring the country (1880, 1891) as the prelude to his famous work *Historical Geography of the Holy Land* (1894), which was followed by a two-volume study of Jerusalem (1908). Smith was appointed Professor of Old Testament Language, Literature, and Theology at the Free Church College, Glasgow, in 1902 and became Principal of Aberdeen University in 1909. The close succession of these scholars had increasing impact; they rendered generations of students and readers more aware of the potential significance of contemporary Jewish history and modern Jewry in the divine design, and helped to relate that significance to the fate and future of the Holy Land.

OLD JEWRY AND NEW JEWRY

In two respects, the historicity of the Jewish People was often associated with the Christian sense of their own history in modern times. First, there were the examples of warning and divine intervention set out in numerous biblical narratives. Such examples were often regarded as retaining their resonance and relevance in contemporary situations. Second, there was often an assumption or notion that British society should act as though it were in some way continuing the drama of the Hebrew Bible.

This sense of continuity was felt in both England and Scotland. It was especially marked among the Puritans of seventeenth-century England, and it was discernible in later periods within the Established Church as well as among the Dissenters. The Anglican poet and cleric, John Keble, was a serious exponent of this view, and his widely debated and published sermon entitled *National Apostacy* (1833) forcefully illustrates this state of mind.

The ideological implications of these sentiments and attitudes toward the old and new roles of the Jews took many forms. The policy of seeking their conversion did not exhaust the aspirations and philosophies of Christians. Was there a continuing role in history for Jews? What was now to become of the Restorationist element in covenantal theology? In the 1840s, public discussion in the national press and various literary periodicals transformed the debates on the future of the Holy Land from the distant, imponderable reaches of time to the here-and-now, and from the allegorical or chimerical to the actual. Such transformation was occasioned by a variety of factors: the Napoleonic forays into North Africa and the Holy Land; the sights and sounds of the Holy Land as experienced by soldier, pilgrim, diplomat, and traveler; the new forms of transportation that made travel so much easier; the Damascus Affair; the plight of the Ottoman Empire; the expectations of the millenarians; the aspirations of the conversionists; and the ambitions of the Great Powers. The mutual influences of these trends and events remain fruitful subjects for study.

Those nineteenth-century scholars who frowned on the German schools of Bible criticism and on their English followers or adapters retained an acute sense of the original chosenness of the Jews. Whatever may have been the precise nature of their Christian conviction as to the new dispensation, the old promises— as St. Paul had affirmed—had not been abrogated. How did they, in their respective ways, resolve their predicaments in relation to the Jews and the Holy Land, in an age where the future of the Middle East and its possible practical connection with the Jews were under public discussion?

Consider for example John Bird Sumner, Bishop of Chester from 1828 to 1848 and Archbishop of Canterbury from 1848 until his death in 1862. Sumner, widely respected by Conservatives and Liberals (formerly Whigs) as an authoritative exponent of the Anglican position, consistently opposed admitting Jews to Parliament and believed in the literal accuracy of the Hebrew Bible. What were his private conclusions and his official policies regarding the changing Jewish scene and the much-debated prospects for the Holy Land—in which British governments were, from time to time, invited to adopt a role?

How did men of Sumner's situation and attitude view the interpretations of prophecy that flowed freely from the pens of esteemed and influential contemporaries? Herbert Marsh was, in the early decades of the century, the most prominent divine in Cambridge, serving as Bishop of Peterborough for twenty years, until he died in 1839. He sought to combine the new techniques in biblical scholarship with a sharply self-conscious conservatism. His works, *The Interpretation of Prophecy* (1816) and *The Authority of the Old Testament* (1823) could hardly be ignored when the succeeding generation was evolving a position on related public issues such as Restorationism. How were such works received in lay and clerical circles which helped to mold opinion?

To those who adopted the "historical" approach, such as Henry Hart Milman in his celebrated *History of the Jews* (1830), the biblical narratives were no less real than history. These accounts aroused curiosity over the nature, survival, and future of the Jews, as well as a sense of awe tinged with respect and compassion and a deep sense of mystery. No intelligent reader of Milman's *History*, which was published in several editions, could fail to note the author's sense of divine interventionism, his reverence for the Jewish strand in history, and his intimations of their continuing, if inscrutable, role.

Leaders of conservative opinion in the Anglican communion, whose published works contain a detailed repudiation of the Jewish interpretation of prophecy, nevertheless transmitted to their pupils and readers a considerable body of Jewish tradition and exegesis. For example, Edward Bouverie Pusey, Regius Professor of Hebrew at Oxford, not only gave public lectures on the Jewish interpretation of prophecy (published in his collected sermons, 1872), but he also urged upon his students the importance of understanding the idiomatic meaning of the Hebrew Bible. His addresses and published commentaries on many books of the Prophets reinforced his practice of deliberately encouraging his students and readers to become familiar with the Hebrew tradition.

INFLUENCE OF HOLY LAND *REALIA*

This sense of the need for familiarity with the Holy Land influenced travelers to seek to acquaint themselves with its geography. Davidson, later Archbishop of Canterbury, records, on the second of his two visits to Palestine (1873, 1876), that during the illness of his companion he kept himself fit by "taking long hard rides in the early morning and at sundown, so that I came to know the country for six or seven miles round Jerusalem better almost than any part of England or Scotland."[1] Acquisition of this kind of familiarity with the Holy Land was thought to provide benefits to scholarship and establish personal virtue. Such were the essential motivations in Arthur Stanley's expeditions, which resulted in publication of his *Sinai and Palestine in Connection with Their History* (1856).

How widespread within English society was such knowledge of the geography and topography of the Holy Land? Was there a relationship between such familiarity and an interest in remedying the "desolation" of the Holy Land? Did such interest actively or theoretically encourage British involvement in plans to ameliorate conditions in the Holy Land, in alliance with the People of the Book?

George Curzon—later Viceroy of India, member of the British Cabinet at the time of the Balfour Declaration, and Foreign Secretary—visited the Middle East in 1882–1883, at the age of 23. He expressed in detail his genuine interest in the biblical sites and his admiration for the poetry of the Hebrews. He described the sight and sound of the Jews at prayer at the Western Wall as "the most impressive sight I have seen abroad." But in a letter to his Oxford friend, Richard Farrar, Curzon wrote:

Palestine is a country to see once, not to revisit. The scenery is not often picturesque or even pretty. There is much greater need of cultivation than in Greece and much less chance of making it pay. For the surface is in many places all rocks and stones. No Jew with his eyes open (and you never see one with them shut) would think of going back; and if the Millennium is only to arrive when they have returned, our descendants will still be expecting it in 3000 A.D.[2]

Curzon retained a sense of antipathy to the Zionist aspiration and doubts as to the feasibility or wisdom of its achievement. In the 1890s he had supported the Conservative Party's policy of seeking to restrict the entry of East European Jewish immigrants into the United Kingdom, in which restrictive efforts Balfour had been a prime mover, together with Joseph Chamberlain. However, whatever ideology and expectation might have prompted Chamberlain, when Colonial Secretary, to proffer to Theodor Herzl certain prospects of a Zionist nature in the El Arish area, and whatever impelled Balfour's conversion to Zionism, Curzon appears to have remained immune to any kind of restorationist venture.

In the Cabinet, this leading Conservative expressed strong reservations on the proposed Balfour Declaration. Upon succeeding Balfour as Foreign Secretary in 1919, he wrote to his predecessor: "I shudder at the prospect of our country having to adjust ambitions of this description (i.e., Zionism) with the interests of the native population or the legitimate duties of a Mandatory Power."[3]

How far was Curzon representative of nineteenth century Conservative opinion? To what extent was familiarity with the geography and history of the Holy Land conducive to a sympathetic interest in the notion of Return? What factors induced a Liberal historian and politician like Professor Goldwin Smith to advocate encouragement of Jewish settlement in Palestine, even while expressing disdain for the Jewish character as he perceived it, displaying an inveterate hostility to the influence of Jews in politics and finance, and maintaining a deep-seated suspicion of the "English" pretensions of the emancipated Anglo-Jewish community? How far was such a combination of attitudes an expression of Smith's (and others'?) opposition to Disraeli's style and politics, even when he adopted, in part, Disraeli's theories of race and his belief in the practicability and virtue of the return of the Jews to the Holy Land? Goldwin Smith compared the Jewish right to independence and statehood to that of the Greek people. He was the principal literary antagonist of Hermann Adler, a senior spokesman of the established Jewish community in the 1870s and 1880s who responded continually to Smith's publicly expressed doubts about the Jewish capacity for patriotism, and his assertion of the Jewish proclivity for "tribalism."

THE PLACE OF THE JEW IN BRITISH SOCIETY

Examination of these personal views and ideological stands reveals that the issues of Jewish emancipation, integration, nationality, international kinship, and restorationism were interlinked. These questions were part of the legacy of the preceding century, and even of far lengthier prior historical conditioning.

Eschatological enthusiasms centering upon Palestine were engendered or heightened by the Napoleonic era. Directly and indirectly, they were sustained thereafter by Britain's increasing involvement in the affairs of the region. Worldly interests became intertwined with hopes for a British association with the restoration of the Jews to the Holy Land. In many instances conversionism was the dominant motive. In other instances biblical prophecy mingled with compassion for Jewish suffering and/or with a sense of Christian guilt toward the Jews for past ill-treatment. There were both instinctive and conscious links between such sentiments and British political and practical concerns, against a background of belief in Britain's providential role as a moral factor in history.

All these diverse strands of involvement and aspiration are evident in the parliamentary debates on the Jewish Emancipatory Bills between 1830 and 1858. Some Christian emancipationists (such as Sir Robert Grant) saw the bestowal of emancipation upon the Jews, and British encouragement of Jewish restoration to the Holy Land, as part of Christian duty. Others (such as Sir Robert Inglis) found in the assumed Jewish belief in and a desire for the much-discussed Restoration an added ground for withholding emancipation from them. Still others (such as Lord Shaftesbury) promoted the idea of Restoration, evinced strong Judeophile sentiments, and yet opposed the admission of unconverted Jews to Parliament.

To what extent was Edward Augustus Freeman representative of university opinion in his responses to the Jewish predicament and Jewish hopes? This Regius Professor of Modern History at Oxford, who supported Gladstone's policy for Irish Home Rule, was described as an "independent radical" and was said to have "the constant habit of deciding all moral questions by reference to duty." He supported British representations against the treatment of Cretans and Armenians under Ottoman rule, where "we have promised to make them (the Turks) do otherwise." Yet, in a private letter (1891), he repudiated the right of British public figures to seek, or to appear to seek, to interfere in Russian affairs through protest of the treatment of the Jews in the Czarist Empire. He described the issue as "Jew humbug . . . (and) . . . simply got up . . . (to deflect) . . . our thoughts from Armenia and Crete." This doyen of English historians added: "I don't want to wallop anybody, even Jews. The best thing is to kick them out altogether."[4]

An early academic predecessor of Freeman at Oxford was Thomas Arnold (more famous as headmaster of Rugby School than for his short-lived Regius tenure). Both men were Anglicans of liberal disposition in church matters and in public policy. They shared an acute sense of nation and regarded the social order as having a moral character reflecting the temper and aspirations of the people. The standards shared by the people were an important cohesive factor, and a common religious outlook was a vital ingredient in national cohesion. History defines the outlook and the study of history strengthens the cohesion. They further believed that the people are judged by their reactions to the moral issues posed in society.

Such a conception enables one to understand Arnold's doubts concerning the desirability and propriety of the political emancipation of the Jews. Those doubts were directly connected with his uncertainty as to whether the Jew could become an Englishman, and they raised the specter of a query of Jewish entitlement to residence in the land of the Englishman. In 1836 Arnold wrote that, while pleased that Parliament had done away with distinctions between Christians and Christians, he "would pray that distinctions be kept up between Christians and non-Christians." He added:

The Jews have no claim whatever of political right. . . . the Jews are strangers in England and have no more claim to legislate for it than a lodger has to share with the landlord in the management of his house. If we had brought them here by violence and then kept them in an inferior condition, they would have just cause to complain; though even then, I think, we might lawfully deal with them on the Liberia system and remove them to a land where they might live by themselves independent; for England is the land of Englishmen, not of Jews.[5]

How prevalent were these ideas in political and religious circles? Was there an intentional (or an unwitting) alliance forged by polemics and history between restorationists imbued with philo-Judaic convictions (whether conversionists or otherwise), and "restorationists" influenced by religious, political, and personal antipathies to Jews and Judaism?

In the 1890s, Arnold White was perhaps the best known and among the most authoritative critics of the allegedly adverse influences (especially on housing and employment) of unrestricted Jewish immigration. He achieved fame as an industrious agent of Baron de Hirsch in arranging for an orderly exodus of Russian Jews for resettlement, particularly in South America. He combined his public critique of Jewish influence and habits with advocacy of Jewish settlement under the auspices of the Great Powers in selected regions in the Eastern Mediterranean.

The ideological relationship of the anti-emancipation and anti-immigration schools of thought merit close study. Both sets of ideas impinged upon major issues concerning Jewish identity, Jewish purpose, and Jewish and Gentile responses to the comparatively open society that followed the Age of Reason and the French Revolution.

Throughout the nineteenth century there was ever-mounting interest among the reading public in the Jews, their history, their role in European society, and their future. In 1859 Lord Macaulay wrote to his sister that in his recollection as a boy at the outset of the century, no one "doubted that Buonaparte was the principal subject of the prophecies of the Old Testament." He noted his father's statement that when Napoleon went to Egypt, "the prophets were then wilder than ever he remembered them."[6] Disraeli had a public for his Zionistic novels. Recollections of the long and regular debates in Parliament on the many bills dealing with the emancipation of the Jews were still fresh. Matthew Arnold was proud to make it known that he was studying Hebrew the better to understand the Book of Isaiah. George Eliot was a keen student of Spinoza; indeed, there was a boom in Spinoza studies. The reality of Jewish power and of Jewish poverty was plain, as was the reality of intense Jewish introspection and of the strong Jewish desire for social integration. These paradoxes aroused curiosity, speculation, and a mixture of respect and perplexity.

Pervading these sentiments and phenomena was the ever-present debate concerning Jewish Restoration, the need for it, its viability, alternative auspices, respective motivations, and possible British roles.

The memoirs, papers, and diaries of public figures who were involved in the public debates on these Jewish issues have much to tell us about the factors influencing their respective positions. The emancipationist Grant was much affected by his belief in the continued chosenness of the Jews and the divine protection (despite appearances) under which their contemporary history was determined. By what features of temperament, family history, education, political affiliation, and social outlook were he and others moved to adopt their attitudes toward the Jews and toward restorationism? What impact did millennarianism have upon individual parliamentarians and churchmen? (We are aware, for example, that Shaftesbury was profoundly affected by Edward Bickersteth's millenarianism.)

TRAVEL LITERATURE ABOUT THE HOLY LAND

The earliest travel guide to the Holy Land that I have seen (by courtesy of Mr. Harry Schwab of London) is dated 1824. In that year an announcement appeared in London of the intended publication of a series of "Popular Descriptions" of "the various countries of the globe." The series was to be entitled "The Modern Traveller" and was to be concerned with the "geographical, historical and topographical" features of the respective lands. The volume on the Holy Land was the first volume in the series. It is a 372-page, pocket-size book entitled *Palestine or the Holy Land*. "Every acre of the Holy Land," declared the editor, James Duncan, in the preface, "is connected with associations interesting to the antiquary, biblical critic and Christian reader." Accordingly, it was "thought necessary to go far more minutely into topographical details than will be either requisite or desirable in the case of other countries. . . . There is ample scope for the investigation of future travellers."[7]

Among the contemporary explorers relied on by the editor for information and illustrations were the brothers-in-law Capts. James Mangles and Charles Leonard Irby. Their letters concerning their travels in the region in 1817–1818 were privately printed in 1823 and then published in 1844 in John Murray's famous "Home and Colonial Library," where they attracted wide attention. Prominent among travelers whose works were used in the travel guide of 1824 was James Silk Buckingham. James Duncan, who produced that guide, was undoubtedly aware of what would attract purchasers. Thus, the book provides detailed accounts of past explorations and recent surveys. The historical, especially biblical, background of numerous sites and buildings is set forth, and a welter of information of current interest to the traveler is included.

Such publications illustrate the increase in extensive foreign travel, which was not possible during the long years of war, on the part of the wealthier classes in Britain, particularly the rising middle class in the new age of expanding industry and commerce. The fact that the first volume in the series related to Palestine was more than a matter of piety, although that element was undoubtedly present. The sheer weight of detail in the book reflects the sharp interest that was rightly thought to exist among intelligent circles concerning the history of the Holy Land, its future, its "desolation," its possible "rebirth," and the prospective political and commercial roles of the West in the Eastern Mediterranean. The opening words of the book are eloquent of the age: "Palestine, the land of Israel, the Kingdom of David and Solomon, the most favored and the most guilty country under heaven.''[8] Intellectual curiosity was stimulated by knowledge of the Bible, a familiarity with the narrative of divine promises, and a declared or undeclared presentiment of things to come. No reader of the travel guide could fail to detect the sense of mystery with which the pages endowed the Land of Israel and the People of Israel within the pattern of human history.

What was the character of succeeding travel guides to the Holy Land, to whom were they directed, how widely were they read, what uses were made of them, and by which sections of society? Between such a compendious travel guide, the formation early in the century of the Palestine Exploration Society, and the later creation of the London Society of Biblical Archaeology, there are many links in outlook and motivation—implications that call for scrutiny and exposition.

Among the prominent public figures who traveled in Palestine and wrote accounts of what they saw and experienced were John Carne, the Cornish-born *litterateur* whose descriptions of his tour of 1821 were first published in serial form in the *New Monthly Magazine* before appearing as a book (in three editions); William John Bankes, Tory Member of Parliament and friend of Lord Byron; John Madox, who in 1834 published an extensive (two-volume) record of his *Excursions* to the Holy Land and neighboring territories; and Lady Egerton, who in 1841 printed for private circulation a diary of her tour of the Holy Land during the previous year. The diary included copies of illustrations drawn by her husband, Francis, who became the first Earl of Ellesmere.

In 1877 the London publishers, Bentley and Son, produced a volume on behalf of the committee of the PEF entitled *Our Work in Palestine: An Account of the Different Expeditions Sent Out to the Holy Land* (by the Committee since the formation of the Fund in 1865). However varied were the reasons that led Englishmen to travel to Palestine—curiosity, the resumption of the Grand Tour, adventure, commercial interests, military survey—the pervasive inspiration is to be found in the first chapter of this work:

> Small as this theatre of the most stupendous drama in the world's history is, it has never to this day been scientifically or even superficially explored. . . . the first clear grasp of Palestine geography . . . shows us as men and women those who were before puppets; it makes their actions intelligible which were before obscure or even fantastic. . . . To know this country intimately . . . and to illustrate by its present condition the narrative of the Old and New Testaments, is the aim of every earnest student of the Bible, and more especially of those who, by assuming the duties and responsibilities of teachers, may influence the young so powerfully to feel either repugnance or love to the Sacred Books.[9]

What effect did visits to Palestine have upon the views of the travelers regarding the idea of Jewish Restoration and the practical area of relations between Jews and Christians? How widely read were the travelers' accounts, how widely reviewed were they and by whom, and what was their impact upon Christian opinion, lay and clerical?

On July 23, 1866, Arthur Penrhyn Stanley, Dean of Westminster and an influential advocate of the cause of the PEF, presided at a widely publicized public meeting at the Royal Institution in London. At this meeting Stanley reported on the latest activities of the teams of surveyors and archaeologists sent out by the Fund. In the course of his address he reported on recent discoveries showing that ancient synagogues had been built with deliberate regard to beauty. The point would not have been lost on those accustomed to the conventional wisdom, much reinforced by the well-meant writing of Matthew Arnold, that "the synagogue lacked aesthetic sense."

Such meetings were often attended by ladies and gentlemen of high social rank and a wide spectrum of the educated public. To assemble the reports and comments of such meetings, published or otherwise, would throw a light upon the nature and extent of practical interest in the stated purposes of the Fund, and in Jewish-Christian relations both generally and with respect to Palestine-oriented projects.

Cleric and secularist, politician and traveler, businessman and soldier, the plainly curious and the avid explorer, all had their respective reasons for an interest in the Holy Land—not solely in the Land as it was in their day, but as it once was, and especially in what it might yet become. History is concerned not only with major trends, but also with the many and ever-varying microcosms of attitudes, beliefs, hopes, and deeds—which, in their impact and mutual interactions, contribute to the whole. Thus, further study of the several issues touched upon in this chapter is likely to be a multifaceted process that will prove to be most revealing.

NOTES

1. George K. A. Bell, *Randall Davidson*, 2d ed. (Oxford: Oxford University Press, 1938), 36.

2. Kenneth Rose, *Curzon: A Most Superior Person* (London: Macmillan, 1969), 89.

3. Letter dated 25 March 1919, ibid., 89.

4. William E. W. Stephens, ed., *Life and Letters of Edward Augustus Freeman* (1894), 427-28.

5. Letters dated 12.5.1834 and 27.4.1836, in Arthur P. Stanley, ed., *Life and Correspondence of Thomas Arnold* (London: B. Fellowes, 1844), 220, 273.

6.Thomas Pinney, ed., *Letters of Thomas Babington Macaulay*, vol. 6 (London: Cambridge University Press, 1974), 253.

7. James Duncan, ed., *Palestine or the Holy Land* (London, 1824), Preface.

8. Ibid., p. 1.

9. *Our Work in Palestine: An Account of the Different Expeditions Sent Out to the Holy Land* (London: Bentley & Son, 1877), 2-3.

REFERENCES

The author refers to the subjects discussed in this chapter and related topics in the following sources:

"Some Conversionists in Hull in the 19th Century," *Gates of Zion* 1, no. 4 (London: Synagogue Council of English Zionist Federation, 1957).

"Matthew Arnold and the Jews," *Jewish Quarterly* 23, no. 4 (1976).

"A Modern Examination of Macaulay's Case for the Civil Emancipation of the Jews," *Transactions* 28 (London: Jewish Historical Society of England, 1984).

"Some Modern Themes in the Emancipation Debate in Early Victorian England," in *Tradition and Transition, Essays Presented to the Chief Rabbi*, ed. Jonathan Sacks (London: Jews' College, 1986).

"Early and Middle Nineteenth Century British Opinion on the Restoration of the Jews," in *With Eyes Toward Zion–II*, ed. Moshe Davis (New York: Praeger, 1986). See also, in that volume, the chapters by Vivian D. Lipman and Lionel Kochan.

Comment

Aubrey Newman

In many ways the British section of this book treats a number of themes first hinted at in *With Eyes Toward Zion–II*. Comparing the chapters that examine a number of West European societies provides evidence of considerable links between them. Such links carry with them parallels with, but also significant differences from, the other Western societies with extensive Holy Land links. Not least of all there are significant differences from the America–Holy Land experience.

One of the important features of these countries was that their experience with the Holy Land goes back far longer than their experience with Jews. All of them had religious, diplomatic, and cultural links with the Holy Land, reflecting their own national interests. Another feature of most of these countries was the existence of an established church, and in that respect it does not matter very much whether it is Roman Catholic or Protestant. These church relations inevitably influence national policies toward the Holy Land; they create archaeological connections as well. Given the growth of "modern" science, there was a strong desire within the nineteenth century to confirm (or challenge) the teachings of the Bible, and this in turn led to a strong interest in the Land of the Bible.

Yet there are variations among the countries considered in the chapters. For Germany, the Holy Land was not a central area of action within the Middle East, as it was to be for Britain and France. Even then, however, French interest was gradually diverted toward Syria and North Africa, leaving Britain with almost a free hand in Palestine.

These various issues have been discussed in the chapters presented in this section. V. D. Lipman's essay is central to all the others. In it he has continued his earlier work on the archival resources available in Great Britain for Holy Land Studies in general, by looking specifically at a wide range of British activities in the Holy Land. He puts Britain's interests into their political, geographical, and economic context, as the growth of strategic interests in the area gave it new significance and stimulated activity by the Great Powers. Britain's interests, however, were not based solely upon such economic and political factors; the development of various missionary activities, culminating in the creation of a Protestant Bishopric in Jerusalem, is considered in detail. Complementing that religious work were the activities of the British consuls, one of whom, James Finn, made Britain the leading force in Jerusalem at the time of the Crimean war.

One of the crucial features of Lipman's chapter is the way in which attention is directed to various aspects as yet under-researched. Not enough is known about the growth of tourism; many individuals made well-publicized journeys to the Holy Land, but the development of the much larger "middle-class" tour, evidenced by the growth of popular Guides and the provision of Cook's Tours, had a potentially important effect upon the area. The figures that he quotes, suggesting almost a "flood" of tourists by the end of the century, and an increase in British shipping out of Jaffa at the same time, certainly provide a direction for additional research.

Two other chapters in this section offer additional points for further consideration. Rupert Chapman examines in detail the activities of the PEF. There was a striking growth of archaeological science all over Europe, but archaeology in the Holy Land developed independently of its growth elsewhere. Chapman points to important new areas; for example, the need to look at the individuals who took part in the foundation meetings of the PEF. At the base of his chapter however, is the urge to use more adequately the archives of the PEF and the light it throws upon the ways in which individuals in Britain, Jew and Gentile alike, displayed an enthusiasm for exploration in the Holy Land.

Israel Finestein emphasizes personalities and other themes for study. Of special interest is the deep and continuing interest of the Scottish Church, all the more important because of the long tradition of Hebrew scholarship among that Church's ministers. Other questions raised by Finestein are the extent to which individuals in British society had a knowledge of the geography and topography of the area, and the ways in which issues such as Jewish emancipation, integration, and restorationism were linked. Finally, he suggests a study of tourism and the plethora of travel literature about the Holy Land, and he raises the allied question of to whom these works were directed.

The intense discussion that followed these presentations at the workshop sessions held in Jerusalem in 1988 illustrated the considerable amount of work that all felt needed to be done in this area, from both the British and Israeli sides. The issues raised included the question as to how far the nineteenth century could be regarded as a unity. Since all agreed that it could not be so regarded, where should the divisions be made? It was also felt that the extent to which all these policies were dominated essentially by the "holiness" of the Land should be more fully considered. How extensive would have been the same involvement by the Great Powers in the strategic problems of the area, had there not been this complicating factor of its holiness to all faiths? How much did its sacred character serve merely as a cloak for more pragmatic issues?

Another important group of questions worthy of study concerns the specific part played by British Jewry in the Holy Land. What was the general approach of the Jewish community in Britain toward Palestine? How does the attitude of British Jewry compare with that of communities in other Western societies? While much of this is closely linked with the history of Zionism in Britain, there is sufficient that cannot be so viewed, and can only be studied within the general context of Britain–Holy Land studies. There is clearly a need for the parallel development of Britain–Holy Land studies and similar studies involving other West European societies and communities.

AFTERWORD

Chapter 18

Some Reflections on the Present State of Holy Land Studies

Lloyd P. Gartner

After reviewing the chapters in this book, it is difficult to point to any discipline in the humanities that is not somewhere represented in them. Be it philology, archaeology, geography, religion, or history, one or more of the contributors has put it to use. One also notes that attention has been paid to town and country planning, sociology, government, and other subjects that lie outside the humanities. History, the most pervasive discipline applied here, is represented not only by its traditional political, diplomatic, and intellectual modes with an archival emphasis, but also by newer methods and approaches, such as the study of images and perceptions in time, architectural history, women's history, and cultural migration and transplantation.

One hopes to see even more disciplines employed in Holy Land Studies. Everyone may offer suggestions. I, for example, would suggest paying more attention to international law and to economics. International law affected the status of the Holy Land and the complex of privileges that the subjects and institutions of foreign states enjoyed under Turkish and then British rule. As to economics, the revival of the Holy Land after 1800 was possible because of revolutionary improvements in travel, communications, and banking, as well as more gradual improvements in agriculture and manufacturing. The hardship and expense of travel, and the kinds of accommodations travelers could expect, obviously influenced the number who came, pilgrims included.

The abundance of disciplines signifies that the field has taken root and that it has become the subject of serious scholarly attention. As the French contributions stress, Holy Land Studies may take their place in the university curriculum within several departments, depending on particular conditions and the interests of the teaching staff. There can be little doubt of its adaptability and inherent significance, as these many excellent chapters decisively demonstrate.

Healthy interdisciplinary diversity also ensures that Holy Land Studies will not congeal into a dominant doctrine or accept ideological postulates in research. Rather, it will remain flexible and responsive to new approaches. This merits mention because ideology, whether political or theological, surfeits the Holy Land. One will get to the heart of issues only by a degree of reserve and self-distancing from them.

It appears important to set some boundaries, or at least to define the field by what lies outside it. If Holy Land Studies are not defined, at least negatively, the fruitful atmosphere of growth and maturity may dissipate in undisciplined roaming and speculation. Thus, we may state for a start that Holy Land Studies are distinct from the history of Zionism, which is a Jewish movement with political goals. Holy Land Studies are not a branch of the history of Judaism or Christianity, for all their sanctification of the Land. These two examples are necessary because Holy Land Studies do intersect and partly overlap Zionism and Western religious history. Therefore, it is all the more essential to hold boundaries in mind.

One's attention is also drawn to a gallery of arresting personalities, men— perhaps women, too, but they have not yet sufficiently been brought to center stage—who functioned with vision and daring near the outer edge of their native societies as spiritual and intellectual explorers and persons of action. Men like C. C. J. Bunsen stir the historian's imagination.

Several basic areas should be examined: Periodization, political and diplomatic factors, travel, comparison of empirical data, religious-theological dimensions, and Jewish Restoration to the the Holy Land.

There is a question of periodization: At what point does the modern history of the Holy Land commence? Its medieval origins have been illustrated by the French examples. Most of the chapters seem to place modern origins around 1800, when the ripple effects of the French Revolution reached the Eastern Mediterranean, aided materially by General Bonaparte's campaign. Once the Holy Land was accessible to the Western world, the ancient spiritual interests in the region could become tangible. The campaigns of Mehmet Ali out of Egypt exposed the Holy Land to the attention of the European powers after 1840. World War I brought an end to the Ottoman Empire, and the Balfour Declaration of 1917 was one step in the parcelling out of the lands formerly under Ottoman rule. Likewise, the State of Israel's founding in 1948 is in one respect the outcome of the Great Powers' withdrawal from the Middle East following World War II.

The State of Israel, secular though it is, expresses to the fullest extent the Jewish conception of the Holy Land up to the point of the messianic advent. As a turning point in the history of the Jews, the founding of Israel also deeply affects the relation between Jewish and Christian ideas of the Holy Land. Probably the idea of the Holy Land will endure as long as Christianity itself. But although some Christian ideas anticipated the Jews' return, they never contemplated the physical settlement of Christian masses—as did Jewish ideas of "ingathering of the exiles." The time may not yet be ripe, but it appears clear that Holy Land Studies must sooner or later consider their relation to Zionism and the State of Israel. Until then, there is a century-and-a-half of modern times before 1948, during which the idea of the Holy Land gradually attained physical reality alongside spiritual conception.

The political and diplomatic aspects of the Holy Land's emergence into modern history are burdened with controversy. Since this was the era of British dominance in world affairs, and one of Britain's central purposes was the preservation of the Ottoman Empire, it is not surprising that British presence in the Holy Land became pervasive. In examining the varying attitudes of British churches to the Holy Land, Israel Finestein notes how their interest became enhanced after the critical year of 1840. V. D. Lipman shows the British presence in the Holy Land being strengthened through exploration, scholarship, and religious endeavor, in close connection with one another. Only the Church of England set up its own ecclesiastical structure, at first in collaboration with the Prussian Lutheran church.

One repeatedly sees the combination of politics and salvation, most remarkably in the case of Bunsen, when the native land was called upon to support religious efforts in the Holy Land. The temptation at this point to resort to the term "imperialism" ought to be resisted. The methods employed contemporaneously by states without imperial interests, such as Prussia and the United States, did not differ much from those of the imperial British.

Travel, as mentioned previously, is a dimension of Holy Land Studies that requires fuller attention. My own studies of Jewish migration have made clear to me that with all the good reasons Jews had to emigrate to other lands, were there no railroad transportation from East European towns to Atlantic ports and fleets of steamships to cross the ocean, there would have been no Jewish mass migration in the nineteenth century. Today, with all our secularization, I should guess that more Christians set foot in the Holy Land, now the State of Israel, in one year than during the entire previous century. A worthwhile beginning concerning the economics of travel has been made here, and at a different level, in David Klatzker's analysis of what that experience meant to the traveler when he set out, and later when he returned home. The history of mail service to and from the Holy Land is yet another aspect of communication that ought to be examined.

Valuable attention has been devoted to the history of the empirical study of the Holy Land. With everyone in agreement that more should be known about the Land, it became possible to generate an extensive literature, much of which is of enduring scientific value. This literature includes detailed physical surveys, architectural studies, and descriptions of the native population—sometimes almost at an anthropological level. The methods of acquiring knowledge of the Holy Land are a function of general intellectual history, as Rupert Chapman has well illustrated. More specifically, it was necessary to have on hand experts as well as their tools—from the humanist's library to the laboratories required by the botanist, archaeologist, and geologist.

A comparison may be made between exploring the Holy Land and exploring North America. It is almost a micro-macro contrast. North American exploration took place on a primordial, enormously extensive, richly varied terrain, while that of the ravaged, tiny Holy Land required an attempt to reach backward into biblical and early Christian times. To set Yehoshua Ben-Arieh's study alongside the works of John Bartlet Brebner, *The Explorers of North America, 1492–1806,* and William H. Goetzmann, *Exploration and Empire: The Explorer and the Scientist in the Winning of the American West,* makes the point.

Holy Land Studies exist as a field because of their religious-theological dimensions, and that is the central concern of many of the chapters here. They deal, however, only with Catholic and Protestant interest in the Holy Land. It may be hoped that research will also focus on Eastern Orthodoxy and other Christian groups. Since these studies already suggest differences between Protestant and Catholic ideas of the Holy Land, there seems reason to expect still other differences to come to light once the Holy Land attitudes of other Christian churches are probed.

We have had intimations of a spiritual tension within the Roman Catholic Church between the idea of Rome and the idea of Jerusalem. Rome symbolizes the institutionalized Church and its traditions, whereas Jerusalem recalls Christianity's founding era and its pristine message. Thus, it may be easier for Protestants than for a great many Catholics to feel interested in the Holy Land; but more research on this subtle question is obviously needed.

The leaders in Holy Land endeavors among Protestants appear to have been the millenarians. We may divide them into millenarians who stayed home and waited—obviously the large majority—and those who made *aliyah.* It would be interesting to know the views regarding the Jews held by the former group in their native lands. It has been suggested that they looked upon the Jews somewhat more sympathetically than did "establishment" religious leaders.

A recurring point, emphasized in Erich Geldbach's chapter, is the transfer of millenarian energies into improving the conditions of life in the Holy Land while awaiting the realization of eschatological hopes. Certainly the nineteenth-century German efforts of the Templers in agriculture and social welfare were of enduring importance. A fine illustration of the inextricable combination of millenarianism and diplomacy is the founding of the Anglican Bishopric of Jerusalem. The effects all these efforts had in the native lands of the Holy Land activists also merit attention.

The Jews occupy a special place among all the people and religions to whom the Land was holy. Putting the matter rather crassly, it had once been theirs and they lost control of it and ultimately left it, for reasons that preoccupied some of the finest Jewish and Christian religious minds. The Jews hoped and believed they would have their land back. This would come about by miraculous as well as worldly means. To what extent each of these means was necessary and legitimate was always a matter of considerable discussion.

How did Christians regard the idea of the Jewish Restoration? Some rejected it outright, while others advocated it and even sought to be of aid to the Jews. Yet is there any symmetry—as Gershon Greenberg argues there is—between the Jewish and the Christian conceptions of the methods and timing of the destined Restoration? A spectrum of attitudes toward Jews actually living in the Holy Land is documented here; they range from sympathy to belittlement. Christians learned to be wary in missionary attempts because Jews bitterly resented them and more than once physically assaulted missionaries.

The Jewish Restoration in the Holy Land, which commenced during the nineteenth century, has become the subject of occasionally sharp debate. Was it "proto-Zionist"—or just the continuation of the old pious ways without a substantial change of outlook? In other words, is there a direct line between the growth of the traditional Holy Land community and the Zionist endeavors that started during the 1880s? Or does Zionism constitute a revolutionary change in Holy Land Jewish life? Did Moses Montefiore, that famous nineteenth-century figure, consider himself to be assisting the old Jewish settlement, or was he attempting to initiate a transformation in the future Zionist direction?

In my own view, what Montefiore did resembled somewhat the Anglican and Lutheran endeavors emphasized by Geldbach and Yossi Ben-Artzi, but of course within a different religious faith. They all sought to train the poor to become self-supporting, rather in the mode of "scientific philanthropy" and "charity organization." Perhaps this ultimately leads to Zionism, but Montefiore was neither a Zionist nor a proto-Zionist. What happened to the Holy Land idea when Zionism overshadowed it? As Ben-Arieh asks, can the Holy Land idea persist in secularized form? This brings us near 1948, our stopping point for the present.

Selected Bibliography

GENERAL

Books

Ben-Arieh, Yehoshua. *The Rediscovery of the Land in the Nineteenth Century*. Jerusalem and Detroit: Magnes Press and Wayne State University Press, 1979.

Davis, Moshe, ed. *Israel: Its Role in Civilization*. New York: Harper & Bros., 1956.

———. *America and the Holy Land*. Reprint Series of 72 volumes. New York: Arno Press, 1977.

———. *With Eyes Toward Zion*. Vol. 1. *Scholars Colloquium on America–Holy Land Studies*. New York: Arno Press, 1977. *Vol 2. Themes and Sources in the Archives of the United States, Great Britain, Turkey and Israel*. New York: Praeger, 1986.

Friedman, Isaiah. *Germany, Turkey and Zionism, 1897–1918*. Oxford: Clarendon Press, 1977.

Handy, Robert T. *The Holy Land in American Protestant Life 1800–1948*. New York: Arno Press, 1981.

Kaganoff, Nathan M., ed. *Guide to America–Holy Land Studies 1620–1948*, Vol. 1. *American Presence*. New York: Arno Press, 1980. Vol. 2. *Political Relations and American Zionism*. New York: Praeger, 1982. Vol. 3. *Economic Relations and Philanthropy*. New York: Praeger, 1983.

Kaufman, Menahem, and Levine, Mira, eds. *Guide to America–Holy Land Studies 1620–1948*. Vol. 4. *Resource Material in British, Israeli and Turkish Repositories*. New York: Praeger, 1984.

Lipman, V. D. *Americans and the Holy Land through British Eyes 1820–1917: A Documentary History*. London: V. D. Lipman, 1989.

Maoz, Moshe, ed. *Studies on Palestine during the Ottoman Period*. Jerusalem: Magnes Press, 1975.

Nir, Yeshayahu. *The Bible and the Image: The History of Photography in the Holy Land 1839–1899*. Philadelphia: University of Pennsylvania Press, 1985.

Sandeen, Ernest. *The Roots of Fundamentalism: British and American Millennarianism, 1880–1930*. Chicago: Chicago University Press, 1970.

Stevens, Mary-Anne, ed. *The Orientalists: Delacroix to Matisse, European Painters in North Africa and the Near East*. London: Royal Academy of Arts, 1984.

Tuchman, Barbara. *Bible and Sword: England and Palestine from the Bronze Age to Balfour*. London: A. Redman, 1957.

Articles

Ben-Arieh, Yehoshua. "Pioneering Scientific Exploration in the Holy Land at the Beginning of the Nineteenth Century." *Terrae Incognitae: The Annals of the Society for History of Discoveries* 4 (1972).

———. "Lynch's Expedition to the Dead Sea (1847–48)." *Prologue: The Journal of the National Archives* 5 (1973).

Kark, Ruth. "Millenarism and Agricultural Settlement in the Holy Land in the Nineteenth Century." *Journal of Historical Geography* 9 (1983).

Lipman, Vivian D. "The Origins of the Palestine Exploration Fund." *PEQ* 120 (1988).

OVERVIEW

Books

Aamiry, M. A. *Jerusalem: Arab Origin and Heritage*. London: Longman, 1978.

Arberry, A. J. *British Orientalists*. London: William Collins, 1943.

Bennet, M. *Catalogue of Exhibition, William Holman Hunt*. Liverpool/London: Walker Art Gallery & Victoria and Albert Museum, 1969.

Davies, William D. *The Gospel and the Land*. Berkeley: University of California Press, 1974.

Epp, Frank W. *Whose Land Is Palestine: The Middle East Problem in Historical Perspective*. Grand Rapids, Mich.: W.B. Eerdmans, 1974.

Friedman, Saul S. *Land of Dust: Palestine at the Turn of the Century*. Washington, D.C.: University Press of America, 1982.

Hunt, W. Holman. *Pre-Raphaelitism and the Pre-Raphaelite Brotherhood*. London: MacMillan, 1905.

Hyamson, Albert M. *British Projects for the Restoration of the Jews*. London: British Palestine Committee, 1917.

Newton, Frances E. *Fifty Years in Palestine*. Wrotham, England: Coldharbour Press, 1948.

Roberts, David. *The Holy Land, Syria, Idumea, Arabia, Egypt & Nubia*. London: F. G. Moon, 1842–1849.

Rose, Andrea. *The Pre-Raphaelites*. Oxford: Phaidon, 1981.

Schattner, Izak. *The Map of Palestine and Its History*. Jerusalem: Bialik Institute, 1951.

Searight, Sarah. *The British in the Middle East*, 2d ed. London: Weidenfeld & Nicolson, 1979.

Tristram, Henry B. *The Land of Israel: A Journal of Travels in Palestine*. London: Society for Promoting Christian Knowledge, 1865.

Vogel, Lester I. "Zion as Place and Past—An American Myth: Ottoman Palestine in the American Mind Perceived through Protestant Consciousness and Experience." Ph.D. diss., George Washington University, 1984.

NORTH AMERICA

Books

Bond, Alvin. *Memoir of the Rev. Pliny Fisk, A.M., Late Missionary To Palestine*. 1828; reprint, New York: Arno Press, 1977.

Cohen, Naomi W. *The Year after the Riots: American Responses to the Palestine Crisis of 1929–1930*. Detroit: Wayne State University Press, 1988.

Fishman, Hertzel. *American Protestantism and a Jewish State*. Detroit: Wayne State University Press, 1973.

Goren, Arthur A. *Dissenter in Zion*. Cambridge: Harvard University Press, 1982.

Hale, Edward Everett & Hale, Susan. *A Family Flight Over Egypt and Syria*. Boston: D. Lothrop, 1882.

Kay, Zachariah. *Canada and Palestine*. Jerusalem: Israel Universities Press, 1978.

King, Philip J. *American Archaeology in the Mideast: A History of the American Schools of Oriental Research* [ASOR]. Philadelphia: ASOR, 1983.

Klatzker, David. "American Christian Travelers to the Holy Land, 1821–1939." Ph.D. diss., Temple University, 1987.

Madsen, Truman G. *The Mormon Attitude Toward Zionism*. Series of Lectures on Zionism, no. 5. Haifa: University of Haifa, 1981.

Mencken, H. L. *Erez Israel*. New York: B. F. Safran at the New School, 1935.

Onne, Eyal. *Photographic Heritage of the Holy Land, 1839–1914*. Manchester: Institute of Advanced Studies, Manchester Polytechnic, 1980.

Parsons, Helen Palmer, ed. *Letters from Palestine, 1868–1912, Written by Rolla Floyd*. Dexter, Maine: privately printed, 1981.

Pfeiffer, Rev. James. *First American Catholic Pilgrimage to Palestine 1889*. Cincinnati: Joseph Berning & Co., 1892.

Rausch, David A. *Zionism Within Early American Fundamentalism, 1878–1918*. New York and Toronto: Edwin Mellen Press, 1979.

Twain, Mark. *The Innocents Abroad, or The New Pilgrims' Progress*. Hartford: American Publishing, 1869.

Walker, Charles T. *A Colored Man Abroad: What He Was and Heard in the Holy Land and Europe*. Augusta, Ga.: John M. Weigle & Co., 1892.

Articles

"America and the Holy Land: A Colloquium." *American Jewish Historical Quarterly* 62 (September 1972). Reprinted as a pamphlet by the Institute of Contemporary Jewry, 1972.

Brown, Michael. "The Americanization of Canadian Zionism." *Contemporary Jewry—*

Studies in Honor of Moshe Davis. Ed. Geoffrey Wigoder. Jerusalem: Institute of Contemporary Jewry, Hebrew University, 1984.
———. "Divergent Paths: Early Zionism in Canada and the United States." *Jewish Social Studies* 44 (Spring 1982).
Elmen, Paul. "The American Swedish Kibbutz." *Swedish Pioneer Historical Quarterly* 32 (1981).
Fox, Frank. "Quaker, Shaker, Rabbi—Warder Cresson, The Story of a Philadelphia Mystic." *Pennsylvania Magazine of History and Biography* 95 (April 1971).
Handy, Robert T. "Holy Land Experiences of Two Pioneers of Christian Ecumenism: Schaff and Mott." *Contemporary Jewry: Studies in Honor of Moshe Davis*. Ed. Geoffrey Wigoder. Jerusalem: Institute of Contemporary Jewry, Hebrew University of Jerusalem, 1984.
Kark, Ruth. "Annual Reports of United States Consuls in the Holy Land as a Source for the Study of 19th-Century Eretz Israel." *With Eyes Toward Zion–II*. Ed. Moshe Davis. New York: Praeger, 1986.
Klatzker, David. "American Catholic Travelers to the Holy Land, 1861–1929." *Catholic Historical Review* 74 (January 1988).

IBEROAMERICA

Books

Aizenberg, Edna. *The Aleph Weaver: Biblical, Kabbalistic and Judaic Elements in Borges*. New York: Scripta Humanista, 1984.
Grünberg, Carlos M. *Mester de Judería*. Buenos Aires: Argos, 1940.
Herman, Donald L. *The Latin American Community of Israel*. New York: Praeger, 1984.
Kaufman, Edy, Shapira, Yoram, & Barromi, Yoel. *Israel–Latin American Relations*. New Brunswick, N.J.: Transaction Books, ca. 1979.
Kibrik, Leon, ed. *Fundación Catedra República Argentina en la Universidad Hebrea de Jerusalém*. Buenos Aires: Leon Kibrik, 1940.
Liacho, Lazaro. *Sionidas desde las Pampas, y Sonata Judí a de Nueva York*. Buenos Aires: Candelabro, 1969.
Marín, Rufino. *Lo que piensa America del problema Judío*. Buenos Aires: Editorial America, 1944.
Primér Congreso Sionista Latinoamericano, Informe General. Buenos Aires: Consejo Central Sionista Argentina (CCSA), 1946.
Senkman, Leonardo. *Identidad Judía en la Literatura Argentina*. Buenos Aires: Pardés, 1983.
Sicron, Moshe. *Immigration to Israel from Latin America*. Tel Aviv: Tel Aviv University, 1974.
Tov, Moshe. *El Murmullo de Israel: Historial Diplomático*. Jerusalem: Semana, 1983.
Windmuller, Kathe. *O Judeu no Teatro Romántico Brasileiro, Una revisão da tragedia de Gonsalves de Magalhães, Antonio José ou O Poeta e a Inquisicão*. São Paulo: Universidade de São Paolo, Centro de Estudios Judaicos, 1984.

Articles

Borges, Jorge L. "Una vindicación de la Cabala." *Obras Completas*. Buenos Aires: Emece, 1976.

Mirelman, Victor. "Zionist Activities in Argentina from the Balfour Declaration to 1930." *Studies in the History of Zionism.* Jerusalem: Hasifriya Hazionit, 1976 (Hebrew).

Mistral, Gabriela. "Mi experiencia con la Biblia." *Chile escribe a Israel.* Santiago, Chile: Andrés Bello, 1982.

Schenkolewski, Silvia. "The Relationships between the Zionist Movements and the Jewish Community in Argentina, 1934–1943." *Zionism* 11 (1986, Hebrew).

WESTERN EUROPE

Books

Bensimon-Donath, Doris. *Les juifs de France et leur relations avec Israël, 1945–1988.* Paris: L'Harmattan, 1989.

Berchet, Jean-Claude, ed. *Le Voyage en Orient, anthologie des voyageurs français dans le Levant au 19e siècle.* Paris: Robert Laffont, 1985.

Carmel, Alex. *Christen als Pioniere im Heiligen Land.* Basel: F. Reinhardt, 1981.

———. *German Settlement in Palestine during the Later Periods of Turkish Rule: Political, Local and International Problems.* Jerusalem: Israel Oriental Society, The Hebrew University, 1973 (Hebrew).

———. *Die Siedlungen der württembergischen Templer in Palästina, 1868–1918.* Stuttgart: W. Kohlhammer, 1973.

Eliav, Mordechai. *Love of Zion and Men of Hod: German Jewry and the Settlement of Eretz-Israel in the 19th Century.* Tel Aviv: HaKibbutz Hameuchad, 1971 (Hebrew).

Friedman, Isaiah. *Germany, Turkey and Zionism 1897–1918.* Oxford: Clarendon Press, 1977.

Ginossar, Shalev. *Voyage littéraire en Terre Promise.* Paris-Geneva: Champion, Slatkine, 1986.

Gradenwitz, Peter, ed. *Das Heilige Land in Augenzeugenberichten.* Munich: Deutscher Taschenbuchverlag, 1984.

Khalidi, Rashid I. *British Policy toward Syria and Palestine, 1906–1914.* London: Ithaca Press, 1980.

Las, Nelly. "Les juifs de France et le sionisme de l'Affaire Dreyfus à la second guerre mondiale (1896–1939)." Ph.D. diss., Israel, 1985.

Lazar, David. *L'opinion française et la naissance de l'Etat d'Israël, 1945–1949.* Paris: Calmann-Levy, 1972.

Minerbi, Sergio I. *L'Italie et la Palestine, 1914–1920.* Paris: Presses Universitaires de France, 1970.

Neuville, René. *Heurts et malheurs des consuls de France à Jerusalém aux 17e, 18e et 19e siècles.* Jerusalem: [n.p.], 1947–1948.

Nicault, Catherine. "La France et le sionisme (1896–1914)." Ph.D. diss., Sorbonne, 1985.

Samuel Gobat: Evangelischer Bischof in Jerusalem, Sein Leben und Wirken meist nach seinen eigenen Aufzeichungen. Basel: Verlag von C. F. Spittler, 1884.

Sauer, Paul. *Uns Rief das Heilige Land: Die Tempelgesellschaft im Wandel der Zeit.* Stuttgart: K. Theiss Verlag, 1985.

Schütz, Christiane B.H. Preussen in Jerusalem (1800–1861): Karl Friedrich Schinkels Entwurf der Grabeskirche und die Jerusalempläne Friedrich Wilhelms IV. Inauguraldissertastion zur Erlangung der Doktorwürche, vorgelegt der Philosophischen Fakultät der Rheinischen Friedrich-Wilhelms-Universität zu Bonn, Berlin, 1986.
Sinno, Abdul-Raouf. *Deutsche Interessen in Syrien und Palästina 1841–1898.* West Berlin: Baalbek, 1982.

Articles

Carmel, Alex. "Historical Sources on the History of Eretz Israel during the Ottoman Period in Archives in Austria and Germany." *Cathedra* 1 (September 1976, Hebrew).
Delpech, François. "Les chrétiens et la Terre Sainte: suggestions pour une meilleure approche du problème de Jérusalem." *Sur les juifs, études d'histoire contemporaine.* Lyon: Presses Universitaires de Lyon, 1983.

GREAT BRITAIN

Books

Albright, William F. *The Archaeology of Palestine and the Bible.* The Richards Lectures Delivered at the University of Virginia. New York: Fleming H. Revell, 1932.
Blumberg, Arnold, ed. *A View from Jerusalem 1849–1858: The Consular Diary of James and Elizabeth Finn.* London and Toronto: Associated University Presses, 1980.
Goldschmidt-Lehmann, Ruth. *Sir Moses Montefiore, Bart., F.R.S., 1784–1885: A Bibliography.* Jerusalem: Misgav Yerushalayim, 1984.
Manuel, Frank E. *Realities of American Palestine Relations.* Washington: Public Affairs Press, 1949.
Shepherd, Naomi. *The Zealous Intruders: The Western Rediscovery of Palestine.* London: Collins, 1987.
Silberman, Neil A. *Digging for God and Country.* New York: Alfred A. Knopf, 1982.
Watson, Sir Charles M. *Fifty Years Work in the Holy Land: A Record and a Summary.* London: PEF, 1915.

Articles

Hannam, Michael. "Some Nineteenth-Century British Residents in Jerusalem." PEQ (1983).
Vereté, Mayir. "Restoration of the Jews in English Protestant Thought." *Middle East Studies* (1972).
————. "Why was a British Consulate Established in Jerusalem?" *English Historical Review* (April 1970).

Index

About the Editors

MOSHE DAVIS is Academic Chairman of the International Center for University Teaching of Jewish Civilization under the aegis of the Israeli Presidency, Founding Head of the Institute of Contemporary Jewry at The Hebrew University of Jerusalem, and Stephen S. Wise Professor (Emeritus) in American Jewish History and Institutions.

An authority on contemporary Jewish life, Professor Davis specializes in the field of American Judaism. He is Project Director and General Editor of the American–Holy Land Studies. His publications include: *The Emergence of Conservative Judaism*; *Jewish Religious Life and Institutions in America*; *The Shaping of American Judaism* (Hebrew), which received the Louis LaMed Award for outstanding contribution to Hebrew Literature; and *From Dependence to Mutuality: The American Jewish Community and World Jewry* (Hebrew). He is the author of numerous articles and editor of several series of publications, among these thirteen volumes on World Jewry and the State of Israel.

Professor Davis has been recipient of the Guggenheim Fellowship; the Hebrew Union College–Jewish Institute of Religion honorary degree of Doctor of Humane Letters; the Lee Max Friedman Award for distinguished contributions to American Jewish historiography; and the Samuel Rothberg Prize in Jewish Education by the Hebrew University of Jerusalem.

In 1984, Professor Davis' colleagues and associates published a volume entitled *Contemporary Jewry—Studies in Honor of Moshe Davis*.

YEHOSHUA BEN-ARIEH is Professor of Geography at The Hebrew University of Jerusalem. He is currently Head of the Center for the Study of the History of Eretz Israel, at Yad Yizhak Ben-Zvi, Jerusalem, and of the Center for the Study of Zionism and the Yishuv, at the Hebrew University.

Professor Ben-Arieh has been awarded two of Israel's prestigious literary prizes: the Ben-Zvi Prize for the History of the Land of Israel, and the Bialik Prize in Jewish Thought. Among his books are *The Changing Landscape of the Central Jordan Valley*; *The Rediscovery of the Holy Land in the Nineteenth Century*; *Jerusalem in the Nineteenth Century: The Old City*; and *Jerusalem in the Nineteenth Century: The Emergence of the New City*.

Professor Ben-Arieh has written over 100 scientific articles and scholarly papers for international publications and colloquia and has participated in the editing of many books and monographs in his field. He has been a visiting professor at University College, London; the University of Maryland; Carleton University, Ottawa; and at various universities in Israel.

Contributing Authors

RAN AARONSOHN lectures in the Department of Geography, the Hebrew University of Jerusalem, and is Visiting Fellow at the University of Maryland. He is the author of *Baron Rothschild and the Colonies: The Beginnings of Jewish Colonization in Eretz Israel, 1882–1890* (Hebrew).

YOSSI BEN-ARTZI teaches in the Department of Land of Israel Studies at the University of Haifa and is chairman of the Center for the Study of Eretz Israel (Yad Yizhak Ben-Zvi and University of Haifa). He is the author of *The Moshava Settlements of Eretz Israel, 1882–1914* (Hebrew).

MICHAEL BROWN, Associate Professor of Humanities and Hebrew at York University, Toronto, Canada, is the author of *Jew or Juif? Jews, French Canadians, and Anglo-Canadians, 1759–1914.*

ALEX CARMEL, Professor in the Department of Land of Israel Studies, University of Haifa, is head of the Gottlieb Schumacher Chair and Institute for Research into the Christian Contribution to the Development of Nineteenth-Century Palestine. His most recent books are *The Life and Work of Gustav Bauernfeind, Orientalist Painter, 1848–1904* and *German Settlement in Palestine in the Late Ottoman Period* (Hebrew).

RUPERT L. CHAPMAN III is Executive Secretary of the Palestine Exploration Fund, United Kingdom.

DEBORAH DASH MOORE is Professor of Religion at Vassar College and editor of the *Yivo Annual*. Her most recent book is *East European Jews in Two Worlds*.

ISRAEL FINESTEIN, Q.C., is Major Scholar Trinity College, Cambridge, and former President of the Jewish Historical Society of England. He is Vice-President, Board of Deputies of British Jews, and former Senior Crown Court Judge. He edited James Piciotto's *Sketches of Anglo-Jewish History*. His own *Collected Volume of Studies on Anglo-Jewish Life in the Nineteenth Century* is to be published.

LLOYD P. GARTNER is the Spiegel Family Foundation Professor for European Jewish History at Tel-Aviv University. Among his books are *The Jewish Immigrant in England* and *The Jewish Community in the United States* (the latter in Hebrew).

ERICH GELDBACH is a consultant to the Ecumenical Research Institute in Bensheim, Germany, and Professor of Church History and Ecumenics at Philipps University in Marburg. His most recent books are *Ökumene in Gegensätzen*, and *Freikirchen*.

HAIM GOREN is Director of Academic Studies at Tel-Hai Regional College, Upper Galilee, a branch of the University of Haifa. He lectures on the history of the Land of Israel in the nineteenth century.

GERSHON GREENBERG is Associate Professor of Philosophy and Religion at The American University, Washington, D.C., and Research Fellow at the Institute of Holocaust Research, Bar-Ilan University. He is the author of *Holy Land and Religion in America*.

ROBERT T. HANDY is Henry Sloane Coffin Professor Emeritus of Church History, Union Theological Seminary. He is currently undertaking research for the Project on Church and State at Princeton University. The most recent of his books are *A History of the Churches in the United States and Canada* and *A History of Union Theological Seminary in New York*.

ABRAHAM J. KARP is Joseph and Rebecca Mitchell Adjunct Research Professor of American Jewish History and Bibliography, The Jewish Theological Seminary of America. He is curator of "Haven and Home, Jews and Judaism in America," an exhibit mounted by the Library of Congress.

ANDRE KASPI teaches American history at the Sorbonne and directs a seminar on French-Jewish history. Among his publications are *Les Americains*, *Franklin Roosevelt*, and *The Jews in France from 1940 to 1944* (all in French).

SOPHIE KESSLER-MESGUICH teaches at l'Ecole des Hautes Etudes du Judaïsme, Paris. She is doing research and writing on Hebrew language and grammar of the sixteenth–eighteenth centuries.

DAVID KLATZKER is Academic Liaison, U.S.A., for the America–Holy Land Project of the Institute of Contemporary Jewry, The Hebrew University of Jerusalem, and serves as Rabbi of Beth Tikvah–B'nai Jeshurun in Philadelphia. He writes extensively on America–Holy Land Studies.

VIVIAN D. LIPMAN (1921–1990), was Honorary Research Fellow at University College, London, and co-editor of the Littman Library of Jewish Civilization. *A History of the Jews of Britain Since 1858* was published posthumously.

FRANKLIN H. LITTELL is Professor Emeritus of Religion, Temple University; Adjunct Professor, the Institute of Contemporary Jewry, The Hebrew University of Jerusalem; and Distinguished Visiting Professor, Stockton State College, New Jersey. He is the author of *From State Church to Pluralism: A Protestant Interpretation of Religion in American History*.

AUBREY NEWMAN is Professor of History at Leicester University and a Fellow of the Royal Historical Society of Britain. His books include *Provincial Jewry in Victorian Britain* and *The Jewish East End, 1840–1939*.

CATHERINE NICAULT is Assistant Professor of Contemporary History, Poitiers University, France. She is currently doing research on French-Zionist political relations from 1897 to 1948.

LEONARDO SENKMAN lectures in the Department of Spanish and Latin American Studies, The Hebrew University of Jerusalem, and is a research fellow at the Truman Institute there. His most recent books are *Argentina y el Holocausto*, and *El Antisemitismo en la Argentina* (editor).

LOTTIE K. DAVIS is Editorial Coordinator for the *With Eyes Toward Zion* series and a co-author of *Land of Our Fathers*, a map and study of Bible place-names in America.

PRISCILLA FISHMAN is Editorial Associate for this volume and Director of Publications, International Center for University Teaching of Jewish Civilization.